MY FATHER
RUDOLF HESS

MY FATHER
RUDOLF HESS

Wolf Rüdiger Hess

Translated by
Frederick and Christine Crowley

A Star Book
published by
the Paperback Division of
W. H. Allen & Co. Plc

A Star Book
published in 1987
by the Paperback Division of
W.H. Allen & Co. Plc

First published in Great Britain by
W.H. Allen & Co. Plc 1986

Copyright © 1984 by Albert Langen Georg Müller
Verlag GmbH, Munich–Vienna

Translation copyright © by Frederick and Christine Crowley

Printed and bound in Great Britain by
Anchor Brendon Ltd, Tiptree, Essex

ISBN 0 352 322144

Dedicated to my children
Friederike Andrea
Wolf Andreas
Katharina Charlotte

The publishers thank Verlag, Leoni, for permission
to print extracts from Ilse Hess, *England–Nurnberg–
Spandau, Gefangener des Friedens* and *Antwort aus Zelle
sieben*, and S. Fisher Verlag, Frankfurt am Main, for
permission to print extracts from Bradley F. Smith,
*Der Jahrhundertprozess (Reaching Judgment at
Nuremberg)*.

CONTENTS

[v]

CONTENTS

FOREWORD

WHEN I READ the manuscript of this book, an incident from long ago came to mind which plays a part in the story – perhaps I can even say it sets the theme. As I spoke English in my childhood, from 1933 onwards I often acted as a kind of interpreter, as the lady who took important British visitors in to dinner at receptions. During the 1936 Olympic Games in Berlin, I acted in this role very frequently for Sir Robert Vansittart, Permanent Under-Secretary at the Foreign Office, whom my husband and I met not only at the Reich Chancellery receptions but also in the capacity of hosts on outings with a handful of people into the country around Berlin. On one of these occasions, Vansittart, who was fully aware of his unequivocal reputation as a German-hater, told me that as a child he had for many years had a German 'nanny', and that as a result he was quite fond of the German people. This can scarcely have been a calculated remark for my benefit, as it came out quite naturally during an almost intimate chat.

At the end of the Games, at the final Reich Chancellery reception, we were standing beside one another in a large doorway as Michael Bohnen of the Berlin State Opera sang the Loewe ballad *Archibald Douglas* as a kind of tribute to the British people present:

'. . . do not think of the old Douglas feud
Which relentlessly pursues you.
Think rather of your childhood
When I comforted you on my knee. . .'

When it ended everyone applauded, but Vansittart seemed to be strangely lost in thought. I asked him with a smile, 'Sir Robert, why don't you try to think a bit more about your childhood?' He immediately understood what I meant. This was made even more clear by a little hand-written note I received before he left. The 'arch-enemy' of the German people thanked us for our frequent hospitality, for my thinking of him '. . . in sending flowers, as if you had cut them in the garden yourself for your beautiful vases; but above all for the sincere urging of me to think more "about my childhood", to think more about so many things . . .'

When my husband read the letter, he waved it happily backwards and forwards before my eyes and – locked it up in his safe! 'Do you realize that you have dabbled in "high politics"? This letter could be important!'

Unfortunately I no longer have this letter; I can turn only to my memory for the extract I quote. In 1941, after my husband's flight, Martin Bormann took away the safe, and no protests on my part brought back what had belonged to me.

I have no doubt that Martin Bormann recognized the value of the letter. He probably kept it as circumstantial evidence against my husband – his horizon would have been too limited to grasp the faint possibilities it concealed. But it is true that, in fact, my husband made no use of these possibilities. How often were we just about to visit England! How often did our plans come to nothing for a thousand different reasons, reasons which now seem so unimportant! It is futile to brood on this. I have often thought in the past years that my husband's way of expressing himself – so very close to the proverbial 'understatement' of the British – and my own candour – strongly averse to any claptrap, any pathos, in fact completely apolitical – might perhaps have succeeded in breaching the convictions of those circles for whom 'Germaniam esse delandam' has been the guide for decades on end.

In this context, a word from Lady Vansittart may sound curious. Shortly after Jesse Owen's third victory, she said, almost scornfully, 'One fine day the Americans will regret letting niggers run for them!' She meant this sincerely. The words came out quite naturally in the normal course of conversation, and surprised me not a little. Neither my husband nor I would ever have entertained such a thought, let alone have expressed it.

All this was merely an incident whose far-reaching possibilities remained purely speculative. When my husband arrived in Britain in 1941, he was no longer the guest who had conversed so easily around the tea-table just a few years before. It was war-time. The paths towards compromise had meanwhile been rendered almost impassable – under the dominant influence of America. Less so for us than for the British, who had long ago fallen into the hands of those Americans who wanted the British to 'pull their chestnuts out of the fire'.

As I have said, this was just an incident, but in it lay the seeds of 'that rashness that sometimes serves an end', as my husband said in a letter many years later.

My son, the publishers and their historical adviser, who have taken over the baton of historical truth as in an Olympic relay and are trying to carry it onwards, have brought to light little that may be described as human – like the incident I have described – and much that must be seen as inhuman. Inhuman, in that the door is kept barred to the Spandau cell, to the lonely man who has been allotted, as the Bible says 'by reason of strength', not eighty years but ninety years of life, years which have certainly been 'toil and trouble', for he has come through them unbroken.

And we, the powerless onlookers? 'It is no use weeping where tears are forbidden', as the Japanese epigram says.

Ilse Hess
Gailenberg, April 1984

PREFACE

WHEN MY FATHER flew to Scotland on 10 May 1941 I was three-and-a-half years old. I can still see his worried face as he pulled me out of the garden pond, and I can still hear his comforting voice as he disentangled me, screaming in panic, from a bat that had caught itself in my hair and carried it to the window, releasing it into the night. These are my only personal memories of my father from that time. I remember nothing at all of my godfather, Adolf Hitler.

In 1943 we were bombed out of our house in München-Harlaching, and my mother moved with me to Hindelang in the Allgäu, where she still lives. Here I spent what was for me a carefree country childhood. I was scarcely aware that I had a famous father. The true meaning of the angry exchange with a neighbour's boy, who shouted at me from a safe distance, 'Your father was a Nazi!', upon which I screamed, 'So was yours!, and he yelled back, 'Yours was a bigger one!', never dawned upon us boys at the time.

Although my father was not present in person, he was always with the family in our minds. But at that time my mother told me very little about my father's special situation, so that my child's mind should not be burdened with the tragic details of his lot. The bridge between him and us was the letters he wrote from England and from Nuremberg. My mother tells me that I had a special urge to learn to write so that I could communicate with him. His letters have always radiated peace, strength and confidence; above all, they are evidence that his sense of humour has never deserted him. On 27 July 1946, already in Nuremberg, he wrote to me (*Volume of Letters*, p. 109), 'My dear Buz (my nickname); thank you for your letter in which you inform me that you no longer wish to be an engine-driver for Munich's rubbish-disposal goods trains but the real, big railway. I now give you my consent to this. I fully understand that you would like to 'scorch along', but of course you will be able to do this even better as an aircraft pilot.'

When the victorious powers' International Military Tribunal opened at Nuremberg in November 1945, my father, Rudolf Hess, was among those sitting in the dock, thin and hollow-cheeked, quite different from the picture I had before me from my childhood memories. As a nine-year-old, the emotional stress of the Nuremberg trial communicated itself to me only through the oppressive atmosphere of my surroundings. The journey my mother undertook with me to Nuremberg before judgment was passed was, for me, an exciting adventure; I did not sense in it my mother's courageous determination to see and speak with her husband and my father after five years of separation. We were refused admission.

My mother was arrested by the American authorities in June 1947 and taken to the 'Labour and Internment Camp' at Göggingen near Augsburg. The only reason for her arrest was that she was the wife of Rudolf Hess. At almost the same time we were being taught at school that *Sippenhaftung* – liability of a family for the crimes of one of its members – was an utterly objectionable process, employed only during the Third Reich. I gradually realized that there was something different about my father; something that did not apply to the fathers of my playmates and school-fellows. These other fathers came home from the prisoner-of-war camps, or were eventually reported dead or missing. But I had to cope with the fact that I had a father whose appearance I knew, whom I knew to be alive, whose whereabouts I knew, who was often talked about, but whom I was never allowed to meet.

At the end of the 1950s I travelled with a school friend to South Africa. During the trip we soon came to recognize that conditions there were quite different from what we had gathered from the newspapers of Federal Germany. Encouraged by this surprising discovery, I began to take a deeper interest in the political background to my father's life, and to look critically at what I had learnt about the Third Reich at school and from the media. I slowly began to understand the political dimension of my father's fate.

In 1959 I was called upon to perform National Service in the Federal Armed Forces. I refused to report for duty on the grounds that the only tangible reason for sentencing my father to life imprisonment at Nuremberg had been his co-signature of the Law of 16 March 1935 introducing universal military service. While my father continued to be imprisoned in Spandau, therefore, I reasoned that to assist in the build-up of the German Armed Forces represented, according to the victors' case law as established at Nuremberg, a 'crime against peace' involving a threat of life imprisonment. My case was considered by two Examining Boards, and was finally rejected on the grounds that there was no paragraph in the Armed Forces Act on which to base a judgment on my claim. For my part, I concluded the sitting of the second Examining Board by declaring that if they wanted me in the Armed Forces they would have to send the police to fetch me! The whole case had already raised some dust in the press, and the higher authorities prudently rejected police action. Thus, to my regret in fact, I have not performed National Service.

In the early 1960s I completed civil engineering studies at the Munich Technical University with distinction, and in the late summer of 1964, after a probationary period, I passed my second civil service examination and became a government engineer.

Throughout all these years, the spiritual bond between my father and myself remained unsevered. With his characteristic intuition he gave me good advice, and with his subtle sense of humour he commented on what was expedient or inexpedient, what was good or bad, what was to be striven for or avoided in life. He recommended to my mother Eduard Spranger's 'Psychology of Youth,' referring with a twinkle to the chapter on seventeen-year-olds: 'I see myself as a proper paterfamilias, hovering white-haired over all the fuss. How would this father of a seventeen-year-old really act?' Unfortunately he was never able to have this question answered.

So I formed a mental picture of my father from the letters that passed between us or from stories told by other people who knew my father, and I noticed that the respect they showed towards Rudolf Hess was transmitted to me. In fact, many striking virtues are combined in my father: willpower, enterprise, sincerity, resolution, and honesty towards himself and his ideals. What he has to endure is so severe that I can assimilate it only in a few moments of awareness; for the rest of the time I have to push it aside if I am to survive. But my father bears it quite alone, 24 hours a day, 365 days a year; today, 43 times 365 is already more than 15,600 days . . . an inconceivable stretch of time.

My father's unique lot means that my normal life differs from that of other people. His courage as a prisoner in Spandau has laid an obligation on me, his son. In 1967 – I was then 30 years old – I initiated a systematic campaign for my father's release. The family's hopes had concentrated on 1 October 1966, the release date for Schirach and Speer, his last two fellow-prisoners in the Allied Military Prison. When Christmas 1966 had passed, it became clear to us that the victors were doing what was inconceivable; they were continuing to hold him alone in custody.

It was clear to me from the outset that the chances of success in my efforts and those of our family and friends were minimal because of the victors' brutality. There were – and still are – periods filled with weariness and despondency. But how can I give up if my father, in his much more difficult position, has not given up? These thoughts have continually heartened me and spurred me onward. Although success has so far been denied us, we have triumphed in one important respect: the mantle of oblivion and silence has not been allowed to descend upon my father.

In all my years of effort to secure my father's release, I have been continually questioned in countless interviews on my attitude towards the Third Reich and National Socialism. I have always answered from my conviction that of all people I, the son of Rudolf Hess, must keep an open mind while there still exists a possibility of talking to my father about this. I feel a special responsibility in expressing any opinion on this matter, based quite simply on the fact that a well-reasoned and balanced verdict will be expected from the son of a man who played such a leading role in the Third Reich. This is all the more true if this son adopts a very positive attitude towards his father and his father's qualities. I cannot therefore approve or judge as easily as others, since any opinion that I deliver – negative or positive – also affects my father directly or indirectly.

The longer my concern with his life continues, however, the deeper for me become the elementary contradictions between what we Germans are being taught about our recent history and what a leading representative – namely my father – contributed to this history at the time.

The fact that until this very day he has suffered, unbroken and with head held high, the indescribable mental persecution inflicted on him by the victors of the Second World War proves that this man in Spandau bears no guilt. If there were even a grain of guilt in him he would long since have broken down under the endless solitude surrounding him.

For me, the son of Rudolf Hess, the question arises: to what extent are the allegations against us Germans really true if it can be proved that my father has been kept imprisoned until now with no legal justification, and quite obviously only because the victors wish to silence with him, their accessory and victim, a political crime committed not by the Germans but by themselves?

All the victors' actions after both the First and Second World Wars were conducted on the moral foundation that peace and harmony could prevail only if the 'incarnations of evil', the German people, were excluded. This exclusion was totally successful after the Second World War. The peace which then prevailed in the world is impressive: more than 40 million people have died since the end of the Second World War in some 140 wars and 'conflicts' – the modern word for war. In Africa alone five million children a year die of hunger, while simultaneously millions of tons of food are destroyed to keep up prices; this also is part of the victors' new, equitable world order.

The Germans can scarcely be held responsible for these innocent and pitiful victims of this new world order. We are forced to recognize that the victors of both the First and Second World Wars – they are in fact almost identical – are anything but the arbiters of law, morals and humanity they made themselves out to be in their treatment of Germany, which, when necessary, they continue to treat as an 'enemy state' without rights under Articles 53 and 107 of the United Nations Charter, and for which, following territorial dismemberment and deprivation, there now looms apocalyptically on the horizon only extermination in the 'world's first nuclear battlefield'.

All this is either reality or malevolent fancy, and the man who, by staking his life, tried to end the war before it broadened into a world war has been imprisoned for decades for a 'crime against peace'.

If we consider dispassionately the fundamental relationships – as I try to do in this book – we cannot avoid recognizing that my father Rudolf Hess, by his flight to Scotland, staked his all in an effort to make peace a possibility – not only peace with Britain but with the Soviet Union also; world peace. This peace mission was not the 'fanatical deed of crack-brained naivety' which Winston Churchill, then the ruler of England, belittled in his memoirs. Churchill belittled it for good reason, because by doing so he hoped to conceal that in May 1941 there was in fact a chance of preventing world war if only London and Washington had been seriously interested in this. Imagine the situation that would have arisen if Churchill had reacted positively to my father's arrival and, for example, had called a peace conference to include the United States of America and the USSR! Hitler would have been unable to dodge such a conference, and it is scarcely believable that the Powers taking part in it would not have succeeded in holding Hitler down to the justifiable demands arising from the Versailles Diktat. The world would have been spared 50 million dead and endless devastation . . .

To explain the significance of his peace mission, this book describes in some detail the history of Germany, and world history as it affected Germany, up to my father's flight in 1941. It then concentrates on his lot at Nuremberg and Spandau in order to prove the injustice and inhumanity of the action taken against him by the victorious Powers. The imbalance so arising between the first part of the book and the two later parts was consciously accepted for the sake of continuity.

In the book, therefore, I quite deliberately refer very rarely to 'my father', but to Rudolf Hess. This is to typify my efforts to evaluate matters dispassionately and soberly.

The book also gives me an opportunity to thank all those who have acted on behalf of my father for the untiring efforts they have exerted – and are still exerting – for his release and vindication. Besides the members of the Executive Committee of the Hilfsgemeinschaft (Support Association), who are separately referred to later, my gratitude also goes out to the many members, friends and sympathizers of the Hilfsgemeinschaft 'Freiheit fur Rudolf Hess' (Freedom for Rudolf Hess Support Association), a registered society, whose donations, assistance and activities have made the work of the Association possible.

The unflagging and exceptional efforts of my father's solicitor, retired Secretary of State Dr Alfred Seidl, deserve my special gratitude and respect. What Dr Seidl has achieved for my father in nearly forty years of activity is equalled only by his client's bearing during this period.

Compared with the 40 million dead whose lives must be laid at the feet of the Second World War victors' world-system, the fate of one individual such as my father may appear insignificant. Nevertheless, his is the very example which characterizes the hypocrisy of the former Allies: in the name of justice and morality, the 'ambassador of peace' receives worse treatment than any common criminal. At the same time, the three Western Occupying Powers have asserted for nearly twenty years that nothing is of more importance to them than the release of Rudolf Hess. If this is really so, why have they bowed for so long to the Soviet veto?

As early as December 1967, the well-known Jewish journalist Bernard Levin wrote in the *Daily Mail*: 'The time has come to declare that twenty years of carefully regulated torture, which is what solitary confinement is, is sufficient and should be ended. And that the three nations which are prepared to do so – namely England, France and the United States – should act without delay. If the fourth government concerned, the Soviet Union, refuses to give its consent, it should be invited to start a Third World War on these grounds. Since the Four Powers take turns monthly in providing the guard, there is no problem in making the necessary announcement during a month in which the Western Powers are responsible for Spandau. Also, if Kosygin should really be alarmed, the thought of a Third World War is scarcely tenable. Our Foreign Office would doubtless find an acceptable and sonorous explanation.'

Bernard Levin's words clearly show that the high-sounding promises of the Western Occupying Powers are nothing but tinsel.

But if it must be that my father is to drain the cup of revenge to its bitter dregs, then I ask myself why the Western Powers compromise their position and demonstrate *ad absurdum* their so often affirmed moral, legal and human values in the form of this life-long imprisonment. Since this pitiless and solitary torture mocks these values in a manner nothing short of grotesque, there must be very weighty reasons which conceal even today, 43 years after my father's flight, highly dangerous political explosive.

We can only guess at the nature of this explosive material as long as my father's voice is silenced, and as long as the British and American governments embargo documents on my father's case until the year 2017. We can, however, steer these conjectures in a certain direction in the light of what has been found – in spite of the embargo – in British archives, and, with other pieces of the mosaic, assemble all this into a convincing picture of the Hess affair.

In brief: by incarcerating Rudolf Hess for life, the victors are probably trying to conceal the fact that at the very least they were accessories to the continuation of the war, a war which did not reach its full measure of horror until after 1941.

To conclude this introduction, I wish to make a few further comments on my father's case. They are intended to help the reader to understand the political connexion between the flight to Britain and his imprisonment for more than forty years:

1. Whether or not my father flew to Britain with Hitler's direct consent is unimportant. It suffices that Rudolf Hess acted in political concord with Hitler and in accordance with the desires of the German people in his wish to prevent the European war expanding into a world war.
2. If this readiness to make peace had not been abused in such an abominable way, there would probably not have been a Second World War, with its fifty million dead.
3. The unleashing of the Second World War became unavoidable once Churchill and Roosevelt gave priority over all other considerations to the destruction of Germany. Hess was not there-

fore enticed to Scotland by the British Secret Service because the Prime Minister had in mind peace with Hitler but because he wished to weaken Hitler by a loss of prestige and to goad Stalin into war.

4. This state of affairs broadens into the dimensions of an atrocity the perfidiousness with which my father has since been treated by the British. His capture, his extradition to Nuremberg, his conviction and his martyrdom in Spandau are what a man must suffer whose good intentions were exploited – under false pretences – in a perilous but hopeless undertaking. The argument that, because of his gullibility, my father should himself be blamed for what happened to him ignores the fact that, if this were true, the desire for peace would have to be seen as naive, and planning for war seen as a superior concept.

5. The four victorious Powers hold my father prisoner because he knows too much. That Rudolf Hess has not broken down during four decades of imprisonment presents the Four Powers with an ever-increasing dilemma: to prevent Rudolf Hess from recounting in freedom the historical truth, they have to accept, against all sense of justice and of humanity, that he must be kept prisoner to the end of his days. Because the Four Powers are unable to find a way out of this dilemma, they simply hope for the death of Rudolf Hess.

6. With a few exceptions, the Germans ignore the fact that on German soil a German named Rudolf Hess is slowly but surely being tortured to death. To be sure, all Bonn governments since Konrad Adenauer's have courteously appealed to the Four Powers for my father's release. Indeed, some politicians – Helmut Schmidt and Helmut Kohl in particular – penetrate quite far behind the scenes in their efforts, but as yet no one has dared to ask in public what is the real meaning of the Rudolf Hess affair, this slow and repulsive enforcement of one of the most malicious judicial murders of all time.

7. In spite of all this, Rudolf Hess has not bowed his head in Spandau. This book is intended to ensure that this scandalous and anachronistic outrage is not forgotten. It is also intended to sharpen the perception of present and future generations of German youth in their differentiation between the propaganda of victors and the truth. It is also an attempt at an interim balance sheet in the Rudolf Hess affair.

I call upon the Four Occupying Powers to release my father from Spandau immediately, if only so that he can express an opinion on the testimony given in this book.

If the Four Occupying Powers continue to hold my father in prison, I accuse them before world opinion of:

SUBJECTING RUDOLF HESS TO SLOW AND AGONIZING DEATH, CONTRARY TO JUSTICE AND HUMANITY, IN ORDER TO SUPPRESS THE HISTORICAL TRUTH.

Wolf Rüdiger Hess
Munich, 15 March 1984

**ON 17 AUGUST 1987 RUDOLF HESS DIED
IN SPANDAU PRISON AT THE AGE OF 93.**

Part I

THE FLIGHT

'WHEN ARE YOU COMING BACK?'

SATURDAY, 10 MAY 1941. For more than a year-and-a-half there has been war in Europe. Nevertheless, the peace of a sunny spring day lay over Bavaria when my father said goodbye to my mother at his home in München-Harlaching.

She had not felt very well that day and had stayed in bed that morning, so this midday scene she has so often told me about took place in her bedroom. My father was dressed in a blue shirt, matching dark blue tie, blue-grey breeches and high top-boots. This was his Air Force uniform. It all spoke of a departure, and he told my mother that during the lunch break he had received a telephone call ordering him to Berlin. After a short 'detour via Augsburg', he would 'go up there' in the evening.[1]

His wife was surprised – above all by the blue shirt and the matching tie. My mother had always thought that blue suited her husband, but 'the big chap', as she liked to call him, had so far refused to follow his wife's advice.

My mother asked in surprise why he had decided to wear a blue shirt on this very occasion. He replied with an engaging smile, 'To make you happy!'

'When are you coming back?' she asked.

'I don't know precisely; perhaps tomorrow. But I shall certainly be home again by Monday evening', he answered.

'As early as tomorrow? Or Monday? I don't believe it – you won't be back so quickly!'

As my father wrote later from Nuremberg, he turned hot and

[17]

cold. He took his leave by kissing my mother's hand and quickly turned to go. He was afraid that his wife might question him further. Perhaps she already sensed that her husband was about to set out on the longest, most adventurous and most tragic journey of his life.

Accompanied by his adjutant, Lieutenant Karlheinz Pintsch, his personal orderly, Josef Platzer, his security officer, Frantz Lutz and his driver, Rudolf Lippert, my father arrived at Augsburg-Haunstetten late in the afternoon. Here was located a Messerschmitt production plant manufacturing fighter and bomber aircraft for the Luftwaffe. Rudolf Hess had addressed the assembled workforce here on 1 May, National Labour Day. Here in the preceding weeks and months he had been taught to fly the Me 110. Here, as always, his plane stood on the runway ready for take-off.

The rest was routine. Over the official telephone of Messerschmitt's senior pilot, Helmut Kaden, he was given the weather forecast for the North German coastal region and the northern part of the North Sea by the Meteorological Office at Hamburg. He then went to the pilots' changing room, forced himself into a leather pilot's uniform without badges of rank, and slipped on the heavy fur boots. Accompanied by Pintsch, he walked across the runway to the aircraft and shook hands with the ground staff. Before he climbed the ladder into the Luftwaffe-grey aircraft, Hess handed his adjutant a sealed envelope which he, Pintsch, was to deliver to Adolf Hitler at Obersalzberg four hours after his departure.

The mechanics had meanwhile started the two engines. While they were warming up, Hess lifted his hand in farewell. The chocks were removed. The aircraft shuddered slightly as it slowly began to move. Hess taxied out to the take-off point, carried out the various engine tests and opened up the engines to full throttle. Then, on the grass track which served as a runway, the great plane accelerated and took off. It was just 17.45 Middle European Time.

The Me 110 E-1/N, serial number 3869, in which Rudolf Hess took off for Great Britain to salvage world peace on this Saturday evening, was a heavy fighter-bomber. With its two reserve tanks, it had a range of 4,200 km or 10 flying hours. Its two engines totalling 1,400 HP gave the Me 110 a cruising speed of

420 kph. If nothing intervened, flying time to the Scottish coast would be about four hours.

Across the North Sea it was 'magnificently lonely . . . with a fantastically beautiful evening light already affected by the high latitude', as Hess later recalled.[2] 'The little clouds far below me were like ice floes in the sea, crystal-clear, everything lit with red. The sky was clear – alas, too clear; of the Meteorological Office's "solid cloud cover at a height of 500 metres" into which I could if necessary withdraw there was nothing – nothing whatsoever.'

Rudolf Hess had not expected this, and for a moment he thought of turning back. But as an experienced pilot he calculated the risks involved in such a decision. With a probability approaching certainty, to return to Augsberg with reserve tanks almost empty and to land at night on the factory's unlit airfield would mean disaster. Even if the Deputy Führer himself survived this, the Me 110 would be destroyed and he, Rudolf Hess, would thus lose any further chance of carrying out his mission. So he decided to see it through – 'come what may'.

One great problem was of course the air defences' radar and interceptors. But Hess was lucky; no one seemed to detect him. As he approached the Scottish coast, he noticed a haze reflecting the evening sun. He began to circle in its shelter for a time over the open sea until dusk fell. He then dived at full throttle from a height of a few thousand metres towards the coast. This caused the Me 110 to gain so much speed that the two Spitfires which had been chasing him were apparently unable to keep up.

Shortly after 22.00 hrs., at the breathtaking speed of 750 kph, Hess crossed the coast at Farne Island, thundered with screaming engines over a sleepy village and began hedge-hopping. He flew at low level over houses, trees and cows, up-hill and down-hill, as if he wanted to trace the contours of the Scottish Highlands in his desperate flight. It was the surest – but somewhat dangerous – way of escaping the enemy air defences.

Hess had no need even to look at his map. In the months before his flight, at home in München-Harlaching, he had fixed a road map to the wall which he studied repeatedly when he could not sleep. Thus, Hess had the most important landmarks in his head as he flew across Scotland in the evening light: the Cheviot Hills, a little reservoir lake in the mountains, and around the peak of Broad Law.

Shortly before 23.00 hrs. he was gliding over Dungavel House, the country seat of the Duke of Hamilton. To rule out any error – it had by then become dark – Hess flew on for a few minutes to the west coast of Scotland. He later recalled almost passionately that moment when he reached the Atlantic: 'In the light of the rising moon, there lay the glassy sea. Rising sheer from it to a height of some five hundred metres was a granite dome bathed in a magnificent red glow, beautiful and peaceful in contrast to my somewhat daring and alarming enterprise, shortly before the first parachute jump of my life. I shall never forget that picture.'[3]

Convinced of the accuracy of his navigation, Hess then banked and flew eastwards across Scotland, recognized the railway line with its curve at Dungavel, saw the little lake south of the country seat, and the road leading past it. He then spiralled upwards to reach the safe height of 2,000 metres necessary for a parachute jump, switched off the ignition and set the propeller blades at zero pitch. This stopped their rotation in spite of the slipstream, and he could safely allow himself to fall. Now, however, a number of circumstances intervened which Hess had not foreseen.

First, one of the propellers continued obstinately to rotate because the gas mixture was repeatedly ignited by the cylinders, which had overheated. When the engine finally calmed down, Hess unstrapped himself, opened the cockpit hood and tried to get out. But the air pressure produced by the Me 110 even at low speed forced him so firmly against the back of the seat that he felt as if he was glued down. Later, in explaining this difficulty, he said: 'I had asked the good Messerschmitt people at Augsberg everything, except how to jump out. I suppose I thought it was too simple a question.'[4]

The fierce thunder of the night air and the confused situation which had so surprisingly arisen did not cause Hess to panic, but it made him forget to reduce speed further by lowering the landing flaps. He was therefore gliding without power but still at some speed towards the ground. At this moment, he thought of a piece of advice once given him by an experienced pilot: If you want to get out of a plane but can't because of the speed, put it on its back. Then you simply let yourself fall out.

Hess had never carried out this manoeuvre in his flying

training, but he now began gradually to turn the heavy Me 110 on to its back. In doing this, however, he instinctively pulled the elevator control as if for a half-hoop instead of setting it for horizontal flight. The plane therefore suddenly plunged into a steep downwards curve, and the Deputy Führer, pressed down into his seat by the enormous centrifugal force, was suddenly thrown forward. For some moments he saw 'stars', as all fighter pilots report, then everything went black.

Hess has two circumstances to thank that his mission did not end in his death at this early point. First, he was pressed so firmly down into his seat that the air pressure could not break his neck. Second, he regained consciousness just as the plane reached the top of its flight path, which had meanwhile again become an ascent, and for a moment the speed was approaching zero. 'I got up and out in one go – at the same moment the plane plunged downwards vertically', he said later, with a sigh of relief.

It was precisely 23.09 hrs. when Deputy Führer and Reich Minister Rudolf Hess landed by parachute on British soil, spraining his right ankle. In spite of his adversities, Hess had missed his target, Dungavel House, by only twelve miles.

The man he was looking for would not however have been there on the night of 10–11 May. The Duke of Hamilton was then a group-captain commanding an RAF fighter group at Turnhouse airfield, a sector in Scotland's Air Defence. Shortly after 10 p.m. his comrades in the Observer Corps at Inverness, a little further north, had detected a lonely plane on their radar screens in the grid 1/AC. This plane was pursuing a strange zig-zag course westwards. They sent up two interceptor fighters towards it as a precaution. When Hamilton heard that it was a German Me 110 he thought it must be a mistake, because every RAF officer knew that this type of plane carried sufficient fuel to reach Northumberland at most, if the pilot was to avoid crashing on his return flight because of lack of fuel.

In a little village south of Glasgow, the well-known and respected engineer Mr Ramsay was out for a walk with his son on this evening in early summer when they heard above them the noise of a strange plane. Ramsay briefly remarked: 'That's probably Rudolf Hess.' Scarcely had he uttered these words when he broke off in alarm, and turning to his son he went on,

'Forget what I have just said and talk to no one about it.' Until his death, in fact, Mr Ramsay senior never again mentioned this incident.[5]

At the Baird family's Floor Farm, the manager David McLean was preparing for bed when he heard a plane roaring frighteningly low over the house. Shortly afterwards he heard a dull crash. When McLean looked out of the window into the hazy moonlight he saw across the field a parachute coming down like a silver cloud. He could clearly see the figure of the pilot beneath it. McLean alerted Farmer Craig Baird and, as Baird had first to get dressed, he ran alone towards the stranger. Meanwhile, the crashed plane went up in flames 300 metres away.

McLean helped the pilot out of his parachute harness, supporting him as he had obviously injured himself in the jump. On the way to the farm, Hess said in English, 'I am German. My name is Captain Alfred Horn. I am here on a special mission. I want to give the Duke of Hamilton of Dungavel House an important message.' He was apparently unarmed. Leaning on McLean's shoulder. Hess alias Horn limped into the farm manager's sitting room. Baird had meanwhile alerted the soldiers of an Intelligence Unit stationed not far from the farm at Eaglesham House. Within a short time, two men in battle dress came thundering into the sitting room. In their hurry, they had forgotten their rifles. A little later, two oddly dressed members of the Home Guard arrived, to whom Hess repeated his request. Of course, they all knew the Duke of Hamilton, Scotland's premier peer.

The two Home Guard members, pistols drawn, arrested my father and drove him to the Home Guard Headquarters at Giffnock, where the guard started by giving the prisoner a bottle of milk to drink. My father repeated that he wished to speak to the Duke of Hamilton. He at first kept to his assumed name so as not to be recognized too soon and thereby endanger his mission. However, the Major who interrogated him thought he looked just like Rudolf Hess, but Horn-Hess did not let this tempt him into abandoning his reticence. The prisoner was then taken to Maryhill Barracks at Glasgow and from there to the nearby military hospital, where his sprained ankle was treated.

Later in the night of 10 to 11 May, Group-Captain Hamilton received a telephone message at Turnhouse airfield that a German pilot named Alfred Horn, who had just bailed out of his aircraft, wished to speak to him. The Duke, who we must remember was commanding a combat unit of RAF Fighter Command, did not at first know how to react to this overture on the part of the enemy. The military regulations for behaviour in wartime had nothing at all to say about such rare events. Nevertheless, Hamilton made his way to Glasgow, arriving at Maryhill Barracks on Sunday 11 May just before 10 a.m.

With the Interrogation Officer and the Duty Officer, Hamilton first went into a room where Rudolf Hess's belongings were held: a Leica camera, a few family photographs, some medicaments and the visiting cards of a certain Dr Karl Haushofer and a certain Dr Albrecht Haushofer, two German scholars who were friends of Hess and whom Hamilton also knew. The three Britons then went to see Rudolf Hess.

My father immediately demanded a talk with Hamilton alone. At the Duke's request, the two other officers withdrew. The German opened the conversation by saying that he had met Hamilton in 1936 during the Berlin Olympic Games, and that he, Hamilton, had also on one occasion had lunch with him, Hess, at München-Harlaching. 'I don't know whether you remember me', my father added, 'I am Rudolf Hess.' 'He then continued', as Hamilton later reported to Prime Minister Churchill,[6] 'that this was a mission of humanity, and that the Führer did not want to conquer Britain but to put an end to the war. Albrecht Haushofer had told him that I was an Englishman who would understand his (Hess's) point of view. He had therefore tried to arrange to meet me in Lisbon . . . . He had tried to fly to Dungavel, and this was his fourth attempt; the first had been in December (1940). On the first three occasions he had had to turn back because of bad weather. During the period that Britain was victorious in Libya he had done nothing, because his visit might then have been interpreted as a sign of weakness. But now, following the German successes in North Africa and Greece, he was glad to have come.

'The fact that Reich Minister Hess had come personally to this country, he pointed out, must be evidence of his sincerity and of Germany's readiness for peace. The Führer, he continued, was convinced that Germany would win the war – perhaps very soon, but certainly within one, two or three years. He wanted to end the unnecessary bloodshed which would otherwise unavoidably result. He asked me whether I could assemble leading members of my party so that we could together discuss practicable peace proposals. I replied that there was now only one party in this country. He then said that he could tell me Hitler's peace conditions. He would first insist on an agreement which excluded for ever another war between our two countries. I asked him how such an agreement could be achieved and he replied that, of course, one of the conditions would be that England abandoned its traditional policy of always opposing the strongest power in Europe. I then said to him that if we were to make peace now we would probably be at war again within the next two years. He asked why, and I answered that if a peace agreement were possible it would have been concluded before the war began. However, as Germany had preferred to make war instead of peace, and this at a time when we were very earnestly seeking to preserve peace, I could not now put forward a peace agreement as a matter of course.

'He asked me to request the King to grant him safe-conduct because he had come unarmed and of his own free will.

'He also asked me if I could send a telegram to Rothakker, Herzogstrasse 17, Zürich, informing his family that he was safe by writing that Alfred Horn was safe and well. He also requested that his identity should not be revealed to the press.

'During the entire interview Hess was able to express himself quite clearly, but he did not understand enough of what I said. I therefore suggested that I should return with an interpreter and conduct a further conversation with him.'

Throughout the conversation, Hamilton had turned over in his mind whether he was in fact dealing with Deputy Führer and Reich Minister Rudolf Hess. By the end, however, he was quite sure. 'I believed that this prisoner was in fact Hess in person.' Only Rudolf Hess himself was not so sure about this. As he later confided in a letter to his wife, he often asked himself at the time 'whether this is really me . . . whether I may be dreaming, lying peacefully in bed in Berlin in the Wilhelmstrasse or at home in Harlaching, and would suddenly wake up with only the road map illuminated on the opposite wall of my room. On the other hand, I dreamt repeatedly that I was still at home and that I had not yet succeeded in carrying out the planned flight; or that I had already returned from England without having achieved my purpose. Each time it was like a horrible nightmare; in my dream I did everything to reach my goal, and ended in the most dreadful despair because I was back without having attained my objective.'[7]

Who, then, was this Rudolf Hess? A dreamer? Or a politician who genuinely wished to make peace?

'A NEW ERA HAS DAWNED'

MY FATHER, RUDOLF WALTER RICHARD HESS, was born in Alexandria, Egypt, on 26 April 1894, son of the respected and wealthy merchant Fritz Hess. His birthplace is not very far from Abukir where Admiral Nelson once sank Napoleon's fleet and established British naval supremacy in the Mediterranean. The Hess family were representatives of the German Reich of that time which had achieved by the turn of the century power, riches and self-assurance. It therefore provoked the envy, fear and fighting spirit of the Anglo-Saxon powers.

Fritz Hess owned an imposing property and a beautiful garden on the Mediterranean coast. The family, which came from Wunsiedel in the Fichtelgebirge, also owned a country house at Reicholdsgrün, where they regularly spent their summer holidays. The source of this wealth was the trading firm of Hess & Co., which Fritz Hess had inherited from his father and which he managed with great success.

His son Rudolf was a pupil at the German Protestant School in Alexandria. In addition, he received tuition from private tutors. His future appeared to be predetermined by the family tradition and the strong hand of his father: he would inherit the property and the firm, that is, he would become a merchant. Young Hess, however, was not very much inclined towards this aim in life. He felt drawn towards the sciences, above all physics and mathematics. His ability in these fields became clearly evident at the Bad Godesberg Educational Institute, a boarding school for boys which he entered on 15 September 1908 and left at Easter 1911. Nevertheless, at the behest of his father, he was required to end his high school education by passing the school-leaving examination so as to enter the École Supérieur de Commerce at Neuchâtel in Switzerland, followed by an apprenticeship in a Hamburg trading company.

The defeat of the German Empire in the First World War and the victors' Versailles Diktat represented a deep, even catastrophic, turning point in the life of the Hess family. They had spent the crucial July crisis in their holiday home at Reicholdsgrün, and Rudolf Hess, then 20 years of age, did not hesitate for a moment before reporting to the Bavarian Field Artillery as a volunteer. Soon afterwards he was transferred to the infantry, and as a poorly trained recruit he was at the Front by 4 November 1914, where he took part in the trench warfare on the Somme.

Like most young Germans sharing his lot, Rudolf Hess had gone to the Front as a fervent patriot acutely conscious of Germany's cause, which he saw as just, and determined to defeat the British-French arch-enemy. After six months of front-line service, Hess was promoted lance-corporal. To his men he was an exemplary comrade, always the first to volunteer for raids and reconnaissance patrols, and distinguishing himself in bloody battles among the barbed wire, trenches and shell craters by his cheerful composure, courage and bravery.

My father Rudolf Hess fought on the Western Front in Flanders and before Verdun; he fought on the Eastern Front in the battles around Rimnicul-Sarat and on the Putna, in the Siebengebirge and on the Moldau. He was awarded the Iron Cross, Second Class, for his outstanding conduct and courageous efforts. However, in 1916 and again in 1917 he paid the price of his career as a soldier, in which he reached the rank of Lieutenant of Reserves, suffering two severe wounds. A rifle bullet penetrated his left lung, and for some time he was fighting for his life.

Scarred by the dangers and privations of war, Rudolf Hess was 'discharged from active military service to Reicholdsgrün without maintenance', as the Army List somewhat baldly reads, on 13 December 1918, i.e. after the humiliating armistice of Compiègne.[1] Meanwhile, his father had lost the Egyptian part of the family fortune as a result of British expropriation. But for Rudolf Hess the political fate suffered by his Fatherland under defeat and revolution weighed more heavily than this private misfortune. Defeat led to the Treaty of Versailles, enforced upon Germany by the victorious Powers by maintenance of the hunger blockade. It was a 'peace of annihilation'. In reality, it was a victors' Diktat which the German National Assembly accepted only under protest and following threats of violence. The Social-Democratic Reich Chancellor, Philipp Scheidemann, employed moving words in his address, since famous, of 12 May 1919: '. . . Allow me to speak entirely without tactical considerations. What our discussions are concerned with, this thick book in which a hundred paragraphs begin with "Germany renounces, renounces, renounces", this most atrocious and murderous hammer of evil by which a great people is extorted and blackmailed into acknowledging its own unworthiness, accepting its merciless dismemberment, consenting to enslavement and serfdom, this book must not become the statute book of the future. . . . I ask you, who as an honest man – I will not even say as a German; only as an honest man loyal to the terms of a treaty – can submit to such conditions? What hand would not wither which submits itself and us to such fetters? Moreover, we must stir ourselves, we must toil, work as slaves for international capitalism, work unpaid for the entire world! . . . If this treaty is actually signed it will not be Germany's corpse alone that remains on the battlefield of Versailles. Beside it will be lying equally noble corpses, the right to self-determination of peoples, the independence of free nations, belief in all the fine ideals under whose banner the Entente purported to fight, and above all belief in loyalty to the terms of a treaty! An unequalled degeneration of ethical and moral concepts would be the consequence of such a Treaty of Versailles.'[2]

The words of the Social Democrat Philipp Scheidemann leave scarcely any doubt that the *vae victis* of the allied and associated governments had become a question of whether the German Nation was to continue to exist or not. As a result of his 'withered hand' words, Scheidemann resigned. He did not wish to bear the responsibility of shaking hands on the 'enslavement of the German people'. The new Bauer Government eventually signed the Treaty. By taking this decision, the Weimar Parliament itself directed its eventual downfall – of course without then expecting it – while its Constitution was still under debate. Far-sighted critics uttered at the time the wise and true doctrine: the Weimar Constitution was not that actually adopted by Parliament on 11 August 1919 but the Versailles Diktat of 28 June 1919. In fact, the innumerable Reich Governments engendered by the Weimar Republic – from Bauer to Brüning and Schleicher – were repeatedly faced with the continuing and insurmountable dilemma that they were required to act as 'agents' of the victors in enforcing the countless suppressive and destructive conditions of the Versailles Diktat. They thus unavoidably and continually discredited themselves in the eyes of their own people, which was as good as political suicide for these governments.

One party and one man adopted from the very outset the watchword: they would not allow themselves to be blackmailed. This man was Adolf Hitler, and his party was the National Socialist German Workers' Party.

The fundamental difference between 'agent' on the one hand and radical and uncompromising rejection of the Versailles Diktat on the other hand may be seen as the main reason for the final seizure of power by Adolf Hitler on 30 January 1933. Hitler came to power because his principles of self-respect and self-assertion were adopted more vigorously by the people than were the 'fuddled representations' of the 'Weimar appeasement politicians'.

Rudolf Hess was appalled and deeply shocked by the conditions that had developed in Germany, and he decided to fight against the Diktat. The state of affairs he found in Munich when he returned from the Front defied description in his terms. Like most of his comrades, Hess was drawn into the war in 1914 to fight for a free, strong and proud Germany. Now, 26 years of age, he had to witness the establishment in Bavaria of a republic governed by communists and socialists, which in his eyes created national catastrophe out of military defeat.

In a letter to a cousin – although written in 1927 – Hess graphically described his mood at the time: 'You know how I suffer under the situation to which our once proud nation has been brought. I have fought for the honour of our flag where a man of my age had of course to fight, where conditions were at their worst, in dirt and mud, in the hell of Verdun, Artois and elsewhere. I have witnessed the horror of death in all its forms, been battered for days under heavy bombardment, slept in a dugout in which lay half a Frenchman. I have hungered and suffered, as indeed have all frontline soldiers. And is all this to be in vain, the suffering of the good people at home all for nothing? I have learned from you what you women have had to live through! No, if all this was in vain I would still today regret that I did not put a bullet through my brain on the day the monstrous armistice conditions and their acceptance were published. I did not do it at the time solely in the hope that in one way or another I might still be able to do something to reverse fate'.[3]

From then onwards his belief that he could 'reverse fate' and his will to do so dominated his thought. During the winter of 1918/19, in a humiliated Germany shaken by communist riots, tormented by workers' and soldiers' soviets, he still recognized in spite of his depression the possibility of a renewed effort for his country and his people, for whom he had been prepared to lay down his life in the years past.

He wanted to fight against the visible subjugation of Germany, and his initial despair was transformed into indignation and motivating anger.

These feelings led him almost unavoidably to the one force that, as he had correctly sensed from the beginning, was alone in a position to burst the fetters imposed upon the Germans at Versailles. Like millions of other Germans, he followed this man, and he followed him earlier and with more dedication than most of the rest. Like everyone, he was convinced of the justice of the cause for which he fought: the restoration of Germany's rightful position by throwing off the Versailles Diktat.

Sometime in May 1921, at an evening meeting of the German Workers' Party in a room adjoining the Sternecker brewery in Münchner Tal, Hess first heard Hitler speak. When he returned home to the little Pension von Schildberg, he reported enthusiastically to the girl in the next room, Ilse Pröhl, whom he was later to marry: 'The day after tomorrow you must come with me to a meeting of the National Socialist Workers' Party. Someone unknown is speaking; I can't remember his name. But if anyone can free us from Versailles he is the man. This unknown man will restore our honour.'[4]

Rudolf Hess's enthusiasm for Hitler had various causes. First, there were reasons of practical policy, which Hess formulated as follows in a letter written in 1921:

'The core of the matter is that Hitler is convinced that resurrection (of Germany) is possible only if we can succeed in leading the great mass of people, in particular the workers, back to national awareness. But this is possible only in the context of reasonable, honest socialism.'[5]

Second, Hess had a personal reason, which was Hitler's eloquence. In a letter to a friend written in 1924, Rudolf Hess described clearly the effect of this gift: 'You won't find more than once a man who at a mass meeting can enrapture the most left-wing lathe operator just as much as the right-wing senior executive. This man, within two hours, made the thousand communists who had come to break up (the meeting) stand and join in the National Anthem at the end (as in Munich in 1921), and this man, within three hours, in a special address to a few hundred industrialists and the Minister President, who had come more or less to oppose him, secured their full approval or speechless astonishment.'[6]

Rudolf Hess was convinced that Hitler could not fail to succeed in bursting the chains of Versailles and in bringing about the political change of direction in Germany which promised a better future. A long paper written in 1921 sets out how he saw this happening:

'If we want to look for future probabilities, we must look to the past. History repeats itself along general lines. The outbreak of similar illnesses demands similar doctors.

'What is the German nation suffering from?'

'The body was unhealthy even before 1914. White-collar and blue-collar workers decried one another instead of respecting one another. The intellectually creative looked down with some arrogance upon the manually creative. Instead of providing them with leaders from their own ranks, they left them to themselves and even to alien seducers, seducers who skilfully exploited the injustice present to widen the gap.

'This led to a fearful revenge, when after the stupendous efforts of four years of war nerve suddenly broke. The collapse was primarily the work of these same seducers and their helpers among the enemy.

'Since then Germany has writhed in agony. It can scarcely stand. Years of blood flowing from the arteries as a result of the Treaty of Versailles; wasteful state administration – empty coffers; wild printing of banknotes – grotesque inflation. Among the population, brilliant parties alongside flagrant misery, gluttony alongside hunger, profiteers alongside starving honesty. The last morsel of strength has disappeared.'[7]

In this broad context, Hess then referred to Hitler and his role as the 'doctor' of critically-ill Germany: 'His arguments lead the workers towards relentless nationalism; he destroys the Marxist ideology of international socialism. He replaces it by National Socialist ideals. To this end, he educates both manual workers and the so-called intelligentsia: the common interest is superior to one's own interests; first comes the nation, then me personally. This unification of national ideals and social ideals is the pivot of our times . . . The Führer must assimilate healthy philosophies for his time and hurl them back at the masses concentrated into electrifying ideas.'

Hess believed that Hitler was capable of this, and in his conclusion he describes the gifts of the ideal leader, which he accepted that Hitler possessed. 'Over and above the economy, the destiny of a people is determined by politics. All internal reforms, all economic measures, are ineffective as long as the Treaties of Versailles and St. Germain continue to exist. The ruler trained in political geography has a comprehensive conception of the world. He knows the nations and the influential individuals. He can if necessary trample down under jackboots or tie threads with careful and sensitive fingers to reach as far as the Pacific.'

'The noblest of duties is the rehabilitation of Germany's standing in the world. He knows the meaning of the imponderable. He knows that the old flag under which millions gave their life's blood in their belief in their country will fly high once again, that the battle against the war-guilt lies must be fought by all available means. Strong national feeling within the country, faith in oneself, strengthens a nation, as does vindication in the eyes of the world.' Seldom has the attitude then adopted by many towards the tasks facing German politics and their conduct been more impressively and sharply defined.

The concept of 'threads tied by careful and sensitive fingers to reach as far as the Pacific' awakened memories of the geo-political theories of Hess's tutor, Professor Karl Haushofer, in his lectures, and seminars and in his Zeitschrift für Geopolitik (Journal of Geo-politics). Apart from Hitler, this man most strongly influenced Rudolf Hess's conception of the world.

Returning from the First World War with the rank of Major-General, Haushofer dedicated himself, as successor to Ratzel, Kjellen and Mahan, to the role of a scientist pursuing a theory of political geography which he named 'geo-politics'. According to this theory, each state in the world is engaged in a harsh battle for existence, which it can determine for itself by the mastery of space. Using political, economic and strategic criteria, Haushofer attempted to explore the intrinsic legality of such spaces so that the results of his analyses might serve practical politics.

Hess became a close personal friend of Haushofer during his years as a student in Munich. Hess referred to his tutor in a letter to his parents dated 17 June 1920: 'I hear and learn about very interesting things from General Haushofer. He is a wonderful man. If the weather is fine he always picks me up for a stroll before lunch or supper. We were recently walking through the English Garden from 7 a.m. to 8.30 a.m. . . . He is exactly the opposite of what Uncle Alfred (Hess) describes as a 'militarist'. He was an outstanding member of the General Staff, but was more a scholar in soldier's uniform. . . . He was a father to his soldiers, and was so popular that his men protected him from insult during the revolutionary period, and he was able to lead his artillery division home as a complete unit. He has travelled a lot around the world. . . . I sometimes go for a walk with his only son [this refers to Albrecht Haushofer – W.R.H.], and we speak English together.'[8]

Rudolf Hess was able to observe at close quarters the professor with the melancholy eyes and the strong bushy beard as he formulated his theory of 'German living space' and as he talked about 'Germany's spatial destiny' – concepts that both Hitler and Hess adopted in their political terminology. Supported by his very far-reaching connections with political personalities in Japan, Italy and Britain, Haushofer also later influenced National Socialist foreign policy. Thus, in the 1930s, he sponsored preparations for the German–Italian and German–

Japanese alliances, the so-called Berlin–Rome–Tokyo Axis, the cornerstone of Hitler's policy of alliances.

On 5 January 1919, the writer Harrer founded the German Workers' Party in Munich, which Adolf Hitler joined as Member No. 7 in September 1919. The National Socialist German Workers' Party (NSDAP) was founded in Munich in 1920 under Hitler's influence, and my father became its Member No. 16 on 1 July 1920. From that time onwards my father began a slow but steady turn towards Hitler, counterbalancing to a certain extent his hitherto very exclusive friendship with Karl Haushofer. The friendship itself remained intact until the old gentleman's death in March 1946.

The NSDAP, before its great successes with the voting public, was a small Bavarian party, and Hitler's importance in national politics was insignificant. This could not at first be changed even by Hitler's great abilities as a speaker. His rise between 1928 and 1933 was not because he was against the Republic as an institution but solely because he opposed the policy of appeasement. In the period from 1924 to 1929, when it appeared possible to normalize conditions in Germany in spite of Versailles, Hitler was little known. The only exception to this in the early years was the 'March on the Feldherrnhalle' of 9 November 1923. The result of this attempted coup, in the course of which my father was to arrest three Bavarian ministers, was the confinement of Hitler and later also of my father in the fortress of Landsberg.

In Landsberg, Hitler and my father served out their sentence, only part of which was in an environment that might be described as 'cheerful'. Here was established between the two men that relationship of confidence which characterized the image of the party leadership over the coming years. Here, too, Hitler wrote his seminal work *Mein Kampf*. My father edited the pages of manuscript and checked them for errors. Professor Karl Haushofer often called for discussions and to bring literature. After his early release on 13 December 1924, my father rejected Haushofer's offer of a post as his assistant at the 'Germany Academy', and instead, in April 1925, became Adolf Hitler's private secretary at a monthly salary of 500 RM.

Hess wrote to his parents two days before his thirty-first birthday giving the reasons that had persuaded him to take this fateful decision:

'Here (close to Hitler), I remain on the path I have been treading for years . . . I acknowledge the Tribune (which is what the Hess family jokingly called Hitler) as Führer. I have a personal and confidential relationship with him and no-one is going to interfere with that. I represent him in many matters. . . . The respect I enjoy is based on this. . . . Also, it was important to him from the outset that I am not a Party employee, and that my position is quite independent of the Party. This is necessary if only because of the authority located there.'[9]

The letter continues: 'If anyone says that I am standing on a narrow platform, I ask where in these times is there a safer and broader platform on which one can settle? We should not forget that we are in a build-up period, and this will accelerate when the bad years, which are certain to come, are upon us.'

Hess also felt that he was particularly suited to his new post, for he wrote: 'In fact, there are probably not many people in whom are united, as in me, what he (Hitler) needs. I have been in the Movement since the time when it consisted of less than a hundred members. I am therefore aware of the external build-up, the external effects, and I know the Tribune's innermost thoughts, his attitude towards all questions, his whole nature. He knows me; our mutual trust to the very utmost; we understand one another.'

Finally, Hess saw that he had a certain role to play in his vocation: 'Thanks to my studies, which I have, of course, in part consciously, adapted to the Movement, I am in a position to discuss with intellectuals matters they have not been quite clear about; I am qualified to act as a link between the mass movement and the intelligentsia. On the other hand, I am far too convinced of the necessity of the often unpleasant methods and nature of the struggle in terms of mass psychology to allow this to frighten me away from participation in this Movement, as are so many other members of the intelligentsia. I am convinced that by exerting influence in many directions I can do some good in *that* respect. After all, it doesn't bind me for ever to the Tribune . . .'.

But this time was to come. The Party's offices were originally in a building at the rear of Schellingstrasse in Schwabing. Only in 1929, when people rushed to join the Party at the beginning of the world economic crisis and the simultaneous agonies of the Weimar Republic, did Hess and his small staff move to the

[35]

fashionable Brienner Strasse. Here, Paul Ludwig Troost the architect converted the Palais Barlow into the Braunen Haus (Brown House).

Towards the end of the 1920s, when the NSDAP had succeeded in becoming a party enjoying mass support, Rudolf Hess had so far extended his position that his control of the growing Party apparatus was unchallenged. In this process, in contrast to other Party personalities such as the Propaganda Minister-to-be Dr Joseph Goebbels in Berlin, he avoided establishing a power base. He enjoyed the unrestricted trust of his Chief, and the good, quiet and balanced character which nature had given him looked after the rest.

Thus Hess became the second man at the apex of his Party. He knew all Hitler's secrets, but his personal loyalty and his conviction of the political necessity of the Führer principle prevented him from ever thinking of abusing Hitler's confidence. Hess was present when sections of German industry and high finance decided to support the NSDAP financially. Hess consoled Hitler when his great love, his nineteen-year-old niece Geli Raubal, committed suicide in 1931. And when one day the police appeared at the Brown House to confiscate the most important documents in Hitler's safe it was Hess who tricked them. When no one was looking, he unscrewed the sealed handles, emptied the safe and screwed the handles back on again, so that when the police opened the safe they believed Hess when he said that not a scrap of paper had ever been in it. As late as February 1942, Hitler said appreciatively, when remembering this episode during table-talk, 'Hess was always a technical fiddler.'[10]

In December 1932, Hitler deprived the champion of the left, anti-capitalist and revolutionary wing of the NSDAP, Georg Strasser, of any influence. Until then he had served his Party as Reich Leader of Organization. The vacancy arising from his removal from power was filled by a Central Political Commission, whose leader was thereafter Rudolf Hess. He could now also co-ordinate the work of the NSDAP in the Parliaments of the German Länder, into which it had meanwhile been introduced.

In the early 1930s, the disintegration of the Weimar Republic and the burden of the world economic crisis created the political framework necessary for Hitler to seize power. At the same

time, because of its election successes, its propaganda cam-
paigns and the proof of its military unity, it achieved that degree
of attraction which caused widening groups of the population to
vote National Socialist. As unemployment increased, more and
more workers were also turning to the NSDAP, some directly
from the KPD (the German Communist Party). During the hectic
days of January 1933, Hess never left Hitler's side. He took part
in the secret negotiations at the Cologne villa of the banker Kurt
von Schröder, the so-called 'Schröder breakfast', which decisively influenced Reich President Hindenburg's appointment of
the leader of the strongest group in the Reichstag, the NSDAP,
as Chancellor of the Reich on 30 January 1933. On 31 January
1933, 'the day after the entry into office of Adolf Hitler', Rudolf
Hess, in a hand-written letter to his wife, recorded the feelings
that had seized him at this moment of triumph: 'Am I dreaming
or am I awake – that is the present question! I am sitting in the
Chancellor's office in the Wilhelmsplatz. Senior civil servants
approach noiselessly on soft carpets to submit documents "for
the Reich Chancellor", who is at the moment chairing a Cabinet
meeting and preparing the initial government action. Outside
the public stands patiently, packed together and waiting for
"him" to drive off – they start to sing the National Anthem and
shout "Heil" to the "Führer" or to the "Reich Chancellor". And
then I start to shake and I have to clench my teeth – just as I did
yesterday when the "Führer" returned from the Reich President
as "Reich Chancellor" and summoned me to his bedroom in the
Kaiserhof from among the mass of leaders waiting in the reception room – when what I had considered impossible right up to
the last moment became reality. I was firmly convinced that
everything would *of course* go wrong at the last moment. And the
Chief also admitted to me that a few times things were on a
knife-edge because of the intransigence of the old weasel in the
Cabinet [this refers to the coalition partner and Chairman of the
German National Peoples' Party, Alfred Hugenberg–W.R.H.].

'The evening torchlight procession marched before the
delighted old gentleman, who bore it until the last SS-man had
passed at about midnight. . . . Then came the jubilation directed
at the Führer, mixing with that directed at the Reich President.
The hours of men and women pushing past, holding up their
children towards the Führer, young girls and boys, their faces

[37]

radiant when they recognized "him" at the window of the Reich Chancellery – how sorry I was you were not there!

'The Chief behaves with incredible assurance. And the punctuality!!!! Always a few minutes *before* time!!! I have even had to make up my mind to buy a watch. A new era and a new time schedule has dawned!'

All this was written on a sheet of paper headed 'The Reich Chancellor'. Hess had, however, deleted the Gothic lettering with his pen. In a continuation of the letter dated 1 February, he wrote in conclusion: 'One stage towards victory is now I hope finally behind us. The second difficult period of the struggle has begun!'[11]

'THE PARTY'S CONSCIENCE'
OR
'DEPUTY FÜHRER OF THE NSDAP'

THE SECOND REICH of 1871, successor to the Holy Roman Empire, had perished at the end of the First World War in defeat and revolution. The Third Reich of 1933 tried to eradicate the humiliation of Versailles, to expunge the fourteen years of the Weimar Republic and to establish continuity with Germany's thousand-year history. The result was that there arose again in the heart of Europe what the Western Powers had wished to destroy once and for all in 1918/19 – i.e. a unified and strong Germany as good as its neighbours. Hitler had therefore to expect maximum opposition to his rule from the outset.

On 21 April 1933, the Führer appointed Hess Deputy Führer of the NSDAP. It was his duty to lead the state party as Hitler's representative and to preserve its national and social principles. Eight months later, on 1 December 1933, Hess was appointed, on Hitler's proposal, Reich Minister without Portfolio by Reich President Hindenburg. Although at the outbreak of war Reich-Marshal Hermann Göring was made Hitler's deputy leader of the state, this did not alter the fact that Hess remained Hitler's closest confidant, a confidant he could trust without reservation.

My father's unchallenged position at the summit of the Party was thanks to his attitude towards his career, which was in contrast to the overt or covert lust for power of other leading members of the Party. Shortly before the 'seizure of power', he wrote in December 1932 to his father: 'Making a career is akin to the American "making a dollar": "Make dollars, my son – if possible honestly – but above all make dollars!" The career-maker is often not far removed from the career-racketeer. He more resembles a phoney than an able man . . . "Making something for its own sake" and making a successful career do not go hand-in-hand. The man rising on the strength of his ability comes up against the career-makers. He does his duty without thinking about his career . . . rising upwards, assured and erect – the career-maker tries to get hold of a free seat on the cable car!' – 'To get ahead by his own efforts' – this was the secret of Hess's career.[1]

Even after he had accepted the rank of Minister, nothing changed in my father's modest and confident attitude towards his position. In Autumn 1933 he spent his holiday incognito, so well equipped with horn-rimmed spectacles, a false passport and a false name that the other holidaymakers confused him – mistakenly as they finally decided – with the 'genuine Hess'. Hess even went as far as to declare to an irritating passer-by that he did not like always being taken for the Deputy Führer; he really wasn't him! The false name under which he rented a room in a boarding house was in fact 'Alfred Horn of Nuremberg'. It was the name Hess was to use eight years later on his peace-flight to England.

Beside the gruelling double life he led in the Brown House at Munich and at his Wilhelmsplatz office in Berlin, Hess's attitude towards his duties was so relaxed that he, the Deputy Führer, still had time for a hobby, rare and expensive at the time: flying. In the 1920s, in fact, he had induced the publishers of the Party newspaper to buy a Messerschmitt 25 for publicity purposes. But it was none other than Rudolf Hess who then took his place behind the controls of the aircraft, its fuselage decorated in large letters with the legend 'Völkischer Beobachter', the paper's title.

Hess even succeeded in persuading Hitler that he should not always accompany him in special trains or the official car to distant meetings and conferences. 'To save time', as Hess tried to make the Führer believe, he would rather use his 'air vehicle'; the result, however, was that he often wasted much time or arrived late because of adverse weather or technical hitches.

The following is reported to have been said by Hitler to his flying fool: 'Hess, next time I am due to speak at Hamburg I shall tell you to go to Cologne; then at least there is a chance that I'll meet you in Hamburg.'[2]

At that time, private flying was still a dangerous pastime, needing – apart from money – a good deal of sporting spirit. Hess developed so much enthusiasm that in 1932 he won second prize in the 'Round the Zugspitze' amateur pilots' competition, and in 1934, already a Reich Minister, he won first prize. He also nearly matched Colonel Lindbergh's first Atlantic crossing from America to Europe by the first solo flight from Europe to America. The venture failed because the insurance companies refused to cover the risk. Hess wrote sadly to his parents: 'Now the dream is finally at an end – not exactly to the regret of the Tribune, who saw with very muted enthusiasm his Secretary pushing on towards the danger of an ocean flight.'[3]

Hitler reacted to his deputy's flying escapades with mixed feelings. After the first flight around the Zugspitze, he telegraphed Hess as follows:

IN SPITE OF MIXED FEELINGS, I WISH TO EXTEND TO YOU, MY DEAR HESS, MY WARMEST CONGRATULATIONS. I HOPE THAT NOW YOUR FLYING ABILITIES HAVE BEEN FINALLY RECOGNIZED YOUR DESIRE FOR FURTHER FLYING ACHIEVEMENTS WILL ABATE. WITH THIS CALM BUT SINCERE HOPE I SEND YOU ONCE AGAIN MY WARMEST CONGRATULATIONS.

YOURS, ADOLF HITLER[4]

But he was to be disappointed.

Rudolf Hess kept open-house at München-Harlaching, and leading figures in the politics, finance and culture of the Third Reich came and went as they pleased. At the naming ceremony of his son, Wolf Rüdiger, who was born in 1937, Hitler and Haushofer acted as sponsors. But although Hess found time, beside his official duties, for flying, hiking and mountain-climbing, this should not be allowed to give an impression that he was less than earnestly, eagerly and fully behind the National Socialist cause.

The National Socialists believed that the red revolutionaries' 'stab in the back' of the front line troops had caused Germany's defeat in the First World War. From this, and from the 'infamous

Diktat' of Versailles, they drew two conclusions: never again would the 'November criminals' succeed in weakening German fighting strength; never again would Germany be so weak that it could be defeated in war and forced to accept a peace not only unjust but dishonourable.

As they considered all communists, socialists and former wartime opponents as enemies united one with another – united above all through the international press and international finance, often controlled by Jews – the battle against the internal enemy was, in the eyes of the National Socialists, at the same time a battle against the external enemy, and vice versa. Hitler's slogan – and that of his rank and file – was German unity and strength at any price, a two-fold objective which they wished to enforce, if necessary by drastic employment of the police and the military. Any internal and external opposition resisting Germany's resurgence was to be broken.

Hitler pursued his objectives with such resolution that he increasingly challenged the covert and overt resistance of his opponents inside and outside the Reich. This resistance eventually became a growing obstacle to the consolidation of the Third Reich. An added factor was that at first the National Socialist Movement was not totally in agreement. Whereas the radicals wanted to turn the 1933 seizure of power into a 'real' revolution – with the Party troops of the SA and SS as an armed forced responsible for law and order – Hitler formed a precautionary alliance with the conservative Reichswehr (Armed Forces) and the middle classes.

These disagreements came to a head in the so-called 'Röhm Putsch' of 1934. The intracacies of this affair have still not been clarified, in particular the role played by the Reichswehr leadership at the time.

There is no doubt, however, that the Chief of Staff of the SA, Ernst Röhm, and many other senior SA leaders were dissatisfied with the course and outcome of the National Socialist revolution. They wanted a 'Second Revolution', which was apparently to be strongly socialist. But above all Röhm and his friends intended to replace the Reichswehr by a 'People's Army', whose basis was to be the Storm Troopers. As in 1934 the SA had more than four million members, it would in practice have swallowed up the much smaller Reichswehr.

The designs cherished by Röhm and his friends did not of course remain hidden from the Reichswehr leadership. The generals were understandably opposed to these plans, especially as Hitler in his speeches had left no doubt that the Reichswehr, which had become the Wehrmacht following the introduction of conscription in 1935, was to remain the nation's sole bearer of arms. For its part, however, the SA had secretly hoarded arms. The 'Hochland' group stationed in Munich and Upper Bavaria was said to have 40,000 weapons.

On 28 June 1934, particularly trustworthy SA members were summoned to a 'specially important operation'. Heinz Haushofer, Albrecht Haushofer's brother, who commanded a troop of SA cavalry, thereupon travelled to Berlin to warn Hess and the National Socialist leadership. On 30 June 1934, on Hitler's orders, Röhm, other SA leaders and some non-SA members were shot. Hitler said shortly afterwards, in a speech to the Reichstag, that he had dealt with a state emergency, and he was probably not far from the truth. Haushofer visited Börries Freiherr von Münchausen on his return journey, and agreed with him that 'a seizure of power by the SA and the men representing it would have been a catastrophe for the Germany we both love'.[5]

In implementation of the Führer's Decrees of 27 July 1934 and 6 April 1935, Rudolf Hess was given the post of Reich Minister without Portfolio. Only foreign policy and the Armed Forces were excluded from his field. Basing himself on the Law on the Unity of Party and State of 1 December 1933, Hitler furthered, by this decision, his intention of instilling National Socialist ideology into all legislation.

In the course of his duties under this appointment, my father signed the so-called Nuremberg Laws of 1935 under which the Jewish minority was made the subject of a special law. In assessing these Nuremberg Laws – which incidentally were drafted by Globke, later Adenauer's Head of Chancery – it is of some interest to consider what the well-known Jewish philosopher and writer Hannah Arendt says in her book on the Eichmann trial.[6]

Mrs Arendt had been sent to Jerusalem by the American periodical *The New Yorker* as an observer at the Eichmann trial. She attended all hearings, and her articles were subsequently published in book form:

'. . . Israeli citizens, religious and nonreligious, seem agreed upon the desirability of having a law which prohibits intermarriage, and it is chiefly for this reason – as Israeli officials outside the courtroom were willing to admit – that they are also agreed upon the undesirability of a written constitution in which such a law would embarrassingly have to be spelled out. Whatever the reasons, there certainly was something breathtaking in the naivité with which the prosecution denounced the infamous Nuremberg Laws of 1935, which had prohibited intermarriage and sexual intercourse between Jew and Germans. The better informed among the correspondents were well aware of the irony . . .'

Although the Nuremberg Laws were intensified under the influence of many an NS leader, Rudolf Hess advocated in many instances properly balanced treatment of the Jews. He issued to his friend Haushofer, who had married a half-Jewish woman, and to her family a so-called 'letter of safe-conduct' protecting them against persecution.

Compared with other champions of the NS regime, Rudolf Hess was in many respects exceptional. In his secluded and homely life-style, he did not enrich himself with the property of others, and he took part in no excesses. He kept the Party's finances within proper limits, and he was always mindful of the need for differentiation in and just treatment of the individual case, which he often went into in detail. If only for this reason, many called him the 'the Party's conscience'. Hess also repeatedly found himself in trouble with other personalities of the NS regime in enforcing his point of view.

As the projection of the Führer within the Party, Rudolf Hess's power may have appeared to many observers as merely implied or even insignificant. It was in fact great, because Hess had Hitler's unrestricted trust. Moreover, Hess's influence did not extend only to matters of internal Party policy; his Party headquarters had at its disposal its own foreign-policy apparatus.

This consisted primarily of the Foreign Organization of the NSDAP, which co-ordinated the Party's foreign activities through some 350 groups in various countries. Its Chief was Secretary of State Ernst Wilhelm Bohle, an active Party manager who had been brought up in England. His deputy was Alfred Hess, a brother of the Deputy Führer. Then there was the

Foreign Policy Office of the NSDAP under Alfred Rosenberg, which concerned itself with foreign propaganda and Germany's foreign trade relations. Finally, until Ribbentrop's appointment as Foreign Minister in early 1938, it included the Ribbentrop Department, where the eventual Foreign Minister at first dealt with disarmament matters and German–British relations.

The NSDAP's foreign-affairs apparatus, which up to the outbreak of war never achieved a coherent capacity to act, was still complemented by various other organizations. In the first place, there was the Volksbund für das Deutschtum im Ausland (VDA) (National Association for German People and Culture Abroad), whose president was Professor Karl Haushofer. His duty was to care for citizens of foreign countries whose origins were German.

Although as a result Hess had a certain amount of access to foreign policy matters, no instances are known in which he crucially influenced or even criticized any of Hitler's foreign policy decisions. In essence, the Deputy Führer must have fully agreed with the foreign policy of the Third Reich up to his flight to Britain. The NS leadership in general was of the opinion that Greater Germany, including Austria, was entitled to a position equivalent to that of the Anglo-Saxon maritime powers, America and Britain.

Hitler's foreign policy began with withdrawal from the League of Nations, denunciation of the Versailles Diktat and German re-armament. The German Reich Chancellor's principle was: since we do not interfere with the affairs of the British Empire, do not compete with Britain on world markets and do not aspire to become a maritime power comparable with Britain, Britain should not interfere with our interests on the Continent of Europe. This applied in particular to those questions which Hitler rightly considered to be German domestic matters or overdue corrections of the injustice of Versailles, such as re-unification into the Third Reich of the Saarland, Austria, the Sudetenland and Danzig. In Austria, for example, the Austrian National Assembly had convened on 12 November 1918 and had adopted the following resolutions:

'Article 1: German-Austria is a Democratic Republic. All public authorities are appointed by the people.

Article 2: German–Austria is a constituent part of the German Republic. Special laws regulate German–Austria's participation in the legislation and administration of the German Republic as well as the extension to German–Austria of the jurisdiction of laws and institutions of the German Republic.'

This policy accorded not only with the ethnic relationship but also with the principles of reason and justice, since no sensible person had any doubt that these regions were territories indisputably affiliated to the German people, and since many impartial observers in London, Paris and Washington had meanwhile realized that it had been wrong to take these regions away from Germany at Versailles.

If only, in 1919, President Wilson had succeeded in getting his 14 Points, and in particular the 'right to self-determination of peoples', accepted not only in order to destroy the Habsburg monarchy but throughout Central Europe, then the German yearnings of 1813, the dreams of 1848, would have been fulfilled in the Weimar Republic! A victory for democratic principles out of the defeat of two Empires – what a scenario!

The result of Versailles was to ensnare the Third Reich in a whole network of international relations which at first it could not break by its own efforts without itself suffering irreparable damage. The greatest damage imaginable would have been war before Germany was strong enough to take up the struggle with adequate prospects of success. The risk of war had always been latent since 1933, because the resurgence of Germany as a great power was observed with mistrust by its former opponents of the First World War. Versailles threatened to disintegrate into nothing, and that had to be prevented!

In 1937/38, Hitler was faced with a momentous decision, the vital factor being Britain. What was most likely to make Chamberlain agree to a substantial compromise – Germany's continued hesitation or a determined grab to take back what had unjustly been taken away in 1918/1919? This was the crucial question which then occupied Hitler's mind. But he took no final decision on this, and during the so-called Sudeten crisis of 1938 he continued to negotiate instead of simply launching a military occupation of the disputed area. The matter oscillated backwards and forwards dramatically in September, and Hitler had the greatest difficulty in avoiding the outbreak of a European war.

The real significance of the Munich Agreement of 29 September 1938 was to win time for Britain. Although the conference which then took place between Europe's 'Big Four' – Chamberlain, the French Prime Minister Daladier, Hitler and the Italian Dictator Mussolini – was claimed, to some extent against their better judgment, by the Western politicians and media to be a great victory for Germany, Hitler did not consider it so. It is true that the Sudetenland represented for Germany a substantial weakening of Czechoslovakia and a notable prestige success, but it in no way gave Hitler a free hand for a final revision of Versailles.

On the whole, Hitler had in fact lost more than he had gained. However strange it may sound, he had above all lost the possibility that in the end Chamberlain might have decided on tacit acceptance of the German policy of revision without military countermeasures. After Munich, this was gone for ever – if such a possibility had ever existed – since Chamberlain now came under such domestic and foreign pressure that he was forced to set Britain openly on a course of confrontation with Germany if he wished to keep office.

The most important result of these developments was that Britain continued to strengthen its ties with America, Roosevelt demanding from Chamberlain as a condition of American assistance in the event of war certain commitments in the field of political stability. It was under this pressure that Britain and France then concluded a military agreement in February 1939. In addition, the two West European democracies, bowing to Roosevelt's claim to lead world policy, gave guarantees to Holland, Switzerland, Poland, Rumania, Greece and Turkey, i.e. to all Germany's neighbours in the West and East, which Hitler considered his own domain.

To compensate for these losses, all that remained for Germany was military occupation of the so-called Remainder of Czechoslovakia, i.e. that part of Czechoslovakia remaining after the surrender of the Sudetenland and the cession of Slovakia in mid-March 1939. However important was this event, the real turning-point in pre-war history was the Western Powers' commitment to Poland. It had already been set in motion before the German march into Prague, and was only accelerated by this event. As a result, the whole development of world politics took a sharp downwards turn in the direction of war. Since the British and French guarantees to Poland of 31 March 1939 were followed in early April by Poland's reciprocal guarantees to Britain and France, Hitler was faced with encirclement, a deadly danger to the German Reich.

From now on, Britain, France and Poland, with America behind them, decided which of Hitler's revisions of Versailles they would consider reason for, or even merely a pretext for, war against the German Reich. Even had Hitler refrained from further revisionist policies, from now onwards the question of war or peace was no longer solely in his own hands.

In this situation, Hitler decided to destroy Poland at the first opportunity that offered, to secure his rear for the conflict he expected with the Western Powers. The German attack in autumn 1939 was not of course as yet finally planned, but it was a vital step closer, and not a politician in the West was unaware of this before the guarantee to Poland. On the contrary, in certain Western circles and among the German opposition, the expectation that Hitler would react to Poland's dependence upon the West by military measures, and unleash not only war but perhaps his own downfall at the hands of the disappointed German people, was the true calculation behind the guarantee policy. Chamberlain confirms this in his diary entry of 10 September 1939: 'My hope is not a military victory – I doubt very much whether that is possible – but a collapse on the German home front.'

At the wish of leading Western politicians, Roosevelt above all, 'toleration' of the return to the Reich of Danzig, the Corridor and certain parts of Upper Silesia was no longer on offer. This was repeatedly made clear to Hitler in summer 1939, particularly by Roosevelt. This meant that, without a conference, without political compensation, with the West's rearmament being completed before his eyes, Hitler would have to wait for an unforeseeable period until the Western Powers condescended to resume negotiations, or until the hot-headed Poles created an opportunity for war under the pretence that Germany had provoked them.

The British Prime Minister's hope of a revolution in Germany was not entirely unfounded. The same was true of the expectations of Lipski, the Polish Ambassador in Berlin, who stated in August 1939 that in the event of war the Polish Army would march into Berlin in not more than a week. In fact, before the war began, the British Government received hints from German Resistance groups that, in the event of war, it was intended to take up arms against Hitler, to arrest him or eliminate him, to liquidate the National Socialist regime and to create lasting peace by negotiation with Germany's adversaries.

For example, during the Sudeten crisis in autumn 1938, Counsellor Theo Kordt – who was then Chargé-d'Affaires in London – submitted declarations on these lines to Lord Halifax. He also stated this in giving evidence for Secretary of State v. Weizsacker, who was himself a leading member of the Resistance movement, at the so-called Wilhelmstrasse trial (Military Court of Justice IV, Case XI) in June 1948. According to his testmony, Kordt had assured Lord Halifax that 'the political and military groups for which he then spoke would take arms against a sea of troubles, and by opposing end them'. The utmost caution was necessary, and the British Government should not flinch from employing, in agreement with them, drastic measures to prevent Hitler's continuing his criminal policy.

Besides Kordt, other members of this Resistance group included his brother, Erich Kordt, who was then head (Chef de Cabinet) of the Reich Foreign Secretary v. Ribbentrop's office; the Chief of the Army General Staff, Colonel-General Halder; his predecessor, Colonel-General Beck; the head of the Foreign and Defence Office of the Supreme Command of the Armed Forces, Admiral Canaris; and the head of Department Z, General Oster.

The longer Hitler hesitated, the more unfavourable became his position. He knew that the USA would intervene sooner or later in a European war, and he considered it advisable to seek a decision in Continental Europe before such an intervention. The Reich would then have at least a chance at last of attaining its territorial desires in the East, and so acquire the strength needed for an armed conflict with America. After the intervention of America, or even after the full mobilization of its economy on behalf of the French armies and the British fleet, Germany would no longer have such a potential unless it gained space, economic strength and a defensive capability.

On 1 September 1939, the German Armed Forces commenced the attack on Poland. Two days later, Britain and France declared war on the Reich. Four weeks later, Poland was shattered and the country shared between Germany and Russia without a single shot being fired in the West. Britain and France had done nothing for their allies, and Hitler began to plan the attack on France. Following Poland's prostration, and at the latest following the victory over France, he hoped that Britain would make peace with him and leave the regions of Eastern Europe to a now-powerful Germany.

My mother later told me of my father's attitude towards the war: 'He considered himself a front-line soldier, and in all the years since 1933 he had acted as one, in his passionate appeals to his German, French and British comrades of the First World War who had responded vigorously. He saw a renewal of armed conflict as a disaster for all European peoples, and moreover for the world. To be sure, when the die was cast and the war machine running, he unswervingly did all he could within his field to achieve a German victory as quickly and as bloodlessly as possible, a victory which in his opinion would end centuries of fruitless and destructive wars between the peoples of the Continent of Europe and inaugurate a long period of peace between nations enjoying equal rights. From the very first day of the war, his innermost thoughts were aimed at the early realization of such peace . . .'.[7]

After Germany's lightning victory over Poland, and before the German attack on France, Hitler made his first attempt to end the war in the West. His peace offer of 12 September 1939, accompanied by the assurance that under his leadership Germany would never capitulate, was a feeler. It was supported by Stalin, but rejected by Chamberlain and Daladier.

Hitler's specific offer of 12 October 1939, which included the re-establishment of a rump Poland, a guarantee of neutrality for neighbouring western states and no claims whatsoever on France, fared no better. Hitler reacted to this 'rejection of Germany's hand of peace' by ordering definite preparations for a German attack in the West.

However, the Russian attack on Finland and Britain's plans to occupy the Norwegian coast so as to cut off Germany from its vital ore exports from Sweden extended the war into the winter of 1939/40, through no fault of Germany's. But the German Navy anticipated the British Navy by only a few days, or even hours, and occupied Denmark and Norway.

For his part, Hitler postponed the German attack on France more than 29 times before it actually began in the early summer of 1940. This was not only because of uncertain weather conditions; rather, the Führer still hesitated to allow the war, declared on the Reich by Britain and France, to escalate in the West.

Only when all hopes of peace with France and Britain had been dashed did Hitler order the attack on France for 10 May 1940. In the morning of that day, 133 German divisions formed up between Emmerich on the Lower Rhine and Bitburg in the Eifel. The tank units advanced with breath-taking speed, separating the British Expeditionary Force from the main French forces. Catastrophe would have resulted for the British at Dunkirk if Hitler had not given his famous order of 24 May 1940 for the spearheads to halt. As a result of this, nearly 340,000 British and Allied troops were able to escape across the Channel, leaving behind all their equipment. This fateful order is attributed to Hitler's – unfortunately false – assumption that Britain would interpret this as a gesture towards the conclusion of a peace with Germany reconcilable with its honour. We now know that destruction of the encircled troops, which could then have been achieved without difficulty, was more likely to have brought peace, and perhaps have prevented world war.

France collapsed on 21 June 1940 and signed an armistice with the Third Reich in the historic saloon railway carriage in which the Germans had been humiliated in 1919.

A little-known fact told me by my mother is that it was my father who, before the armistice was signed in the historic railway carriage at Compiègne, requested in a long and earnest discussion with Hitler that the armistice conditions should contain no item which might injure the honour of the defeated enemy and so increase the difficulty of reaching a final German–French understanding. Only when he had gained this pledge did he participate at Compiègne.

No one had expected German victory over France with such speed. Hitler had thereby made himself ruler of the Continent of Europe from the Atlantic to the Bug and from the North Cape to Sicily. But Britain still stood in the way of his objective of a free hand on the Continent. When, therefore, in June 1940, Hitler visited the sites of Germany's lightning victory he again referred to his desire to reach world-wide understanding with Britain. It was then that his Deputy, Rudolf Hess, decided that if it became necessary he would make a personal attempt to achieve the vital peace in the West.

WAR OR PEACE WITH BRITAIN?

THE EVENTS IMMEDIATELY preceding Hess's flight began with Hitler's final peace address of 19 July 1940 in the Kroll Opera House at Berlin. Paradoxically, it no longer included a specific offer of peace, as a few weeks earlier the former First Lord of the Admiralty Winston Churchill had taken office as Prime Minister in London.

On 15 July, with unequalled aggressiveness, the new man uttered the watchword 'War until Victory' in the House of Commons. At this signal, the first freighters carrying arms for Britain left the American east coast ports. The day before the Führer's address, Roosevelt, then President of America, anticipated it with an unparalled challenge. In response, Hitler deleted from his address the intended offer of peace. While during the subsequent weeks and months the German Führer was still oscillating uncertainly between war against or peace with Britain, the alliance of Anglo-Saxon maritime powers began to be formed.

The first nail was hammered home on 2 September 1940. Following months of negotiations, the governments in Washington and London signed a treaty under which, in exchange for 50 old destroyers, the USA received rights of use in eight British possessions for the next 99 years. In this, Churchill not only extended his hand to Roosevelt and sold out the British Empire; the Head of Government in London at the same time declared publicly that, even in the event of Britain's military defeat by Germany, he would neither sink the Royal Navy nor hand it over to Hitler. This could only mean war to the bitter end, if necessary using Canada as a base.

Three days before this crucial turning-point in world history, the Deputy Führer had met his old mentor and friend Professor Karl Haushofer in the Alps. In the savant's secluded mountain hut, Rudolf Hess asked the fateful question: Is it still possible with any prospect of success to put out peace feelers towards Britain through a British intermediary in a neutral country? The professor, who in this context first mentioned the name Hamilton, passed the enquiry on to his son, Professor Albrecht Haushofer, who also knew a number of prominent Britons. A week after the American–British agreement, Rudolf Hess met Albrecht Haushofer at Bad Gallspach and asked him to make contact with Hamilton. The timing alone indicates that Hess's initiative was evoked by the eventual and increasingly feared entry of the United States into the war. In mid-June, even before France's capitulation, Thomsen, the German Chargé-d'Affaires in Washington, had reported to Berlin: If the German Reich were to defeat the two West-European democracies, US President Roosevelt would delay action for two or three years in order to rearm the United States. And then he would make war alone against Hitler.[1]

But there was a further reason for the Hess initiative: the impossibility of Hitler's ending the war in the West awoke fears in Berlin that in the long run Russia would re-orientate itself towards the West simply in order to march with the victorious battalions, since the whole world – including Stalin – knew that without 'living space in the East' the Third Reich would in the long run have no chance against the Anglo-Saxon maritime powers. In the summer of 1940, therefore, Hitler ordered the military to make 'mental preparations' for resolving the Russian problem.[2] Hitler hoped to make Britain also finally ready for peace by overcoming the Soviet Union and Bolshevism.

When in late-summer 1940 Hess began to plan his peace initiative, he therefore had in mind the danger of a war on two fronts, because if Britain could not be eliminated from the war in time by political or military means the Third Reich would in the end have to fight in the West as well as in the East. No great feat of imagination was needed to see that this would result not only in the defeat of Germany but also probably in its destruction.

The probability that Hess allowed himself to be guided by such notions is all the greater in that, in making contact with Britain, the Deputy Führer had in fact taken the advice of Professor Karl Haushofer's son. Albrecht Haushofer had followed in his father's footsteps. He had studied geography, and in 1940 he was the head of the Geographical Society in Berlin. Albrecht Haushofer had long been corresponding with Hamilton, whom he familiarly called 'My dear Douglo' in his letters. The two had also met personally on various occasions. Shortly before the outbreak of war in 1939, Albrecht Haushofer had pleaded in a letter to the Scottish Duke for a 'genuine peace plan on the basis of complete equality and with substantial (but mutual) security measures of a military nature', by which he also meant Germany's protection from Britain. When in September 1940 Albrecht Haushofer put himself at the disposal of the Deputy Führer in connection with his peace initiative, he was under the impression 'that there was reluctance in the highest places [i.e. Hitler – W.R.H.] to enter into a final conflict with the island [i.e. Britain – W.R.H.] for very long-term world policy and race policy reasons'.[3] Albrecht Haushofer's great analytical clear-sightedness had made him recognize Hitler's dilemma: under the pressure of the world alliance between America and Russia against Germany which loomed on the horizon, Hitler had to drive Britain from the field as soon as possible – if necessary even by attack from the air or a landing on the island.

But on the other hand, Hitler wished to preserve the British Empire intact at any price, because Germany, the land power, could not in any event govern it. If, therefore, he wished to bring together his desire to end the war against Britain and his racial-ideological objectives, Hitler could in fact work for peace with Britain only by political means, i.e. by negotiation. The war alternative was in practice excluded, quite apart from the fact that Germany, the land power, lacked the means for victory over Britain, the maritime power.

Young Haushofer at first had misgivings about making his British contacts available to the Deputy Führer. He believed that the 'complete absence of trust [between Britain and Germany – W.R.H.] would condemn to failure even the most skilful or sincere attempts'.[4] When on 10 September 1940 Hess pursued the matter by writing to the Haushofers asking them to take definite action to contact Hamilton, Albrecht Haushofer felt compelled to reconsider from basic principles the possibility of paving the way to an understanding.

The result was a memorandum headed 'Are there still possibilities of a German–British peace?', which he sent to his father on 15 September 1940.[5] However, after the victories over Poland and France, Albrecht Haushofer did not believe that the British would still accept the Führer as a suitable negotiating partner. They would rather transfer their Empire to the USA than allow Germany to rule over Continental Europe. But in the final analysis Haushofer also believed that only partition of the world, that is 'fusion' between Germany and Britain 'with common Armed Forces and a common distribution of property' – i.e. 'precisely what the British now seem about to agree with the United States' – would represent a true way out of Hitler's dilemma. Although he again emphasized his fundamental scepticism towards any attempt to reach an understanding, Haushofer finally gave the names of a number of British diplomats who appeared to him to be willing even now to reach an understanding. 'As a final possibility', reads the last sentence of the memorandum, 'I then referred to the possibility of a personal meeting on neutral soil with the closest of my British friends: the young Duke of Hamilton.'

Hess accepted this plan. He originally considered sending Albrecht Haushofer to Hamilton; this came to mind immediately because the two had long known each other. They were to meet on neutral soil, for example Switzerland, Spain or Portugal; but the Haushofers suddenly objected to this. They considered such an undertaking too risky. All contact with the enemy was officially prohibited at the time, and this was strictly monitored on both sides of the Channel. Anyone, whether civilian or military, who dared to make contact – and moreover for a political purpose – could expect the most unpleasant consequences.

Contact between Haushofer Jnr. and Hamilton would of course have presented no difficulty at all had Hess been able, as Deputy Führer, to give him official protection. But in wartime this was quite impossible. Haushofer would therefore have to take a roundabout route if he wished to avoid endangering both himself and Hamilton. Hess had already suggested bringing in an old acquaintance of the Haushofers, Mrs Violet Roberts, daughter-in-law of the former viceroy of India, who was living in Lisbon. After long hesitation, Albrecht Haushofer came to accept this suggestion. He thought he would be able to encode a letter to Hamilton in such a way that Mrs Roberts, as the sender, would encounter no difficulties if British postal censorship intervened. The German peace initiative could therefore commence.

Under the date of 3 September and using his usual form of address, 'My dear Douglo', Albrecht Haushofer drafted an apparently innocuous letter, beginning by assuring the Duke of his eternal friendship. He then carefully reminded him of his peace feeler of 1939. Haushofer linked this with the hope that 'you – and your friends in high places – may find some significance in the fact that I am able to ask you whether you could find time to have a talk with me somewhere on the outskirts of Europe, perhaps in Portugal'.

He, Haushofer, could go to Lisbon in the near future without difficulty. Hamilton had merely to indicate that this suited him by using a double envelope – 'Inside address: "Dr A.H." Nothing more! Outside address: Minero Silricola Ltd., Rua do Cais de Santarem 32/1, Lisbon, Portugal'. The letter concluded simply: 'Yours ever, "A" '.[6]

The letter was written on about 19 September 1940. Albrecht Haushofer sent a copy to his parents on that day from Berlin. His reason for backdating the letter to 3 September is not known. Perhaps he wished to make even clearer to Hamilton and his 'friends in high places' the political context of the American–British understanding of 2 September. In any event, it was not until 23 September that the letter was sent – via a confidant in the Foreign Organization (presumably his brother, Alfred Hess) – to the Portuguese cover address. In Lisbon, Mrs Roberts, as requested, entrusted the peace feeler to the postal services of Messrs. Cook, probably enclosing a few lines of her own.[7] The letter was not however to reach its addressee, and then under peculiar circumstances, until nearly six months later.

Over the following weeks and eventually months Hamilton's reply failed to arrive, and Rudolf Hess changed his plans. He no longer wished to leave making contact with the Scottish Duke to Albrecht Haushofer alone; he now wished to meet Hamilton himself for the sake of world peace. This meant that, if need be, the Deputy Führer was prepared to stake his own life.

It is not certain what gave Hess this idea. It seems that Göring had said to Hitler shortly after the war commenced: 'We must fly to Britain and I'll try to explain the position . . .'. To which Hitler is said to have replied: 'It will be of no use, but if you can, try it.' Thereafter the rumour persisted for some time that Göring wanted to fly to Britain.[8]

If this rumour was true, Hess could have received encouragement from Göring as early as 1939. In any event, the idea of intervening as 'bearer of the flag of truce on his own initiative' entrenched itself in Hess's mind in the summer of 1940.[9] The longer his attempt to reach an understanding with Britain by the roundabout route of Albrecht Haushofer dragged on unsuccessfully, the stronger became his determination 'to cut the Gordian knot of ill-fated entanglements', if necessary by a spectacular flight.[10] The preparations themselves began in September 1940. Until then, the word of honour to cease flying given by Hess to the Führer shortly after the outbreak of war was binding. At that time, the former First World War aviator had wanted to go to the Front as a Luftwaffe officer. This, however, Hitler refused, and at the same time he bound Hess by his word of honour, because he was aware of Hess's obstinacy. But Hess succeeded in incorporating a time limit in his promise, which expired in the early autumn of 1940. Until then, Hess, who would never have broken his word to Hitler, did not feel himself at liberty to convert his decision into action.

Hess had by no means always been determined to fly to Britain to meet the Duke of Hamilton. He originally thought of neutral Switzerland as a meeting place.[11] When the period of waiting proved too long for him, Hess in fact asked Bohle, the head of the Foreign Organization, to come to his official residence in Berlin, Wilhelmstrasse 64, on the evening of 9 October 1940. Hess then told his colleague, in the strictest secrecy, that he intended to 'take a step to end the war with Britain', and to this end to meet Hamilton in Switzerland. Hess handed Bohle the draft of a letter he wished to send to the Duke to pave the way for the meeting. This letter began with the sentence: 'I am approaching you on the recommendation of my friends, Professor Karl Haushofer and his son Albrecht.'

Hess had asked Bohle to come to see him because he had the greatest confidence in him as a colleague. Also, unlike Hess, Bohle spoke and wrote fluent English. At Hess's request, he sat down immediately at a typewriter already to hand to translate the beginning of Hess's draft into English. Hess put the final result into his pocket. As Bohle left, Hess said that he would ask him to come again when he had completed the next part of the letter, which would of course be longer. In fact, Hess asked Bohle to come again at the end of October, and from then on he came at irregular intervals until early January 1941. Meanwhile, Hess completed his message step by step, and Bohle finally had the impression that 'the letter was more or less complete apart from a few general concluding remarks'. Bohle was not told what eventually happened to the letter – it is significant that the document has not as yet emerged – since 'after about 7 January 1941' he was 'never again involved in the matter'. But even at the time, Bohle, in full knowledge of the letter, assumed that 'Hess and the Duke intended to meet in Switzerland'.

The technical preparations were going on alongside this. Even for the Deputy Führer, it was of course not at all easy in the middle of the war to get an aircraft for a non-military purpose which, because of its nature, had to remain secret. Every aircraft was needed for operations at the Front and was on the delivery-requirement lists of the Bauaufsicht-Luft (BAL) (Building Inspectorate – Air) of the Luftwaffe High Command. Each aircraft was immediately handed over on completion, checked against the list and delivered for its intended military use.

In the summer of 1940, my father had already put out feelers to the Messerschmitt factory at Augsburg-Haunstetten about a single-seater Me 109 – then the Luftwaffe's most successful fighter plane.[12] But the head of the company, Willy Messerschmitt, and his chief test pilot, Willi Stöhr, convinced him that this aircraft was too difficult to fly for even such an experienced pilot as Hess. After this the Deputy Führer drew back. During the following period, he apparently tried to get a plane of this type at Wiener-Neustadt, Warnemünde and Kassel, where the Me 109 was being built under licence.

However, in August or September 1940, while he was consulting the Haushofers about making contact with Hamilton, Hess reappeared at Augsburg-Haunstetten. This time he wanted to fly the new Me 110, a two-seater aircraft which made it possible for a trained pilot to accompany him as instructor. Stöhr considered that, under such circumstances, he was justified in meeting the Deputy Führer's request, particularly as Hess gave the reason that he wanted to be trained so that he could ask the Führer for permission to go into action at the Front as a fighter pilot. Finally, he wanted to set an example to his fellow Germans in this field also.

Since Hess was accustomed to flying a government plane of the Focke-Wulf 'Condor' type on official flights assisted by a co-pilot, he proved an apt pupil. In the first trial flights with the Me 110, he sat behind Stöhr looking over his shoulder. Hess subsequently took the controls himself on some ten occasions, while Stöhr sat at the rear. When he had the feel of the plane he made solo flights of various distances, mostly practising take-offs and landings.

This training period lasted from September 1940 to April 1941. During this time, at Hess's request, radio apparatus and, at the flying associations' request, reserve tanks, were incorporated. In the same period, during which Stöhr was replaced as chief test pilot by Helmut Kaden, Hess even succeeded in having a specific aircraft reserved for him by the factory management. For the sake of appearances, this plane was reported to Berlin as a 'test plane for trial flights by Messerschmitt AG' and deleted from the delivery-requirement list. At this time, Hess also arranged for weather reports for two secret locations, 'X' and 'Y', to be sent to him more or less regularly by the Meterological Office at Hamburg. A few days before his departure for Britain, he also finally acquired, through Hitler's chief pilot Hans Baur, a secret map showing the German prohibited flying areas.

Before his fateful take-off on 10 May 1941, Hess had already made two earlier attempts on 10 January and 30 April 1941.[13]

In the late 1950s, Hess's adjutant Karlheinz Pintsch told the British journalist James Leasor[14] that, 'on 10 January 1941' the following scene took place at Augsburg-Haunstetten: Before taking-off in the Me 110, Hess had handed him a sealed letter. Pintsch was to open the letter four hours after the plane had left if he, Hess, had not returned by then. Pintsch had waited the four hours with Hess's escort, and then opened the letter. Enclosed were a sealed letter to Hitler and a message to Pintsch that Hess had flown to Britain to conclude peace; would Pintsch please put the enclosed letter into Hitler's hands by the quickest method possible. The driver and the security officer had also read the message.

Shortly afterwards, however, Hess returned without achieving what he had set out to do, and later in the evening, at München-Harlaching, he confided to Pintsch that he could of course pass on to the other members of the escort what he was about to tell him.

Hess is then said to have disclosed his peace plans in a kind of lecture on world politics, expressly emphasizing that Hitler as yet new nothing about his flight. Hess then apparently went on to say that when he landed in darkness directly on the Duke's threshold he would have just ten minutes to carry out his mission before the police arrived to arrest him.

When the butler asked the stranger what he wanted of the Duke so late in the evening, he would simply hand over Haushofer's visiting card at the door. Hamilton, who would of course at first think that he was Haushofer, would then be utterly surprised when he suddenly saw the Deputy Führer before him. Even though the police, who would probably have seen his parachute descent, might by then have arrived, he, Hess, would still have time to make his request to see the King of England.

On the whole, this story is so improbable and in some points factually so questionable that it does not deserve belief. However, Pintsch's original statement, which unfortunately cannot be traced, is itself not open to doubt; rather is its rendition by Leasor and later by the illustrated periodical *Revue* questionable. Pintsch was undoubtedly a man of integrity who was quite clearly unequal to modern journalistic probing after ten years of harrowing imprisonment in Russia. He is now sadly dead and can no longer be questioned personally.

It is scarcely worthwhile going into the many points at which the factual accuracy of Pintsch's alleged account must be doubted. Kaden, in a sworn statement made after the War, describes quite accurately Hess's attempts to take off. Kaden normally sat with Pintsch and a few men of the ground crew in the flight operations manager's office until the Deputy Führer returned. It is correct that one day Hess – Kaden says 21

December 1940, but this can be ruled out as a date – had to cut short a flight because his signal pistol broke loose from its holder and jammed the rudder.

Although it is also correct that Hess handed a letter to his adjutant before the actual flight to Britain – the letter that Pintsch was to deliver to the Führer and that contained the formal message about Hess's flight – it is scarcely believable that Hess had already disclosed something about this message in the letter containing Pintsch's directions to deliver it to Hitler. Apart from the risk that unauthorized persons might also read the letter, it would be against all military rules to entrust him with more information than was absolutely necessary for him to be able to carry out his orders.

Towards the end of the war, Hess's adjutant went into Russian captivity, where he underwent much suffering. He was cruelly tortured for months in the Ljubljanka basement during interrogation by the Soviet secret police. The Soviets wished Pintsch to sign a faked document which they intended to use to have sentence of death passed on Rudolf Hess at Nuremberg. In spite of all the torture, Pintsch did not sign the document and did not surrender his former chief to the treacherous intentions of the Soviets.

Pintsch's stand deserves the greatest respect. It is entirely in line with that of his former chief.

Unlike Hess's first confirmed take-off attempt on 10 January, there is a witness to the second, on 30 April 1941, whose evidence is beyond doubt. This is Kaden's detailed report, confirmed under oath, of 4 May 1981; this, however, discloses nothing about Hess's target destination on that day. Leasor, incidentally, simply ignores this second unsuccessful attempt.

On this 30 April, a Wednesday, the Messerschmitt factory at Augsburg-Haunstetten was decorated with bunting and garlands. It was the day before 'National Labour Day', and on the Thursday, 1 May 1941, no less a person than the Führer and Reich Chancellor Adolf Hitler was to address the staff. To give additional emphasis to the importance of the day, it was the first May Day celebration since the 1933 seizure of power at which Adolf Hitler was not to speak at the Tempelhofer Feld in the capital, Berlin.

On the day before this important address, Hess and his escort suddenly appeared at the factory's airfield. Shortly before, one of the Deputy Führer's adjutants had, as usual, telephoned the factory management to arrange for the auxiliary tanks of the Me 110 to be filled. This being done, Kaden carried out the routine test flight. When the Deputy Führer arrived, everything went according to plan. Hess received the weather report, changed into flying kit, went across to his aircraft, greeted the ground staff, climbed up the ladder, sat in the cockpit, strapped himself in, allowed one of his adjutants to photograph him, and opened up the left engine and then the right engine. Then something quite unexpected happened.

Unnoticed by those present, on arrival at the factory one of Hess's adjutants had taken up position at the factory management's telephone. He now ran excitedly across the runway, waving his arms and signalling to the Deputy Führer to stop the engines. Without hesitation the young officer seized the ladder placed against the grey fuselage of the aircraft and climbed up to give Hess a message. Hitler had just telephoned; the Führer was unable to speak on 1 May at the Messerschmitt factory; Hess must give the address.

And so it happened that on 1 May 1941 Hess awarded Messerschmitt the 'Honorary Ring of Labour' and made an address to the workforce which was relayed by all transmitters in the German Reich. This was his penultimate appearance in public before, nine days later, he finally set out on his journey.

Hitler's order to stop raises the question: did the Führer know on that 30 April that Hess wished to fly to Britain? If not, what made him telephone Augsburg-Haunstetten literally at the last moment before take-off? If the answer is yes, why did Hitler stop Hess? What in fact did he know of his deputy's planned peace mission?

THE APPROACH TO THE MISSION

HITLER'S MAIN PROBLEM in 1940/41 was to end the war in the West so that Germany could have a free hand in the East to solve its living-space problems with as little risk as possible. Although in attacking Poland the Führer had taken into account that Britain and France would then declare war on him, he would have preferred to avoid this reverse order of battle and to have gone into the living-space war against the Soviet Union together with the West. In his efforts to persuade or force Britain to make peace, however, Hitler had come to realize in 1940/41 that this – like making war – rested with two people – himself and Winston Churchill. And Churchill had no intention of making peace with Hitler.

In 1940/41, Germany's war against Britain was stamped by indecision. During the campaign in France, Hitler had allowed the British Expeditionary Force to escape across the Channel to avoid blocking the chances of peace. He now lacked the courage and the means to bomb the island into total collapse, or to land on it. Berlin even had no plan for action in the event that Britain was determined to continue the war, so certain was the government that Britain would be prepared to compromise after the victories over Poland and France.

For the moment, Hitler did not know what to do. However, while preparing for his great peace address on 19 July 1940 he had begun planning 'Operation Sea Lion', i.e. an invasion of the island following an amphibious landing. But this had more to do with his usual procedure of supporting any political onslaught with military contingency planning than with the available facts, since a successful landing leading to the conquest and occupation of the British Isles needed both an efficient navy and unchallenged superiority in the air. Neither of these preconditions existed.

After a few attacks by the Luftwaffe on the British capital in May/June 1940, the true air offensive against Britain began on 13 August 1940. But by November the attempt to break the British will to resist by bombing London had collapsed. Although the air attacks were thereafter extended to other British towns, Reich-Marshal Göring and the Quarter-master-General of the Luftwaffe, Ernst Udet, had simply not made available sufficient aircraft, weapons and bombs. As a result, the Battle of Britain was lost in the course of 1940.

At this time, the war at sea looked rather more encouraging for the Reich. Simultaneously with the air offensive, on 13 August 1940 Hitler declared a 'total blockade of Britain and unrestricted submarine warfare against British shipping'. The tonnage of ships sunk by German submarines, destroyers and cruisers increased between June and October 1940, decreased somewhat between November 1940 and February 1941, and then rose again steeply. Although this seriously endangered supplies to the island, and in the long term could mean great difficulty for Britain unless the USA intervened, it was no substitute for the large, strong and well-commanded fleet that Hitler would need to carry out land operations such as, for example, the subsequent 'Operation Overlord'. Germany had no such fleet.

At the end of June 1940, Hitler had already conjectured: 'Britain will probably need a demonstration of our military power before it yields and leaves our rear free so that we can turn against the East.'[1] But during the summer and early autumn of 1940 he was forced to recognize that he lacked the means for such a policy of strength against Britain because, behind the island, there was emerging ever more strongly and theateningly the true main opponent of the future: the United States of America. Under these circumstances, Hitler did three things: on 27 September he concluded a defensive alliance with Japan to tie down the USA in the Pacific; he began planning for the war against Russia; and he searched for ways of making secret contacts with Britain to prevent the eventual disaster of a war on all fronts.

After Roosevelt and Churchill had successfully undermined Hitler's official peace initiative, on 29 and 30 July 1940 the Führer, in spite of the continuing war in the West, ordered his military commanders to start planning a blitzkrieg against Russia lasting about five months. This was expected to begin in May 1941. The plans of the Army High Command were ready by early December, and two weeks later, on 18 December 1940, Hitler issued his directive for 'Operation Barbarossa', which initiated the detailed preparations for the planned campaign against Russia.

At the same time, the Reich – with or without Hitler's knowledge – put out secret peace feelers to Britain. The first of these contacts had been made before and after the Polish campaign. After the German victory over France, in July 1940 the German Foreign Office began a new peace initiative through the British Ambassador in Washington, Lord Lothian. Churchill, however, without hesitation forbade Foreign Secretary Halifax to conduct unofficial peace talks on this basis.[2]

In spite of his victories over Poland and France, in late summer 1940, when Rudolf Hess once again urged peace with Britain, Hitler was in fact left rather empty-handed. It is not known precisely whether or when Hess let the Führer into the secret of his plan to arrive at an understanding, if necessary by a personal sacrifice, and it is not known when Hess took the irrevocable decision to achieve his objective by flying to Britain. But historians are in general agreement that Hess acted on the 'direct orders' of Hitler when, at the end of August or beginning of September 1940, he first asked the Haushofers, father and son, about the chances of making unofficial contact with Britain.

Bernd Martin, in his standard work 'Peace initiatives in the Second World War', even goes as far as to assume that in the summer of 1940 Hitler had entrusted his Deputy with the 'role of messenger of peace', and had given Hess 'vague instructions' to 'open up a way to negotiations acceptable to the British by staking his own prestige'.[3] Martin also believes that Albrecht Haushofer's letter to the Duke of Hamilton of 19 or 3 September came into existence 'following consultation (by Hess) with Adolf

Hitler'.[4] All these statements can be accepted, although in detail they leave room for interpretation.

Until we have proof to the contrary, therefore, it must be assumed that:

1. Hess acted on Hitler's orders when he discussed with the Haushofers the possibility of an unofficial peace probe;

2. Hitler knew about Albrecht Haushofer's letter to Hamilton, or at least knew its general content or intention;

3. Hitler was informed of and agreed with Albrecht Haushofer's intention to meet Hamilton in Lisbon.

Beyond this the uncertainties commence. Can Bernd Martin's assertion that Hitler ordered Hess 'to open up a way to negotiations acceptable to the British by staking his own prestige' be interpreted to mean that Hitler knew something of Hess's plans, approved of them, or even initiated them? And if Hitler knew something of Hess's plans, of what did this knowledge consist – his Deputy's intention to go to Switzerland, which must be regarded as certain for autumn 1940 and probable for spring 1941, or Hess's intention to fly to Britain?

This differentiation between the various objectives of Hess's mission has so far been avoided by all historians interested in the matter. It is however particularly important because upon it depends the answer to the two other questions: Did Hitler approve of his deputy's plans; or did he accept them as, at least, a stop-gap? In war, of course, it made all possible difference whether the Deputy of the German Führer was going to neutral Switzerland or to enemy Britain to put out a peace feeler. It is conceivable that Hitler might agree under certain conditions to Hess's travelling to neutral Switzerland – this, after all, was in line with his sending his own special emissary on certain important occasions to focal points. And as we shall see later, at that time Switzerland was a highly suitable place for paving the way to peace talks between Germany and Britain.

But a flight by his Deputy to enemy Britain was quite another matter. Apart from the risk of life and limb for Hess, was such a step a contradiction of the entire strategy then employed by Hitler in his efforts to make peace with Britain? This strategy was based on 'making Britain come' to the negotiating table by a demonstration of military strength, as the Führer liked tc express it. A flight by Hess to Britain was clearly contrary to this, particularly if the venture went wrong and became public, because then the event could be seen by world opinion as an admission that the Reich no longer felt able to continue the war, i.e. as a sign of Germany's weakness. Moreover, it was also to be feared that British propaganda would exploit the intentions and utterances of the Deputy Führer in Britain and use them in other ways against the Germany Reich. The damage all this would cause to German morale during the run-up to the Russian campaign was incalculable.

Hitler's reaction to Hess's flight to Britain confirms our assumption that when he learned of the undertaking he did not agree, at least at the time, whether or not his Deputy informed him that he intended to fly off on 10 May 1941 precisely. On the other hand, Hitler would surely have agreed if Hess's secret flight had been successful. The fact that on 30 April 1941 he called Hess back at the last moment by a telephone call only proves that the Deputy Führer had intended to take off for Britain on that day, and that Hitler's misgivings still at that time predominated. But then, in early May, Hess had a personal meeting with Hitler lasting about four hours at the Reich Chancellery. At the end of this talk, during which voices were sometimes raised, the Führer accompanied his Deputy to the ante-room, put his arm soothingly around his shoulders and said: 'Hess, you really are stubborn!'[5]

From all this, it must be concluded that:
1. on this occasion, Hess informed Hitler of his plan to fly to Britain;
2. in view of Churchill's intransigent attitude, however, Hitler still had misgivings;
3. Hitler nevertheless agreed in principle with his Deputy's peace mission.[6]

Indeed, we may perhaps even go as far as seeing the heaviest of all bomb attacks carried out by the Luftwaffe during the night of 10/11 May 1941 as a demonstration of force ordered by Hitler to give his Deputy's peace mission the emphasis it needed. But how was it that Hitler and Hess initially came to seek contact with Britain through a roundabout Swiss route? The reason for this bore a very specific name: Professor Carl Jakob Burckhardt. At the outbreak of war, this well-known Swiss historian and former

League of Nations Commissioner in Danzig had become Vice-President of the International Red Cross (IRC), with its head-quarters at Geneva. In 1940 and 1941, Burckhardt, who had already been concerned in European crisis management before the outbreak of war, was one of the few internationally recognized and trusted people who might be considered as a mediator. Through him, many contacts passed between the enemy powers – officially and unofficially.

Indeed, this serious and thoughtful Swiss had been in touch with the Secretary of State at the German Foreign Office, Ernst von Weizsäcker, and with the British Foreign Secretary, Halifax, since autumn 1939. In summer 1940 he had examined the possibility of a compromise peace through the German and British Consuls in Geneva. Although in December 1940, after the sudden death of Lord Lothian, the British Ambassador in Washington, Churchill had transferred Halifax to the American capital, in January 1941 Burckhardt received unofficial information from London that Britain was still prepared to make peace if:[7]

1. Germany would quit and reinstate the Netherlands and Belgium,
2. 'Some kind of Poland (without the former German provinces)' were re-created; otherwise Britain had no special interest in the European East, nor in the re-establishment of Czechoslovakia.
3. As far as Britain was concerned, there was no special interest in France, which would of course, because of Britain's control of the Eastern Mediterranean, have to be maintained as a power factor *vis-à-vis* Italy.
4. The former German colonies would be returned to the Reich, provided the British Empire remained unmolested by Germany.

This offer – if indeed it was an offer, which had of course first to be explored – was a genuine sensation. Its realization would not only have given promise of far-reaching satisfaction for Germany's ambitions on the European Continent but would also have come very close to Hitler's concept of a division of the world between Germany and Britain. It contained only one – but very bitter – touch of gall for the Führer: Hitler was no longer considered an acceptable negotiating partner, even by the British

[69]

circles making this extremely favourable offer. But – and this puts us on the track of Hess – Burckhardt announced in the context of this offer an interest in meeting Albrecht Haushofer.

Hamilton having by now been silent for four months on the Haushofer/Hess/Hitler letter, a new and apparently more promising initiative had unexpectedly emerged for German-British peace negotiations, provided that in some way Hitler could be excluded. In autumn 1940, Hess had already turned his eyes towards Switzerland as a location for a personal meeting with Hamilton, an enterprise towards which he, with Bohle's help, continued to work until early January 1941. We do not know precisely when the Deputy Führer learned about Burckhardt's continuing peace feelers, but it is certain that during spring 1941 Hess contacted Burckhardt through Albrecht Haushofer. What purpose could such a contact have had other than the exploration of this offer from certain British circles? And did Hamilton belong to these circles?

Albrecht Haushofer was with Rudolf Hess between 21 and 24 February, between 12 and 15 April and on 26 April 1941 – on this occasion with his father – to prepare for the contact with Burckhardt. These at least are the meetings that were recorded in one form or another. But strangely enough, although there are detailed records in the Haushofer archives of the early meetings with the Deputy Führer, the publisher of the Haushofer documents, Professor Hans-Adolf Jacobsen of Bonn, could find no documentary evidence of the content of these final and probably crucial discussions. This indicates their highly explosive, and therefore highly secret, nature.

One fact only is indisputable: on 28 April 1941, Albrecht Haushofer went to Geneva to see Carl Jacob Burckhardt, not only on the orders of Rufold Hess but also on the orders of Adolf Hitler. This was incontestably evidenced by Karl Haushofer. He asserted expressly in a letter that his son had repeatedly asked Hess 'whether this order [to meet Burckhardt in Geneva – W.R.H.] originated from the Führer', to which Rudolf Hess had replied in the affirmative.[8]

As his mother noted in her diary, Albrecht Haushofer reported back on 3 May 1941 'from his not entirely unsuccessful diplomatic mission'. On 5 May, Martha Haushofer writes, with relief: 'His talk with . . . [Burckhardt – W.R.H.] in . . . [Geneva –

W.R.H.] was not entirely fruitless, which is more than we had expected.'[9] Five days later, Hess set out on his flight to Britain.

It is still of course impossible fully to explain the background to this event as long as we do not know what was discussed between Haushofer and Burckhardt. The trip to Switzerland appears not to have been completely unsuccessful, but what was its actual significance? Did they discuss specific points, i.e. the political points bearing on post-war arrangements in the British offer? And did they also talk about individuals – perhaps who would if necessary replace Hitler to negotiate with the British and become the future head of government in Germany?

At first glance these questions may seem somewhat misleading, since Rudolf Hess had certainly never even dreamt of taking Hitler's place for the sake of peace. He was far too loyal and unambitious for that; it would have been contrary to his entire personality. But for him also there was no way of ignoring the fact that peace in Europe and in the world then depended, on the British side, on the exclusion of Hitler beforehand. Hess's intention of preventing this may have been the vital motivation for his flight to Britain. However, such an intention becomes comprehensible only when one knows that Albrecht Haushofer's negotiations with Burckhardt in Geneva also had other backers.

Albrecht Haushofer, then a bachelor aged 38 with strong artistic leanings, was a very complex character. In the early 1930s, his mother had been worried that nothing very much would become of her eldest child. With the National Socialist seizure of power, however, Hess, who had until then been a protégé of father Haushofer, took young Haushofer under his wing. After a 'discussion between K(arl) and R(udolf) about the future of the sons', the Deputy Führer assisted them in finding work.[10] Four days later, Albrecht Haushofer was offered the post of lecturer at the Berlin College of Politics, while three years later his younger brother, Heinz Haushofer, slid into a backwater as an 'agricultural expert' in the Foreign Service of the Third Reich.

Although Albrecht Haushofer valued and claimed the friendship of Rudolf Hess, he could not deny a deep-rooted dislike of the National Socialist regime. He consequently played a kind of double role. In one role he advised Hitler and the

German Foreign Office on world-policy matters. He had been on first-name terms with Hess since 1938, and had also met the Führer privately. At the Munich Conference, Albrecht Haushofer even participated as 'geographical consultant' to the German delegation in the surrender of the Sudetenland. But in his other role, the closer war approached the further did Albrecht Haushofer distance himself mentally from the NS Regime.

This attitude was rooted in both moral and political causes, which also had an effect upon his father, Karl Haushofer. For example, the Professor later noted in his 'Memoirs'[11] that up to October 1938 he and 'wise observers' from Britain, America and Japan had been of the opinion that 'from the teething troubles of National Socialism there might emerge a pacified Central Europe, satisfied for centuries to come, with moderate access to Africa's raw materials. Unless I am completely deceived, this is what Rudolf Hess also believed up to the time of my last personal meeting with Adolf Hitler at the naming ceremony of young Wolf Rüdiger Hess on 10 November 1938 . . .'

But after the Reichskristallnacht (Night of Broken Glass), the first open excesses against the Jews in Germany, a page turned for the Haushofers. After this night of violence there was a rapid and dramatic change of opinion in the West, which made war against a resurgent Germany as good as certain. 'At the turn of 1938/(1939), I tried in vain, and again for the last time in early August 1939', Karl Haushofer continues, 'to make clear to R.H. the full gravity of the world situation and his responsibilities in this direction. When he was alone with me he certainly saw reality as I presented it to him; but he could not assert himself in the presence of Hitler, Ribbentrop or even Bormann, who in my opinion sold him down the river seven times a day, and in the face of Göring's blind pleasure in rearmament in the air'. This was written by the father. The son would have thought along similar lines; the pair were very close.

Although war had meanwhile broken out, from December 1939 onwards Albrecht Haushofer continued in his post in the Information Department of the Foreign Office, offered him by Foreign Minister Ribbontrop. In early 1940, however, Dr Carl Langbehn, a Berlin solicitor working for Messerschmit AG and a neighbour of the Reichsführer SS, Heinrich Himmler, on the Tegernsee in Bavaria, introduced him to the so-called Wednesday Society – a centre of German resistance. This gave Albrecht Haushofer a foot in two camps; a position from which he could carry out his double role, and perhaps even triple role, in the Hess affair.

The Wednesday Society met once a month at the Berlin homes of its members in turn to discuss more or less expertly the problems of the time. It was a circle of Prussian-German Conservatives focusing on the former Prussian Minister of Finance (until 1932) Johannes Popitz, an advocate of resistance. Other members included the former Chief of the German General Staff Ludwig Beck and the former German Ambassador to the Quirinal in Rome Ulrich von Hassel, also a dedicated opponent of Hitler. They also had connections with Karl-Friedrich Goerdeler and General Hans Oster, focuses of civil and military opposition to the regime.

Not every member of the Wednesday Society was of course a Resistance fighter. Many belonged to it for non-political reasons. But although even now little is known about the details, it may be assumed that the recruitment of Albrecht Haushofer through Dr Langbehn, which must certainly have been with the approval of Popitz and Hassel, was for political reasons, if not for specific political purposes from the outset, since it is unlikely that the Berlin opponents of the regime had failed to notice that the young man possessed two rare but enormously important advantages: he was on first-name terms with Hess and had access to the Führer, and he knew a number of influential Britons who belonged to their country's 'peace party'. Indeed, Hassel, Popitz and other Resistance groups were already seeking to contact the British. Douglas-Hamilton – the son of the Duke whom Hess wished to meet – even writes in his book[12] that, after the failure of Hassel's peace plan, Haushofer offered Hassel his services as an expert on Britain.

The German Resistance had tried to overthrow Hitler and to make peace with the West even before war began. Of the three initiatives taken after the outbreak of war, Hassel's attempt must receive particular attention because it forms the bridge leading to the 'Hess case'.

The former Ambassador, who in the plans of the German Resistance ranked as Foreign Secretary in a post-Hitler government, had had loose contacts since early 1940 with Halifax, the British Foreign Secretary, through the British amateur diplomat and globetrotter James Lonsdale Bryans. Hassel's objective was to obtain from Britain an official declaration in writing to the effect that:

1. it would not exploit militarily the overthrow of Hitler;
2. it would enter into negotiations with the successor government for an acceptable peace with the German Reich.

His initiative therefore amounted to a barter deal: 'overthrow of Hitler against peace with the West', an objective on which earlier efforts of the Resistance had without exception foundered. To attain his objective, Hassel wrote a so-called 'Statement' setting out the German opposition's ideas on the content of the intended peace arrangements, which Lonsdale Bryans was to deliver to the British Government. The tall, lean German added by way of qualification:

1. This proposal would be valid only if agreement on it were reached with Britain *before* the 'phoney war' in the West came to an end.
2. The change in the form of government in Germany and the withdrawal of certain personalities – this was a gloss for the overthrow of Hitler – was a purely internal German matter. It could not become the subject of British demands.
3. If Britain could not grant any of the pledges desired, there would no longer be any further prospect of a change of regime in Germany in favour of a negotiated peace.

The details of Hassel's peace plan were as follows:

1. Peace in the West as soon as possible, so that Europe would not be Bolshevized by a Russian military victory over a weakened Germany or a communist revolution in the German Reich resulting from long-continuing wartime shortages.
2. Creation of a 'Greater European Fatherland', in which Germany was to receive a secure and acknowledged place, on a basis of ethnic grouping (not free self-determination) modified by historical realities.
3. Austria to remain part of the Reich (i.e. recognition of the controversial 'Anschluss'), as should the Sudetenland (i.e. break-up of Czechoslovakia). As regards Poland, the 1914 fron-

tiers to be restored (after Britain and France had guaranteed Poland within its 1939 frontiers and, for that reason, had gone to war). The establishment of a Czechoslovakian Republic (without Slovakia). In the West, no changes in the territorial position of 1937 (i.e. renunciation of Alsace-Lorraine).

4. General and equal restrictions on armaments (i.e. no renewed disparity of armaments to the disadvantage of Germany as after 1918/19).

5. Economic co-operation between Germany and Britain (the colonial question therefore remained open).

6. Various principles of international co-existence, which were largely in accordance with Western criteria.

This was the first peace plan committed to paper by the German Resistance Movement, and it went further than anything that their intermediaries had hitherto submitted to the British. If Prime Minister Chamberlain, who was still in office at the time, had agreed to this, Britain would have had to renounce everything for which, with France, it had gone to war in 1939 – and without having Hitler's head served up on a silver platter in return. This last point, according to Hassel, was a purely German internal matter, and no one could say whether the Resistance would ever resolve this to Britain's satisfaction.

The whole plan was rather hypothetical, and Chamberlain had in fact no intention whatsoever of agreeing to it. When Lonsdale Bryans delivered the German plan in London he was not even allowed to see Foreign Secretary Halifax, but was received merely by his Secretary of State, Cadogan, who refused to give the assurances demanded by Hassel. Hassel later thought that the British who were prepared to negotiate 'no longer really believed in the possibility of achieving peace in this way, i.e. by a change of system in Germany'.[13] He was right; although the British were, as ever, interested in overthrowing Hitler, they wanted to continue the War – until Germany disappeared from the scene as a European power factor. The extension of the War in the West by the German-British race for Norway, the German attack on France and Churchill's entry into office radically altered the basic tenets of the German Resistance. The 'drôle de guerre', the phoney war, in which German and Allied troops had faced one another almost peacefully, had now

[75]

escalated into bloody conflict on a large scale. As a result, Hassel's peace plan, as set out above, became invalid. From now on it was quite clear that Britain, having lost its most important ally on the Continent, would insist on the removal of Hitler and the NS regime as preconditions for any peace talks. National prestige alone demanded this. But how could a Dictator and Commander-in-Chief, who had just reached the peak of his reputation among the German people by his glorious victory over France, be overthrown?

From the Resistance aspect, the situation was hopeless – unless Hitler's opponents finally roused themselves for the decisive act: the overthrow and murder of a tyrant. In fact, the question of how Hitler could be effectively removed began from now on to occupy the German Resistance in a new and more radical form – until the attempted assassination of 20 July 1944. And time was running short. As Hitler did not succeed in summer 1940 in ending the war in the West by reaching an understanding with Britain, it was clear to any perceptive observer that the moment for a German attack on Russia was drawing closer and closer. And this raised the threat of the two-front situation again, the situation that had sealed the fate of the German Reich in the First World War.

This was roughly the position when Albrecht Haushofer was introduced to the Popitz/Hassel/Beck Resistance group by Dr Langbehn. Good advice was now at a premium, and the young scholar had unique access to a wealth of contacts with Britain. These essentially consisted of four lines or 'tracks':[14]

1. The Conservative track:

Contacts with young and old Conservatives in Parliament and in the Conservative Party (Hamilton, Stanley, Derby, O. Stanley, Astor), with connections of the British Royal Family (the wife of Hamilton's younger brother was related to the Queen).

2. The Government track:

Contacts with the Government and Ministers (Halifax – Foreign Secretary until December 1940; Lord Dunglass – Chamberlain's Parliamentary Secretary; Balfour – Undersecretary of State at the Air Ministry; Lindsay – Undersecretary of State at the Ministry of Education; Wedderburn – Undersecretary of State at the Scottish Office; Strang – head of the Central European Department at the Foreign Office; O'Malley – former head of the South-East

European Department at the Foreign Office, Ambassador to Budapest in 1941).

3. The Lothian track:

Contacts with Lord Lothian, the British Ambassador in Washington, one of the most influential personalities of his time, with access to President Roosevelt.

4. The Iberian track:

Contacts with Sir Samuel Hoare, the British Ambassador in Madrid.

Of these four tracks, two were obliterated by the end of 1940: the Government track and the Lothian track. In May 1940 Chamberlain was toppled by Churchill; Lothian died in December, and Halifax went to Washington as Ambassador. His successor as Foreign Secretary was Churchill's intimate friend Sir Anthony Eden, who, like the Prime Minister, was a dedicated opponent of any negotiated peace. Albrecht Haushofer was thus left with only two practicable tracks – the Conservative track and the Iberian track. And now began his double game, since in early September, while Hess was being put into contact with Hamilton by Haushofer, the young man tried himself to contact Hoare in Madrid.

Albrecht Haushofer's intentions here were presumptuous. He had set his mind on a place in history as a kind of 'German Talleyrand'; that is, as the statesman who, after Hitler, would lead Germany as a Great Power back into the family of Great Powers, as the famous Frenchman had done for his country after Napolean's banishment. He was driven not only by anxiety for this country but also by power-hunger, ambition and a passion for intrigue. He had once written – significantly – to his father: 'I want to have a say, but not at the front of the stage. I am still too young for that, and the general situation is not as yet tense enough. Do you perhaps know things about Hess which are not confidential but would still be interesting and could be passed on. . .?[15] The question is, to whom?

As one of the few outsiders who knew about Hitler's Russian plans, in summer 1940 Albrecht Haushofer's thoughts ran as follows: If Germany attacks Russia without first having made peace with Britain, it will end with communism penetrating into Central Europe. To prevent this and to initiate negotiations with Britain, Hitler must be overthrown, provided Britain will guarantee:

1. that it will not intervene militarily in Germany while this is being done;
2. that it will negotiate with a German successor government recruited from the ranks of the Resistance Movement for a just and lasting peace.[16]

In this context, Albrecht Haushofer, the National Conservative, developed a peace plan which was, on the one hand, in accordance with the ideas of the German Resistance, as represented by, for example, the Hassel/Popitz/Beck group, but was, on the other hand, not far from Hitler's ideas of a division of the world between Britain and Germany.[17] This plan envisaged the reorganisation of Europe along the following line:

1. Germany vacates all territories in Western and Northern Europe which it has conquered up to now – except part of Alsace-Lorraine, the details of which must be left to a German-French frontier agreement;
2. Germany recognizes the British Empire and Britain's dominion over the seven seas;
3. Britain recognizes German interests in Central and South-Eastern Europe;
4. Germany regards the 'adjustment of the (German) Eastern Frontier as a special problem which must be resolved exclusively by the states directly affected without the participation of other nations';
5. economic unification in Europe;
6. formation of a European constabulary;
7. transfer of colonies into European common ownership.

To realize this plan – depriving Britain of everything for which, together with France, it had gone to war and, apart from the overthrow of Hitler, giving Britain nothing that might protect it from German hegemony on the Continent – Albrecht Haushofer decided in late summer 1940 to play a double game: he wanted to reach his goal with the aid of Hess and also by his own efforts. As a consequence, Albrecht Haushofer became, as Hamilton jnr. rightly says, 'one of the most fascinating and mysterious figures lurking behind the scenes of the Third Reich'.[18]

This is not to say that he would have deceived Hess directly and crudely. From the beginning, Haushofer dutifully pointed out to the Deputy Führer that 'the complete lack of trust [between Britain and Germany – W.R.H.] would condemn to failure the most skilled and sincere attempts to reach a settlement'.[19] But this was more in the nature of a formality, as Albrecht Haushofer confided to his father when he wrote: 'We have said what we have to say on important points.' Moreover, that Albrecht Haushofer finally encouraged the Deputy Führer to make contact with Hamilton, that he gave Hess his active support in this, and that he eventually asserted that he did not know Hoare 'very well', while at the same time seeking contact with the British Ambassador in Madrid, suggests a grave element of deception. And in view of all this it was certainly strange that after starting off the Hess initiative Albrecht Haushofer washed his hands of it with the icy words: 'The whole thing is a fool's errand – but it's nothing to do with us.'[20] In fact, all these reservations by Albrecht Haushofer were perhaps merely intended as 'justification with an eye to history' – a formulation which may rather be interpreted as 'justification with an eye to his friends in the Resistance'. Indeed, Albrecht Haushofer meticulously deposited with his parents everything in the way of documents connected with his efforts on Hess's behalf, as if he wanted to have it to hand as evidence of his political reliability the moment the hour of change struck in Germany. In line with this, he gave great importance to these documents in establishing that 'it [making contact with Hamilton – W.R.H.] was an action in which the initiative was not mine . . .'.[21] In fact, Haushofer saw 'not the slightest prospects' in this plan, and he was fully aware that he would have 'a political future' in the post-Hitler era only 'if my Cassandra utterances are proved correct . . .'

In terms of his own political future in a different Germany, Albrecht Haushofer, in participating in the Hess venture, behind which indeed stood Hitler, certainly realized the 'danger of time slipping uselessly away'. But he had also recognized clearly 'that I can no longer refuse' without endangering his relationship with the Führer and his Deputy.

While, then, in September 1940, Hess started on the weary and troublesome road that finally led him to Britain via Haushofer, Mrs Roberts and the Duke of Hamilton, his most important adviser sought and gained access to Hoare in Madrid. Albrecht Haushofer invited his former pupil, Heinrich Georg Stahmer, who was Secretary to the German Embassy in Madrid, to come to see him in Berlin. He asked him to make personal contact in the Spanish capital with the British Ambassador, who at the time was occasionally mentioned as a possible successor to Churchill at the head of a British government prepared to negotiate.[22] He gave as reason for this that he, Haushofer, had had 'a very good and friendly relationship with Hoare in times past'. During this conversation, Albrecht Haushofer showed Stahmer and explained to him copies of his letters to Hess and Hamilton. Upon his return, the young Secretary of Embassy acted as he had been asked and, with the help of the Swedish Minister in Madrid, conveyed to Hoare Haushofer's request for a meeting in Spain or Portugal. It is uncertain whether Stahmer also told the British diplomat that this initiative was made against the background of a feeler which Hitler and Hess were extending to Britain via Hamilton, but it is probable that he did so. Otherwise, why should Haushofer have told him about it? In the course of these discussions, which took place in the winter of 1940/41 through the Swedish Legation in Madrid, Haushofer and Hoare reached agreement that the exclusion of both Hitler and Churchill was a precondition for an armistice; that is, for a provisional end to the state of war in the West. One can of course cast doubt on the seriousness of this agreement, since Hoare later asserted that he had restricted himself to accepting information from the German Resistance group without going seriously into details. But according to Stahmer's evidence there is no doubt that Haushofer was serious in his intention to exclude Hitler, and hoped from this to gain support from the military opposition in Germany. He planned, at the very least, to wrest 'crucial liberal concessions' from Hitler via Hess which might make it possible to begin discussion, perhaps at first unofficially, with Britain.[23]

There is nothing to indicate that Hess was at any time informed by Haushofer of the approach to Hoare. Until the contary is proved, therefore, it must be assumed that Haushofer's 'Conservative' and 'Iberian' tracks were running side by side for quite a time without the Führer and his Deputy knowing anything of the double-tracking of their adviser on British politics. It is possible that this changed in spring 1941 as 15 May drew closer, the date originally planned by Hitler for his attack on Russia. (A postponement became necessary because of the Italian campaign in the Balkans.) Stahmer reported, however, that the German side had proposed a secret and informal meeting between Hoare and Halifax on the one hand and Hess and Haushofer on the other for February or March 1941 at the Spanish Escorial or in Portugal. This was to discuss the possibility of an armistice between Britain and Germany. As Hess was among the individuals seen as taking part in the discussions, it cannot be ruled out that he might have known of Haushofer's Iberian contacts.

Whatever the answer may be, either the prospect of making headway along this track was weak or the Haushofer-Hoare contact was outbid by the sensational information that Burckhardt received from Britain in January 1941. In any event, Rudolf Hess and Albrecht Haushofer, united once again, had been moving chiefly along a 'Swiss track' since early in that year, a track which perhaps gave more promise of success. But the British had placed on this track an obstacle of enormous weight: before negotiations began, Hitler had to be removed as leader of the Third Reich.

Because of the lack of documents, it is not as yet possible to disentangle these various tracks and to establish the points at which they crossed. It may also be that many of these contacts were running in parallel for longer than previously assumed, or that they were temporarily in abeyance. This appears to apply mainly to Haushofer's contact with Hoare, although it was revived during the dramatic hours of 10 and 11 May 1941. Only one point can be established with certainty: when Burckhardt sought to make contact with Albrecht Haushofer in January, he did so through the agency of Hassel, one of Adolf Hitler's most determined opponents. From now on, Albrecht Haushofer was clearly playing his double game once again.

On 30 January 1941, Burckhardt had visited Ulrich von Hassel, who had gone to Geneva with this in mind, and informed him that, for the sake of peace, Britain was prepared to make far-reaching concessions – provided the negotiating partner did not bear the name of Hitler. This was the same result as from Haushofer's roundabout discussions with Hoare: peace with Britain was possible – but only without Hitler. Hassel told Haushofer what he had heard from Burckhardt, and the two men considered how they could get certain assurances from Britain in the event of a revolution in Germany.

Haushofer now included Hess in the discussions, who in turn informed Hitler. The details of when this took place and who discussed what with whom are not as yet available. But it does not need much imagination to believe that all discussion turned on the one paramount question: should – or could – Hitler be sacrificed for peace with Britain? This question was given additional weight by the fact that in spring 1941 'one of Himmler's confidential agents' unexpectedly approached Burckhardt 'about whether Britain would make peace with Himmler instead of Hitler'.[24] Who was this confidential agent? Was it Himmler's Tegernsee neighbour, the Messerschmitt solicitor Dr Carl Langbehn, who had introduced Albrecht Haushofer to the Wednesday Society?[25] This is a possibility. And did Albrecht Haushofer have a hand in the game here also? This also appears possible.[26] If this was so, then this enigmatic man would have played not only a double game but a triple game in the run-up to the Hess mission.

Whatever may be the truth, in early summer 1941 Hitler's position was no longer unchallengeable from the aspects of both domestic and foreign policy. If we call to mind all that was at stake – peace with Britain, the imminent war with Russia, the destiny of Germany, of all Europe – then even dedicated Party members might also have come to consider the replacement of Hitler by one of his deputies, Göring or Hess, in order to initiate discussions with the other side. Would it not have been appropriate under these circumstances to encourage Hess in his plans, so that at least one high-ranking representative of the Third Reich who was still fairly untainted and not personally disliked moved abroad in good time? Was not this the only way of offering world opinion and the German people an alternative to Hitler? Perhaps this is what Himmler had in mind. The behaviour of the Reichsführer SS after Rudolf Hess's departure for Britain suggests this. He displayed sympathy for this peace mission, although he was also certainly aware of its risks.

On 28 April 1941, two days before Hess's second attempt to leave, matters at all events came to a dramatic head. Albrecht arrived – 'two-faced' – in Geneva[27] to talk to Burckhardt as emissary of the German Resistance *and* as ambassador for Hess and Hitler, perhaps also with Himmler's approval. Ilse von Hassel, Ulrich von Hassel's wife, had prepared the visit from Zürich. She later met Albrech Haushofer at Arosa, the winter-sport resort, where he told her everything while it was still red-hot. As ever, the Vice-President of the International Red Cross was convinced – and this had recently been confirmed by his discussions with British diplomats 'that Britain was still pre-pared to make peace on reasonable terms, but (1) not with our present Regent [i.e. Hitler – W.R.H.] and (2) perhaps for not much longer . . .'.

A certain amount of time pressure was therefore added to the demand for Hitler's removal. On Monday, 5 May 1941, Hess called Albrecht Haushofer to Augsburg to report on his mission. The information brought by the young scholar from Burckhardt in Switzerland appeared so promising to the Deputy Führer that he 'instructed my son to pursue the matter and to make immediate arrangements for a second trip to Switzerland', Karl Haushofer later recalled.[28] On 8 May, Hess was to be seen once more on the Government bench in the Berlin Reichstag, listening with crossed arms to a speech by Hitler. The next day he wrote to Reichsleiter R.W. Darré telling him that unfortu-nately he was unable to keep an appointment arranged for mid-May. The reason was: 'I am going on a long trip and don't know when I shall be back.'[29] On Saturday, 10 May, Hess took off for Scotland to save Hitler and to save peace. Of course, these twin motives will remain speculative as long as nothing is known of all that transpired on both sides of the arras in the twelve days between the 28 April and 10 May. But it is possible that Hess wished to forestall the German Resistance, who of course wanted peace with Britain without Hitler. The increasing time pressure of the planned campaign against Russia also prob-ably played a part.

In any event, the Hess mission was highly inopportune to various people. The Hassel/Popitz Resistance group – perhaps in direct agreement with Himmler, perhaps with his tacit approval, perhaps independently of him – had in fact intended to send Albrecht Haushofer to Burckhardt again after a few weeks. Meanwhile, the Vice-President of the Red Cross was to push ahead with his feelers in Britain, and the Hassel/Popitz group, which during this period might have enquired of the military opposition about the possibility of Hitler's violent overthrow, would 'then assess the overall impressions'.[30] Later on, in June, July or August 1941, it might already be far too late to overthrow Hitler, as by then his order to attack Russia would long since have been given, if only for reasons dictated by the time of year.

Faced with the choice between waiting until Hitler was overthrown or until Germany sank into the Russian mud, Rudolf Hess decided to save Hitler, peace and his country by putting himself personally at stake.

And he had probably received a secret sign from Britain which made him believe that his dangerous mission had more prospects of success than was in fact the case.

DID HITLER KNOW?

ABOUT AN HOUR after take-off on 10 May 1941, shortly after 19.00 hrs., Hess's adjutant, Lieutenant Karlheinz Pintsch, left the Messerschmitt airfield at Augsburg-Haunstetten, taking with him the letter the Deputy Führer had entrusted to him for delivery to Hitler at the Obersalzberg. This letter was to inform the Führer that Rudolf Hess had begun his peace mission.

Pintsch drove to Munich in his chief's official car and took the night train to Berchtesgaden, where he arrived during the late evening. Above Berchtesgaden on the Obersalzberg, Hitler had bought Haus Wachenfeld as far back as the 1920s. It was originally an old farmhouse, which over the years the Führer had extended to become the Berghof.

In the early 1940s, the extensive property consisted of a complex of houses, barracks, and asphalted roads covering the wooded foothills of the Kehlstein. It was one of the tourist attractions, drawing hosts of curious people, particularly during the summer. Although from time to time Hitler condescended to appear at the barrier of the inner security area to pat a child's head or allow himself to be photograhed with the trippers, he loved the seclusion of the Berghof with its wonderful view of the Untersberg, where legend says that the Emperor Charlemagne sleeps.

Several times a year, Hitler withdrew to the Berghof for long periods to unwind and to consider fundamental decisions. Here, during the Czechoslovakia crisis in late summer 1938, he had received Chamberlain, still then Prime Minister. After the outbreak of war, the Führer had to renounce his country house for the lengthening periods he spent at his headquarters on the Western Front, and later on the Eastern Front. In early May 1941, however, he was again at the Berghof.

In contrast to the description given by the British journalist James Leasor, which contains many absurdities, the Führer did not learn about his Deputy's departure on 11 May, but late in the evening of 10 May 1941, when Pintsch arrived at the Obersalzberg.[1] The Führer probably asked the adjutant into his study, where he took his reading glasses from the desk and read Hess's letter. This letter, which covered about two pages of typescript,[2] began with the lines: 'My Führer; when you receive this letter I shall be in Britain.' And it ended with: 'And if, my Führer, my plan, burdened – I must admit – with very slight chance of success, should fail, if fate should decide against me, it can have no evil consequences for you or for Germany. You can drop me at any time – say that I am mad.'

When he had finished reading, Hitler looked up at Pintsch. Then he asked: 'Where is Hess now?' Pintsch was able to answer this question only by saying that Hess had taken off from Augsburg shortly before 18.00 hrs., with Scotland as his destination, to meet the Duke of Hamilton. As far as he could judge, Hess should already have landed there – or had crashed or been shot down over the open sea. Perhaps the Deputy of the German Führer had already been taken prisoner in Britain.

Hitler may also have suspected that Himmler was hatching something against him. Next day he sent for Göring and Ribbentrop – but not for Himmler, the Reichsführer SS and Chief of the German Police, and not for Propaganda Minister Goebbels. The Führer was apparently determined to keep the reins of this political dynamite in his own hands for as long as possible. When, in the course of the 11 May, Hess had still sent no word from Britain, Hitler's doubts about the success of the peace mission increased.

Before he left, the Deputy Führer had provided for the possibility that he might be able to send a message. If his mission went according to plan, he would telegraph an appropriate message to his aunt, Emma Rothacker, in Zürich, Herzogstrasse 17, for her to pass on.

When Hitler did not receive this message, he gradually came under increasing pressure to act. Although Hess's adjutant was still allowed to sit at the Führer's dining table on 11 May, he was soon arrested. It was one of the Führer's principles that 'measures' had to be taken when something went wrong.

Göring and Ribbentrop arrived at the Berghof during the afternoon and evening of 11 May.[3] Goebbels and Himmler were still kept away from the Führer's headquarters.[4]

Relations between Ribbentrop and Himmler, who was inclined towards a negotiated peace with the West, were strained; they were both competing for influence in Germany's foreign policy.[5] But, as it happened, on that Sunday the Reich Foreign Secretary and the Reichsführer SS were together at Ribbentrop's Schloss Fuschl near Salzburg when the news of Hess's flight reached them.[6] Ribbentrop, uninformed, saw the whole thing as 'running away', while Himmler, informed, knew something of the Deputy Führer's farewell letter to Hitler and of the several letters that Haushofer had written to Hamilton via Burckhardt. He was not without sympathy for Hess's step.[7]

On Sunday, 11 May 1941, there was no further action on the German side. The consultations at the Berghof were extremely difficult, as Hitler, Göring and Ribbentrop still did not know what had happened to Hess. Britain was also wrapped in silence.

Next day, Monday 12 May 1941, Hitler's hopes that Hess might have been successful had sunk to zero. The Führer now gathered himself together for action, but still displayed no decisiveness. He ordered Albrecht Haushofer, who was in Berlin, to come to the Obersalzberg immediately, arranged for Reich Press Chief Dietrich to publish a first communiqué and ordered Martin Bormann to carry on with the duties of his former chief 'in the name of the Party Chancellery'.[8] All Reichsleiters and Gauleiters, i.e. the leading NSDAP officials, were ordered to report to the Berghof on 13 May at 16.00 hrs., and Ribbentrop was to hasten to Rome to brief Hitler's ally, the Italian Dictator Mussolini, on this highly embarrassing affair. It was within the bounds of possibility that the Duce might allow himself to be led astray, take Hess as an example, and also extend peace feelers towards Britain.

All these hectic activities concealed Hitler's intention of

regaining as quickly as possible from Churchill the initiative in the Hess affair before Hess in Britain – voluntarily or under pressure – gave away anything 'that might make a great impression here'.[9] The watchword was: damage limitation.

Hitler of course summoned young Haushofer to learn the precise details of Hess's flight. After all, the Führer had used him when he launched his last great peace initiative against Britain in September 1940, and he had certainly heard of Albrecht Haushofer's visit to Burckhardt in Switzerland at the end of April. But Hitler did not know of Albrecht Haushofer's double – or triple – dealings.

For the young and ambitious academic, it was now all or nothing. On the very evening of Hess's flight he had received a telephone call from his friend Stahmer in Madrid, who told him there was an opportunity to leave Berlin and to meet the British Ambassador, Hoare, on the pretext of giving a lecture in the Spanish capital.[10] It is still not clear whether this was fortuitous and coincidental, or whether it was an attempt to save Haushofer. The latter explanation is probable, but assumes that the date of Hess's flight was known in Madrid. It would be interesting to know how this information reached the Spanish capital.

For reasons we do not know, Albrecht Haushofer rejected the saving hand thus extended to him. On 12 May at 10.00 hrs. he was picked up by one of the Führer's courier planes at the Berlin-Staaken air base. When he arrived at the Berghof, however, Haushofer was not admitted to Hitler. He was instead placed in a room under guard, provided with paper and pencil, and ordered to give an account of himself in writing to Hitler.

The draft he prepared during these midday hours bore the innocuous heading, 'British contacts and the possibility of their utilization'. As Hamilton jnr. rightly says, this was 'a plausible and convincing mixture of truths, half-truths and camouflage designed not to implicate any of his friends in the Resistance'. Although Haushofer did not for a moment believe that Britain would ever make peace with Hitler, he skilfully gave an impression, reading between the lines, that without him and his many connections talks would never take place. Even in this crucial situation, therefore, Albrecht Haushofer had the nerve to continue his daring double or triple game.

In a cool and detached manner, Haushofer set out again his many connections with Britain. He emphasized the political importance of the Duke of Hamilton, and maintained that Hess, faced with the choice of making contact with Hoare, Lothian, O'Malley, or the Scottish Duke, had decided on the Duke. However, he, Haushofer, did not know whether the letter he had written to Hamilton in September 1940 had ever reached its addressee. He wrote ambiguously: 'The possibility of loss on the way from Lisbon to Britain is of course not insignificant.'

Haushofer also mentioned his contact with Burckhardt, the beginning of which – in fact contrary to the truth – he gave as April 1941. The Vice-President of the Red Cross had told him on 28 April in Geneva that 'leading Conservative and City circles' in London continued to be interested in 'examining the possibility of peace'. These circles had brought him, Haushofer, into the game as a possible information broker. He had said that he was willing to take on this duty, and at a later date to meet one of Burckhardt's British contacts in Geneva.

Haushofer summarized the content of British peace ideas as follows: The British interest in Eastern and South-Eastern Europe was merely 'nominal', but British interest in the 're-establishment of the Western European States' was irrevocable. The colonial question would not present 'any excessive difficulties'. However, a precondition for real peace talks would be a 'general basis of trust'. But this would be very difficult to find, wrote Haushofer, because 'the conflict with "Hitlerism" ' was seen by Britain 'as a religious war'. In this way he alluded to the British reluctance to negotiate with Hitler. 'Only the long-established section of the plutocracy' was really prepared to make peace, continued Haushofer. But if this section were by-passed, any chance of 'the reasonable forces in Britain compelling Churchill to make peace . . .' would be lost. 'With Roosevelt and his circle, however, . . . it was quite impossible to talk sense.' This was also Burckhardt's opinion.

It is difficult to say what Hitler thought when faced with these lines. Basically, they contained no surprises for him. He had no further need for Haushofer, and ordered that he should be arrested and taken back to Gestapo headquarters in Berlin, where he was interrogated and kept prisoner for eight weeks. But nothing drastic happened to him. Himmler appeared to shield him, and Ribbentrop sacked him. 'I am fully aware that at the moment I am a little beetle thrown on its back by an unexpected and unforeseeable gust of wind', wrote Albrecht Haushofer to his parents from his prison.[11] He at first appeared to bear his lot with composure, and was eventually released on Hitler's orders. But the influence he and his father had exercised on the foreign policy of the National Socialists was broken once and for all.

The old Haushofers continued to live unmolested for some years at the Hartschimmelhof, while their son Albrecht carried on as a professor in Berlin. Later, after Colonel Stauffenberg had tried to assassinate Hitler in summer 1944, he was arrested and eventually shot by an SS detachment without trial on a bombed site in Berlin on 23 April 1945. Karl Haushofer and his wife Martha committed suicide in 1946. It appears that towards the end of his life the father began to doubt whether his son had always acted correctly in the Hess affair. In any event, at the end of 1944 Karl Haushofer wrote that Albrecht Haushofer had 'perhaps toyed with the fate of well-meaning people . . . which worries me much more than it did him.'[12]

What happened next on 12 May 1941? In the evening, at 20.00 hrs., the German radio transmitted the communiqué which Dietrich had drafted on the instructions of Hitler, Göring and Ribbentrop. It informed the German people and the world that, in spite of sickness, 'Party Member Hess' had got hold of an aircraft and taken off against orders. He had as yet not returned from this flight. It said that 'a letter he left behind unfortunately showed, by its confusion, signs of mental derangement, which gives rise to fear that Party Member Hess was the victim of delusions'. It had therefore to be expected that he 'had crashed somewhere or met with an accident during his flight'.[13] Without disclosing that Hess had flown to Britain to make peace, Hitler then made use of the formula which his Deputy had put into his mouth; he declared that Hess was mad. This was a concealed admission that Hitler already considered the Hess mission a failure.

My mother received the first hint of her husband's flight on the evening of 12 May as she was watching a film with friends in her house at München-Harlaching; an adjutant happened to have heard the radio announcement. She immediately tried to put through an urgent official telephone call to Hitler at the Obersalzberg. She wanted to protect her husband against the imputation that he had acted against orders. But she could only speak to Bormann, who insisted that he knew nothing. He instead sent to Frau Hess Ministerialrat Dr Hansen, who arrived at München-Harlaching shortly after midnight. Hansen had come for more information. When my mother protested that she knew nothing, Hansen reacted with incredulity, and threatened the Deputy Führer's wife with arrest if she said anything about the matter in public.

This was the beginning of a long and bitter quarrel between Ilse Hess and Martin Bormann, mitigated only by the fact that the Führer shielded the wife of his Deputy and old comrade-in-arms. On 31 May 1941, Frau Hess was granted 'an appropriate monthly pension', together with a lump-sum payment to assist her in reorganizing her household to conform to that of a normal citizen.[14]

My mother later described how she felt about all this, even when she learned that her husband was still alive: 'He was of course unable to protect us against the fact that the world which had been ours henceforth enclosed us in a magic circle from which there was no longer any return to the former affiliations. Adjutants, orderlies, secretaries, driver, my brother-in-law Alfred and Albrecht Haushofer were all arrested. Some of them disappeared into concentration camps for years, and were not set free until 1943/44. We had all been transformed from individuals in an organization into objects liable to arbitrary treatment – this was a bitter pill we had to swallow day after day, week after week, year after year . . .'.[15]

On Tuesday 13 May, three days after the disappearance of the Deputy Führer, the Reichsleiters and Gauleiters of the NSDAP assembled at the Obersalzberg; among them was Reichsführer SS Heinrich Himmler. The British Government had meanwhile announced in a laconic press statement that Hess had landed by parachute, slightly injured, in Scotland – nothing more. Sixty or seventy men gathered in the large hall at the Berghof, with its view of the Salzburg massif, to be received by Bormann.

In the presence of Hitler and Göring, Bormann, who took this opportunity to introduce himself as the new leader of the Party organization, read Hess's farewell letter. Hitler then took over and condemned his Deputy's action in strong words: Hess erred if he believed he could enlist Britain alongside Germany in the struggle against Bolshevism. As Churchill had once said, this was a British war whose objective was the destruction of Germany as a leading power in Europe. The war had therefore become a war of existence or non-existence.

In his address, Hitler betrayed the reason for his increasing agitation: 'Fellow Party members, Hess has left me at a time when the commanders may at any moment receive orders for the most difficult military operation to date. How can I expect my generals to obey this order when my most senior political leader leaves the battlefield on his own initiative . . . ?'[16] From this, the leading Party figures learnt that the German attack on Russia was now imminent. Because of this insubordination, Hitler continued, the Party must strike the name of Hess from its memory. All pictures of his Deputy were to be removed from the offices of the Party. All who had participated directly or indirectly in the preparation of the flight must be punished.

The Party's official announcement on the Hess affair had led to unpleasant reactions among the German population, and Hitler defended the announcement by arguing that the British Secret Service would be able to confuse Germans – women in particular – by arranging for a Hess impersonator to agitate against Germany on the radio. It was intended to prevent this by declaring that the Deputy Führer was no longer of sound mind. Finally, Hitler urged his Party leaders to do all they could to ensure that 'this mad deed would disappear as soon as possible from political discussion'. He here used the words: 'We take the gamble of flying at the throat of our real world enemy, Bolshevism, before it is fully prepared, as the beneficiary of this war, to fly at the throat of a Europe weakened in battle.' In this 'struggle for life or death, the battle for the coming century will be fought'.

When Hitler had finished his address, turning his attention to the far future in his concluding words, he sank back exhausted into his chair. At this moment Reichsleiter Bohle pushed forward to report to the Führer on his participation in the preparations for the Hess mission. When Hitler caught sight of the chief of the National Socialist Foreign Organization, he exclaimed: 'Tell me, Bohle, did you really know nothing about this?'

Bohle admitted that he had helped Hess draft a letter to the Duke of Hamilton containing peace proposals.

This information appeared to agitate Hitler. He stood up and approached Bohle with raised fists, saying: 'What have you done? Have you lost your senses? Are you mad?'

At that moment Göring intervened, saying with measured emphasis: 'Herr Bohle, I think it would be best if you were to tell the Führer quite calmly what you have done.' Upon this Hitler calmed down, and when Bohle had finished he was asked to show Hitler the items in Hess's farewell letter which, as far as he could remember, had also appeared in the letter from Hess to Hamilton. Although Bohle was summoned for routine questioning to Gestapo Headquarters on his return to the Reich capital, he was neither arrested nor dismissed. He concluded from this 'that Hitler [already before the meeting at the Obersalzberg – W.R.H.] knew about my participation and had been asked by Hess not to punish me if the venture failed and he, Hitler, was forced to disown Hess.'[17] Everyone who knew the Führer agreed that he was a consummate actor.

Ulrich von Hassel noted soberly in his diary: 'The impression . . . was indescribable, although increased immeasurably by the . . . foolishness of the official communiqué . . .'. Hassel considered that, in contrast to the 'eccentric intention' of Hess, whose decency was not basically doubted even by the German Resistance, his peace mission would have the effect of 'prolonging the war'. From the aspect of domestic politics, it was a 'blow against the authority of the system', and from the aspect of foreign policy it was 'a plus for the radicals and for Ribbentrop'.[18]

In comparison, Propaganda Minister Goebbel's unvarnished indignation made it difficult for him to calm down. He foamed with rage after Hitler had telephoned him. 'It is too idiotic! A fool such as this was second to the Führer! It scarcely bears thinking about. Yesterday evening's communiqué was necessary. The matter must be attributed to delusion. How otherwise can it be explained? . . . No one will believe that this is just a crazy excursion on Hess's part. For Hess it shows lack of discipline. He is finished as far as the Führer is concerned.'[19]

Goebbels was wrong. When Rudolf Hess's father died on 2 October 1941, Hitler sent a personal telegram of condolence to his widow. When Bormann noted from this that Hitler had not broken with the Hess family, he also sent the widow a telegram of condolence two days later.

Because of the 'awful' mood of the German people, which the Propaganda Minister realized, Goebbels and Hitler decided to issue a second communiqué on the evening of 13 May. One way or another, there had to be some reaction to the British statements; the confused population had to have an explanation of what the Deputy Führer had really tried to do in England or Scotland. The result was an announcement in the National Socialist Party Press, which in fact only paraphrased the madness theme:[20] a search through his personal papers had established that 'Hess appears to have been under the illusion that by taking personal action among Britons he had known in the past he could bring about an understanding between Britain and Germany.' As if they still wished to leave a tiny back door open, Hitler and Goebbels actually admitted that Hess 'knew better than anyone the Führer's numerous peace proposals, stemming from his most upright heart'. They regretted however 'that this idealist had fallen victim to such a disastrous illusion'.

How Hitler would have reacted if, against all expectations, his Deputy had in fact met with success cannot be imagined. If only Hitler and Goebbels had known that Churchill had no intention whatsoever of making anything out of the affair! Hess was neither presented to the public nor used as a propaganda weapon on the British radio. No one in Germany learned what he had said and what he had not said in captivity. Instead, there came from Britain – apart from the hectic speculations of the ill-informed press – this impenetrable, hostile and perfidious silence. It forced the German leadership to distance itself from Hess, if only as a precaution, and to maintain this distance, both from Hess and from any thought of peace. 'A great military success, and the whole schoolboy prank will be forgotten', said Goebbels, wisely.[21] Perhaps he had in mind the campaign against Russia.

The Propaganda Minister noted as early as 16 May that the affair had lost its 'dramatic character'. He recorded with amazement that the government in London 'has apparently not hit on the obvious idea of simply issuing statements in Hess's name, without consulting him,' which would incense the German people against the Führer. 'This is the only – but a dreadful – danger to us', wrote Goebbels. If he had been the British Propaganda Minister, he would no doubt have made very much more of the whole incident.

Goebbels was now able to watch the rumours gradually dying down as the world's attention turned to other matters. The Minister also adopted the tactic of remaining silent in his domestic propaganda. On 18 May 1941, only eight days after Hess's flight, Goebbel's diary reads soberly and coldly: 'The Hess case is liquidated. . . . This is how fast everything passes in these easy-going times. Hess should have known this beforehand. What will become of him now?'

This question could in fact be answered by only one person: Winston Spencer Churchill.

'HAS SOMEBODY ARRIVED?'

AFTER THE DUKE OF HAMILTON had identified the Deputy Führer in Glasgow on the morning of 11 May, he returned to Turnhouse airfield. On the way, he made a detour to Eaglesham to inspect the crashed Me 110. Back at his station he asked his superior officer for leave, and telephoned the Foreign Office in London. But the Duty Officer at the British Foreign Office on that Sunday morning was reluctant to accept Hamilton's unreasonable request to speak to Secretary of State Sir Alexander Cadogan on an urgent matter about which he could not go in detail over the telephone for reasons of secrecy. Thereupon, Hamilton immediately telephoned the Prime Minister, whom he knew personally.

Like his predecessors, Churchill lived in London, No. 10 Downing Street, a modest brick house which always seemed rather smoke-blackened and had served the heads of the British Government as official and private residence for very many years. In addition, of course, he could use at weekends the British Prime Minister's official country house, Chequers, unless he preferred to spend his scanty leisure with friends or at his own country house, Chartwell, on London's threshold. This weekend, however, the Prime Minister was at Ditchley Park, the country seat near Oxford of his friend Ronald Tree. It was therefore his Personal Assistant Jock Colvin who took the call when Hamilton telephoned No. 10 Downing Street.

The Duke had no need to beat about the bush when Colvin

asked him immediately: 'Has somebody arrived?' Hamilton replied simply: 'Yes', whereupon they both agreed that Churchill should be informed directly.[1] It appeared that Rudolf Hess had been expected in Britain. At least, the sensational news of his landing had already reached Churchill's circle.

Be that as it may, Colvin asked Hamilton to go to Ditchley Park as quickly as possible. The Duke, himself an experienced pilot – in the 1930s he was the first person to fly over the highest mountain in the world, Mount Everest in the Himalayas – took a Hurricane and dashed in the fighter plane to Northolt, an air base west of London. Here he was directed on to Kidlington, where a black limousine was waiting for him beside the runway. Soon after dinner, i.e. in the early evening, the premier peer of Scotland arrived at his destination.

Ditchley Park was an impressive property dating from the 18th century belonging to Churchill's old friend and political comrade-in-arms Ronald Tree, a Conservative member of the House of Commons and half-American. Standing among extensive estates in the immediate neighbourhood of Churchill's birth-place, Blenheim Palace, the mansion had seven reception rooms, twenty-four bedrooms and ten bathrooms. As if by accident, an illustrious party of some thirty people was gathered here this weekend, including, in addition to Churchill, his closest adviser Brendan Bracken, Professor Frederick Lindemann, General Hastings Ismay and the Air Force Minister Sir Archibald Sinclair. They were wearing dinner-jackets and dress uniforms while London was at that moment being bombed.

Hamilton, who was of course known to Churchill from the political everyday life of London, asked the Prime Minister for a private meeting. Churchill, however, considered it proper to include his Air Force Minister. The three men withdrew from the party, and the head of the British Government asked the Scottish duke for his report. Four days later, Churchill asserted in the House of Commons that 'in view of the surprising character of the occurrence I did not believe it', although he had found it 'very interesting',[2] but he could in fact no longer reasonably doubt Hamilton's report that he had positively identified Hess that morning. Of course, anything like official verification was still lacking.

Meanwhile, the Sunday evening went ahead. In happy mood,

[97]

the other guests gathered in one of the elegant drawing rooms to watch the film 'The Marx Brothers Go West'. The cinema-film medium was still then comparatively young and, in spite of everything that otherwise distinguished the two, the British upper class apparently shared with the National Socialist leadership a certain passion for the flickering pictures that jolted across the screen in the darkened room. In any event, there was now, in the middle of the night, nothing more to be done than to make a prisoner of the Deputy Führer, who had just flown in. Churchill said to his two companions, as he rose from his chair: 'Well, Hess or no Hess, I'm going to see the Marx Brothers.'[3] The Prime Minister here tried to give an air of unconcern. In fact, as will be seen later, he was so electrified that he telephoned President Roosevelt the same night.

After the film – it was now midnight – Churchill returned to what was for him potentially fatal political dynamite. He telephoned his Foreign Secretary Sir Anthony Eden and invited Hamilton to a further conversation, which – this time apparently with no third party – lasted until three o'clock on Monday morning. The Duke produced the letter containing peace proposals which he had received from Albrecht Haushofer in July 1939, as well as a copy of the fateful letter of 19 September 1940 which Haushofer had written on the directions of Hess and Hitler, and all the political aspects of the matter were again discussed. Churchill then bound Hamilton to the strictest secrecy. The Scotsman was to remain overnight at Ditchley Park and return to London on the Monday morning with the Prime Minister, when discussion would be continued with the appropriate people.

Apart from a few rumours circulating in the Eaglesham area of Scotland, on the morning of 12 May 1941 the public still knew nothing of the Deputy Führer's peace mission. On the Sunday, the chief editor of the Glasgow *Daily Record* had investigated the night-time parachute descent, but by the Monday his report had not yet appeared; the local censor had blocked the story. As Hitler also hesitated to make an announcement, the London consultations could go ahead quite undisturbed.

On Monday morning, just before 10.00 hrs., Churchill resumed his official duties at Downing Street in London. He first arranged for the Duke to see the Ministers for the Navy, Army and Air Force. The Duke was asked to tell them everything he could remember of his first encounter with Hess on Sunday morning, and what might be of importance to the British in the conduct of the war. It was certainly not an everyday event for such a high-ranking figure from the enemy's side to switch over to their camp. However, the yield appeared to be infinitesimally small, since Hess was no traitor.

Before Churchill joined the regular meeting of the War Cabinet, he discussed with Eden whether there was anyone in the Foreign Office who could incontestably identify the German prisoner up in Scotland as Rudolf Hess. The Prime Minister thought it possible that Hitler might have sent a double instead of the genuine Deputy to create confusion among the British. Churchill and Eden finally hit upon Sir Ivone Kirkpatrick, who had been First Secretary at the British Embassy in Berlin up to the end of 1939. Kirkpatrick had met Hess personally on various occasions, and as he was now working as foreign policy co-ordinator at the British Broadcasting Corporation he appeared to be the right man for the task. Not only was he a sworn enemy of Hitler and National Socialism, but the former Secret Service man and ex-diplomat now employed by the Ministry of Information was also the best judge of whether the Hess story could be exploited for propaganda purposes.

In fact, Churchill at no time intended to use this peace mission as a means of ending the war with Germany. On the contary, his only objective was destruction of the German Reich, and in May 1941 the Prime Minister already had good reason to believe that he would achieve this aim in the not too distant future by the entry of America and Russia into the War. His awareness of this and the resulting determination to hold on at any price until final victory conditioned Churchill's entire behaviour in the Hess affair.

The Head of Government, 67 years of age, half-American by birth, stemmed from one of the oldest families in Britain. He was descended from those imperialists who had created the British Empire in Africa, America, Asia and Australia. In essence, the Empire's existence was based on Britain's ability to play off the strongest power on the European Continent against the second-strongest power. The balance of power thus resulting enabled the Government in London to dominate the world, while the other European powers held one another in check and no longer represented a danger to the island nation.

This changed, however, when at more or less the same time, at the beginning of the twentieth century, the USA and the German Reich rose to the status of world powers. It changed once again in 1917 when Russia became Bolshevist. Problems now arose for a Britain which was becoming relatively weaker, problems which in the long term threatened its position as a world power. Should it support France and Russia against Germany? Or should it take the opposite option and ally itself with Germany against France and Russia? The one would sooner or later lead to war between the European Continental powers and weaken Europe *vis-à-vis* America. The other would have united Continental Europe under German supremacy and have strengthened it *vis-à-vis* America. And a Europe united from Gibraltar to the River Bug would have prevented Bolshevism's expansion as far as the Elbe.

Large sections of the British upper class were fluctuating between these two possibilities up to the outbreak of the Second World War, a factor which explains the scattered nature of British politics at the time. But for Churchill the decision had been clear from the outset: he supported the anti-German alliance, and to this end he unscrupulously accepted the weakening of Continental Europe. He deluded himself here in regard to Britain's ability to maintain itself and its Empire as a world power in alliance with America. After 1917, Churchill deceived himself into believing that the Anglo-Saxon naval powers could together prevent the Soviet Union from penetrating into the heart of Central Europe. With this in mind, the West had already eliminated Germany as a Central European power factor at Versailles. Britain had to pay for these errors and delusions of Churchill by the loss of its Empire; Europe had to pay for them by its partition. The Red Army today stands in the centre of Germany on the Elbe, and all the peoples behind the Iron Curtain have been enslaved. This is particularly true of the Poles, for whose freedom Britain allegedly went to war in 1939.

By the premature mobilization of the British Navy in 1914, Churchill, as First Lord of the Admiralty, had assisted in pushing hesitant Britain into war against Germany on the French and Russian side. Although at first his glittering career received a sharp reverse in the rash attempt in 1915 to unite the British and Russian Navies in the Bosporus, Churchill had already made a substantial contribution to America's entry into the war in the *Lusitania* incident, in which he manoeuvered the British vessel with its American passengers into the path of the torpedo tubes of a German submarine. With the assistance of his powerful friends, who included American and British Jews, Churchill rose again to national prominence during the 1930s. His great topic was, as ever, 'the German menace', a battle cry which he now illustrated by the horrific image of a Nazi Europe subjugated by Hitler.

Churchill agreed fundamentally with his predecessor Chamberlain, that the most important task in British politics was 'to liberate Europe from the perpetual and repetitive danger of German aggression, and to enable the peoples of Europe to assert their independence and freedom'.[4] They differed only as regards the methods, speed and energy with which this aim was to be pursued. While British re-armament and the alliance with the USA remained incomplete, Chamberlain would have preferred a time-limited and restricted understanding with Hitler. From the beginning, however, Churchill was against any compromise, and he exerted all his effort to involve the United States of America in the European conflict as quickly as possible. For example, 'The first thing we must do is to draw the United States into the War', he said on 17 February 1941.[5]

In a tortuous way, Britain and America were linked. As long as Britain did not have a formal commitment from the USA to enter the war, the military conflict with Hitler was a hazardous venture involving the risk of national ruin, because since the First World War the whole world had known that Britain and France could no longer win a war against a militarily re-armed and politically united Germany without the inexhaustible resources of American aid. On the other hand, Roosevelt, the American President, hesitated to give the necessary assurances until Britain and France had proved that they were determined to defeat Hitler decisively at any price. This proof could of course be best provided by the two West European democracies going to war. This in fact occurred on 3 September 1939 after the German attack on Poland, when Britain and France declared war on the German Reich.

Chamberlain had long hesitated to give his approval to this development, although at the turn of 1938/39 Roosevelt had already secretly promised him all America's resources in the event of war. The Prime Minister knew that war against Germany would mean the advance of Communism towards Eastern Europe, the end of the British Empire and the end of his own political career. Finally, he knew in 1939 that Churchill was already favoured by Roosevelt as his successor. It has not as yet been possible fully to clarify the background to all this, but Churchill returned to the bridge of the British Navy as First Lord of the Admiralty on 3 September 1939. 'Winston is back – it's Winston's war', rejoiced the British at the time, and in some way they were correct.

To some extent the European war accorded with Roosevelt's interests. He would certainly have preferred Hitler's overthrow to war; this would have been the cheapest solution. But as the German Resistance could not rouse itself for the crucial deed war was the second-best solution, since any war lost by Germany against overwhelming superiority would eventually mean the downfall of Hitler's government. This had already been demonstrated by the dethronement of the Kaiser after the German defeat of 1918/19. Moreover, a new world war would still further weaken the European colonial powers, whose empires stood in the way of the global economic and security interests of the USA.

This did not of course mean that Roosevelt steered a direct course for war. Had he done so, he would have risked removal from office by Congress, since under the American Constitution the Senate alone decides on matters of peace and war. But the US President also did nothing to support Chamberlain – who of course wanted peace for the time being – in the latter's appeasement policy. Quite the contrary: whenever he could, he put a spoke in Chamberlain's wheel. Like the imperialist Churchill, for the liberal-democratic and internationalist Franklin Delano Roosevelt compromise with Hitler's non-liberal, dictatorial and nationalistic principles was out of the question. In the eyes of both the American President and the British Prime Minister, it was probable that the Third Reich would capitulate – before or after the downfall of the Dictator – in the face of the overwhelming superiority of the Anglo-Saxon naval powers.

As Churchill had the British Navy, Roosevelt had in practice directed the American Navy in the First World War. The 1914 to 1918 war years, with German successes at the beginning and German disaster at the end, represented the crucial experience in the education of these two most important 20th century politicians. In their judgement, Germany could be defeated if only it could be maneouvred into a two-front dilemma, and if the neutral United States entered the war in good time.

In contrast to Kaiser Wilhelm II, Hitler based his policy on an unequivocal decision to achieve world-wide understanding with Britain and on unilateral expansion of the German Reich eastwards. Since his policy was founded on the necessity of a Western crusade against Bolshevism, how could American and British public opinion join in a Western crusade against National Socialism? Most Britons and Americans were less afraid of National Socialism than of the communists, and in fact during the period up to 1939 the West was ready to accept the German Reich's dominion over the European Continent.

But Churchill and Roosevelt thought quite differently. In their opinion, Hitler, the resurgence of Germany into world-power status and the imminent hegemony of the Third Reich over the Continent resulted solely from the West's having dealt too leniently at Versailles with the arrogant, ambitious and aggressive Germans, a race obsessed with Prussian militarism. They did not greatly fear another war against Germany, which they had good reason to believe they would win. Roosevelt and Churchill were much more concerned that Hitler might in fact succeed in reaching at least a temporary agreement with Britain and France, and that Germany would then reach critical mass in the centre of Europe, endangering not only Russia's existence but also Anglo-Saxon naval power and thus world equilibrium. And their fears were not without foundation, since in fact, in 1939, until his attack on Poland, Hitler was well on the way to achieving this objective. Roosevelt and Churchill believed that such an undesirable development could be prevented only by an alliance of the Anglo-Saxon maritime powers, enlarged by France and Stalin's Russia. The First World War had shown that this was an invincible combination against the 'German menace'. Churchill had striven unswervingly for this Grand Alliance since the mid-1930s. But at the turn of 1938/39, Roosevelt settled temporarily on Poland as a flanking power, crediting that country with high preparedness for war and great fighting power. But Stalin upset their plans by entering into a non-aggression pact with Hitler in 1939, giving them the possibility of liquidating Poland together.

Although, in relations with Russia, the American President had for the time being taken a path that by-passed the Grand Alliance, he continued to agree with the British Prime Minister on the necessity for the Anglo-American alliance. Roosevelt also shared with Churchill the false doctrine that in the long run the West, which of course dominated the Seven Seas, world trade, world finance and the world's raw material resources, would succeed in keeping the Soviet Union in check. Only on this basis can the territorial concessions granted by the two Western politicians to Stalin on Teheran and Yalta be explained, and at that time, in the early 1940s, before the atomic bomb was ready, the nuclear stalemate was still unforeseeable. In any event, Roosevelt and Churchill's common determination to eliminate Germany entirely as a power factor so strongly outbalanced any other considerations that they underestimated the risks associated with the inclusion of the Soviet Union in the Western Alliance.

The outbreak of war in 1939 brought the alliance between America and Britain several steps closer. The fact that Churchill was now at the head of the British Navy strengthened his influence upon the entire Anglo-French policy in both war and peace. It was then that the First Lord of the Admiralty – an office corresponding to that of Minister of the Navy on the Continent – began his secret correspondence with the American President. This led over the next few years to a steadfast relationship of trust between the two politicians. The next step came with the defeat of France; the German armies had now crossed the Rhine, which even before the outbreak of war Roosevelt had declared to be the United States' front line of defence, and his friend Churchill had become Prime Minister in London.

Nevertheless, in 1940/41 great uncertainty persisted within the Anglo-American alliance. Would Hitler be able to end the war against Britain? This was the question Churchill and Roosevelt were continually asking themselves in the period between the defeat of France and the German attack on Russia. But they were as relentlessly determined as ever to continue the war until Germany's unconditional surrender – whether or not the German Resistance succeeded meanwhile in overthrowing Hitler. But could the British people be trusted? If they were to capitulate to Hitler the Anglo-American alliance would come to nothing – and so would any chance of bringing in Stalin, who would then certainly have to move even further towards appeasing Hitler.

From a tactical aspect, Britain's position in 1940/41 was poor. It had lost, in France, its only ally on the European Continent. The other possible ally, Russia, was still in the enemy camp, and the most powerful potential ally, the USA, was still neutral. This prevented Roosevelt from providing Britain officially with the weapons, munitions and war equipment it needed for effective and long-term continuation of the war. Even worse, Britain's finances were in ruins; without dollars it was internationally insolvent. For good measure, since summer 1940 Britain had a second opponent in addition to Germany, i.e. Italy, and if the conflict between Japan and the USA came to a head it must expect a third opponent. Britain was thus involved in two – possibly three – theatres of war, and that situation might easily lead to catastrophe.

But, as the course of events of 1940/41 during the Battle of Britain and in the Mediterranean area showed, the situation was not completely hopeless. By September 1940, Britain had won the war in the air against Germany, which from then onwards lacked the most important prerequisite for a landing on the island. But fear of invasion continued, and 'the Blitz', as the British called the German bombing campaign against their towns and cities, strained their nerve. But by spring 1941 the worst had been withstood and was past.

After the defeat of France, Germany's Italian ally in the Mediterranean region had begun a large-scale pincer-movement to exert pressure on the British position in the Near East and to create an empire for itself. British Somaliland and the French possessions in North Africa had been lost, the Suez Canal was blocked, and the Axis Powers threatened the British Protectorate in Egypt, the French Mandate in Syria, Iraq and the entire Balkans. Britain had thrown 50 per cent of its tanks into North Africa to protect Egypt, but had to draw troops away from there to defend Greece against the invading Italians. Coverage was too scanty everywhere.

During 1940, it became clear that Mussolini's plans were far too ambitious, that his troops would not reach their objectives and that the Italian ally had become a liability to Hitler rather than an asset. At the turn of 1940/41 the British launched a counter-offensive in Cyrenaica, and Hitler had to form the Africa Corps under General Erwin Rommel to get the Italians out of their mess. In the Balkans also, matters did not progress without German assistance. Four weeks after the beginning of the Italian attack, which immediately faltered, Hitler had to intervene militarily in Greece and later in Jugoslavia in order to stabilize the Balkan front.

It was a bitter experience for the British to leave Greece, whose independence they had once guaranteed. After the failure of Churchill's Norway adventure and the near-catastrophe at Dunkirk, this was the third time that British soldiers had had to withdraw defeated – and this of course reduced the nation's morale. Moreover, the strip of desert west of Egypt was lost again in spring 1941. Tobruk and Crete were at risk, but the general situation was not too serious for Britain in the land theatres of war. Hitler had tied down part of his forces in Africa and the Balkans, his Italian ally had been militarily humbled and his war against Britain seemed to continue endlessly.

There was, however, one sphere of war that greatly disturbed Roosevelt and Churchill – the Battle of the Atlantic. Here, in spring 1941, the German U-boats, which had hitherto operated individually, changed to 'wolf-pack' tactics. They extended their range of action further and further into the Atlantic, until British fighter planes could no longer pursue them, and the German Luftwaffe bombed all sea convoys between Dover and Narvik, and above all in the western approaches to the Irish Sea. This had truly devastating consequences for the ships transporting the vital supplies of food, arms, ammunition, war equipment and raw materials from America and the Empire to Britain. In spring 1941, the British lost more tonnage than they could replace or repair in their shipyards.

And it was in the waters surrounding the British motherland that it became even more forcibly apparent that the country was fighting on two or three fronts at the same time. Of the 14 battleships at Britain's disposal, seven were employed on con-

voy protection, three were chasing enemy warships in other
waters and three were cruising in the Eastern Mediterranean,
leaving only one to protect the British Isles. Not one of the four
aircraft carriers had been assigned to the Home Fleet. Of 45
cruisers, 39 were stationed away from home waters. In spite of
the fifty old destroyers Britain had received from the USA, this
part of the Royal Navy was so weak that no more than four
destroyers could accompany a convoy. Experts believed that the
British Navy was just too small to cope with its world-wide
problems without help. But in the final analysis the security of
America had for the past 150 years always rested on British naval
power. For this very reason, Roosevelt's support for Churchill
became increasingly apparent in the Atlantic. Although, officially, the United States was still neutral, it was already conducting a regular secret war against Germany by allowing its naval
units to patrol further and further eastwards on convoy protection, by establishing several naval bases on the North Atlantic
coast and finally even by occupying Iceland with its own troops.
Moreover, America exchanged with the British naval authorities
all information on shipping movements, both their own and the
enemy's. When at the end of May 1941 the *Bismarck*, flagship of
the German Navy and one of the most powerful battleships in
the world, was sunk in the Atlantic, it was apparent that Hitler's
control of the seas was in fact restricted to the North Sea, in spite
of his successful U-boat campaign.

The alliance between the two Anglo-Saxon maritime powers
was, in practice, in being by January 1941 under various secret
agreements and their joint operations in the Atlantic. In January
1941, on the orders of Roosevelt and Churchill, the commanders
of the two navies agreed to defeat first Germany and then Japan
after America entered the war. In spite of this, it was still questionable whether the British people were prepared to withstand
a war lasting several years. Roosevelt therefore sent no less than
three of his closest and most important advisers to London in the
period between late summer 1940 and early summer 1941. These
were the head of the Secret Service, Colonel William Donovan;
his confidant, Harry Hopkins; and the millionaire Averell Harriman, who at the President's request co-ordinated the American
supplies for Britain. All three had broadly only one assignment:
they were to investigate Britain's will to continue the war until

victory, because only if this precondition were present could Roosevelt, in the face of strong opposition in his own country, risk demanding from the United States' economy and military the effort and sacrifice necessary to provide Britain with effective assistance. The result of these 'quality tests' was so convincing that the American Congress passed the Lease-Lend Act on 11 March 1941. This opened for Britain, which paid for it by the loss of its status as a world power, the largest cornucopia in history of arms, ammunition and war equipment.

With some accuracy, this step was referred to at the time as 'Roosevelt's declaration of war against Hitler'. It was a triumph for Churchill's long-term policy of winning the confidence of the American President and of drawing the United States into the war. It meant in practice that Hitler had already lost the war. Chamberlain's Britain may have forfeited United States' sympathy because of his readiness to compromise, but all the American visitors were agreed on Churchill's intransigence, fighting spirit and determination to hold out. 'Churchill is the only person you should fully consult', enthused Hopkins to the hesitant President on his return. Britain was behind its Prime Minister 'to the last man'.[6]

Backed by this, Roosevelt decided to act. On 11 April 1941, the USA took over the direct supply of the British troops in the Middle East. In the first half of May, America transferred almost its entire Pacific Fleet to the Atlantic. On 31 May, Lease-Lend supplies from the USA commenced. The West's pressure on Hitler thus became progressively more severe. But what in fact happened in the East to complete the two-front situation for Germany?[7]

Roosevelt and Churchill had reacted with contempt to the pact between Hitler and Stalin, but not without comprehending the dangers it involved. What would happen, for example, if the German Wehrmacht and the Red Army together marched to war against the Western Powers? But Hitler had no intention whatsoever of weakening the British Empire in concert with Stalin. It at first appeared that the two Dictators had their hands full in demarcating their spheres of interest. The Russian attack on Finland, the incorporation of the Baltic States into the Soviet Union and Stalin's persistent pressure on south-east Europe disturbed Hitler. But Germany still appeared to get all the raw materials from Russia it needed to continue the war. For this reason, the Supreme War Council of Britain and France had decided, before the French defeat, on a gigantic pincer-movement against the Soviet Union. While a British Expeditionary Force in the far North was to fight its way to Finland via Norway and Sweden to occupy Murmansk, the Russian port on the Arctic Ocean, the British Air Force was to destroy the Soviet oil fields in the deep South around Baku and Batum. In the winter of 1940/41, France was to assemble in Syria an army of 150,000 men with the most modern equipment, which was to invade Russia after the bombardment. This plan for an offensive war was on an entirely equal footing with Hitler's subsequent plans for 'Barbarossa'. The objective in building up this military threat was to make Stalin aware of the price he must pay if he continued the alliance with Hitler.

Realization of this plan was thwarted literally at the last moment by the German attack on France. But its psychological effects nevertheless continued. After the Western Powers had exploited the Russian October Revolution of 1917 by tearing Russia to pieces in a war of intervention, Stalin's constant concern was to avoid falling victim again to British and American aggression. This objective was his first priority. Although we as yet know little about Soviet policy in these years, it may be concluded that the Hitler-Stalin Pact was merely an interim solution, in the eyes of the Soviet Dictator. It was intended to keep away from Russia's western frontier the inevitable war between Germany and the Western Powers, which had been awaited since the turn of 1938/39. But the Pact did not signify that Stalin had lost his long-term interest in Central Europe. In fact, in the long run Russia could protect itself effectively against attack from the West only by gaining territory. We do not know what Stalin thought about Hitler's lightning victory in France. The German Dictator's inability to make peace with the West probably impressed him more than the efficiency and speed with which the Third Reich had succeeded in defeating the mightiest land-power in the world. This may be the origin of the Soviet Union's gradual re-orientation. Stalin had to accept that the more probable it became that the West would overcome Germany the less chance had Hitler of making peace with Britain. To prevent the West then reviving its sinister plans against the Soviet Union, Stalin gradually decided to change camps.

During 1940, Roosevelt and Churchill began to court the Soviet Dictator once again. The American Secretary of State, Cordell Hull, recommenced the talks in Washington with the Soviet Chargé-d'Affaires which he had discontinued in 1939. In London, there were informal talks with Maisky, the Soviet Ambassador. When Molotov, the Soviet Foreign Minister, came to Berlin in November 1940 to discuss the future of the German–Russian Alliance, he did not allow himself to be persuaded to join the Berlin–Rome–Tokyo Axis, nor did he allow Russia to be fobbed off with India as a possible region of expansion for the Soviet Union. The star of German–Soviet friendship, which had brightened in 1939, was about to be extinguished.

At the end of March 1941, Churchill came to the conclusion, on the basis of Secret Service information, that Hitler would attack Russia in May. For the Prime Minister, this knowledge was 'too good to be true',[7] because it promised fragmentation of the German forces. On 13 April, Stalin ensured by an agreement with Japan that his hands were free to give Hitler, if it became necessary, the long overdue lesson that Napoleon had once had to learn. On the other side, in the West, Roosevelt pushed his Pacific Fleet forward in the Atlantic. By May 1941, therefore, Germany was falling with increasing severity under the two-front pressure Churchill had always intended for it.

At this inconvenient moment, the Deputy Führer, Rudolf Hess, literally fell out of the sky to make peace.

THE PEACE PLAN

AFTER SIR IVONE KIRKPATRICK has offered to identify Rudolf Hess up in Scotland, he left on Monday 12 May 1941 at about 17.00 hrs. from Hendon Airfield in London in a Flamingo plane, with the Duke of Hamilton at the controls. Because of the plane's slow speed and other handicaps, they did not arrive at Turnhouse Airfield until shortly before 22.00 hrs. Meanwhile, the German Radio had announced in a first communiqué that the Deputy Führer had disappeared, and Foreign Secretary Eden telephoned Kirkpatrick urging him to carry out his assignment as quickly as possible. Kirkpatrick had been instructed to identify Hess, to report on this to London and to accept any explanation the curious prisoner wished to give.

After their arrival, Kirkpatrick and Hamilton went to the military hospital at Buchanan Castle, to which the Deputy Führer had been moved. There, in the attic of the house in what had been a servant's bedroom, Rudolf Hess was at this late hour already asleep, dressed in grey flannel pyjamas beneath a brown woollen British Army blanket. A naked light bulb glowed in the ceiling, shielded only by an old newspaper. Twenty-four hours had now elapsed since the German had left Augsburg.

Kirkpatrick and Hamilton awakened Hess, who after a moment's reflection recognized and greeted the former Secretary of Embassy. The two visitors sat down on hard wooden chairs, and the Deputy Führer produced a bundle of handwritten sheets. He then began to give vent to a long dissertation on British policy towards Germany, past and present. Kirkpatrick left the room only once to inform Churchill and Eden in London by telephone that it was indeed Hess who was lying in bed before him.

In his analysis of British policy towards Germany, Hess went back to the turn of the century.[1] Referring to a well-known British historian, the Deputy Führer said that since the Entente Treaties of 1904 Britain had supported France against Germany, well-knowing that in the long run this would lead to a conflict. Britain was therefore responsible for the First World War. After the War and Versailles, British Governments had failed to grant the German Weimar Democracy those concessions necessary for its existence. This was the explanation of the rise of Hitler and of National Socialism.

Hess then referred to the recent past. Hitler had at first sought for peaceful union with Austria by negotiation. Only when this failed had he felt forced to occupy this Alpine country in accordance with the wishes of its population. The Czechoslovakia crisis had been provoked by France's attempt to develop that country into an air base directed against Germany. Hitler had been unable to accept this. He had, however, welcomed with grateful relief Chamberlain's mediation at the Munich conference. Since Britain and France had continued their attempts to rearm the rest of Czechoslovakia, the Führer had finally felt bound to take action to counter this threat.

Britain's opposition to Germany, Europe's strongest Continental power, then provoked the Polish crisis, Hess continued, since without Britain Poland would have accepted the German demands. 'The clear conclusion is, therefore, that Britain is responsible for the war', said the Deputy Führer. When, subsequently, in May 1940, Britain began to bomb Germany, 'Herr Hitler first saw this as a temporary aberration, and he had waited with commendable patience – partly to spare the world the horror of unrestricted air warfare and partly from a sentimental regard for British culture and its monuments. Only with the greatest misgivings and after weeks of waiting had he given the order to bomb Britain. 'The bombing of residential areas as well', said Hess, 'had been a necessary means to make Britain prepared for peace'. Since the British continued to lack understanding, Hitler had no other choice but 'to continue the struggle to the bitter end'.

Hess gave his views on why Germany could not fail to win the war. Germany was producing huge numbers of aircraft and U-boats. Britain could no longer catch up with this lead in armaments, and would therefore have to accept mortal blows against its supplies by sea. The conquered territories gave Germany rich deposits of raw materials. Germany was economically self-sufficient. 'There is not the slightest hope of a revolution in Germany', said Hess in regard to the activities of the German Resistance. 'Hitler has the blind trust of the German masses.'

The Deputy Führer then turned to his peace proposals. The thought of the great shedding of blood which might now be necessary was unbearable to him. He had therefore come without Hitler's permission 'to convince those responsible in Britain that it would be best to make peace now, since Britain could certainly not win the war'. Because of his many years of friendship with Hitler, he, Hess, could affirm on his word of honour that the Führer 'had never hatched underhand plans against Britain, neither was he striving for world supremacy. He believed that Germany's sphere of interest was in Europe, and that dissipation of German forces outside Europe would only weaken the Reich, and indeed would carry within it the seeds of ruin'. Hitler had only recently confirmed in public that he would make no unacceptable demands on Britain.

The solution of the German-British conflict proposed by Hess was the already known division of the world into spheres of interest. Britain must leave to Germany 'a free hand in Europe', while Germany would give the British 'absolute latitude in the Empire' – 'with the exception of the colonies, which were important because of their raw materials. These would have to be given back'. It was not advisable to allow Hitler to wait even longer for peace, Hess added in support of all this, since the Führer might become very impatient, although at the bottom of his heart he was good-natured.[2] On the basis described, the German Wehrmacht and the Royal Navy could together control the world. This combination of powers was so strong that Britain could detach itself from the USA without risk, 'and that would be an advantage to the whole world', said Hess.

Up to this point, Hamilton and Kirkpatrick had listened to the Deputy Führer in silence. Only twice did Kirkpatrick interrupt. He wanted to know more about a possible invasion of Britain and about the German plans towards Russia. Kirkpatrick had of course heard the rumours going around about an allegedly imminent German attack on Russia.

As concerns the invasion of Britain, Hess said[3] that he did not know precisely whether Hitler still intended this. The Führer would probably prefer to throttle Britain gradually by a total sea and air blockade until the Government in London begged for peace. But that of course would be pure suicide. He, Hess, therefore proposed a road 'promising honour, security and a glorious future'.

On the subject of Russia, Kirkpatrick fished more skilfully for information. He asked Hess whether in his opinion Russia was in Europe or Asia. Kirkpatrick hoped from his reply to discover whether Hitler's demand for 'a free hand in Europe' meant that Britain would also have to accept without objection a German war against Russia.

'In Asia', said Hess. Thereupon Kirkpatrick tried to satisfy himself even further by replying that Russia would not then be attacked by Germany. 'Hess reacted quickly, with the response that Germany still had certain claims against Russia which had to be satisfied either by negotiation or by war', reads Kirkpatrick's subsequent report. 'He added, however, that all the rumours about an early attack on Russia were without any basis whatsoever.'

After about three hours, Hess came to the end of his discourse. Kirkpatrick, who was one of the sworn enemies of Germany in Britain and hated Hitler, could scarcely contain himself from sheer impatience. The Briton, tired and hungry as he was, had so far restricted himself to interrupting the German only when he considered that he was departing too far from the truth or in order to learn more about Russia and the invasion of Britain. In general, Kirkpatrick kept to the instructions he had received in London, which, purely superficially, made him a neutral listener. But in fact he felt it an imposition to have to sit there for hours and listen to what in his opinion would in any event change nothing in Britain's determination to continue the war until victory over Hitler. On this point Kirkpatrick agreed with Churchill one hundred per cent. He had therefore enquired about Hess's peace conditions purely for information, and somewhat brusquely.

At the end of this night-time encounter, the Deputy Führer succeeded in producing one more surprise. Before Kirkpatrick and Hamilton left, he remarked that he had forgotten to mention earlier that 'Germany would not negotiate on these peace proposals with the present British Government. Churchill, who had worked for war since 1936, and his colleagues, who were associated with his war policy, were not people with whom the Führer could sit around a table'. Kirkpatrick had to check himself at this provocation, and refrained from reply. He had no wish to provoke a further dispute with Hess which, as he remarked ironically in his report to Churchill, 'would have certainly deprived us of our breakfast'.

Towards four o'clock in the morning of 13 May, Kirkpatrick and Hamilton took their leave of Hess, who at that moment produced a dirty scrap of paper on which was written the name and number of a German prisoner-of-war. This man, the Deputy Führer said, must stand at his side as his personal assistant during the coming negotiations. This request of Hess's was not met. Real negotiations on his peace offer never materialized.

At daybreak, Kirkpatrick and Hamilton drove back to Turnhouse to snatch a few hours' sleep. When at half-past eight Kirkpatrick spoke to the Foreign Office in London by telephone, he heard that the Hess affair had greatly embarrassed the Government, which was uncertain about the attitude to adopt towards the public. Meanwhile, the *Daily Record*, on the front page of its Tuesday edition, under the headline 'Nazi leader flies to Scotland – Official: Rudolf Hess in Glasgow', had published a sensational report with photographs of the Deputy Führer and his crashed aircraft. Uproar now broke loose in communications between Whitehall, the seat of government in London, and Fleet Street, the newspaper district of the British capital. Reporters fanned out to discover the whereabouts of the prominent guest; editors asked for interviews and photographs; telephone lines buzzed.

Kirkpatrick had quickly to provide some local colour so that the Government offices responsible could at least answer the journalists' simplest enquiries. Although they were fobbed off with trifles, the fact that roast chicken had been served to Hess provoked general indignation. After all, in the eyes of many British people he personified 'the enemy'. Towards eleven o'clock, Kirkpatrick telephoned a preliminary report on his night-time talk with the Deputy Führer, intended for the personal information of Churchill and his closest advisers. He reported correctly on the rough content, without going into detail about the German attitude towards Russia. Nevertheless, the British Head of Government learnt that Hitler had no intention of negotiating with him about peace, which probably reinforced Churchill's intention to suppress the Hess initiative.

In Kirkpatrick's mistaken opinion, Hess did not appear to be very well informed about Hitler's strategic plans. Although the German seemed fairly calm, reported Kirkpatrick, he had nevertheless probably lost some of his mental balance. Kirkpatrick believed that, before his flight, Hess had continually turned his plan over and over in his mind until it had become a kind of 'monomania'. Hess, who repeatedly emphasized that he had come on his own initiative, had quite simply got it into his head that only he could bring peace and save mankind from bloodshed.[4]

The Hess affair represented an incalculable danger to Churchill in both domestic and foreign policy. If it became known that the Deputy Führer had come to Britain with a peace offer, all those forces would be re-aroused which had always advocated an understanding with Germany. And what would the United States say, upon whose determination to supply the island, and if necessary protect it, depended Britain's existence? It did not bear thinking about that an understanding might be reached between the British 'peace party' and Hitler, and that Roosevelt, in reaction to this, might turn away from Europe. And finally, that Stalin might also climb down in the face of Germany's demands for room to expand. In that event, Germany would truly become the strongest power from the Atlantic to the Urals, which America and Britain had prevented only with difficulty in 1914–18. Churchill's entire life's work would be in ruins.

Outwardly, of course, the Prime Minister acted as if he did not take Hess's 'escapade' very seriously.[5] He propagated from the outset the theory that the Deputy Führer had come to Britain to ingratiate himself once again with Hitler by a great achievement. Hess allegedly suffered under a strong inferiority complex because at the outbreak of war the generals had driven him from his special position as the Führer's intimate friend. It is not known where Churchill found this psychological theory. But it was recognizably in line with the objective of depriving the German peace initiative of all political significance and turning it into the psychopathological problem of an individual consumed

[116]

by jealousy and a craving for recognition whose political ideas could at best be described as 'naive' (Churchill).

The truth was, however, that on this 12 May 1941 Churchill was faced with a problem similar to Hitler's. Since the German leadership also shrouded itself in silence, he did not know precisely what Hess wanted, who were his contacts in Britain and what might still come out of the affair. What would happen if Hitler publicly acknowledged Hess's peace mission? This uncertainty persisted in London throughout Monday. Only when the Reich radio published its first communiqué that evening, and in practice declared that Hess was mad, did Churchill breathe a sigh of relief. As the press had meanwhile latched on to the matter, the Prime Minister arranged for a statement to be published on the evening of 13 May at about 23.00 hrs. This confirmed, in plain terms, the crash of the aircraft near Eaglesham, Hess's landing by parachute, and his identity. But nothing was said about the peace proposals the Deputy Führer had brought with him.

Although at the time Churchill only knew Hamilton and Kirkpatrick's version of these proposals, and above all nothing of their Russian aspect, on 13 May he had already taken a decision in principle on Hess's future status, a decision of extremely far-reaching significance. It in fact made clear how the British Prime Minister intended to treat leading National Socialists after victory, for he arranged for Hess to come under the responsibility of the War Ministry as a prisoner-of-war and not under the responsibility of the Home Office as a bearer of a flag of truce or a refugee. The Foreign Office's responsibility for all foreign-policy matters raised by the Hess affair was unaffected by this. In a note to Foreign Secretary Eden, Churchill gave as his reasons for interning Rudolf Hess that, 'like other Nazi leaders, this man is potentially a war criminal, and he and his confederates may well be declared outlaws at the close of the war. In this case his repentance would stand him in good stead'.[6] Thus, from the early summer haze over London in this second year of war, the outline of Nuremberg was already emerging. Churchill's instructions expressly ordered that Rudolf Hess was to be treated as a person against whom 'grave political charges' might be raised. The prisoner was therefore to be strictly isolated from his surroundings, preferably in a suitable house not too far from London. He was to be given everything in the way of food and accommodation, books, writing materials and recreational facilities necessary for his comfort and the maintenance of his health. He was to be watched by specially selected guards. He was not allowed to listen to the radio or to read newspapers, and 'every endeavour should be made to study his mentality and to get anything worthwhile out of him'. Summarizing, Churchill declared: 'He should be treated with dignity as if he were an important general who has fallen into our hands.'

On Wednesday 14 May, Churchill also, of course, arranged for Foreign Secretary Eden to brief him on the progress of the affair. From Buchanan Castle, Kirkpatrick continued to keep contact with the Foreign Office. During the morning he prepared his first report on his night-time encounter with Hess, which was flown by courier plane to London in the afternoon. Receiving no new instructions – the Government's uncertainty persisted – Kirkpatrick and Hamilton decided on a lightning visit to Britain's newest aircraft carrier HMS *Victorious*, which was in the neighbourhood. On their way, however, they were recalled by the Foreign Office to continue the dialogue with Hess. The Government in London apparently wanted to gain time until the grass had grown over the whole matter.

During the 36 hours since their last visit, the Deputy Führer's spirits had of course become distinctly lower. Hess was manifestly disappointed that 'nothing at all had happened to meet his reasonable request for German–British negotiations', as Kirkpatrick maliciously recorded.[7]

The German rested all his hopes on the presence of the Duke of Hamilton, whom in fact Kirkpatrick had kept with him only to keep the prisoner talking. Perhaps something would be revealed of use to the British conduct of the war.

Lacking specific instructions, Kirkpatrick allowed the talk with Hess simply to run on. The Deputy Führer complained about certain conditions of his imprisonment – above all about his being constantly guarded by a soldier. He asked for certain books, his medicines, his camera and a fragment from the wreck of his aircraft as a souvenir. He then gave details of his flight. Finally, he turned to political matters.

Hess said that there were two other peace conditions which he had forgotten yesterday. The first point concerned Iraq, which a few weeks earlier had rebelled against British rule before being 'pacified' by military intervention. The Deputy Führer now demanded that the British should vacate this strategically important region, across which ran the crude oil pipeline from the Persian Gulf to the Mediterranean. Kirkpatrick replied that this significantly contradicted Hess's statement that German interests were restricted to Europe; from Iraq, Hitler would be able to threaten Britain's entire position in the Middle East. But Hess defended himself by arguing that Germany could not just abandon the Iraqis, who had fought bravely. All in all, his peace proposals were more than fair. A further point was that a peace agreement would of course have to provide for compensation for all those British and German people who had lost their property as a result of the First World War.

Finally, Hess expressed his confidence that Germany would win the war against Britain by blockade – if peace was not achieved. This would be ensured by the enormous number of U-boats alone that Hitler was having built. Even after capitulation, the Führer would continue to cut off supplies to Britain itself, so that the population would have to starve. Under such circumstances, it would be fruitless to think, like Churchill, that the war could be continued from, perhaps, Canada. Kirkpatrick showed that he was quite unimpressed by this, because he considered that the British did not need much to survive. But Hess believed that not even one or two ships a day could break through the German blockade.

The Deputy Führer apparently continued to hope that negotiations would begin, since as they took their leave he asked for a qualified interpreter to be made available and, on the British side, that not too many people should participate in the discussions; this would overtax him in view of the many questions and observations which might be expected.

The British public remained very uncertain in their interpretation of the affair, because the Government created an artificial absence of information. On the following Wednesday, the British Ministry of Information divided into three categories the speculation circulating in the national press about Rudolf Hess's motives:[8]

1. One section of public opinion considered the flight to Britain to have been caused by a swing to the left in the National Socialist leadership, which would strengthen co-operation

between Hitler and Stalin. Under these circumstances, Hess had fled from Germany because he did not wish to participate in the spread of communism in Europe.

2. Another section of public opinion considered that the Deputy Führer's flight to Britain was simply the result of a personal quarrel among political 'gangsters'. Hess had wanted to save his skin.

3. Finally, there was the view that the Hess venture resulted from a deep split within the National Socialist leadership. It was the consequence of a violent conflict on Hitler's war policy, and a feeling among an increasing number of Party members that Germany could no longer win the war and was drifting towards national catastrophe.

This last assessment strengthened Churchill and his advisers' already unfavourable opinion of German morale, and the Ministry of Information, which organized psychological warfare against Germany and stiffened the morale of the British people, made every effort to encourage similar views in the press and the BBC.

Not even Information Minister Duff Cooper had been accurately informed on this. The details of the whole affair were kept so closely under lock and key by Churchill, Eden and their closest advisers that the other Ministers teased and mutually praised one another for not asking indiscreet questions in Cabinet. This edifice of silence had its good side, in that the Government did not feed the conflagration of speculation raging among the public by adding further information. On the other hand, silence alone would not help Churchill to extinguish the blaze. In fact, Roosevelt and interested groups in the British Parliament saw it as evidence that Britain was after all, and in all secrecy, preparing a negotiated peace with Hitler. Since at that time the Prime Minister's main objectives were not to dishearten the American President and not to hearten the advocates of a negotiation policy, he was forced to take some action. Churchill, in his aggressive way, had at first seriously toyed with the idea of taking the bull by the horns. By giving the matter maximum publicity, he would remove from the beginning any doubt about his will to continue the war until victory under all circumstances, and present the Deputy Führer's flight to Britain as – which indeed it was in his eyes – an escapade that need not be taken too seriously. On the very night that Hamilton visited him at Ditchley

Park, the Prime Minister tried 'quite excitedly' to win over his Foreign Secretary to this line of action.[9] But Eden, who did not think much of the idea, was able to restrain him. The result was the noncommittal communiqué of 13 May.

On 14 May, however, the Hess matter so dominated domestic debate that the Prime Minister saw himself as forced to give a formal explanation to the House of Commons at Westminster. Anything less would have caused Parliament to rise against him. But it appears that Eden was able even now to secure a continuation of the strategy of silence, since the words Churchill addressed to the Speaker on this Wednesday were in fact more than frugal: 'I have at present nothing to add to His Majesty's Government's communiqué, but in the near future there will certainly be a further explanation of the flight to Britain of this high-ranking and influential Nazi leader.'[10] But this explanation was not given until a year-and-a-half later in a completely different context.

The entire episode was for Churchill 'one of these matters in which reality surpasses imagination',[11] and apparently the old hand in British politics had the greatest difficulty in coping with the public relations aspect of the matter. He was certainly determined from the beginning not to make a hero of this 'potential war criminal'. But how could this be avoided without raising suspicions of secret peace feelers? Churchill prepared as early as 14 May a detailed explanation which he intended to present to the House of Commons next day to allay any such suspicions. But Eden's hard line once again prevailed, urging the Prime Minister to leave the Germans completely in the dark about all that Hess might finally have revealed. In any event, the second communiqué published by the German leadership on that day had shown that Hitler himself had no wish to follow the Hess line.

Churchill, however, was offended, and demanded that his Foreign Minister should himself think up a suitable text. But although Eden sat down to this the same night the result of his efforts convinced neither the Prime Minister nor his Minister of Information, and finally the whole plan was allowed to drop. 'This means no explanation', growled Churchill into the telephone, banging down the receiver. This was at two o'clock in the morning of 15 May 1941.

Churchill had wanted full publicity for the Hess affair, although of course only in a destructive sense, probably with an eye to the United States and Roosevelt. Indeed, although the British press was already full of wild speculation, the American newspapers and radio stations outdid one another in their craving for sensation. Something of this was continually splashing across the Big Pond to Britain.

For example, one American radio commentator alleged that he had been told by German sources that Hess's flight resulted from a quarrel between Göring and Hess on the one hand and Hitler and Ribbentrop on the other about Germany's policy towards Russia, which culminated in an attempted assassination on Hitler's special train. Himmler had foiled the plot at the last minute and had advised Hess to commit suicide with the assistance of an aircraft, but instead the Deputy Führer had flown to Britain. The Australian Embassy in Washington warned the British Commonwealth Office that Hess had arrived in Britain under such dramatic circumstances only so as to gain access to Churchill and to assault him. This shows the extent of the fantasies in circulation.

On Thursday 15 May, the American President himself intervened in the affair. In one of his routine secret messages to Churchill, which were always dispatched under the apocryphal heading: 'Message for Former Naval Person [i.e. a reference to Churchill's former office as First Lord of the Admiralty – W.R.H.] from the President', Roosevelt suggested that, if Hess were to talk, could he please be prevailed upon to state what Hitler had to say about the United States and what Germany was really hatching up as regards the USA – including any plans in the fields of commerce, infiltration, military supremacy and – no less – 'the encirclement of the United States'. This would have a 'very valuable' effect on public opinion in America, by which Roosevelt doubtlessly meant stimulation of America's preparedness to enter the war against Hitler. 'From this distance I can assure you', he wrote to Churchill, 'that the "Hess flight" [the wording "Hess flight" could also be interpreted as "Hess's fleeing" – W.R.H.] has gripped the imagination of the Americans, and the story should be kept at the boil for as many days or even weeks as possible.'[12]

Kirkpatrick up in Scotland was promptly told to go and see Hess again, although he no longer had any desire to do this. The Deputy Führer again complained about bad treatment, the noise at night and that he was not given certain books to read. Kirkpatrick led on to political subjects such as Iraq and Ireland in order to reach, discreetly, the subject of America. In his now-regular report to Churchill and Eden, he summarized Hess's statements as follows:

'1. The Germans were reckoning on American intervention, and were not afraid of this. They knew everything about American aircraft production and the quality of the aircraft. Germany could produce more than Britain and America together.
2. Germany had no designs on America. The so-called German menace was a ridiculous invention of the imagination. Hitler's interests were European.
3. If we were to make peace now, America would be furious. In fact, America wanted to inherit the British Empire.'[13]

This was the last talk between Hess and Kirkpatrick at Buchanan Castle. Meanwhile, there were serious misgivings at the Scottish headquarters responsible for the safety of the high-ranking prisoner. They had already stationed an infantry batallion in the park against any attempt by the Germans to hack a way out for the Deputy Führer by an audacious Commando operation. There were twelve men alone keeping guard over the entrance to the hospital, which housed three hundred patients. But what would happen if the Germans – by accident or design – bombed the hospital? The safety measures were insufficient for this contingency.

At the request of the Scots, therefore, the head of the War Office department responsible for prisoners-of-war asked Churchill on 15 May whether Hess could be moved to Mytchett Place at Aldershot, a spacious country house not far from London. It bore the code name 'Camp Z'. But this accommodation had still to be prepared, which would take some time. The official therefore asked for permission to lodge the Deputy Führer in the Tower of London until then. The Prime Minister agreed to these two proposals immediately, merely asking for the strictest secrecy and the strictest isolation of the prisoner.

Before his removal on 16 May, Rudolf Hess was again examined medically. A medical report of three days earlier had declared that Hess was not mentally disturbed, and now a different Army doctor confirmed that, from a medical aspect, there was no reason why he should not be moved immediately.

Escorted by eight officers, Hess was taken by train to the British capital under cover of night. One of these officers, a certain

Major Sheppard, summarized his impressions as follows: 'Up to the last moment (Hess) had not been informed of the move. He appeared to be quite beside himself at the news, and adopted an air of great importance. He was keen to know his destination, but he was weary and quiet on the way to the station. On the train he became refractory, objected to any lighting in the compartment and demanded the withdrawal of the officer on guard. These requests were of course refused, whereupon he raised his voice in anger, saying that he would make no attempt to sleep while he was being guarded. When he discovered that his demands were in vain, he appeared to sulk for most of the night.'[14]

The train was stopped for some hours on the way because of a German air attack on the midlands. Meanwhile, there had been rumours in London of Rudolf Hess's imminent transfer to the British capital. A small number of curious people had gathered at the arrival station, and to avoid any complications the train with its prominent passenger was shunted into a siding. Hess was then driven by ambulance, as a form of camouflage, through the London evening to the Tower.

Sheppard wrote: 'He remained very quiet in the ambulance, and did not say one word until he was lodged in his new accommodation, when he stated that he felt well.' At about 18.00 hrs., the Deputy Führer was installed in the house of the Governor of the medieval fortress high above the banks of the Thames. 'Placid and pleasant, and ate his food', recorded Sheppard. 'Appears quiet and reasonable.' The escorting officers were ordered back to Scotland the same night to give any resourceful reporter no opportunity of picking up an indiscretion.

At this point, the Hess affair had reached a stage which allowed a summary to be prepared. Kirkpatrick returned to London on 17 May to report to Churchill and Eden personally. In a very limited circle, the matter was considered once again from all angles:

1. Hess had obviously come to Britain on his own initiative and without a formulated plan. However, it was probable that, in general, he had presented Hitler's views. But the Führer did not identify himself with his Deputy's mission. For the time being, therefore, the danger that might have arisen if Churchill were asked publicly whether or not he wanted peace was removed.
2. Hess also appeared not to represent any other important

segment of the National Socialist leadership. His knowledge of Germany's strategic plans appeared weak, although it was possible that the Deputy Führer was keeping something to himself for purely tactical reasons.

3. The evasive answers given by Hess on the subject of Russia did not convince Churchill. Churchill's knowledge of Hitler's plan of attack was too accurate for this. Neither did Churchill intend for one moment to keep Germany from the Russian adventure by making peace with Russia a condition for peace with Britain.

4. The peace offer Hess had brought with him did not impress Churchill. Apart from the fact that the Premier was in any case firmly determined to continue the war until victory, Britain had indeed already rejected the German offer of a division of the world before the outbreak of war. It might also be said that it was precisely because Britain did not wish to share world supremacy equally with Germany that it had declared war on Hitler.

5. Hess's attempt to force Britain to the negotiating table by the threat of total blockade by sea and air had no effect on Churchill, although a further deterioration in the supply position, and perhaps even a serious national emergency, could not be excluded in the mid-term. But for Churchill, the naval strategist, the certain victory of German land power over British sea power which Hess predicted lacked any credibility. Moreover, the Deputy Führer appeared to have the wrong idea about the relative strengths of America and Germany.

To summarize, Hitler, with his plans for attacking the Soviet Union and with the increasing involvement of the USA, appeared to be facing war on two fronts very shortly, which would destroy him. Britain's situation was therefore quite favourable. As Churchill observed in the discussions of 17 May, 'If Hess had come a year ago and told us what the Germans would do to us we should have been very frightened – and rightly, so why should we be frightened now?'[15]

Kirkpatrick confirmed Churchill's impression that Hess 'represented no one', and that he was not in possession of all Germany's war secrets. But, he reflected, might it not be possible that the Deputy Führer had come by some useful information, perhaps in the field of U-boat and aircraft production or other technical developments? In this context, Kirkpatrick recalled a proposal he had made after his first talk with Hess: shouldn't someone with unquestioned authority meet Hess to 'ensure that he is sucked dry before he is cast aside'?

Churchill played the ball back, asking Kirkpatrick if he would be prepared to see Hess once again. Kirkpatrick countered this, arguing that the Deputy Führer's sole aim was to speak to a representative of the British Government. In any other circumstances he would stay sullen and silent. After some discussion, Churchill and the group he had gathered around him agreed: the former Chancellor of the Exchequer and Foreign Secretary, Sir John Simon, who had been an 'appeasement' politician under Chamberlain, would talk to the Deputy of the German Führer.[16]

In Churchill's opinion this was not at all urgent, and he took the view that the purpose of the meeting would be very limited. 'The public will not tolerate any billing and cooing with this notorious war criminal, except for Secret Service purposes.'[17]

Following this, the problem remained of presenting the matter to the public. Roosevelt and the Psychological Warfare people in Britain urged that the affair should be exploited for propaganda purposes. Foreign Secretary Eden and the Minister for Aircraft Production, the newspaper proprietor Lord Beaverbrook, were against this; the edifice of silence erected around Hess and his peace proposals had held up wonderfully. Finally, Churchill agreed that this tactic of silence should be maintained.

Also on 17 May, the Prime Minister informed the American President quite matter-of-factly and objectively, in a secret telegram, of the substance of the three conversations Kirkpatrick had had with Rudolf Hess in Scotland,[18] preferring to omit the information that Germany had nothing up its sleeve for America. This might have reduced American willingness to enter the war. The telegram concluded quite concisely: 'If he is to be believed, he (Hess) expected to contact members of a "peace movement" which he would help to oust the present Government. If he is honest and if he is sane, this is an encouraging sign of ineptitude of the German Intelligence Service. He will not be ill-treated, but it is desirable that the Press should not romanticize him and his adventure. We must not forget that he shares responsibility for all Hitler's crimes and is a potential war criminal whose fate must ultimately depend upon the decision of the Allied Governments.'

That being said, Rudolf Hess's fate had been sealed.

FAILURE OF THE MISSION

IT WAS NEITHER the incompetence of Rudolf Hess nor the unpropitiousness of the moment which caused his mission to fail. It was rather Churchill's firm intention never to make peace with the German Reich – let alone with the Third Reich – on equal terms. As early as 20 January 1941 – when rumours were once again circulating in Europe of an imminent peace offensive by Hitler – the British Head of Government had 'now decided that our attitude towards all these enquiries and proposals should be absolute silence from now on'.[1] The British diplomats in Stockholm and Madrid, until then the preferred locations for unofficial contacts between the warring Powers, were directed by their Governments to report to London everything they heard about German readiness to make peace, but to make no further advances or offers themselves.

The reason for this decree, which condemned the Hess initiative to failure from the outset, was expounded by Churchill in a message to the Japanese Ambassador on 24 February 1941, three weeks before the Lend-Lease Act was adopted by the American Congress: 'His Majesty's Government, which was forced to enter into this distressing contest, has no intention other than to end it victoriously.' It would take some time, however, for 'peaceful communities' such as the British Empire to complete their war preparations. But he hoped that 'within a few months . . . with the rapidly growing supplies of material arriving from the United States, Britain would be overpoweringly strong'.[2]

Two days before Hess landed in Britain, experts in the Churchill Government came to the conclusion that although Hitler, like Napoleon, had indeed achieved certain military successes thanks to his modern methods, these methods would in the long run prove disadvantageous. In comparison with its adversary, Germany had superiority numerically but not technically, and by 1942 Britain would be in the lead in the production of aircraft and tanks, which had so far been Hitler's trump cards.

Because of its naval supremacy, Britain would then be in a position to employ its fleet simultaneously at various points all over the world. If to this were added the British bombing campaign against German towns and the Wehrmacht leadership's difficulties in maintaining its communications network under the growing pressure of continuous attacks, doubts would gradually arise among the German people about Hitler's infallibility. 'The Germans, who are a neurotic race, quickly change from the extreme of self-confidence to the extreme of despair', diagnosed the experts with an undertone of satisfaction. In 1918, in the First World War, they had 'chiefly broken down because they foresaw with mathematical accuracy that, with American help, we would be able to overpower them by a superiority of manpower potential'. In the Second World War, this realization could set in as early as 1942. If this were so – why should one make peace?[3]

The leading personalities in the Churchill Government, and not only the Prime Minister himself, had in any case already committed themselves in early 1941 to a long-term strategic war – to 'total war', as it was called in a memorandum on 'His Majesty's Government's strategic objectives *vis-à-vis* Germany' of 6 March 1941, long before Propaganda Minister Goebbels made his notorious speech in the Berlin Sportpalast.[4] Amateur peace mediators, such as the British globetrotter Lonsdale Bryans, who maintained contact with the German Resistance were whistled to heel by the Foreign Office as 'unwelcome'.[5] Secretary of State Cadogan hoped that no one was giving the impression that 'we are putting out peace feelers'.[6] And when on one occasion an official at the Foreign Office allowed himself to remark that 'Germany alone is responsible for the continuation of the war' he was put in his place by his superior, Roberts: 'It is we ourselves who, for excellent reasons, are in favour of a continuation of the war.' Cadogan settled the argument with the simple words: 'I agree with Mr Roberts.'[7]

And if peace were to come, no one of course had any intention of seeking an understanding with Germany. In the memorandum referred to above, Britain's 'long-term objective' was seen as 'the complete destruction of the German war machine', 'the complete destruction of the existing National Socialist Party' and in general terms 'the complete destruction . . . of the type of state it has established'. Two years before the Casablanca Conference, this was the programme of unconditional surrender. For those who had not yet understood, it was set out quite plainly in the above memorandum: 'We are waging total war against the Third Reich.' And later it read: even if Britain can achieve these aims without a revolution in Germany – and of course without 'the USSR inheriting the territory of the Third Reich' – it was nevertheless, in the medium term, 'a primary objective to create conditions (in Germany) under which a revolution is possible, and to ensure that the result of a revolution is not that Germany becomes more powerful than before'. The National Socialist seizure of power must not be repeated. The short-term aims were economic destruction of Germany and the occupied areas, the introduction and encouragement of all possible forms of sabotage and guerilla warfare, and a lowering of military morale. 'German morale is relatively high, but on the whole it has fallen in the last six months', stated the experts with a sleep-walker's certainty.

The next phase in this merciless war would commence, the memorandum stated, in October 1941 – when the German plans for an invasion of Britain would dwindle away, the Battle of the Atlantic would be lost and the more distant areas of Germany would be devastated by the bomber squadrons of the RAF. 'It will come when the number of Germans who have doubts about victory in 1941 suddenly enormously increase.' Even though Hitler's army might then stand 'before the gateway of India, a sudden and catastrophic change will occur in Germany. British propaganda will then no longer need to suggest the fallibility of the Führer – it will need merely to state it . . .'.

But even then, after the collapse of German morale and the extension of the war to the furthest corner of the world, there would still be no peace with Germany, as by then, the experts believed, it would be time for British propaganda to proceed from the theme of 'the long war' to the theme of 'the fruits'. The time will have arrived to speak of:

1. the consequences of a long war for the German people;
2. the retribution awaiting those who have brought death and destruction to the whole of Europe;
3. the social anarchy and the chaos lying at the end of the road in the direction of Bolshevism.

Then will the time have come to reinforce enormously the antithesis:

young		dictatorial	
free	Britain	belligerent	Germany
peaceful	(and the USA)	feudal	

Then there would at last be a chance for 'social propaganda', i.e. the re-education of the German people along the lines of Western ideals, and the true war aims could be developed in greater detail. If all this had already been decided upon by March 1941, it becomes clear that in May Rudolf Hess represented no more than an interference factor.

The reason for Britain's transformation by this early date from a moderate democracy into a fury spitting blood, iron and gall lay not only in Hitler's victories, not only in the National Socialist dictatorship and its violations of the principles of law and morals as conceived in the West; it lay in the nature of one man, and in a system of bellicosity, lust for power and confidence in victory created by this very man – Winston Churchill. Whereas in the 19th century one spoke of the 'Metternich System' to describe the mixture of suppression, arrogance and sanctimonious hypocrisy of the Holy Alliance of the time, then one must speak of the 'Churchill System' to describe the Britain of 1941.

Not that he would ever have been a Dictator, but for British circumstances he came very close to it. Churchill had come to power on 10 May 1940 at the head of a War Cabinet made up of an equal number of Ministers from the Conservative and Labour Parties supplemented by a few Liberals such as the Minister for Air, Sir Archibald Sinclair. Although in his capacity as wartime

Prime Minister his authority was already extended, the regime immediately introduced by the new man was revolutionary for three reasons. First, Churchill became Minister of Defence, an office that had never before existed in Britain's thousand-year history. Second, he transformed the Cabinet Committee for Co-ordination of Defence so that he could become Chairman. Third, through his closest military adviser General Hastings Ismay he dominated the true centre of the Armed Forces – the British General Staff, with the Chiefs of the Air Force, the Army and the Navy at its head. In short, it was Churchill himself who was Britain's supreme war-lord, with almost unlimited power, and Britain's despot in domestic and foreign policy, a kind of war Dictator.

But that was not enough. Through a network of personal advisers, friends and former colleagues, the much-quoted 'Old Boy Net', Churchill also dominated wide areas of Britain's domestic policy. This led not only to a shift of power between the legislative and the executive but also, within the one year that passed between Churchill's taking over the Government and Hess's flight to Britain, to the disappearance of any thought of moderation, compromise and peace from public discussion of Britain's war aims. The question of a negotiated peace was discussed by the War Cabinet on one occasion only, at the end of May 1940 when the defeat of France was imminent, but never again. At the end of 1940, only eight Members of Parliament in Britain dared to plead in public for an understanding with Germany. Although of course there were many more people who secretly wanted peace, all that counted for Churchill was absolute, final and total victory.

This did not mean that Churchill's influential advisers were not already thinking deeply behind closed doors of Germany's future. There was not a shadow of doubt among the Prime Minister's circle that sometime, and it was hoped soon, Hitler's Germany would collapse, even though the time this would take was all too often miscalculated. As early as 9 June 1940, ten days before the capitulation of France, a year before Hess's flight, the journalist and German-hater Wickham Steed, one of the people liaising with Roosevelt on Churchill's behalf, had started planning for the post-war period on the orders of the Government.

This former Chief Editor of *The Times* had already set out in a memorandum[8] the most important points that would determine the fate of Germany after the war: 'No peace with the German people until it throws out and punishes the Nazis'; division of the country 'either into the former states or into provinces made up of the former states', no 'normal peace treaty'.

Steed's reasons for this Carthaginian programme were that Germany was simply 'not suited . . . for the large-state system'. The post-war planner had been particularly impressed by a book just published, 'Germany, Jekyll and Hyde', in which a German emigrant named Sebastian Haffner had propounded similar theses. Neither had Steed any intention of making peace at the end of Nazi rule with the old German conservative upper class, which represented the Resistance. He thought rather that 'a number of the emigrants [residing in Britain or in other Allied countries – W.R.H.] had a great following in Germany, and it might be possible to nominate a group of these emigrants as Germany's representatives in making peace'.

Steed, who wrote to Churchill on those lines, proposed the appointment of a small unofficial working group. In fact, such a 'War Aims Committee' was set up by the War Cabinet in summer 1940, although Churchill, like Roosevelt, was not in favour of untimely public discussion of war aims because, he said, 'precise war aims would compromise and vague principles would disappoint'.[9] The Prime Minister knew very well that premature publicity for his true war aims would unmask the Western Powers before world opinion as advocates of total war, and would exonerate Germany from the rebuke of insatiable aggression. The committee was in fact dissolved a little later on the threadbare excuse that the world would learn 'only after the war' how Britain 'intended to cope with the problems arising from Germany's attempt to rule the world by force'.[10] But it is nevertheless clear that Britain already had definite ideas on Germany's future, ideas still imprinted on present-day Germany, and that these ideas preceded the demands later presented by Stalin at the Teheran and Yalta Conferences.

The strategy employed by Churchill on the question of war aims also of course had some bearing on the war-criminal trials already envisaged, to which we shall refer in the following chapter. In fact, the longer the Western Powers' real war aims remained concealed from the world, and the longer the Germans were prevented from making peace with Britain, the more might Hitler be expected to intensify the war against the Western Powers, attack Russia and seek to force a decision by employing increasingly brutal means – until he stood 'before the gateway to India'. And the more he became entrapped in the deadlock of total war the more convincingly could he and his people be put on trial after the defeat of Germany, which was seen as inevitable. There was just one problem: Would the British people go along with the war in the long term? In 1940/41 the British supply problem was really serious, fear of the German air assault was intense, and for most of the British who had sent their fathers, sons and brothers to the Front it was of course no pleasure to witness the enforced retreat of British armies in Norway, France, the Balkans and North Africa. But the people around Churchill were well able to handle this problem.

Two days before Hess's arrival, the political leaders of the British Ministry of Propaganda, which bore the euphemistic title of Ministry of Information, discussed long-term strategy in domestic propaganda.[11] It was agreed that the British public were impressed by Hitler's successes, but were not afraid that Germany might win. On the other hand, the public could not yet see how Britain could win. It was decided to counteract this trend. Although those attending the meeting were fully aware of the inherent danger that years of continual war might demoralize the British people, they were agreed that 'public opinion should gradually be brought to accept this'. Under all these circumstances, Rudolf Hess in fact had no chance from the outset of achieving his goal unless he succeeded in reaching the ear of the British public with his peace proposals. However, the directions issued on 16 May 1941 by Secretary of State Cadogan to all important British foreign missions made abundantly clear the line the Churchill Government wished to maintain in this affair:[12] 1. Absolute silence about Hess's peace proposals. 2. The Foreign Office to attempt to get more out of the Deputy Führer. 3. Germany to be kept in the dark about what Hess had said or given away. 4. Dissemination of fear and doubt in Germany about the 'Hess escapade'. 5. 'Hess to be branded as a war criminal, and any attempt at sentimentality on his behalf to be vigorously discouraged.'

The Secret Service section of the Foreign Office, which constantly analysed the Axis Powers' propaganda, recorded with satisfaction, in a survey dated 27 May: The official Party publication Das Reich stated in its edition of 18 May 1941 that events such as the Hess affair 'were of no significance to the development and the ending of the war'. This quotation was approvingly underlined in the report because it indicated that Hitler was determined to continue the war, and the next survey of 10 June stated reassuringly that Axis propaganda had not referred to the matter once since 19 May.[13]

But although Churchill had personally made every effort to persuade President Roosevelt to follow the British line in the Hess affair, there was still a further problem – public opinion in America! The British Consul-General in New York anxiously reported on 19 May 1941 to the Ministry of Information in London[14] that although the Hess story had now disappeared from the American media it had nevertheless had an unfavourable effect on American aircraft production. It could be looked at from whichever angle one pleased, but nevertheless the fact remained that the USA was under the impression that Britain was seeking a compromise peace with Germany.

In the opinion of this diplomat, the 'most serious result' of the whole matter was that doubt was aroused among leading industrialists in America about whether it was still advisable to speed up the armaments factories' production, because it was no longer worth the effort if the rumours of an imminent peace were shown to be true. 'Because of this atmosphere', Campbell urged his Government, 'it is highly desirable that all possible steps be taken to dispel any misunderstanding of the fact that His Majesty's Government has not the slightest intention of reaching a negotiated peace with Nazi Germany.'

So what remained to be done other than to hush up the whole matter? And this is what the Government had been doing all along. In spite of this, for the moment it could not control the problem of America. In early June, this problem became so pressing that the American Ambassador in London, John Gilbert Winant, went to Washington to report personally to President Roosevelt. At a press conference on 6 June in the White House, there was an odd exchange referring to Britain's alleged peace proposals which Winant had reputedly brought with him to the USA to submit to Roosevelt for examination. Whereas the

President maintained that these were no more than malicious rumours propagated by Nazi provocateurs, one reporter would not cease from irritating the sore point: 'Can you definitely state that Winant has not submitted to you for examination any peace proposals of whatever kind?' Roosevelt replied: 'Absolutely no such thing.'[15] It has never been possible satisfactorily to clarify this point.

Matters became even more serious when the American ex-President, Herbert Hoover, Roosevelt's predecessor, zealously circulated in the USA during the first half of June his opinion that 'Hess had brought with him to Great Britain specific and concrete German peace proposals'. Since Hoover was neither an agent of nor a sympathizer with the Nazis, this information caused a stir on both sides of the Atlantic. For the first time, world opinion learnt from a semi-official source that the 'Hess escapade' was in fact a disguised peace mission. And all this had happened nearly a month and a half ago – scarcely believable!

The information circulated by Hoover was all the more explosive because the former President maintained that when the leaders of the Conservative Party learnt about Hess's peace proposals they had exerted great pressure on Churchill to consider these proposals seriously. Moreover, it was said that the Conservatives had threatened to withdraw their support from the Prime Minister in Parliament if he refused to discuss the German peace proposals with them. For this reason, Churchill had sent the US Ambassador by air to Roosevelt to obtain the President's consent.

Halifax, the British Ambassador in Washington, was so alarmed about this hearsay that on 22 June 1941 he called on the Deputy Secretary of State, Sumner Welles, and declared soothingly that all these reports were purely imagination, although the Churchill Government 'was of course aware of the general nature of the statements made by Hess on his arrival in Scotland'.[16] This rumour of a Conservative palace-revolution against Churchill and of his alleged willingness to permit a debate within the Party on the German peace proposals, however improbable this may seem, has also never been confirmed.

On one point, however, Halifax had clearly not told the truth. On his arrival in Scotland, Hess had delivered not only a general statement but, in his three conversations with Kirkpatrick, he had gone into some detail on the German peace proposals, which by this time Roosevelt had of course learnt about from Churchill. It is still uncertain, however, whether the Deputy Führer expressed himself even more specifically on peace in Europe and in the world on another occasion.

At this point, a general comment on the information available about Rudolf Hess's peace proposals is necessary. My father has had silence imposed upon him because he knows of matters whose publication would be highly embarrassing to Britain, and perhaps also to America and the Soviet Union. As long as this remains the position, contemporary historical research is dependent purely and solely on the British documents. As long as important sections of these files dealing with the Hess case remain under lock and key until far into the next millenium, it is impossible to establish precisely what Hess in fact brought with him to Britain in the form of peace proposals. In such a matter, which was handled so secretly that perhaps only a handful of people around Churchill were really in the picture, it has been possible to keep the proposals, plans or offers, made by Hess himself or brought by him on Hitler's orders, concealed in the archives up to the present day. They must of course be taken into consideration in any proper assessment of Hess's flight to Britain.

An indication that Hess said more than is as yet known is contained in a note prepared on 3 June 1941 by Ralph Murray of the PWE (Political Warfare Executive) – a somewhat super-secret organization to which we shall return – for the Head of the Secret Service section of the Foreign Office, Sir Reginald Leeper. According to this, Secretary of State Cadogan also may have spoken to Rudolf Hess at some time and at some place.[17]

The context in which this talk took place and what purpose it served cannot as yet be determined; the source of the information is too incomplete for this. But on this occasion the Deputy Führer appears to have been even more specific than in his conversations with Kirkpatrick. These were his proposals:

1. Germany and Britain to reach a compromise on world-wide policy based on the status quo – i.e. without a German Lebensraum (living-space) war against Russia.
2. Germany to drop its colonial claims and to acknowledge

British rule of the sea. In return, Britain to acknowledge Continental Europe as a sphere of German interest.

3. The present strength relationship between Germany and Britain in air and on the sea to be maintained – i.e. no reinforcement from the USA. Since there is no comment on land forces, maintenance of the strength relationship reached must be assumed here also.

4. Germany to leave 'Metropolitan France' (this probably meant Vichy France) after total disarmament of the French Army and Navy. German commissioners to remain in French North Africa. German troops also to remain in Libya for a period of five years from the conclusion of peace.

5. Germany to establish satellite states in Poland, Denmark, the Netherlands, Belgium and Serbia (sic!). It will however withdraw from Norway, Rumania, Bulgaria and Greece (except for Crete – which German parachutists had taken at the end of May) two years after the conclusion of peace. After some rounding-off in the East, North, West and South (Austria and Czechoslovakia were apparently to remain within the Reich), Germany would thus have abandoned pressure on Britain's position in the Eastern Mediterranean and the Middle East.

6. Germany to recognize Abyssinia and the Red Sea as a British sphere of influence.

7. The person the Deputy Führer was speaking to was somewhat confused about whether Italy had approved Hess's peace proposals. The Deputy Führer said nothing on this. (Points 4 and 6 would have considerably affected Italian interests.)

8. Rudolf Hess admitted that his being of 'unsound mind' had been agreed with Hitler.

This sensational peace proposal, previously unknown, would in fact have brought peace to the world in 1941, because if Britain had negotiated with Germany on this basis the German attack on Russia of 22 June 1941 less than three weeks later – would not have taken place, since Hitler would have obtained what he needed for survival – control of the Continent. The war would have withered away on all fronts. Or was this prescription simply a cunningly contrived feint by which Britain hoped to divide Mussolini from Hitler?

Whatever the truth may be, the penultimate occasion on

which Hess was questioned about his views and intentions by a representative of the British Government was, as far as is known, on 9 June 1941, three days after Roosevelt's press conference and the dispute about the existence of German peace proposals. This probably explains the strict secrecy under which this conversation took place.

On the afternoon of 20 May 1941, Rudolf Hess was moved from the Tower of London to his new domicile, Mytchett Place near Aldershot, not far from Farnborough, where the Deputy Führer was to remain for the next 13 months. The means of transport was again the ambulance that had already taken him from Scotland to London. The prisoner was given two rooms and a bathroom at the end of a passage on the top floor of the spacious country house, previously occupied by a military headquarters. His corner was separated from the rest of the premises by wire-netting, with a sentry before the door. The house was guarded by an army unit.

Lord Simon, whom Churchill had designated to talk to Hess, knew him from a visit of British politicians to Hitler in 1935. As Lord Chancellor, Simon was in 1941 a member of the British Government, but not of the more restricted War Cabinet. Urged by Eden, he finally said, in early June, that he was prepared to meet and to question the German. This had two main objectives: to secure information on Germany's conduct of the war and to clarify the matter of 'whether Hess had been sent here by Hitler as part of some plan for a peace initiative'.[18] The Churchill Government apparently still feared that the German Führer might introduce such an initiative before or after his attack on Russia, and perhaps Hess was merely his skilfully camouflaged agent.

To prepare for his interview, Simon was provided with all the documents that had meanwhile become available in the matter, including the monitoring reports of Hess's private conversations at Mytchett Place with officers of the guard. The entire wing inhabited by the Deputy Führer was festooned with monitoring devices. This advance information indicated that Hess had so far stuck to his line that German victory was as certain as continuation of the war by Britain was futile. Moreover, Hess continued to assert that it had been his own idea to come to Britain, and that Hitler had not sent him.

[138]

A memorandum prepared on 9 June 1941 by Desmond Morton,[19] Churchill's chief adviser on Secret Service matters, indicates the direction of thought on the Hess affair among the Prime Minister's circle when Simon met the Deputy Führer. This document demonstrates the truly phenomenal ability of Churchill's closest advisers to interpret Rudolf Hess's unwelcome peace mission as the action of a mentally disturbed person.

In Morton's opinion, Hess had come to Britain without Hitler's knowledge. Although he was not 'psychotic' or 'mad' in a medical sense, Morton considered him a 'high-grade neurotic' and 'very stupid'. Morton did not believe that he belonged to the innermost circle surrounding Hitler and his generals, although it was possible that he knew more than he at present admitted. On the subject of Britain's morale, Morton considered that Hess was completely on the wrong track. Also, he had 'little or no knowledge of how this country functions and is governed'. As to the nature of Hess's ultimate ideas on peace, the Secret Service man was still groping in the dark, but he hoped for more enlightenment from the talk with Simon.

The following questions were of most interest to Churchill's advisers: What was Hess afraid of – was he afraid for his own person or for the international situation? Why was he at this very moment 'searching so earnestly for a patched-up peace'? How did he view a German–British understanding, and why? Morton found it very interesting that the 'obvious exaggerations' with which Hess had described the superiority of the Luftwaffe and the U-boats accorded with Goebbels' propaganda. Could it be that Hitler was also taken in by these fairytales, and had therefore a fundamentally false picture of the military situation?

Because of Churchill's anxiety about America's attitude, the meeting between Simon and Hess was kept so secret that in internal documents the Lord Chancellor himself referred only to the 'high-ranking political personality whose identity is known to you'. However, a few days before the meeting Hess was given an indication that a member of the Government who was sympathetic towards the peace mission wished to meet him. This was intended to make Hess talk.

But when Lord Simon, accompanied by Sir Ivone Kirkpatrick, arrived at Mytchett Place on 9 June 1941 the two were admitted formally as the psychiatrists 'Dr Guthrie' and 'Dr Mackenzie', and were so named in the minutes of the interview. Hess had been told in advance of these pseudonyms, which were intended to protect the interview from undesirable indiscretions on the part of the assistants involved. The Deputy Führer was referred to as 'J' for 'Jay' in the minutes. The officers of the guard, for their part, appeared to have no idea whatsoever of the grotesque game of hide-and-seek taking place before their eyes.

The interview lasted about three hours. It was conducted in the presence of a stenographer, an interpreter and a certain Mr Maass, an interned German who had been included for appearances' sake to give Hess a feeling of numerical equality. This Kurt Maass did not however once intervene in the interview, which was in fact merely a dialogue between Hess and Simon. Kirkpatrick restricted himself to a few questions, and to assisting with the translation occasionally when the interpreter was in difficulties.[20] Hess's English was not sufficient for communication without an interpreter.

Compared with the information given by the Deputy Führer to Kirkpatrick after his arrival, the interview with Simon produced little that was new. Hess again described the circumstances preceding his flight. The decision to undertake this venture had been made easier for him by the fact that he had constantly seen before him 'an endless row of children's coffins followed by weeping mothers' on both the German and British sides. He brought up once again the history of German–British relations.

·A new aspect was that Hess now openly accused Britain of having forced Germany by a series of violations of international law and aggressions to act similarly. The first was the violation of the armistice after the First World War in the internment of the German Navy. The two 'first territorial violations of international law' in the Second World War had then been committed by Britain in the raid by its destroyer *Cossack* on the German *Altmark* in Norwegian waters and its laying of mines. As was known from captured documents, Britain and France had also planned aggression on Belgium and Holland with a view to conquering the Ruhr from there, which meant making war on Germany. Hitler had not wished to bomb Britain, but he had been forced to begin this, whether he wanted to or not, by the increasing attacks of the British Air Force on the German civilian population.

Hess did not expect Simon to agree with him on all points, and he therefore accepted without emotion the Lord Chancellor's objections to this view of history. He also readily agreed to Simon's request that he should now, at long last, move on to his peace proposals. To lend these the necessary emphasis, however, Hess at first gave vent in great detail to his views on the increasing strength of the German U-boat weapon and the Luftwaffe. This development would in the long run make Britain's position 'hopeless', which had had a 'significant influence' on his decision to undertake this flight.

Here also Simon cut in once again. He wanted more details of the number of pilots now under training and to be trained in the future on the German side, and he asked Hess why in fact he was complaining about losses among German civilians if German air superiority was so great. Hess tried to get out of this by pointing to the future; only in the future would the German Luftwaffe and the German U-boats be so superior that Britain would have to capitulate. But he could not convince Simon, who countered with the question: Why should Britain make peace today if Germany would be stronger only tomorrow?

After two hours, Simon became impatient. But Hess continued to pour out long dissertations to the effect that British reports of their own successes in destroying German U-boat production were exaggerated, and that in contrast to 1917 Germany had every opportunity of starving Britain by the utter destruction of its supply routes. This was certainly 'the vulnerable point' for the island. Germany would win without an invasion simply by sinking more and more of the tonnage that Britain needed for its subsistence, declared Hess. This was followed by a lengthy dispute about the correct tonnage figures. The Lord Chancellor also appeared to be little impressed on this point, since he considered that if Hess's claims were in fact correct Britain would no longer possess a single ship.

Finally, however, Hess began to speak of his peace plan. He had outlined it in writing under four brief points before the meeting with Simon.[21] It was the planned division of the world already put forward, but Italy was now to participate in the German dominion over the European Continent. Germany was of course also interested in the European part of Russia, and if Hitler were to enter into an agreement with Stalin Britain was not to interfere, declared Hess. When Simon asked what the future of the Netherlands, Norway, Greece and Iraq would be under such circumstances, Hess could not answer. He did not know precisely, but of course no one in Germany had any intention of annexing Greece.

Simon also asked Hess to explain the term 'sphere of interest'. Hess understood by this that Britain should conclude no more alliances with the European states lying within the future German sphere of interest, nor should Britain interfere in their domestic policies. This concerned particularly the Balkan countries.

The rest of the Hess peace plan related to the return of the German colonies and reparations for German property losses in the First World War, two points already known from his conversations with Kirkpatrick. An addition was the demand that Britain should make peace with Germany and Italy simultaneously. However, Hess's comments on his proposals remained vague.

When finally he again threatened that Britain would sooner or later be forced to agree to these peace proposals if it did not now do so voluntarily, Simon replied acidly that the British were quite courageous and were not very fond of threats. After this, the Deputy Führer became more reasonable.

Finally, Simon, who like Hess had tried to keep the atmosphere friendly, turned to the questions that interested Churchill most. Why had the Deputy of the German Führer arrived at this very time? Did Hitler have a hand in this? On whose behalf had Hess arrived? But on these points also the German was still vague. Before each of his attempts to take off he had talked to the Führer about his peace ideas relative to Britain, said Hess. But he had come 'without his (advance) knowledge' on his own initiative. The reasons he had not left earlier were of a purely technical and political nature. In the spring, the weather and Britain's successes in North Africa had prevented the flight.

Simon and Kirkpatrick wanted to know whether he had come at least on behalf of other 'important people in Germany'. This was one of the few times that the Lord Chancellor's companion intervened in the conversation. This reference to other possible co-originators of his peace plan, which might of course have alluded to Haushofer and the German Resistance, or even to Himmler, appeared quite irrelevant to Hess. 'The ideas [contained in his plan – W.R.H.] are the Führer's ideas', he replied with some indignation. 'And they are of critical importance; no more, no less.' But he had certainly talked to Göring about them occasionally.

At the very end, Hess asked his visitor for a further conversation in private, whereupon Simon's escorts withdrew.[22] He feared that he was being poisoned, complained Hess when they were alone, and he showed signs of losing some of his self-control, which he had strictly maintained when the others were present. He also believed that the guards outside in the passage intentionally made a lot of noise to prevent his sleeping at night. Indeed, Hess was not even sure of his life, because he feared that he had fallen into the hands of the British Secret Service.[23] Simon tried to comfort the Deputy Führer, telling him to be brave and not to indulge in such misguided thoughts.

Rudolf Hess's suspicions could not of course be rejected completely out of hand, because the British employed certain medicaments and other means of persuasion to harness the Deputy Führer to their own purposes.

Next day the Lord Chancellor sat down and wrote this first report to Churchill on his meeting with the German Deputy Führer. 'Hess came on his own initiative . . . I come to the conclusion from the conversation that Germany does not want any substantially prolonged war . . . And it may be that the sudden appearance of Hess with this bludgeon of an olive branch reveals that Germany feels more uneasy than it admits.' Could there have been any better news for the Prime Minister? If Hess had come on his own initiative, this proved that Hitler was not behind the peace initiative. If Germany did not want a prolonged war, this meant that it must fear a prolonged war, and if it felt more uneasy than Hess admitted, this indicated that time would increasingly work against Hitler the longer the war lasted.

Less than two weeks after the Simon–Hess talks, Germany began its attack on Russia. Six months later, after the Japanese attack on Pearl Harbour, the United States entered the war. Thus Churchill and Roosevelt's dream of the Grand Alliance was realized simply by their refusing to make peace with the Axis Powers and by the determination of Hitler and the Japanese military to enforce peace upon the Western Powers by continuation of the War.

THE TRAP

WHEN CHURCHILL VISITED Stalin in Moscow in October 1944 to sacrifice Poland's freedom on the altar of the Grand Alliance, the Soviet dictator suddenly proposed one evening a toast to the British Secret Service. He very seriously believed that none other than the agents of His Majesty were behind the Hess affair. Stalin contended that, without signals from the Secret Service, the Deputy Führer would never have been able to land in Scotland.[1]

Since then, this conjecture has haunted the literature on the subject. It leads to an aspect of the Hess case that remains impenetrably obscure, more so than many of its political details. But it appears that this fog is gradually beginning to disperse, since what a few years ago was perhaps still considered the product of an over-excited imagination can now be to some extent proved. The scenario is that Hess was in fact lured by Britain to take off on 10 May 1941, and that unexpectedly he fell into a trap.

The question intrudes: Was this trap set jointly by the German Resistance and the British Secret Service?

It is again best to let the facts speak for themselves. The first point to attract attention is that the entire story of the flight to Britain contains a major contradiction. This is, that the Deputy Führer, with the knowledge and consent of Adolf Hitler, prepared a peace initiative for months, culminating in his putting his reputation at stake – and then risked everything, including his own life, by simply taking off on 10 May, crossing the enemy lines and jumping out into darkness over a strange country with no knowledge at all of whether the Duke of Hamilton was in fact staying where he expected him to be! This glaring disparity between a calculated stake and an incalculable risk arouses astonishment in the context of an enterprise which involved such high aims as the salvation of Germany and the restoration of peace.

It is true that in a letter to his wife in 1946/47 Hess himself described his flight as if his enterprise had gone completely according to plan, even the hazardous parachute jump which the otherwise so meticulous Deputy Führer had never before practised; in fact, it nearly miscarried. There is also the Englishman Leasor's description, which recounts that Hess is said to have explained to his adjutant Pintsch in a night-time conversation that in the ten minutes between his landing and the arrival of the police he intended to hand over the crucial peace message to Hamilton.

But what source value have letters when they originate under conditions of political imprisonment and pass through the censorship of the British authorities, and were perhaps written on the basis of false promises? Not very much. And Leasor's description – as has already been indicated elsewhere – is for various reasons implausible in its details.

Thus, only these two questionable 'documents' exist, i.e. the Hess letters from Nuremberg and Leasor's book, which describe Rudolf Hess's flight as an enterprise planned in every detail and then proceeding smoothly. This is an insufficient foundation on which to base historical truth.

It is also striking that during the many interviews with Hess conducted by Hamilton, Kirkpatrick, Simon and Beaverbrook he was never asked for the details of this adventurous flight and landing, how he succeeded in breaking through the Scottish air defences without being shot down, and how in any event he found his way to Hamilton's house. Was there no one in Britain interested in this? After all, there was a war on. Or did the British already know everything? This must be suspected.

Other peculiarities emerge. On 10 May 1941, two-and-a-half hours before my father said good-bye to my mother at München-Harlaching to fly to Britain, he was visited by Alfred Rosenberg, the head of the NSDAP's Foreign Policy Bureau. It is not known what they spoke about during the brief snack they took together. Hess had expressly told his wife to make sure that none of the servants witnessed their conversation. Shortly afterwards, he appeared before my mother in his Luftwaffe uniform.

It may be that the meeting with Rosenberg shortly before Rudolf Hess's departure was purely coincidental. Rosenberg was subordinate to the Deputy Führer, and he may have come to see him on official business that permitted no postponement. On the other hand, the close association in time between Rosenberg's visit and Hess's departure is striking. The supposition that there is a causal connection here grows stronger when we consider what Ilse Hess told Solicitor Dr Alfred Seidl in a letter dated 16 January 1983. According to this, shortly before the British–French declaration of war on the German Reich on 3 September 1939, Rosenberg had been staying with the Welfs in Brunswick when none other than the Duke of Hamilton arrived alone by plane to prevent, at the last minute, an outbreak of war.[2]

This incident, previously unknown, raises several questions. Did Rosenberg, on that 10 May 1941, bring a secret message from Hamilton which caused Hess to set out immediately on his flight, already prepared for months past? How long in fact had Hamilton and Hess known one another, and how close was their relationship? And, indeed, the question must be asked, for how long had the British Secret Service been involved?

This question arises because the letter written by Albrecht Haushofer to Hamilton on 19 September 1940 on the directions of Hess and Hitler did not immediately reach its addressee, but landed first on the desk of the British Secret Service. British postal censorship, which in principle checked all incoming mail, had intercepted it on 2 November 1940 on its way from Lisbon to London.[3] Hamilton allegedly did not learn of this until mid-March 1941, when he was asked to come to the British Air Ministry. Here, Group Captain Stammers is said to have confronted him with the existence of the letter for the first time. Stammers belonged to Military Intelligence; more specifically the Secret Intelligence Service of the Royal Air Force.

It is not clear why Military Intelligence took more than three months to inform the addressee of the letter in question, and what had happened to the letter over this long period. It was said to have been mislaid. But in all the circumstances this is unlikely. It is also uncertain what occurred during the month before Hamilton was again called to the Air Ministry. On this occasion, 25 April 1941, he was asked by two officers of Air Defence, Captain Blackford and Major Robinson, to follow Haushofer's suggestion and go to the proposed meeting in Lisbon. His assignment would be 'to obtain as much information as possible about German intentions and Haushofer's ideas'.[4]

Hamilton at first said that he was willing to carry out this Secret Service commission on two conditions: first, the British Ambassador in Portugal should be informed of his visit, for co-ordination purposes; second, Hamilton wished to speak to the Secretary of State at the British Foreign Office before he set out. A letter from the Duke to the Air Ministry giving these conditions also pointed out that it would be politically 'dangerous' if Haushofer were to conclude from the seven-month delay in replying that 'our authorities had a hand in all this'. He wanted to cover up the fact that Military Intelligence was already party to the matter. This letter was sent by Hamilton just two days before 30 April, when Hess tried for the second time to take off in his Me 110 from Augsburg-Haunstetten, but was held back at the last moment by Hitler.

In his reply of 3 May 1941 to Hamilton, however, Captain Blackford of the Air Ministry backed down.[5] Military Intelligence was no longer prepared to give the Duke the go-ahead for this mission without the consent of the Churchill Government. After consulting his superior, Air Commodore Boyle, Blackford agreed with Hamilton's opinion that 'it was not perhaps the right time to conduct talks whose purpose might be misunderstood'. The matter was therefore postponed. Hamilton replied by letter on 10 May agreeing with this decision and saying that he considered it 'postponed until you take it up again'. This was the very day on which Hess finally set out for Scotland from Augsburg-Haunstetten.

Here also the close coincidence in time is striking. Was it an accident that the Deputy Führer's two attempts to take off, the second of which succeeded because Hitler had no further opportunity to intervene, coincided with the dates of dispatch of Hamilton's two letters? The first letter had contained Hamilton's agreement to a meeting with Haushofer in Lisbon; his second letter agreed to the calling-off of the venture. Nothing had come of the conditional co-operation between Military Intelligence and Hamilton. Could it be that Hess received, via Rosenberg on 10 May 1941, a countersignal to the effect that Hamilton was willing to meet him or Haushofer? If this was so, who dispatched this misleading signal?

In his book on Albrecht Haushofer and Rudolf Hess's flight to Britain, James Douglas-Hamilton took great care to establish that his father had not been in collusion with the Deputy Führer. An impression to the contrary had been aroused in May 1941 by a Government spokesman's unfortunate choice of words to the effect that the Duke had corresponded directly with Hess and had himself received the Haushofer letter of 19 September before handing it over to the security authorities. Among the British public, then committed to 'war until victory', this impression was equivalent almost to character assassination, and the Churchill Government hurried to restore the Duke's reputation without delay by a suitable counter-statement. Did this haste stem only from concern for Hamilton's reputation? Or did it conceal something else – i.e. concern that the gossip about the Scottish nobleman might reveal that, in the Hess affair, Hamilton was acting as a man-of-straw for the British Secret Service?

An incident dating from 1945, to which we shall return in more detail later, provides evidence for our assumption that this was the case: Churchill prevented the Duke from making a private trip to New York because he was afraid that the American press might squeeze out of Hamilton the dirty trick 'involving Hess'.[6] The Prime Minister was concerned that world opinion should not learn 'the low-down on Hess'. In fact, it still does not know even half of 'the low-down'.

What the British Government definitely kept from its own public was that Military Intelligence toyed with the idea of using the Duke as an agent in secret contacts with Hitler's envoy, and that Hamilton, under certain conditions designed to protect himself politically, initially agreed to this. James Douglas-Hamilton's efforts to spare the memory of his father, long since dead, from any taint of collaboration in fact reinforces the supposition that the Duke was far more deeply involved in the whole affair than previously assumed. His role is open to doubt and quite obscure.

It is still impossible to say how close were the contacts between Hamilton and the leading National Socialists, and how far into the past they extended. Hess maintained that he came to know the Duke personally during the Berlin Olympic Games in 1936, but the Duke denied ever having met the Deputy Führer before 11 May 1941. The Duke admitted, however, that he had frequently been in Germany before the war. Whatever may be the truth, Hamilton certainly had contact with Hess through Albrecht Haushofer. And although the Duke assured Air Minister Sinclair personally that he had never received a letter from the Deputy Führer[7] the relatively close link between Haushofer and Hamilton represents one of those channels through which the British Secret Service could have influenced the Deputy Führer's decisions.

That the Secret Intelligence Service (SIS) played a part is supported by the fact that Hess himself repeatedly expressed fears that he had fallen into the hands of the Secret Service. Also, in a programme transmitted on 13 May 1941 within the Reich only, the German radio commentator Hans Fritzsche suggested that the Deputy Führer might have been 'deliberately lured into a trap by Britain'.[8] And the periodical *The American Mercury* in fact asserted in May 1943[9] that since January 1941 the Secret Service had negotiated with Hitler on peace by improperly using the names of Hamilton and other British noblemen, and that Hitler had then ordered Hess to fly to Scotland where a reception committee consisting of officers of Military Intelligence and the Secret Service was awaiting him at Dungavel House. However, because Rudolf Hess missed his target by ten miles the whole plan came into the open and collapsed. Much of this report is probably incorrect. *The Mercury* is a periodical which, at least in the 1930s and 1940s, was under communist influence, and much of what this report had to say about the Hess affair was all too clearly stamped with Stalin's distrust, which until 1945 assumed that the Western Powers might eventually ally themselves with Germany against the Soviet Union. But the slant of the article is probably accurate, as many of its details accord with the actual course of events as evidenced by, or as may be gathered from, the documents now available.

What *The Mercury* reported in 1943 and what Stalin told Churchill to his face in October 1944 amounted basically to the same thing. It is true that the Prime Minister protested strongly and declared that the British Government knew nothing of the flight beforehand, but apart from the fact that Stalin had in no way suggested this, does any government always know what its Secret Service is up to? And if Churchill had known, would he have admitted it? Substantial doubt is permissible here. The version involving the Secret Service with the Hess flight certainly cannot be trusted solely because it originates from a communist source. On the other hand, the authority with which Stalin and *The Mercury* commented on matters involving the British Secret Service should not be underestimated.

What they had to say probably originated from one and the same source: from the Soviet master-spy Kim Philby, who since early 1940 at the latest worked in Section D (later Special Operations Executive – SOE), a sub-division of the Secret Intelligence Service concerned with secret enemy propaganda and disinformation. In September 1941, Philby was transferred to SIS. It is probable that the information *The Mercury* and Stalin had about the British Secret Service's part in the Hess affair originates from him, since, in his notorious fear of an alliance between the West and Hitler, Stalin was interested in any information on secret contacts between London and Berlin.[10] In parts, however, *The Mercury*'s story was painted in almost grotesque colours.

The grotesque aspect of *The Mercury*'s story is certainly the suggestion that a reception committee from all the secret services was awaiting Hess in Scotland, that the whole plan had come to nothing merely because the Deputy Führer missed the Duke of Hamilton's Dungavel House by ten miles, and that his mission had therefore become public knowledge. Military Intelligence and the political secret services controlled by Churchill and his cohorts certainly had no interest in negotiating with Hess about peace; they would have interrogated him only in their professional capacity. And the Hess mission did not fail as a result of publicity but, on the contrary, because the Deputy Führer's peace proposals were kept secret by the British Government.

This story of a secret reception committee and damaging publicity is just as grotesque as Hess's alleged statement that he had intended to carry out his peace mission within the ten minutes that would elapse between his arrival at Hamilton's house and the appearance of the police. Neither the one nor the other is true.

In fact, on 10 May 1941 or shortly before then, Rudolf Hess had received, probably via Hamilton, some secret signal from Britain which, under the pretence of non-existent prospects of success, caused him to start immediately on his peace mission. The Deputy Führer had not planned a parachute descent but a 'soft landing' with his Me 110 somewhere in Scotland, relying on the Duke of Hamilton's offer to guide him in to a landing. It was only when his contact did not appear in the air space over the Scottish coast that Hess had suddenly to change his plans and risk the unforeseen parachute landing. In the absence of an alternative, he decided to aim for the Duke's country house, whose location he had fixed in his mind for any emergency.

Only the two 'documents' already referred to do not in fact support this assumption. But their credibility is very low, for the reasons given. On the other hand, there is abundant evidence for the accuracy of our assumption. This evidence is summarized here for the first time in order to present a plausible picture of Hess's mission. It is admitted that, to be really convincing, our argument calls for one assumption, i.e. that the British Secret Service knew of the Deputy Führer's planned flight.

This, however, is very probable. As we have said, Hess had planned his flight in every detail for months past. Why is it assumed that he said nothing about it to his friends Karl and Albrecht Haushofer? In fact, it can at least be proved that Karl Haushofer, whom Ilse Hess refers to as her husband's 'best friend', learned of the Deputy Führer's proposed flight not later than 25 or 26 January 1941.[11] Since the Haushofers, father and son, were so close that they confided to one another their private thoughts about the peace initiatives of the National Socialist leadership and the German Resistance, why should Karl Haushofer have withheld, of all things, this extremely important fact, particularly as Albrecht Haushofer had heard about it long ago from Hess himself?

Did Albrecht Haushofer pass this information on to the Duke of Hamilton? This question is difficult to answer as long as we do not know the entire correspondence between Haushofer and Hamilton. The letter of 19 September 1940, already extensively discussed, written by Albrecht Haushofer on behalf of Hess and

Hitler, was certainly only one of several letters exchanged between the Berlin academic and the Scottish nobleman. But it would be difficult to establish how many other letters there were and what they contained, since, as Albrecht Haushofer's letter of 16 July 1939 to Hamilton shows, [12] they communicated under the seal of strictest secrecy. Haushofer expressly asked Hamilton to destroy the letter when he had read it and, at Haushofer's suggestion, had shown it to Halifax, the British Foreign Secretary. In this informal way, scarcely reconstructable today, the information that the Deputy of the German Führer intended to come to Britain in person and by plane to sound out the possibility of peace might in fact have reached London. But what motive or interest might Haushofer have had in passing on this information to the British? Here there are as many possible explanations as the number of roles Albrecht Haushofer was playing. Since he was adviser to Hess and Hitler on British policy, it is possible that he wished to do them a favour by trying to secure support within Britain for the flight. The opposite is however just as possible, since Haushofer was of course working for the Resistance at the same time, and perhaps also for the Reichführer SS. Albrecht Haushofer was at all events not unknown to the authorities in London concerned in the Hess matter, which is not to say that he was an agent of the British Secret Service. Like Hamilton, Haushofer belonged to the Anglo-German Fellowship Association, which was infiltrated by agents of various hue. Stalin's Philby was also a member. In these circles, a suitable intimation by Haushofer in good time could have been spread privately, and reached the ears of the Secret Service.

In the final analysis, however, what is important is not whether or how Haushofer passed on the information about Hess's intended flight. It may have reached Britain in quite another way. For example, the former president of the Federal Constitutional Protection Authority, Dr Otto John, who then belonged to the Resistance, told the author that since about 1937 he had met Albrecht Haushofer every Saturday over a tureen of pea soup, followed by a walk in the Berlin Grunewald. In this way he had learned of Hess's intended flight before May 1941. After the Deputy Führer had left, Haushofer had even suggested that John himself should fly to London with a peace message. He, Otto John, had a contact there named Tony Mine-god of the Secret Intelligence Service (SIS).[13] If Hess's flight was spoken about so openly within the Resistance, it is easy to imagine that similar information had reached Britain long before the event.

Whatever the truth may be, Rudolf Hess was expected in Britain when he flew there on 10 May 1941. In this respect, *The Mercury* was basically correct. Walter Ramsey's comment referred to above is evidence of it.[14] The behaviour of Scottish Air Defence on the evening of that day is evidence of it. Above all, the Duke of Hamilton's behaviour is evidence of it; by accident or design, he was on duty that evening in the control room at Turnhouse Airfield on the West Coast of Scotland.

In fact, Rudolf Hess's approach was followed stage by stage by Hamilton.[15] At 22.08 hrs. the enemy plane crossed the coastline at Farnes Island. At 22.56 hrs. it was located north-east of Ardrossan. At 23.07 hrs. it disappeared from the radar screen a few miles south of Glasgow; it had crashed. Each of these flight movements was reported immediately to Hamilton by the air observers. It is true that the Duke later asserted that he had at first been surprised that an Me 110 was involved, because he assumed that an aircraft of this type could not cover the long journey from Germany to Scotland. But he did not say that he was unaware that Hess was sitting in the aircraft.

'The usual steps were taken to intercept the enemy aircraft and to shoot it down', reads Hamilton's report to Churchill. But every doubt is permissible on this very point. What could have been easier than to shoot down an aircraft, roaring in alone across the open sea, that had been detected by British radar many miles south of Turnhouse in the latitude of Northumberland? In fact, two Hurricanes were sent up against it.[16] A fighter of the Defiant type is said to have flown 'in hot pursuit' as close as four miles to Hess's aircraft before it crashed.[17] But unfortunately, reported Hamilton to the Prime Minister, with a note of regret, 'its armament was not fired'. Why not? According to the report in *The American Mercury*, the Commanding Officer at Turnhouse had expressly ordered that the plane should not be shot down. Who was this officer? Hamilton!

The Duke himself had already flown across the Firth of Forth in a Hurricane on the afternoon of 10 May 1941, as if on the lookout for Hess. But when the Deputy Führer arrived a few hours later the Wing-Commander was again sitting in the control room at Turnhouse. Protected by the haze, Hess was circling off shore waiting for his guide. When he failed to arrived, Hess fell into the trap. The Deputy Führer could no longer return to Germany because he would have crashed en route because of lack of fuel. He therefore had to continue and look after himself. Hess decided to fly to the Duke's country house, the only landmark he had in Scotland.

The Deputy Führer in fact flew by no means as directly to Dungavel House as his questionable letter might suggest. On the contrary, it can be shown that he took an aimless zig-zag course across Scotland as though he had great difficulty in finding his way. This is the strongest argument against our relying on his description. It is nothing less than proof that his letter was forged. The flight movements were recorded in detail at the Turnhouse control room: Hess first flew west, then north-east, then south, then north and finally west again.[18]

Then, when his tanks were empty and he believed himself to be in the neighbourhood of Hamilton, the Deputy Führer jumped out into the night. He had never practised this, he later told his wife, but he did not add that it had never been his original intention.

It was quite common during the war for German pilots who had got into difficulties to bail out over British territory. The authorities had a routine for this. But in the present case all was different. As soon as practicable, Hamilton was informed that the German who had bailed out was asking for him, using the name of Alfred Horn. Why was this so important for a Wing-Commander who was merely doing his duty in a responsible post? The message even shot up the chain of command to Air-Marshall Sholto Douglas, who was then at Stanmore, Middlesex; quite a different place. During the night of 10/11 May, Hamilton travelled from Glasgow to Eaglesham and Busby to see first the aircraft wreckage and then Hess, whom he recognized immediately. When next morning Hamilton went to see 'Alfred Horn' at Buchanan Castle he took with him an officer from the Intelligence Service. The quite harmless article on the crash submitted by the *Daily Record* on Sunday afternoon to the censor in Glasgow, and in which the name Hess did not as yet appear, was banned as 'stupid nonsense'.[19] One asks oneself, would the authorities have behaved in this way unless they knew who the as yet unidentified parachutist was?

Scarcely! In fact, when on the afternoon of 11 May Churchill's Private Secretary was informed by Hamilton of Hess's landing he appeared to know immediately that 'somebody had landed', i.e. the Deputy Führer.

It must be assumed from this that Rudolf Hess was expected when he landed in Scotland. If this was so, who in Germany would have been able to convey to him the secret starting signal? To answer this question, we must know more about what Douglas-Hamilton passed over in his book: the Haushofer/Hess letter seized by British postal censorship in early November 1940 was passed not only to the RAF Intelligence Service, which, considering the Duke of Hamilton's position in the Royal Air Force, was perhaps obvious; it also went to MI5[20] – and from there it was only a step to the Secret Intelligence Service (SIS) and other secret organizations.

MI5 (Military Intelligence, Department 5) came under the War Office and was concerned with counter-intelligence inside Great Britain, chiefly in the military field. The authority of the SIS on the other hand, frequently called MI6, was different and much wider. The Secret Intelligence Service conducted Britain's counter-espionage abroad, not only in the military but also in the political field. The SIS was therefore Britain's true Secret Service, perhaps comparable in its importance to today's American Central Intelligence Agency (CIA).

The head of this important and powerful organization, Sir Stewart Menzies, usually referred to only as 'C' (Chief) for reasons of secrecy, was called in on the Hess case by the leading official at the Foreign Office, Secretary of State Sir Alexander Cadogan, on 12 May. Cadogan enquired whether Menzies would be in agreement with Kirkpatrick's flying to Scotland to 'investigate' Hess.[21] Churchill and Eden did not trust Hamilton's assurance that the Deputy Führer was in fact caught in their net; they wanted to be 100 per cent sure.

Cadogan's enquiry of the SIS is in itself strange, since the Secretary of State knew Kirkpatrick very well personally. The former Secret Service man had previously been in charge of the Foreign Office's German-policy department. That the Secretary of State nonetheless consulted Menzies proves that after Hess had landed, if not earlier, the SIS was vitally involved; and at later stages in the affair, when matters were particularly critical, the 'Chief' was repeatedly on the scene.

For the reasons given, however, there is a lot to suggest that the Secret Service background extended very much further into the past, and that Cadogan was among those who were just not informed about it. For a man who, as Eden's deputy, in practice conducted British foreign policy this at first appears surprising. But in 1953 Churchill succeeded in keeping his stroke secret from the entire government, although he was not really capable of action for weeks.[22] The Secretary of State had at first been merely surprised that the Prime Minister had received the Duke of Hamilton at Ditchley Park as early as Sunday 11 May, i.e. directly after Hess's landing.[23] But in the following days and weeks, Cadogan appeared to recognize the full extent of what had been kept secret from him, since he bitterly rebuked the Minister of Economic Warfare, Hugh Dalton, for allowing the uncontrollable activities of the Secret Service to add to the Foreign Office's already heavy workload.[24]

What role did Dalton play? We know that the Second World War was conducted on three fronts simultaneously: the military front, the economic front and the Secret Service front. To be precise, we are referring to a highly differentiated system of secret fronts, particularly on the British side. In this wide-ranging underground system, some organizations were so secret that not even those working for them knew what they were. The Secret Intelligence Service (SIS) was only the tip of the iceberg.

Beside all this, there was an obscure grey zone between classical espionage, counter-espionage, intelligence activities and psychological warfare, which from September 1941 came under the Political Warfare Executive – PWE. This super-secret organization centred on Special Operations 1 (SO1), engaged in propaganda, and Special Operations 2 (SO2), concerned with all forms of sabotage and subversion.

In summer 1940, Churchill had transferred responsibility for these two secret organizations to the Minister of Economic Warfare, Hugh Dalton, with the characteristic comment: 'Now set Europe on fire!'[25] The Labour politician did in fact immediately set about increasing the activities of SO1 and SO2. Until that time, SO1 had mainly carried out 'white propaganda'; it was now increasingly to concentrate on 'black propaganda'.

The purpose of white and black propaganda was to confuse the Germans, to provoke them to act against their leadership and to do everything possible to split them politically. This alone, of course, could not win the war, but it was a way of creating conditions under which the war could be won more easily and quickly. Britain had merely to destroy the self-confidence of the enemy.

White propaganda was the more harmless aspect of this psychological warfare. It consisted in millions of leaflets, thousands of radio programmes and hundreds of more or less targeted items of disinformation of a demoralizing nature, dropped by air, transmitted by radio or circulated in the Reich. Similar methods had already been employed during the First World War.

Black propaganda, on the other hand, represented a completely new concept of secret psychological warfare. It operated by using the most evil means, such as lies, deceit and forgery. Its methods were indistinct from those of the Secret Intelligence Service, the Ministry of Information and the Foreign Office, as well as from those of Special Operations 2, which itself did not balk at bribery, blackmail and murder.

Following the outbreak of war in 1939, propaganda activities and other equally important aspects of counter-espionage, such as the radio listening services, were moved from the British capital to the country to protect them from German air attack. The propaganda and espionage centre's new home was the Duke of Bedford's seat, Woburn Abbey, 69 kilometres from London supplemented by surrounding country houses, inns and villages. Over the next two years, a whole complex of secret intelligence departments, radio stations and forgery workshops arose in this area. More than 400 people were working here in summer 1941, including drivers, cooks and shorthand-typists. In the course of time, a surrogate British government was established here, composed of a close-knit fraternity of a few journalists, officials and German emigrants; a secret underground state whose behaviour was not subject to the control of Parliament and the public.

It was not fortuitous that the operational centre of this surrogate government was Woburn Abbey.[26] It belonged to the Duke of Bedford, and with this British aristocrat the prelude to the Hess affair had begun in August 1940.[27]

At that time, there was a meeting in Geneva between representatives of influential British circles and Professor Albrecht Haushofer, the Berlin academic who had been sent to meet them by none other than Hitler and Hess. It is alleged that in the course of these contacts, which apparently included the Hitler/Hess/Haushofer letter of 19 September 1940 to the Duke of Hamilton, already frequently quoted, the following package was prepared: Britain was willing to conclude a negotiated peace with Germany if, in return, Germany abrogated the Hitler–Stalin Pact of 1939 to relieve the British of the nightmare of a German–Soviet alliance. (The Hitler–Stalin Pact was only a non-aggression pact and not an alliance directed against the Western Powers.) Hitler and Hess were in principle prepared for this because they believed it represented the achievement of their desires – an anti-Soviet alliance with the West. But they wished to wait until the situation in the Balkans became clearer. This was how matters stood in late April/early May 1941 – shortly before Hess's departure.[28]

While, therefore, certain feelers had been going out to the German leadership from Woburn Abbey since August 1940, the Ministry of Economic Warfare, sitting at the other end of the line, had of course nothing like an understanding with Hitler in mind. It used the Dukes of Bedford and Hamilton only as a pretence to delude Hitler into believing that there was an opportunity for the long-desired understanding with Britain. In fact, Germany was merely to be separated from Russia, so that Churchill and Roosevelt could then enter into an alliance with Stalin against Hitler.

The contact-man between the propaganda and espionage centre in the country and the Ministry of Economic Warfare in the British capital was Leonard Ingram, an international banker. He was working for the Minister, Dalton, as an Under-Secretary of State, and he co-ordinated much of the Woburn Abbey activities. Acting for the Chemical Bank of New York, Ingram had travelled throughout Europe in his private plane before the War. He knew the secret game of behind-the-scenes intrigue. Blank cynicism was expressed by his cold eyes and the drooping corners of his mouth.

After the defeat of France, Dalton and Ingram came to the conclusion in summer 1940 that Britain's psychological warfare, with its predominantly 'white' methods, was not very effective. These methods would never set Europe on fire. 'Black propaganda' of maximum effectiveness should now be commenced. Thus, in late summer and autumn 1940, there was brewed in the witch's cauldron of Woburn Abbey, from a combination of bogus diplomatic negotiations and subversive disinformation, the recipe for the most audacious secret service venture of the Second World War – the enticement of the Deputy Führer to undertake his flight to Britain. To this end, Ingram involved the 37-year-old Denis Sefton Delmer, a protégé of Churchill and of the newspaper publisher Lord Beaverbrook. This native of Australia had spent his youth in Germany. In 1928, he became Berlin Correspondent of Beaverbrook's *Daily Express*; in 1937 he was Chief Correspondent for all Beaverbrook's publications in Europe, with his head office in Paris; and in 1940 he was War Correspondent in France. In circumstances that have not yet been fully explained, Delmer had the honour on 19 July 1940 of rejecting within one hour, publicly on the BBC and on behalf of Britain, Hitler's last peace offer.

Delmer thus had intimate experience of the methods of the Churchill Government when he entered its service to assist in bringing the Hess project to fruition. The reason for this lay in the 'phenomenal ability' of the affable and creative Falstaffian figure 'to tune in to the German mentality'.[30] Delmer spoke German as fluently as he did English, preferably in the dialect of the Berlin road-sweeper. In his office hung a notice bearing the ironic inscription: 'No Jews wanted here'.

Following the defeat of France, Delmer, in the guise of a correspondent of the *Daily Express*, went to Lisbon on the orders of the Secret Intelligence Service. Perhaps he had already been commissioned to track down Haushofer, which of course led via Portugal to the German capital and to Hess and Hitler. In January 1941, when German peace efforts via the Burckhardt contact entered a new and decisive phase, Ingram recalled Delmer to the British capital; the task awaited him there of orchestrating the propaganda for the planned Hess enterprise.

To this end, Delmer with a small staff of assistants was to establish a new secret transmitter. It was decided, during the planning discussions, that this highly secret propaganda unit was to corrupt leading officials of the NSDAP by subversive methods. In contrast to the other radio stations already working from Woburn Abbey on British propaganda, the new installation was a 'black propaganda' project, the little word 'black', as an insider remembers, 'having rather a "sinister" meaning at the time'.[30]

The first commission for the new super-secret undertaking was the Hess venture. Delmer was given a small office near the Ministry of Economic Warfare in London and immediately formed his own Research Unit, which to some extent carried out its duties by scientific methods. Preparations lasted throughout spring 1941 under the strictest secrecy, while Hess and Hitler continued to explore the ground in England through Haushofer and Burckhardt.

Delmer's apparatus became available as planned at the very moment that Hess landed in Britain. Two days after his arrival, the 'genius of black propaganda' (Howe) entered his new office at Aspley Guise near Woburn Abbey. Eleven days later, the 'Gustav Siegfried Eins' transmitter (alias 'George Sugar One') announced itself for the first time in a monotonous voice – chiefly over the ether of the Third Reich – running down the departed Deputy Führer: 'Like the whole clique of crack-pots, megalomaniacs, wire-pullers and drawing-room Bolsheviks who call themselves our "Führers" ', said the speaker Peter Seckelmann, a German emigrant who posed as a disappointed patriot, 'he (Hess) had nerves too weak to withstand the crisis'.[31]

Even a hidden reference to Haushofer was not omitted, when the speaker referred to 'men whose only mistake has been to overestimate the strength of nerve of this so-called Deputy Führer, and who at the end of April recited to him the strong misgivings they could not present to the "Führer" himself because he was surrounded by a gang of liars and bootlickers'.

Rudolf Hess was not of course enticed to Scotland by signals from Delmer's secret transmitter. It cannot even be assumed that this journalist in the service of British psychological warfare had himself conceived the idea of tempting the Deputy Führer to fly to Britain. The plan was probably hatched up within the close circle surrounding Churchill, Dalton and Ingram, and Delmer had perhaps an advisory and attendant role.

Moreover, the diplomatic part of the plan was in the hands of those agencies which were making use of the Duke of Hamilton and other aristocrats to delude the German leadership into believing that there were prospects of a negotiated peace with Britain. These agencies might have been either the Secret Intelligence Service or the Intelligence Department of the Foreign Office, whose former head, Sir Reginald Leeper, head of 'Special Operations' in 1941, was also operating from Woburn Abbey.

In fact, *The American Mercury*, referring to 'excellently informed sources' (Philby?), maintained that, without being aware of it, Hitler had negotiated for four months between January and May 1941, via an 'internationally known diplomat' (Burckhardt?), with the British Secret Service, which for purposes of deception had made use not only of Hamilton's name but also of his handwriting. At the beginning of these bogus negotiations, Hitler is said even to have offered, if necessary, to send Hess to Britain.

This offer, however, continued *The Mercury*, had fallen into the hands of the Secret Service. 'From then on [Hitler's offer to send Hess – W.R.H.], the correspondence was handled entirely by astute British agents', the paper continued. 'Replies designed to whet the German appetite, replies encouraging the supposition that Britain was seeking a way out of its military difficulties, were sent to Berlin. The hook was carefully baited that caught the third largest fish in the Nazi lake'.[32]

At first glance, this version strikes one as so fantastic that it can scarcely be believed. But apart from what we have already set out there are two particular aspects which suggest its accuracy with a probability approaching certainty, i.e.:

1. the fact that the peace conditions Hess brought to Britain in 1941 and the preceding course of events correspond precisely to *The Mercury*'s report of two years later, although there had meanwhile been not even a partly correct – let alone full – disclosure of the facts from either the German or the British side;
2. the fact that Stalin had every reason to assume that behind the Hess affair there lay a sophisticated and base intrigue by the

British Secret Service, since Churchill tried in all seriousness to put political pressure on the Soviet dictator by using the German Deputy Führer.

The explosive secret of the Hess case which has as yet not been exposed lies, in fact, in 'the Russian aspect'. The true reason for the life-long imprisonment of a man who must be prevented from opening his mouth and telling the truth about one of the most shameful misdeeds in world history probably also lies here.

And what follows is the truth of the Hess matter:

Since January 1941, Churchill had assumed that, if only for economic reasons, Germany 'had to seek victory in 1941'.[33] Since January, and increasingly from March onwards, the Government in London had been receiving secret information about German preparations for an attack on Russia. This was either the usual war of nerves, by which Hitler tried to extort economic and strategic concessions from Stalin, or it concerned plans for real war. Whichever was true, what was important to Churchill was that under all circumstances the Soviet Union should resist Germany's unreasonable demands, if necessary by force of arms, since the British Prime Minister feared that without a German–Russian war Hitler was certain of victory in 1941. In this situation, which for Churchill was a matter of life or death, he began his major counter-offensive at the turn of 1940/41. He secured the support of Roosevelt; he tried to wrest Japan from its Tripartite Alliance with Germany and Italy; he strove for rapprochement with the Soviet Union; and he allowed the bogus negotiations with Hitler on a separate German–British peace to run on with a view to tempting Hess to Britain at the decisive moment.

By the end of April 1941, Churchill had achieved an impressive measure of success in pushing his master-plan ahead. In March, he secured via the American Lease-Lend Act everything Britain needed by way of raw materials, food, munitions, war equipment and weapons for the long-term prosecution of the War. In April, he induced Roosevelt to offer Japan a bogus secret alliance with a view to splitting the Berlin–Tokyo–Rome Axis. And by late April/early May the bogus German–British negotiations had reached such a stage that Hitler and

Hess assumed that an understanding with Britain was close. Only one thing was lacking: Stalin gave Churchill the cold shoulder.

To change this attitude, in April 1941 the British Prime Minister, for the first time, warned the Soviet Dictator of the danger of a German attack, at the same time indicating the possibility of an Anglo-Russian rapprochement. Relations between the two countries had grown cold since the Hitler–Stalin Pact, the Russian attack on Finland and the incorporation of the Baltic States into the Soviet Union in 1939/40, and on 16 April 1941 Foreign Secretary Eden told Ivan Maisky, the Soviet Ambassador in London, that warmer relations were possible.

But no answer came from Stalin. Moreover, Sir Stafford Cripps, the British Ambassador in Moscow, warned his Government during the night of 23/24 April 1941 that if Hitler's demands on Stalin were not excessive Russia would yield without a fight.

Two days later, a German delegation arrived in Moscow to negotiate on the Third Reich's growing need for raw materials from the Soviet Union. On 26 April, Cripps again warned that the next few days would decide peace or war between Germany and the Soviet Union, the former still appearing to him more likely than the latter. At this dramatic moment, when in London's view the point at issue between Hitler and Stalin was either an alliance or war, the British Secret Service decided to unleash the plan prepared months ago to entice Hess to Britain. In the event, he flew off on the very day the time limit predicted by Cripps ended – 10 May 1941.

When, on 11 May, Churchill learned of the Deputy Führer's arrival, he could not at first believe his good fortune. He was firmly convinced that there was bitter disagreement within the German leadership. Whereas one faction favoured an understanding with Britain, another advocated a settlement with Russia. Hitler and Hess had shown by their peace feelers that they gave priority to an understanding with Britain. But the fact that his Deputy had now made his way to Britain might mean that the Führer had changed his mind, and was now inclined towards an agreement with Stalin. If this was so, then Churchill had to seek contact with Stalin immediately – in fact by using Hess.

To make this plan work, however, three questions had first to be answered:

1. Was this 'Alfred Horn' really Rudolf Hess?
2. Had Hess had a disagreement with Hitler on Germany's future policy towards Britain and/or Russia?
3. If this was so, was Hess ready for (bogus) negotiations on a German–British understanding, even at the risk that this might provoke war between Germany and Russia?

The first question was answered quickly. Secretary of State Cadogan noted in his diary, after Kirkpatrick had identified the German airman: 'It is undoubtedly Hess'.[34] In answering the second question, Hess gave the British leadership quite a headache: there appeared to be no dissension on British or Russian policy within the German leadership. Indeed, Hess told Kirkpatrick stiffly and firmly that Hitler continued to strive for an understanding with Britain, but not with Churchill. On the matter of a German attack on Russia he was silent.

This attitude permitted three possible conclusions: Hess did not know of Hitler's plans to attack, or he misled Kirkpatrick about the plans, or – in Churchill's eyes the worst of all possibilities – Hitler was aiming at an understanding with Britain as well as an agreement with Stalin, and was using the concentration of the Wehrmacht as a means of pressure. Then there would be peace in 1941 and America would draw away from Britain. Under such circumstances, Hitler was assured of final victory.

To attain his objective of an understanding with Stalin in spite of all difficulties, Churchill would stop at nothing – above all, war between Germany and Russia would not deter him. Hitler's Deputy had therefore arrived as if in answer to a summons. At first, the British Head of Government planned to turn 'in the name of humanity' to the world with the peace proposals Hess had brought.[35] He hoped that this would kill two birds with one stone: impressed by the publicity given to his proposals, Hess would be ready to negotiate even with the Churchill Government, and Stalin would believe that Hitler was in fact striving to reach an understanding with Britain while conducting only bogus negotiations with Russia. This would doubtless have severely strained German–Russian relations.

But Foreign Secretary Eden and Secretary of State Cadogan were horrified when, on 12 May, they learned of Churchill's plan. They were vehemently opposed to it for two reasons. First, although Churchill did not of course want an understanding with Germany, his appeal 'in the name of humanity' could be taken as a genuine offer of agreement addressed to Hitler – above all in America where it would have fatal repercussions on the realization of the Lease-Lend programme. Second, senior officials in the Foreign Office considered it wiser to represent the Hess flight before the world as a sign of conflict within the Nazi leadership.[36]

On 14 May, however, as speculation on the Hess affair intensified in the world press, Churchill had not yet abandoned his plan. He decided to inform Parliament next day of Hess's peace proposals, since Ambassador Cripps had cabled from Moscow on 13 May that everything said by Hess must be used to provoke Russia against Germany, so that (1) Stalin's fear of being 'left holding the baby' would increase [i.e. in the event of war, he would receive no help from the West – W.R.H.] and so that (2) it was made clear to Stalin that he had a greater chance of withstanding Hitler's demands successfully today than tomorrow. In Cripps' opinion, both objectives could be achieved if Churchill were to inform the Soviet Dictator of Hitler's peace feelers in Britain, and if he could bring the Soviet Dictator to see that Hitler was attempting to shake Stalin's power to its foundations by war.[37]

But Eden and Cadogan were, as ever, stubbornly opposed to such a statement because they feared that, in the case of Hess, the price of informing the public was far too high. The Secretary of State believed that Hitler 'would then draw a sigh of relief. And the German people even more so! They would say: "Then what our dear Führer said is true. Our worthy Rudolf has gone off to make peace." They (the Germans) may think he is quite mad, but they will not think him a traitor, which is what I would like them to dread'.[38] Cadogan therefore favoured absolute silence even more than Eden. This led to a disagreement with Churchill, until in the night of 14/15 May the Prime Minister, probably under Beaverbrook's influence, gave way and decided not to make a statement. After this, Churchill let matters rest for the time being. The German prisoners-of-war, who had been urgently asked for their views on the Hess flight, were completely confused, and in the opinion of the Foreign Office this was sufficient indication of the devastating effect of the event in Germany. Nevertheless, the Prime Minister persisted in his 'stupid statement on Hess' until 19 May. He even insisted on reading it 'with the greatest pleasure' to the Cabinet meeting on that day,[39] although he had already admitted on 15 May that the Foreign Office was correct in its strategy of silence. It is not clear what made Churchill so irresolute. Apart from his ulterior motives towards Stalin, he was probably impressed by Roosevelt's request of 15 May that he should avoid making the affair public for as long as possible. To Cadogan's great relief, the Cabinet was unanimously against any kind of statement.

Churchill therefore exercised discretion in continuing his attempt to put pressure on Stalin through Hess. With Churchill's approval, it was decided by a very small group on 19 May[40] to send Lord Chancellor Simon to Hess to tempt him out of his reserve by bogus negotiations. As a former politician of appeasement who knew the Deputy Führer personally from past meetings in Germany, the Lord Chancellor appeared to be particularly suitable for this delicate assignment. Churchill wished to shock Stalin with the results of Simon's efforts.

Meanwhile, Germany had commenced the conquest of Crete from the air, which demanded admiration even from some of Germany's bitterest enemies in Britain. The drama of the German battleship *Bismarck* was unfolding, and for the time being the Hess affair was pushed into the background. On 23 May, however, Ambassador Halifax reported from Washington that Stalin was willing to grant large concessions to Hitler at the coming economic negotiations. The rumours about preparations for a Wehrmacht attack might only be a means of pressure applied by Berlin. In the end, the Germans would not only be given a licence to march through the Soviet Union into India but also concessions in the Ukrainian granaries and in the Baku oil fields.[41]

On 1 June, Rome radio even announced the imminent conclusion of a German–Russian military alliance. As a result, Ambassador Cripps was recalled in panic from Moscow to London. Faced with the danger of an alliance between Hitler and Stalin directed against the West, Churchill decided to initiate, alongside the bogus negotiations with Hess, a rapprochement with Russia through diplomatic channels.[42]

On 2 June 1971, Foreign Secretary Eden met the Soviet Ambassador in London again, after a long interval, and on 10 and 13 June they met for a second and third time. The Englishman urged a political understanding with increasing force. He offered economic and military assistance in the event of a German attack, but Stalin remained unmoved. He appeared neither to believe the British offers nor to wish to present Hitler with an excuse for attack.

The British Secret Service had meanwhile come to the conclusion that, if Germany were to attack, the spearhead of German armour would reach Moscow within four to six weeks. After a further four to six weeks, they could turn in their tracks and begin the invasion of Britain. London's view was, therefore, that a German–Russian war was not entirely advantageous. On the other hand, the Secret Service recognized that in such an event Germany would have to split its army, restrict its air attacks on the Atlantic convoys and the British homeland, and reduce the number of its fighter planes on the Western Front. It would become militarily weaker in the critical theatres of the Middle East and North África. A German–Russian war had therefore its good aspects for Britain,[43] and there is no doubt that Churchill was more impressed by these considerations.

While the Anglo–Russian attempts at rapprochement got under way, and London was beginning to comprehend all the implications of a German–Russian conflict, Simon met Hess on 9 June under the pretence of negotiating a German–British understanding. The result was a four-point declaration, which summarized the former Deputy Führer's ideas on peace. This was a document signed personally by Hess which could be shown to the Russians. Since, at least, it included the general statement[44] that Germany claimed supremacy over Europe, it would frighten Stalin. However, during his discussion with Simon the Deputy Führer had not spoken of war against Russia but only of an 'agreement' with Russia – as if he wished to keep open the possibility of a peaceful solution to the German–Russian problem. Simon rightly concluded from this that Germany wanted no significantly prolonged war. But this was precisely the opposite of what Churchill wanted.

Cadogan found 'very interesting' what Simon had to tell him later about his discussion with Hess.[45] He had no doubt that

Hess spoke the truth when he referred to Hitler's wish for peace – 'however strange this may be'. But the ex-Deputy Führer had not passed the decisive test: Hess did not go beyond the four-point declaration. He did not allow himself to be misused as a willing tool in Churchill's sinister attempt to stir up Stalin against Hitler. 'In his present mental and nervous state, he would be quite incapable of playing any part', Simon believed. Hess lacked 'the cool, cold mentality of a clever agent' in the British interest. Cadogan concluded from this: 'Nothing more can therefore be done along those lines, and when we have followed them to their conclusion we must decide how to exploit Hess [in relation to Russia – W.R.H.] – by deceit . . .'.

In order to consummate the 'bluff' of a bogus Anglo–German peace,[46] the British Secret Service ruthlessly harassed Hess in the following days. This forced the German – torn between his desire for peace and his loyalty to Hitler – into a serious mental crisis. On 15 June, Cadogan was warned by the head of the Secret Intelligence Service that Hess was close to a nervous breakdown. The Secretary of State's icy comment was: 'I don't care very much what happens to *him*. *We* can make use of him [in relation to Russia – W.R.H.]. . .'[47]

Then, a day later, after Churchill had misused him to incite Germany and Russia to go to war, the unhappy messenger of peace tried to take his own life at Mytchett Place. In an unguarded moment, Hess jumped over the banister and fell to the stone floor of the entrance hall below. As if by a miracle, he only broke a leg. Once again the wish arose in Churchill to exercise pressure on Stalin by a public statement on the matter. His advisers, however, dissuaded him from this madness. Hess was now temporarily dead as far as Churchill was concerned. 'Not a word more about this', decided the Head of Government at a Cabinet meeting on 16 June.[48]

As long as all British and Soviet documents remain unpublished, it cannot be said with certainty whether the British submitted the four-point declaration on German–British peace to the Russians at that time. In any event, on 10 June, the day after its signature by Hess, Eden and Soviet Ambassador Maisky met again.[49] That the bogus negotiations played a part here may be assumed from Maisky's reaction. He expressly stated that Russia was not negotiating with Germany, and that Stalin would not conclude a military alliance with Hitler – the door to a rapprochement between Britain and Russia was open.[50] This broke the ice between Churchill and Stalin.

In spite of this, the British Head of Government was unsure about the outbreak of a German–Russian war until about 16 June, although he had already learned early in the month that Germany was to attack on 22 June. He also satisfied himself on the attitude Roosevelt would adopt following Hitler's aggression; this was probably the only purpose of American Ambassador Winant's journey to America in early June. But how would Russia react – would it yield at the last moment or would it fight?

After Hess had been pushed to one side by Churchill, on 16 June secret information from Moscow and Prague was received in Britain that the Russians were building new airfields on their western frontier, stocks of equipment and fuel were being built up, and existing aircraft were being replaced by new bombers and fighters. 'This indicates that the USSR is not yet ready for offensive action [i.e. an attack on Germany – W.R.H.] and, as long as it is not attacked, it is trying to avoid war for a considerable time. . .' was the Woburn Abbey diagnosis.[51] This meant, inversely: if attacked, it would fight.

Six days later, however, on 22 June, Churchill received final confirmation, if he had not already received a secret signal from Stalin. The Wehrmacht was attacking, and the Red Army was defending itself. The German–Russian war had begun and, as was soon shown, there was to be no victory for Hitler in 1941 or even later. The strictly secret Operation Hess, which *The American Mercury* not unjustly compared with the military defeat of Germany at Stalingrad, was dead.

The strategy of silence pursued, particularly at home, by Britain, in contrast to Churchill's original plans in the Hess matter, was of course a bitter disappointment to Sefton Delmer. He justly called it a 'miserable farce'.[52] Like the Prime Minister, the journalist and psychological warrior had also at first been in favour of loosening Hess's tongue to make him blab about anything that could be used in public against Hitler. To this end, Delmer even wanted to invent news, or to inject Hess with a truth drug. He would certainly have preferred that someone who 'knew how to combine authority with human warmth and charm' had negotiated with the Deputy Führer instead of the sly German-hater Kirkpatrick or the polished but frosty Lord Chancellor. He had in mind here Lord Beaverbrook, Churchill's Minister of Supply. Delmer was guided in his advice by a psychological assumption that, from the outset, had formed the basis of the entire Hess plan, i.e. that 'the easiest way to the heart of the Nazis was by flattery', even by brutal forgery. But, apart from the transmissions of 'Gustav Siegfried Eins', Delmer had to be content with the invention of a report on a forged page of a London newspaper which was foisted on the imprisoned Deputy Führer to soften him up. This report said that Frau Hess had admitted to the police in Berlin that she had mixed drugs with her husband's food. These drugs had put Rudolf Hess under the influence of British hypnotists and caused him to fly to Britain.

Never again was the enticement upon which Rudolf Hess's peace mission was based expressed so clearly. The subconscious had played a trick on the black-propaganda genius. Indeed, Delmer had disclosed indirectly who it was that Hess really wanted to negotiate with in Britain: Lord Beaverbrook.

In summer 1940, when the Führer and his Deputy opened the last peace initiative of their political lives, Berlin saw Beaverbrook as 'the only man with sufficient courage, power and influence to induce an about-turn in Britain, even against Churchill'.[53] Hitler and Hess pinned on him their hopes of eventually achieving the longed-for peace with Britain. But the questions remained: did they still intend to make war on Russia after such a peace, or would there in fact be world peace following the success of Hess's mission? These are the two crucial questions in any historical evaluation of the flight to Britain. We shall try to answer them at the end of this chapter.

As always in his political career, in 1940/41 Hitler was considering alternative ways of retaining the initiative if Britain did not make peace with him, and of safeguarding the regions of Europe already conquered against the threat of American intervention. He saw here three basic possibilities:

1. a military victory over Britain by combined operations by air and sea, either directly against the British Isles – with a landing of troops to occupy at least the most important airfields in Britain

and Ireland – or indirectly against Britain's power in the Near East and the Mediterranean;

2. the creation of a Eurasian 'Continental bloc' extending from Gibraltar in the west to Vladivostok in the Far East, including not only Japan but also the Soviet Union, which would be in a position to take up the struggle for world hegemony against the two Anglo–Saxon naval powers on a global scale;

3. a war against the Soviet Union, which would end with the destruction of the land bridge between Europe and Asia, provide Germany with the coveted raw materials of the Ukraine (grain) and the Caucasus (oil), and make it possible for the Wehrmacht to advance against the British position in the Near East, and later indeed against India.

The first two options where shattered during 1940, on the one hand by the inability of the Luftwaffe to gain air supremacy over the Atlantic and Mediterranean theatres of war, and on the other hand by Stalin's long-term intention – becoming increasingly apparent – of turning from his alliance with Hitler to a Grand Alliance with Churchill and Roosevelt. The Soviet Dictator apparently intended that this switch of coalitions, which would decide the war, was to be made when Hitler was refused peace with Britain and thus could no longer avert American interven-tion on the European Continent.

In this critical 1940 situation, therefore, when in practical terms his fate depended upon the intentions of Churchill and Stalin, Hitler could choose only between an understanding with Britain or victory over Russia, if he wished to end the war quickly with favourable results for Germany. And on this Hitler was determined from late summer 1940. In the knowledge that he would overtax Germany in the long run if he tried to safe-guard his military successes by military means alone, Hitler is reputed to have said to his Chief of Staff, Franz Halder, at this time: 'A long war is not desirable. We have achieved what is of practical use to us. The bases we have won are politically and economically sufficient.'[54]

But how was Hitler to end the war if Churchill had no wish to end it? Here, in summer 1940 after the lightning victory over France, a dangerous solution occurred to Hitler. He hoped to force Britain to make peace by a lightning war (blitzkrieg) against

Russia. He reasoned that 'if (in London) hopes are dashed as regards Russia, America will also fall by the wayside, since the collapse of Russia will be followed by an enormous increase in the value of Japan'.[55] In other words, Hitler believed that, after a joint victory over the Soviet Union, his Japanese ally would turn against the USA, which would react by refraining from intervention in Europe and, as a result, Britain would finally climb down and reach an understanding with Germany.

But for technical reasons a blitzkrieg against the Soviet Union, as provisionally planned by Hitler for autumn 1940, was impracticable within such a short time. To end the war, all that was left to Hitler, for the moment, was the understanding with Britain he had been hoping to arrange since September 1940 with the British 'peace party', either through Hess's secret negotiations or with powerful individuals such as Beaverbrook. At the same time, as a precaution, preparations for the campaign against Russia, which could not now take place before summer 1941, continued.

At the end of 1940, however, Hitler came under increasing pressure when it became clear to him that he could not put off for much longer the unresolved problems of Britain and Russia. On 17 December 1940, Hitler told General Jodl of his conviction that 'we must resolve all problems on the Continent of Europe in 1941, since from 1941 onwards the USA will be in a position to intervene'.[56] At this point, Hitler's double strategy of seeking an understanding with Britain and preparing for war against the Soviet Union moved into its decisive phase, and the outline of the Hess mission began to come into focus.

In fact, according to the few sources available to us today, certain links between Hess's preparations for his peace mission in Britain or Switzerland and the Barbarossa plan were already apparent. For the first time after a long break, Hitler received his generals on 4 November 1940 to discuss with them the preparations for the Russian campaign (codenamed 'Barbarossa'). On this occasion, he rallied them with the cry that the German Reich was categorically in a position to conquer the Soviet Union. On this very day, Hess was drafting his first farewell letter – the only one to survive – as if his intention to fly to Britain had been triggered off by Hitler's discussion with his generals.[57] We know from notes prepared later by Hess at Nuremberg what he himself thought at the time about the link between an understanding with Britain and the attack on Russia.[58]

The Deputy Führer's view was that Stalin was merely waiting for German troops to land on the British Isles and become entangled there in a long-drawn-out war against the British. Only then would Russia attack Germany. In November 1940, therefore, in a discussion on Germany's policy and conduct of the war in the coming year, Hess suggested to the Führer that he should finally abandon a landing and instead 'forestall Soviet Russia's attack, which was certainly to be expected'. Hess even believed that the prospects of an Anglo–German understanding would be 'better than before' after the outbreak of a German–Russian war. Because Britain could have no interest in seeing 'the whole of Europe falling into the Soviet sphere of influence', it would not support Russia and would so ensure a German victory, i.e. it would finally reach an understanding with Germany.

It appears, therefore, that at the end of 1940 Hess advocated the following priorities:

1. a war against Russia;
2. an understanding with Britain.

As he said in the document we have referred to, he already then planned 'to fly to Britain himself to try to initiate an understanding'. Hess is thought to have kept this secret from Hitler.

In contrast, it is more difficult to say what, at this time, Hitler's priorities were as regards Germany's policy and conduct of the war. Hess wrote laconically in the document referred to, 'It appeared that the Führer had already taken his decision' [to forestall the expected Russian attack – W.R.H.].

This is supported by the knowledge that, in a discussion with Halder on 5 December 1940, the Führer fixed the commencement of the Russian campaign for May 1941. In Winter 1940/41, therefore, Hitler also appears to have given first priority to war against Russia, rather than an understanding with Britain.

It is interesting in this context that, on the day after Hitler announced his detailed operational plans for the Russian campaign to the Commanders-in-Chief of the Army, Hess made his first serious attempt to take off in the direction of Britain. This was on 10 January 1941.

During spring 1941, however, a series of events occurred which reversed Hitler's and Hess's priorities – first, war against Russia; then, an understanding with Britain – or caused the Führer and his Deputy privately to move away from war against the Soviet Union, although externally the preparations continued. Three main events should be noted here:

1. the very wide-ranging peace offer launched in January 1941 by groups in Britain reputedly interested in an understanding with Germany (i.e. the British Secret Service) through the former League of Nations Commissioner in Danzig, Professor Carl Jakob Burckhardt;
2. the adoption of the Lease-Lend Act on 11 March 1941 by the US Congress, equivalent to a declaration of war on Germany by the USA; and
3. the neutralization of Japan by the agreement with Russia of 13 April 1941 and by Japan's negotiations with the USA on a secret alliance, which also became known in Berlin in April 1941.

The events referred to under (2) and (3) above deprived Hitler of the strategic basis for the Barbarossa project. If Japan was unwilling to join with Germany in a two-front war against the Soviet Union, the risks of a German campaign in the East become greater. More importantly, its true objective – keeping the USA out of the European theatre of war and disheartening Britain – apparently became unattainably distant as a result of Japan's secret negotiations on an alliance with the Anglo-Saxon naval powers. Moreover, if the USA was not tied down in the Far East by Japan, its assistance under the Lease-Lend Act just adopted would operate to the full benefit of Britain. In short, whereas Hitler's capacity to continue the war was weakened, Britain's was strengthened. Both events occurred in spring 1941.

In addition, there was the ostensible offer of an understanding from the British peace party. Had the moment now come to end the struggle, not only with Britain but also with the Soviet Union, by a great diplomatic effort? It appears that Hitler did in fact ask himself this question in spring 1941. An indication of this is that in the middle of February reports were accumulating in London from Stockholm and Lisbon that Hitler was planning a new peace initiative. In particular, the British Ambassador, Sir

Robert Campbell, reported on 17 February 1941 to the Foreign Office[59] that Hitler would soon declare:

1. that Germany had already gained what it needed to exist;
2. that, since Britain could not defeat Germany, continuation of the war was senseless;
3. that Germany would submit its peace proposals to an international conference, and place the blame for continuation of the war on Britain if agreement was not reached in such negotiations.

It is of course possible that these were only rumours, which were always making their spectral way through the diplomatic channels during the War. Neither is it at all certain that Hitler was prepared to submit really acceptable peace proposals to an international conference. On the other hand, at least three circumstances suggest that these reports had some substance:

1. Hitler had already said in summer 1940 that Germany had what it needed;
2. the very two documents which directly follow Campbell's report quoted above are embargoed in the British files until the year 2017;[60]
3. Hitler's and Hess's attempts to open discussions with the British peace party via Albrecht Haushofer and Carl Jakob Burckhardt entered their decisive stage long before the campaign in the East, planned for not earlier than May 1941, could begin.

I demand of the British Government that it release the two embargoed documents for publication, because they obviously contain important information on the nature, content and range of Germany's peace feelers. This also applies to the documents which follow the statement by the British Ambassador in Madrid, Sir Samuel Hoare.[61] On 6 March 1941, this British diplomat spoke of a planned 'special mission by Göring' and of Hitler's assurance that he would be considerate 'once there was peace', since it had never been his intention to fight Britain.[62] For the sake of historical truth, these documents must also be released as soon as possible.

Apart from his peace feelers directed towards Britain,

however, there is further evidence that in spring 1941 Hitler was willing to end the war – that is, not only to make peace with Britain but also to abandon any campaign in the East – and that this was his attitude towards the Soviet Union. In spring 1941, Hitler was displaying marked ambivalence. On the one hand, he entered into a new economic treaty with Stalin on 11 January 1941 which bound the Soviet Union to extensive deliveries of raw materials to the Reich, and, on the other hand, he continued to push ahead with his plans for war against the Soviet Union. Without going into detail here, it can however be said, with the Cologne historian Andreas Hillgruber, that 'in spring 1941 Hitler was in no hurry' to attack the Soviet Union.[63]

In his 1978 thesis on the various phases of the Barbarossa project, A. Beer stated that ' "colonization of the East" was the core of Hitler's policy from the beginning. But in 1941, the closer the campaign approached, the more he became aware of the enormous risks. Finally, he would have given anything to have avoided it'.[64]

The final secret of Hess's mission, so far concealed and guarded by the Western Powers as if it were their dearest possession, lies here in Hitler's now uncertain attitude towards the Russians. Let us be open about what is concealed by the embargoing of important documents, far beyond any reasonable date, and by the life imprisonment of Rudolf Hess. Not only would Hess have delivered peace with Britain to his Führer; his flight to Scotland would also have delivered world peace, because for peace with Britain Hitler would have been prepared to renounce war with the Soviet Union.

There are three important indications in support of this assumption:

1. in his discussions with Lord Chancellor Simon in 1941, the Deputy Führer continually spoke of an 'agreement' with, and never of war against, the Soviet Union;
2. Hitler fixed no definite date for the attack on the Soviet Union until 29 May (effective on 22 June) – nearly three weeks after Rudolf Hess's departure;
3. by asserting that he had left without Hitler's knowledge, Hess tried to conceal Hitler's attitude – at that time uncertain – toward the Soviet Union.

In fact, Hitler had for three weeks secretly hoped that an international peace conference would be set up on the basis of the four-point programme outlined by Hess, and he postponed his order to attack the Soviet Union during this period. The only condition he would have made for a 'real understanding' with the Western Powers, Rudolf Hess told Beaverbrook in autumn 1941, was that Britain should renounce forming a coalition against Germany and recognize the Continent of Europe as an Axis sphere of interest,[65] since before the Russian campaign Hitler had abandoned the idea of achieving world-power status. In return for the Soviet Union's surrender of a few areas to Germany – to be agreed by treaty – the world would therefore have reached its well-deserved peace in early summer 1941, a peace from which it is today further away than ever before.

But this is not what Churchill wanted.

Part II

NUREMBERG

'DO YOU REMEMBER?'

When Rudolf Hess took off from Augsburg, he had expected to remain in Britain for no longer than twenty-four hours. He had not even packed a toothbrush. Following his parachute landing and the confrontation with Hamilton, he hoped that the negotiations with the British peace party for which he had been striving could be arranged within the next seven days. But these negotiations never took place, and Hess's request for a safe-conduct from the King so that he could return to Germany was not granted. He had therefore to accept the fact that his stay in Britain would be much longer than he originally intended, and then not as a negotiating partner but as a prisoner.

Hess remained at Mytchett Place near London until June 1942, when he was moved to a former hospital, Maindiff Court, in Abergavenny, South Wales. During the first five months of his involuntary stay in Britain, he had been denied any contact with the outside world. None of his guards was allowed to speak to him about the current events of the war. For the first five weeks, Hess saw no newspapers and received no mail. He was not allowed to write letters. Only once was there a break in this wall of silence: he was told that the *Bismarck* had been sunk.

Meanwhile, Delmer's newspaper hoax about British drugs had had an effect upon the wholly isolated Hess: he became afraid of being poisoned. Before each meal, the officers of the guard had to join him at the table and taste the same food and drink. Plates and glasses were then exchanged between them.

The prisoner was also quite often given inedible food. The light was kept on in his room all night, and from time to time one of the guards checked noisily whether Hess, lying peacefully in bed, was still alive. Under such circumstances regular rest at night was impossible. When Hess noticed that the siren on the roof continually sounded air-raid warnings, while there was no sound of aircraft engines or anti-aircraft fire, he feared a plan to drive him mad.

It is probable that the authorities responsible for his internment conducted this subtle terror only to substantiate the widespread public impression that Hess was in fact mad. Nutritional defects soon caused him to suffer stubborn constipation and urinary retention. When he resisted forced catheterism without local anaesthesia, one of the guards holding him down said: 'Now we are treating you like the Gestapo treats people in Germany. . .'. The doctor smiled sadistically.[1]

Since Hess was not forced to work, he had enough time to keep a diary and to ponder on various matters. He filled no fewer than 15 notebooks with observations on his state of health. He prepared notes on his flight to Britain and, once he was allowed to read newspapers again, on various political problems such as socialism, Germany's reconstruction after the War, the Atlantic Charter and the atomic bomb. He collected cuttings from the London *Times* and passages from books, and he sketched buildings from memory. He also enjoyed good literature and books on history and biology.[2] Hess's hopes were temporarily rekindled in early September 1941 when Lord Beaverbrook wrote to him. Before flying to Moscow to negotiate on arms supplies with Stalin, Churchill's Minister of Supply wanted to form a personal impression of Hess. It was rightly assumed in London that, from a mixture of curiosity and suspicion, the Soviet Dictator would be interested in the fate of the former Deputy Führer. To avoid making Roosevelt suspicious, Beaverbrook announced his visit to Hess under the cover-name 'Dr Livingstone'. It was the old trick of the bogus psychiatrist which Hess already knew from Simon's visit.

Like the conversations that Hess had with Hamilton, Kirkpatrick and Simon, there is an account in the British files of his 75-minute talk with Beaverbrook.[3] Beaverbrook's impression after the talk was, correctly, that Hess had come to Britain under the conviction that 'an anti-Churchill Government could be set up from among a small group of British aristocrats, which would make peace with Germany and would have been welcomed by a majority of the British'.[4] Hess is also said to have spoken of a German–British war against Russia. In fact, he believed that 'a British victory (over Germany) would be a victory for the Bolsheviks also. A victory for Bolshevism would sooner or later mean their penetration into Germany and the rest of Europe'.[5] He was unfortunately to be proved right in this prediction.

Until the turn of 1941/42, when the German attack on Russia was brought to a halt just short of Moscow in the freezing winter, Hess was fighting against what he saw as his scandalous conditions of detention. He wrote several letters to King George VI and the British Government, demanding, for example, the appointment of an independent commission of investigation. Hess pointed out that he had come on his own initiative, unarmed, relying entirely on British fairness, and he was entitled to expect decent treatment. He had meanwhile given up hope of release.

In January 1942, however, Hess suddenly withdrew his complaints, and asserted that his suspicions of poison in his food and drink resulted from auto-suggestion. We do not know what caused him to change his mind. It appears that, after this, Hess ceased using the services of the Swiss Ambassador, Dr Hans Frölicher, who until then had acted as his courier with the British Government.

From 1941, Hess was allowed to write to his wife and to his friend Karl Haushofer. It is alleged that he also addressed a letter to Adolf Hitler.[6] Hess began the letter with five lines from a Goethe poem: 'There are eternal, merciless and mighty laws which demand that we all complete the orbits of our existence. . .'. The lines expressed his acceptance of his fate. Hess swore his unshakable loyalty to National Socialism and his devotion to the Führer. It appears that basically he had resigned himself to the fact that his life was at an end, since he expressed his conviction that 'my flight, in spite of or even to some extent because of my death will contribute to peace and reconciliation with Britain'.

What made it possible for Hess to survive in spite of everything was his awareness that he had accomplished a great deed by his own determination. He did not see himself as a failure, but as a person of historical importance. In a letter of 20 May 1942 written to Haushofer, Hess recalled a lecture given by Haushofer after the First World War at Munich University on the Prussian military reformer Gneisenau. His fatherly friend had commented by quoting his own verse: 'Let the waves surge and roar, life or death is at stake. Whether you fail or succeed, always remain your own pilot.' To these lines, almost prophetic in retrospect, Hess added the comment: 'It cannot be denied that *I* myself was the pilot. In this respect I certainly cannot reproach myself. At least *I* was in control.' The letter continued, obscurely, referring perhaps to external manipulation of his will at the time of his departure: 'You know of course as well as I do that the compass by which we direct our course is influenced by forces that operate unerringly, although we may not recognize them.'[7]

The first letters Hess wrote to his wife sound in no way agitated or particularly sorrowful, but were in general as casual as if he had something to say for which he had not had time before his flight. From what source did this man draw his Stoic serenity? The hope of a speedy reunion appeared somehow to be still alive in him. He congratulated himself on his good fortune in that he had not begun his trial flights in the Me 110 in the neighbourhood of Berlin – since then Hitler would probably have found out about them and forbidden him to fly once and for all.

Hess was concerned about the fight against cancer. He enthused about mountains, and interested himself in the development of his only child, Wolf Rüdiger, who had now reached school age. 'How happy I am made by any little detail you tell me about your immediate circle', wrote Hess to his wife. 'Go on writing like this! It gives me much more than could anything else. I already know what you are *thinking*. And you know that my thoughts move in the same direction, even though we do not write about them. . .'.

Silence gradually surrounded Rudolf Hess. His fate slipped more and more into oblivion under the pressure of the events of war. But in summer 1942 a press report suddenly created much disquiet.[8] It was alleged that Frau Hess had recently visited her husband and had lived with him for several weeks at Mytchett Place. This had been in return for a peace offer which Ilse Hess had secretly brought with her to Britain on behalf of certain German and American business circles.

According to this report, the leading National Socialists were willing to withdraw into private life, to depose Hitler and to dissolve the NSDAP if the Western Powers would content themselves with restoring the status quo ante, as it was before the outbreak of war. Although this report more reflected Stalin's worry about a separate German–British peace – perhaps it was Soviet-inspired – it led to a question in Parliament on 20 October 1942 by the Conservative member Richard Law. A Foreign Office representative, answering this, denied that there was any truth in it whatsoever.

In winter 1942/43, the position on the Eastern Front was obscure, although in November 1942 Stalin's Red Army had succeeded in encircling Hitler's 6th Army at Stalingrad, and by January 1943 had wiped it out. The Führer lost here nearly 200,000 men, as well as the myth of his infallibility. The German front on the Don also disintegrated and the Russians were able to establish a land bridge to Leningrad, which had been cut off for 17 months. But in spring 1943 the Wehrmacht re-established its old front of 1941 between the Donets and the Dnieper.

Meanwhile, in November 1942, American and British troops under the command of US General Dwight D Eisenhower had landed in North Africa, and not in Western Europe as Stalin had steadfastly demanded. The Soviet Dictator was therefore still waiting in vain for the West's 'Second Front' against Germany, and he had not been invited by Roosevelt and Churchill to their conference in Casablanca in January 1943. Although, on this occasion, the two Western politicians initially demanded the 'unconditional surrender' of Germany, it was still possible that ultimately this would be at the expense of Russia.

Stalin manifestly feared that the Western Powers would at the last minute make a separate peace with Germany, and that to this end they might perhaps make use of Rudolf Hess, who was relatively untainted politically. In any event, in autumn 1942 Russia demanded the immediate sentencing of the former Deputy Führer as a war criminal and, to this end, the appointment of an international tribunal.[9]

Then, in late summer 1943, the indiscreet statements of Churchill's new Propaganda Minister, Brendan Bracken, created a stir in New York. First, he made it public that Hess had been firmly convinced that certain circles in Britain would topple the Churchill Government and join forces in crushing the Soviet Union. This disclosure far exceeded anything the British Government had as yet announced on the matter. It plainly ran counter to the War Cabinet's decision to maintain silence. Then – which concerned the Government in London even more – Bracken asserted that the Duke of Hamilton had met Hess in the past. This appeared to belie the words of Sinclair, the British Minister for Air, who in 1941 had denied that there had been any direct contact between the two.

Bracken was promptly reprimanded by the War Cabinet, since the citadel of silence which had been built up around the Hess case with so much effort, perseverance and success was now threatened with collapse. The American newspapers quoted Bracken's statements, and the British censorship authorities were no longer in a position to suppress similar reports in the British press. It was clear that Parliament, which Churchill had fobbed off with anodyne excuses for two years, would now ask uncomfortable questions. And what would Stalin think of the story of a British Minister speculating in America on a joint victory over Russia by Germany and Britain? Under these circumstances, the Churchill Government could no longer avoid revealing more concrete information about the Hess matter. On 20 September 1943, therefore, the Cabinet authorized the Foreign Secretary to take such action, and on 22 September 1943 Eden made a statement to the House of Commons which, for the time being, satisfied the long-accumulating curiosity of the members. He once more gave a brief account of events from Hess's landing in Scotland to Kirkpatrick's conversations with the former Deputy Führer.

In so far as they are known, Eden described Hess's peace proposals more or less correctly, which Hitler had meanwhile apparently adequately rebutted by his insatiable aggressiveness. The statement concluded emphatically, and in line with public opinion which recognized no quarter towards Germany: 'It was made clear to Hess from the beginning that no negotiations whatsoever could be conducted with Hitler or his government. From his arrival in Britain, Hess has been treated as a prisoner-of-war, and will be so treated until the end of the War.'[10]

The 'war criminals' prison at Spandau

The four Directors' room

Changing the Russian-American guard

work-break for the
soners at Spandau:
om left) Neurath, Hess,
hirach, Raeder and
nitz in the prison garden

Alone in Spandau since 1966

ss in the prison garden with the warder

Article by Wolf Rüdiger Hess in the
Daily Express of 8 March 1984

As Rudolf Hess, once Hitler's deputy, nears 90, a remarkable plea from his son

Why must they make my father a martyr?

By WOLF HESS

MY three children have a grandfather they have never met.

To arrange for them to meet him I will have to seek the permission of Britain, America, France and Russia.

For their grandfather is Rudolf Hess, now an old man of nearly 90. He has been a captive of the wartime Allies for 43 years.

Naturally, my father would like to see his grandchildren before he dies. But it is a difficult decision for all of us.

If the children visit him in jail it would have to be one at a time, for he is allowed only one visitor for one hour each month.

They would meet in a small room with a table, my father on one side, his grandchild on the other. There is a partition with a gap in the middle.

Also present would be a guard and the four directors of the jail—one from each nation — who have to witness each visit to make sure that forbidden topics are not discussed.

My father would not be allowed to embrace the children. Touching or any contact is forbidden.

DESIRE

My wife Andrea and I think it would be a bewildering experience for the children because it is very difficult to explain to them what it is all about. Our eldest daughter, Friederike, is only seven, our son Wolf Andreas is six, and Katherina is four.

Yet we are torn by the desire to bring a little joy into my father's last remaining days.

Of course, there is a simpler solution to the problem and

Family man: Hess with young Wolf

❝ Russia doesn't realise it will make him a focus for new Nazism ❞

that would be for the Western Allies—Britain, America and France—to open the gates of Spandau and set Rudolf Hess free.

These three nations have agreed for years that his imprisonment should have ended many years ago.

Only the Russians refuse to let him go, insisting that his life sentence means he must stay in Spandau until he dies.

This week I have been to the Foreign Office in London to meet Sir Ray Whitney, an Under-Secretary, to ask that Britain try once again to persuade the Russians to change their minds.

But I know in my heart that nothing will change, and time is rapidly running out for my father.

Surely, in the name of humanity, it is time for the British to take the lead and end the long torture of a very old man.

It is against all the British qualities of decency and humanity.

The Russians say that Rudolf Hess must remain in Spandau as a symbol of the defeat of Nazism, and that to release him would mean the West has gone soft on Fascism.

But I don't think they realise that by keeping him in Spandau they will make him a martyr, a focus for new Nazis and elements that we all condemn.

If they keep him in Spandau until the bitter end then that contrite prison could be used as a monument to a martyr. I don't think anybody wants that.

All we want is for my father to be allowed to spend his short remaining days with his family and to rejoin my mother. Else, in her home in Bavaria where she has loyally waited all these years.

She is now 84 and too feeble to make the monthly trip to West Berlin to visit my father.

But although she has not seen him since 1961, they remain devoted to each other.

The question always arises of what would happen if the Western Allies broke the Berlin agreements by releasing my father against the wishes of the Russians.

Would the Russians march on West Berlin over this frail old man? I hardly think so. Certainly, there would be a flurry of protests and a lot of hot air.

But I believe the controversy would soon pass and Rudolf Hess would soon be forgotten.

FIGHTING

That is what we want, too, that he simply comes home to be forgotten.

I have been fighting for my father's freedom for all my adult life, nearly 30 years. I know all about his role in the rise of Hitler. But to live to devote my life up to try to secure peace with Britain. I do not believe he wanted the war to continue.

His efforts were in vain and he has spent the rest of his life as a prisoner.

I cannot believe no matter what he did, he deserves to continue this savage punishment.

Often, I am told that my struggle is in vain, that he will never be released and that I am hanging my head against a brick wall.

Sure, there are times when it all seems futile. But I am never tempted to give up.

All I have to do is think of that lonely old man sitting alone in that dreadful prison.

The loneliest man in prison

RUDOLF HESS — Adolf Hitler's deputy and a key figure in the Nazi rise to power — was found guilty of war crimes at Nuremberg and sent to East Berlin's Spandau Prison.

He became the prison's only inmate 18 years ago when two other top Nazis, Baldur von Schirach and Albert Speer, now both dead, were freed.

He is remarkably fit for almost 90, although he has been having problems negotiating a spiral staircase in the gardens where he exercises.

So the prison authorities are spending

£48,000 as a lift to his first-floor cell . . . a strange decision since there are no empty cells in Spandau.

It takes up to 52 men to look after and guard Hess. This is sharing four ways among the wartime Allies—America, Russia, Britain and France—on a monthly rota.

The staff includes 34 armed troops, four governors, four medical officers, four cooks, four warders, four secretaries and four watch.

And it's all costing West Germany £264,000 a year.

JAMES MURRAY

Wolf Rüdiger Hess in London

This appeared to resolve the dilemma. But of course the M.P.s were unaware that Eden had withheld important details – primarily Hess's conversations with Simon and Beaverbrook and the scope for negotiation resulting from them. Understandably, the 'Russian aspect' was not referred to at all by Eden.

It was, however, strange that half of this first and only public statement on the Hess matter made by a British Government before 1945 was concerned with the role of the Duke of Hamilton, a figure who, according to the official version, had nothing at all to do with – or was only fortuitously concerned in – the whole affair. The Minister even spread the fairy-tale that Hess had tried to fly to Dungavel House on three occasions. This did not even correspond to the statement the Duke had made about Hess's arrival after his confrontation with the Deputy Führer.[11] At least, there was nothing in Eden's statement to suggest that Hess had planned his adventurous parachute descent in advance. Neither, of course, was anything disclosed about the co-operation between Hamilton and the British Secret Service.

All this is indirect confirmation that the Duke was deeply involved in the entire affair. The Churchill Government set such great value on his impeccable reputation as a loyal patriot only because it wished to hush up the role of its Secret Service.

This assumption is strengthened by the circumstance that in April 1945 Hamilton was forbidden to take part in an unofficial air-traffic conference in the USA. Information Minister Bracken was in fact afraid that the Scotsman, inexperienced in dealing with the public, would be urged by 'a horde of malicious reporters' to say something about the 'foul trick in regard to Hess'.[12] Hamilton was himself apparently afraid that he would be unable to cope with the rough interviewing methods of the New York press, since he asked Bracken for a kind of covering declaration.

The Minister therefore prepared several letters to powerful American media personalities, such as the editors of *Time* and the *Washington Post*, Luce and Meyer, in which he committed the Scottish nobleman to their care as his 'personal friend'. The text specially drafted to this end, perhaps by Hamilton himself, read: 'In connection with the Hess affair, the Duke of Hamilton's actions befitted in every respect those of a loyal active-service officer, and were of great service to His Majesty's Government. . .'.[13] Aubrey Morgan, head of British Information Services in New York, was directed personally to look after the Duke during his contacts with the press.

But Bracken then overreached himself in this unusual concern for the Scottish nobleman. The Minister suggested to Churchill that he himself should sign Hamilton's covering declaration. This was indignantly rejected by the Prime Minister on 7 April 1945. In a letter to Eden and Bracken, he wrote: 'I have never before been asked to do anything like this. The Russians are very suspicious because of the Hess affair, and I had a long argument about this with Marshal Stalin in Moscow in October; he insisted that Hess had been lured to Britain by our Secret Service.' Churchill brusquely informed his Minister: 'It is not in the public interest that the whole affair should be revived at the present time. It is therefore my wish that the Duke should not – I repeat, not – carry out this assignment (participation in the conference in the USA).'[14] Hamilton therefore had no alternative but to cancel his trip.

On 15 January 1944, Hess had written to his wife: 'I have been sitting for hours – literally – pondering on what I should write to you, and I make no progress. There is – unfortunately! – a special reason for this. Since you will sooner or later sense it or learn about in anyway, I tell you now: I have completely lost my memory; everything in the past has become blurred as if it lies behind a grey fog; I can no longer remember even the most commonplace things. Why this has happened I don't know.'[15] This was Hess's beginning of a strategically-conceived game of hide-and-seek, which was to come to its surprising end only at the Nuremberg Tribunal.

Hess's decision to pretend to have lost his memory made communication with his wife and relations more difficult, for how could he still write meaningful letters if he could remember nothing? There was a long pause in the correspondence, while the War – and so also the German Reich, Hitler and National Socialism – slowly approached its end. It is impossible to say what Rudolf Hess understood of the collapse of his world, or what he really thought, because with an eye to the censorship authorities his letters carefully avoided everything that was on his mind.

On 18 June 1945, when the capitulation of the Wehrmacht was already more than a month past, Hitler was dead and occupied

Germany had ceased to be an independent and unified state, Hess wrote to his wife:[16] 'You can imagine how often in recent weeks my thoughts have gone back to the past years – this quarter century, concentrated for us on one name, but a most beautiful human experience. The story is not ended; one fine day it will again pick up its threads, seemingly for ever torn asunder, and bind them again with steadfast consistency into a new web – the human aspect is at an end and exists only in memory.

'But only a few people, such as we two, have been allowed to participate from the beginning in the growth of a unique personality, in joy and suffering, in sorrow and hope, in hate and love, in all the manifestations of greatness – and also in all the little signs of human weakness which alone make a person completely lovable. This is why my thoughts have been much with you when I thought of him.'

The lines ended with a verse from Nietzsche, which summarizes in one image Hess's feelings at this watershed in history: 'I love all who are like heavy drops falling individually from the dark cloud hanging over Man. They herald the coming lightning and, like heralds, perish.'

After four-and-a-half years of imprisonment in Britain, on 8 October 1945 51-year-old Rudolf Hess was transferred by plane to Nuremberg, escorted by Lieutenant A.J.B. Lacombe. The Allies' proceedings against the so-called 'major war criminals' were to take place there. It was almost the same route as had been covered by the then Deputy Führer on that May evening in 1941 in his Me 110 in search of peace – except that now no peace prevailed but only feelings of hate, sorrow and vindictiveness, as is usual after total war. Apart from the clothes he was wearing, Hess did not have very much to bring to his homeland: a few notebooks, a few files of personal papers, some envelopes and a small packet of food which was once to have been produced as evidence to support his suspicions that he was being poisoned.

Like many German towns, Nuremberg was a heap of ruins in 1945. The Royal Air Force had almost completely destroyed the medieval town in its terror attacks on the German civilian population. The first plans for this bombing assault, which, with the economic blockade and the psychological war, was to wear down the Germans and incite them to revolt against their government, dated from before the Hess mission. These plans were given the discreet designation of 'morale bombing' – bombing directed against the morale of the civilian population – and, with the German extermination camps in the East and the American atomic bombs, were the most immoral aspects of the Second World War.

During the night of 30/31 March 1944, German night-fighters achieved one of their greatest victories of the entire war near Nuremberg. They inflicted true slaughter on 795 four-engined Lancaster bombers approaching Nuremberg with 2,500 tons of incendiary and high-explosive bombs. Ninety-five enemy planes were shot down, 71 were seriously damaged and 12 were forced to crash-land. The remaining 607 bombers then turned around and dropped their deadly load on Nuremberg's suburbs, Grafenberg, Igensdorf, Stöckach, Lauf, Röthenbach, Rückersdorf and Laufamholtz, where damage was extensive. Nuremberg had previously been severely damaged in August 1942 and August 1943, and the air attack of March 1944 was by no means without its effect upon the town centre. Large parts of the inner city were destroyed.

The Nuremberg of 1945 was not only the site of the former Reich Party Congresses but also the only large German town which, apart from law courts, still had a large prison available with relatively undamaged buildings. Moreover, Nuremberg was in the American Zone of Occupation. For these reasons, the Allies chose this town as the scene of their tribunal.

After his arrival, Hess was interrogated on several occasions by the American Interrogation Officer, John H. Amen. With a prisoner who pretended to have lost his memory, this of course was difficult. [17]

According to the records, the dialogue was as follows:

Amen: What is your full name?
Hess: Rudolf Hess.
Amen: And when you came to Nuremberg you brought with you various papers and documents?
Hess: I don't know.
Amen: But you already told me that the other day.
Hess: To this gentleman here (points to Colonel Amen)?
Amen: Yes.

Hess: I don't even know whether I have ever seen this gentleman before.

Amen: You mean you don't remember ever having seen me before?

Hess: No, positively not.

Amen: Don't you remember at all being interrogated after you arrived here?

Hess: Well, I must have been interrogated before because I found among my papers the statement which reads briefly somewhat as follows: 'In accordance with yesterday's interrogation, I declare that I desire no defence counsel.' I must therefore assume that I was asked about this; that is, I could not name one.

Amen: Don't you remember that you left Britain to get here?

Hess: Yes. I know that I came here from Britain.

Amen: And you don't remember what has happened since your arrival?

Hess: Well, I know I am sitting over there in a cell.

Amen: Don't you remember that I have questioned you many times since you have been here?

Hess (turning to the interpreter): You mean the gentleman who is now sitting opposite me and asking me questions?

Amen: Yes, in this very room.

Hess: I don't know.

After the American officer had recovered somewhat from his bewilderment, he went through with Hess the belongings the German had brought with him from Britain. This had to be done under the regulations. But each time Amen presented a folder, envelope or packet Hess maintained rigidly and firmly that he could not remember the contents. Not only that, he could not remember ever having seen the articles before.

Finally, the American officer came to a bag with 'Hess' written on it. Below was printed, 'On His Majesty's Service'. It contained manuscript material, and the Colonel asked Hess whether he had ever seen the documents before:

Hess: It reads here: 'I landed in Scotland on the evening of 10 May 1941.'

Amen: Is this your own handwriting?

Hess: Yes, that is my handwriting.

Amen: Do you remember writing it?

Hess: No, not at all.

Amen: And do you know whether you brought this with you from Britain?

Hess: No, I don't know.

Amen: Do you remember whether you wrote it?

Hess: No.

Amen: Do you know whether or not anything of this is correct?

Hess: What I have been reading up to now was the beginning. I can no longer remember landing in Scotland on the evening of 10 May 1941.

In fact, Rudolf Hess was not only a difficult prisoner; he had the makings of a difficult defendant.

THE TRIBUNAL

ALTHOUGH UNIQUE IN history, the Nuremberg trials did not lack a model. This was Article 227 of the 1919 Versailles Diktat which publicly accused the German Kaiser of 'the most serious viola- tion of international moral law and the sanctity of treaties', and announced the appointment of an international court of justice and the handing over to the Allies of an unnamed number of Germans as well as the Kaiser. In addition to the so-called 'War-guilt Article' (Article 231), which attributed the blame for the First World War exclusively to the Germans, the Peace Treaty, which Germany was forced to sign, also contained a sanctions clause threatening Germany with punishment. By condemning its leaders, the victorious Powers wished to deprive the guilt-laden Reich of any moral opportunity ever to revolt against the world system now established for all time.

Although earlier peace treaties had also included certain elements of Versailles, this process nevertheless had no pre- vious example. Even Bismarck had said, after the Franco- Prussian War of 1870/71 when the victorious Reich tried to fetter its arch-enemy France by reparations and the surrender of terri- tory, 'Politics must leave to Divine Providence the punishment of sovereigns and peoples for sins against moral law'. The Peace of Frankfurt of that time contained no assignment of guilt and no provisions for punishment.

But after their victory in 1919, Britain, France and the United States of America came to the opposite conclusion. Under

Articles 227 and 231 of the Versailles Diktat, they raised themselves to a God-like status as world judges, although both before and during the War they had been disputing among themselves. Because the Allies turned the matters of guilt and atonement into instruments of their world supremacy, and even surrounded this supremacy with the aura of a holy and perpetual right, they themselves created the prerequisites for the next war more than any individual provision of the Diktat, since the moral hypocrisy of victors can permanently pacify nations even less than force of arms, economic exploitation and political blackmail.

As a result, the Western Powers lived through the 1920s in the fear that in the long run the German people would not submit to this Diktat. They would eventually revolt against it politically, and if negotiations did not lead in time to more equitable terms they would once again take up arms. Torn between, on the one hand, their far-overstated claim to be, as it were, nonpartisan 'peaceful powers' and, on the other hand, their egotistical power interests, the Allies certainly tried to avert the worst by all kinds of improvised and temporary solutions. But as they never penetrated to the core of Germany's malaise – the verdict of 'Guilty', which the Germans felt to be unjust, dishonourable and therefore intolerable, and the condemnation deriving from this – they never succeeded in winning over the Germans permanently to the Western principles of international morality. Peace, therefore, remained captive between the hypocritical pusillanimity of the victors and the consuming anger of the defeated.

However, after 1919 the Western Powers wisely did not insist on the surrender of the Kaiser, his Commanders-in-Chief and his leading political advisers. In 1920, when the French representative in Berlin submitted a comprehensive 194-page list of 895 alleged war criminals, at the head of which stood Kaiser Wilhelm II who had meanwhile emigrated to Holland, the Government in The Hague refused to surrender him on the grounds that this ran counter to fundamental principles of law and the tradition of centuries. Even the Allies appeared to doubt the legality of their action, since they had justified it on political principles only. After the courageous refusal of the Netherlands Government, nothing more was heard about the surrender of the Kaiser. He died peacefully at Doorn in 1941.

The West's attempts to round off the fettering of the Germans by legalizing the controversial sanctions policy had, however, already long since commenced. Even before the First World War, leading politicians in London, Paris and Washington had denied the German Reich any claim to legality in pursuit of its interests, if necessary by force of arms. After the War, the League of Nations – a world organization set up by the West in which Britain, France and the USA called the tune, although the USA never joined the League – ensured, through the principle of 'collective security', that Germany did not have its own way politically. In contrast to its bombastic claims to embrace all peoples of the world in a spirit of co-operation and friendship, the German Reich was not accepted into the League of Nations until 1926, and the Soviet Union had to wait until 1933.

But it appeared that the Western Powers themselves did not entirely trust their own League of Nations policy, a policy which regarded war in the national interest as unjustified but war in the international interest as justified. They entered into a series of new treaties, conventions and declarations to provide permanent validity for the principles of their policy – and at the same time for their hypocritical power interests. These agreements included the Geneva Protocol of 1924, the League of Nations Assembly's Resolution of 1927 and – most important of all – the Briand–Kellogg Pact of 1928. These will be discussed in more detail below.

In fact, it could be said that all these were precautionary measures in the event that Germany's will for power, economic recovery and restoration of its standing should reawaken with all the energy, discipline and thoroughness typical of this people. But since there existed no military or economic means by which the political sentiments of a people could be successful and permanently suppressed, moral pressure was to be used to prevent once and for all this nation in the centre of Europe claiming for itself the right to take up arms and to break out of its geo-strategically endangered position. And if nevertheless it were to do so, it would meet with legally incontestable, effective and, as it were, definitive punishment.

For the leading representatives of this imperial and liberal-democratic internationalism such as Churchill and Roosevelt, the real significance of the National Socialist seizure of power was, in fact, Hitler's claim to counter the questionable justice of Versailles with a personal, German, National Socialist justice. Whatever one may think of the National Socialists' arguments, there was more to the 'struggle against Versailles' than a threat to the military, political and economic superiority that the West had secured for itself during and after the World War. Inherent in this struggle was the threat to destroy, not only in Europe but all over the world, all advances achieved in the past twenty years by the imperial and liberal-democratic internationalism of the West. This was a time bomb ticking away which would explode for ever the world supremacy of the Western Powers, if only by reason of its implications under international law.

The West's secret battle against the Third Reich during the 1930s, conducted with much artifice and using all possible means, was therefore nothing but an attempt to extinguish the smouldering fuse as quickly as possible and to overthrow Hitler. In this context, an internationally legitimized war against National Socialism was continually under consideration as a possibility, and was prepared for and striven towards in the Western capitals. The important considerations were certainly once again frontiers, raw materials and regions of ideological influence, but behind these was a struggle of quite a different dimension. This was whether the West would succeed in maintaining the structure of its world supremacy, a supremacy based on the principles of majority rule and therefore seemingly non-violent, or whether individual states, peoples or leaders were to be allowed to shatter this structure in their own interests, to institute an opposing trend in the regulation of affairs and to encroach upon, weaken or even nullify the legitimacy of the West's monopoly of sanctions. This was the end of the world which London, Paris and Washington projected onto Hitler and his – at first successful – movement.

We outlined roughly in the previous chapter the enactment of this struggle in the political arena during the 1930s and early 1940s. Although the Axis Powers emerged here as the demanding, impatient and aggressive parties, the West nevertheless played its part by its suspicion of Hitler, Mussolini and the Japanese military and of the material demands and emotional needs of the peoples they represented, preventing their development and putting them in the wrong. The result was escalation on both sides, conducted with deliberation, cunning and force, and above all with an uneven distribution of the risk of appearing before the world as the aggressor. On the part of the West, which already dominated the world's oceans, world trade, world finance, world reserves of raw materials and large sections of world opinion, this risk was of course relatively limited. Among the 'have-nots', however, it was all the greater.

By attacking Poland, Hitler had taken upon himself the odium of the aggressor, but it should not be forgotten that Britain and France then declared war on him, although they were not themselves under attack. Although they took this action on the basis of their mutual assistance pacts with Poland, the declarations were also acts of aggression. So was the Soviet Union's decision to annex the eastern part of Poland under the Hitler–Stalin Pact. Nevertheless, Hitler's opponents in the War – and later also the Japanese monarchy – could maintain with some justification that it was not they but the Third Reich that had sparked off this chain reaction of aggression. As is said even today, it had 'unleashed' the Second World War.

In so far as this means that, on 1 September 1939 at 4.50 hrs., the Wehrmacht fired the first shot against Poland, this statement is of course correct. But the truth of the 'unleashing' theory must nevertheless be questioned, for three reasons:

First, the Second World War was not initially a world war; indeed, it was to begin with not even a general European war but 'only' a war between Germany and Poland. Hitler would certainly have preferred to localize it entirely to the area between the Oder and the Bug. However, the declarations of war by Britain and France forced him to accept military conflict in the West of the Reich also, i.e. war on two fronts. It was first of all the Anglo–French plans to occupy Norway and to destroy Russia that extended the war; only then did Germany attack France.

Second, the expansion of the European war into a world war was probably contrived by Churchill and Roosevelt as much as by Hitler, Mussolini and the Japanese. It is true, of course, that if we take the commencement of world war as the German attack on Russia and the United States of America's entry into the War – both occurred in 1941 – Germany, followed by Japan, was still then the aggressor. After the Japanese attack on Pearl Harbour,

Hitler, following an old promise to his Asiatic ally, even declared war on the USA. But although the conquest of 'Lebens-raum (living space) in the East' was certainly one of Hitler's most long-standing objectives, it is the Hess affair itself which demonstrates that Churchill also was working towards war between Germany and Russia. And in summer 1941 Roosevelt put the Germans and the Japanese under such pressure as to suggest that he wanted to create the *casus belli* he had long been seeking.

Third, it is reasonable to blame Hitler for unleashing the Second World War only if it can be proved that it was he and he alone who desired, promoted or essentially caused this. Such 'proof' might still perhaps have been available at the time of the Nuremberg Tribunal, when, on the basis of a tendentious selection of German documents, the victors arrogated to themselves the authority of historical researchers. But the more access historians have gained to Allied post-war archives, the more distant they have been in time from those dreadful events. And the more they have learned of the sinister confrontation between America and the Soviet Union, which after 1945 replaced the American-German confrontation, the more have they reversed their original impressions. From the very beginning, Hitler had certainly pursued a long-term objective, i.e. the establishment of an empire on the European continent, with 'African complementary territory', which was to present a bold front to the United States of America, then aspiring to become a super-power. Nevertheless, in the light of present-day research, it can be said that only when Hitler was at the peak of his military successes in Europe, when, following the victory over France, he saw himself as the master of Russia also, did he plan a kind of 'world blitzkrieg', i.e. global war with a quick victory in the East so that he could then turn towards his real major opponent in the West, the USA, still concealing itself under the cloak of bogus neutrality. On the other hand, 'total' war, as far-reaching as possible both geographically and chronologically, and employing all their military, economic and psychological resources, had always been the aim and object of Western strategy, its true content, since it was only in such a war that the USA – the really decisive political, military and economic power of the present century – could fully develop its strategic superiority. Preparations for this occupied Roosevelt for at least as long as Hitler's preparations occupied him, i.e. from 1933 onwards. But Germany had to seek a quicker military decision, if only for strategic reasons; that is, before the United States entered the war.

Long before the outbreak of war, leading Western politicians were asserting that Hitler meant war and nothing but war, and were bringing pressure to bear on world opinion to prevent National Socialist Germany from developing its domestic and foreign policy. And when Hitler attacked Poland in 1939 this operated as further evidence in support of such assertions, although Poland itself had perhaps contributed significantly to the growing aggressiveness of the National Socialist regime. We cannot say what course history would have taken in the 1930s and 1940s if the West had granted Hitler, in good time and peacefully, what any German government could then have demanded with full justification – Austria, the Sudetenland, Danzig, the Corridor, Memel, fair partnership in raw material regions and full readmittance into the League of Nations. But a National Socialist success such as this, was, for the reasons we have described, not in the interests of Western internationalists, and events did not take this form. With the German extermination of the Jews and the Allied air attacks on the German civilian population, the world became engulfed in an orgy of war and barbarism. This was the very outcome that Rudolf Hess wished to prevent by the flight to Britain.

Although the Polish and Czechslovakian governments-in-exile in London issued a public declaration as early as November 1940 protesting against war crimes committed by the Wehrmacht, they still did not demand punishment for these offences. But in Churchill's eyes, as his statement after Rudolf Hess's landing in May 1941 showed, any leading National Socialist, whatever his personal part in the events of the war, must be seen as a 'potential war criminal' who at the end of the war could be declared by the Allies as 'simply outlawed'. As far as he was concerned, the intention to punish was predetermined.

Even before this, in March 1941, the Roosevelt Administration had declared at an Inter-American Lawyers' Association conference in Havana that all wars were not illegal simply because there was no court before which the aggressors could be brought to trial. Referring to the Briand-Kellogg Pact of 1928, it was intimated that the USA considered Hitler's war to be contrary to international law and therefore unjust. It may therefore be assumed that the personal criminalization of the German leadership, coupled with the penal provisions of the Versailles Diktat, was from the outset – i.e. without consideration of the actual events of the war and its consequent intensification by all parties involved – the intention of Roosevelt and Churchill.

We shall show here in a few sentences how this intention became consolidated in the course of time. Before the German leadership decided at the so-called Wannsee Conference of 20 January 1942 to accelerate, refine and extend to the whole of Europe the so-called 'final solution of the Jewish question', the representatives of nine governments-in-exile signed in London the Declaration of St James[1] of 13 January 1942. This elevated 'the punishment of those guilty of or responsible for these crimes in accordance with proper justice' to the status of one of the 'principal war aims' of the anti-Hitler coalition.[2]

The great importance of this conference was emphasized by the fact that Britain, the USA, the Soviet Union and the Empire States of Canada, Australia, India, New Zealand and South Africa sent observers. It was reputedly Charles de Gaulle who here referred for the first time to the 'crime of aggressive war', and laid the sole blame for the Second World War on Germany; there was as yet no kind of agreement in London and Washington on this. Moreover, it was decided to set up an Inter-Allied Conference for the 'punishment of war crimes'. Here began the early history of Nuremberg.

In October 1942, Churchill and Roosevelt invited all states at war with the Axis, which had meanwhile begun to call themselves the United Nations, to join a 'Commission of the United Nations for the Investigation of War Crimes'. Seventeen countries accepted this invitation. The Commission met for the first time in October 1943 in London. Until early 1945, however, it concerned itself almost entirely with matters of organization and principle. But the Commission then began to collect evidence against a total of (up to August 1947) 24,000 allegedly incriminated individuals (of these, 22,000 were Germans). In autumn 1944, the Commission recommended the setting up of a court of justice to try the so-called war criminals, but under the auspices of the United Nations.

The key decisions on the fate of the German Reich, its leaders and the National Socialist movement were not, however, taken by the Allies as a whole but by the major Allied Powers: the USA, Britain, the Soviet Union and later France. At the end of 1943, the Foreign Ministers of the USA, the Soviet Union and Great Britain adopted at a conference in Moscow a Declaration on German Atrocities. Under this, the 'more important criminals' were to be punished by 'joint decision of the Allied Governments'.

Then, at the end of November 1943, at the 'Big Three' Conference in Teheran, there was a personal exchange of views between Roosevelt, Churchill and Stalin. In the evening of 29 November, the three politicians attended a dinner at the Soviet Embassy. The mood was relaxed and cheerful, and drink flowed freely. Suddenly, Stalin demanded that after the war 50,000 German officers and specialists should be shot. Churchill protested, since he feared that the British public would not tolerate such action. (In fact, in April 1945 Churchill was still in favour of mass execution without trial.) Roosevelt rescued the embarrassing situation by suggesting a compromise: not 50,000 but 'only' 49,000 Germans were to be liquidated. After this pouring of oil on troubled waters, the evening resumed its pleasant progress.

Stalin's remark put a finger on a tender spot. What was to happen to the so-called war criminals? Who in fact was included in this category? What were the principles to be employed? Opinion among the Allies was long divided on this point; there was no agreement even between Britain and America. The infamous Morgenthau Plan, for example, which was to extinguish Germany as an industrial nation, envisaged summary execution of the so-called 'major war criminals' out of hand as soon as their identity had been confirmed by the Occupying Powers. President Roosevelt was at first in favour of this plan, but later he allowed himself to be turned against it by Secretary of State Hull and Secretary of War Stimson. It was with Stimson of all people that the mass-education argument played a major role: i.e. that an antecedent judicial process would have a 'greater effect on the future' than liquidation without trial. Indeed, a form of trial would be the 'most effective method . . . of displaying the Nazi terror system and the efforts of the Allies to put an end to this system, and to prevent its return'.[3] This set the *leitmotif* of an 'international tribunal' (Stimson), and when Roosevelt, under pressure from the American public, dropped the Morgenthau Plan the other Allies were also gradually won over. In October 1944, Stalin also came to favour trial before a court.

But who was to be brought before this tribunal? All National Socialists or only the so-called war criminals? Or would it be necessary once again to distinguish between 'war criminals' and 'major war criminals'? These were the next questions. In May 1944, the Commission of the United Nations had recommended the apprehension as a precaution of all leading individuals in Germany, which had yet to be defeated. It also prepared preliminary lists of 'major war criminals', headed by Hitler, Goebbels, Göring, Himmler and Streicher.

Stalin had already asked for the immediate conviction of Rudolf Hess in October 1942, but this was probably no more than an expression of his fear of a separate peace between the Western Powers and Germany, a fear which haunted him until the end – not entirely without justification. In early February 1945, at the Big Three Conference at Yalta in the Crimea, Stalin returned to the subject of Hess. The Soviet Dictator remonstrated that if what Churchill had just said were true, i.e. that all major war criminals must be shot after identification, then the former Deputy Führer should have been a dead man long ago. After this, Churchill acted as though he had changed his mind, and externally he adopted an attitude along the lines that all major war criminals would have to be brought before a court. Stalin immediately agreed, and Roosevelt agreed later. In January 1944, the American authorities set up their own War Criminals Bureau, and developed a two-stage plan for the court proceedings:

1. an international tribunal for major war criminals;
2. a whole series of subsidiary proceedings against the organization of the NSDAP and the authorities of the German Reich.

This established the basic structure of the Nuremberg trials, to which the other Allies agreed over the next two years.

On 12 April 1945 – one month after American troops under US-General Eisenhower had for the first time set foot across the

Rhine at Remagen – President Roosevelt died at Warm Springs, Georgia. On 30 April 1945 – eight days before the Wehrmacht's unconditional surrender – Adolf Hitler took his own life in the Reich Chancellery's bunker in Berlin. In July 1945 – during the Potsdam Conference – Churchill lost the first post-war parliamentary election in Britain. Each of these three events and the end of the Second World War were of course great turning points in the history of the nations concerned – indeed, in world history itself. But the Allied consultations on the future treatment of war criminals and major war criminals appeared not to be greatly influenced by these events. The consultations continued under President Harry S. Truman, Prime Minister Clement Attlee and the only survivor of the Big Three, Joseph Stalin.

Until the end, Churchill had been suspicious of the American proposal for a form of court proceedings. He did not believe it possible to give this such legal acceptability that it would convince world opinion. What if the planned verdicts on the National Socialist regime should turn into a repulsive perversion of justice on the part of the West? The danger that a purely show-trial in a beaten and demoralized Germany might spark off a change of mood in favour of the National Socialists could not be dismissed out of hand. But under pressure from the USA and under the eyes of the Soviet Union – the real victor of the Second World War – there was now no turning back. Two days after Hitler's suicide, the former US Minister of Justice and later Judge of the Supreme Court Robert H. Jackson was appointed chief American prosecutor. Four weeks later, the British appointed Sir David Maxwell Fyfe (replaced by Sir Hartley Shawcross in summer 1945) as his colleague. They were later joined by the Soviet and French chief prosecutors, General Roman Rudenko and François de Menthon. Something like an Allied prosecuting authority had now come into being, and the Nuremberg Tribunal began to take shape.

This, however, did nothing to change the fact that there was as yet no agreement on what was to be included in the indictment. Only crimes against the law of war? Or also the persecution of people on racial or religious grounds, as practised by the Third Reich since 1933?

And what about 'crimes against peace', already so often

invoked; were these independent criminal offences or did they include all other criminal acts? In fact, the legal basis of the planned tribunal was still wholly unresolved in summer 1945, and although the Allies – already disturbed by the emergent East-West conflict – then concentrated all their effort on this matter they came to no convincing conclusion.

The true foundation for the Nuremberg trials was laid at an Allied conference in London in early August 1945 – partly in parallel with the Potsdam Conference and overlapping it to the disadvantage of Germany. The Agreement on the Prosecution and Punishment of the Major War Criminals of the European Axis of 8 August 1945 then fixed Nuremberg as the location of the court, provided for the establishment of the International Military Tribunal (IMT) and contained in Article 2 the Charter of this unique 'court'. (The strange title of the agreement indicated that the USA reserved to itself the conviction of Japanese 'war criminals' under a separate tribunal. This sat from 1946 to 1948 in Tokyo, and was to bring more than 2,400 Japanese military and civilian officials to the scaffold. Italy, which had been a member of the 'European Axis', evaded common punishment, as it had in the First World War, by deserting Germany in good time.)

In London, the definition of aggressive war – the cardinal point in the legitimacy of any conceivable indictment – was the paramount issue. The Americans and the British saw quite clearly that they would be on untenable ground in the planned proceedings if a point were reached, as Jackson and Maxwell Fyfe feared it might, at which the accused Germans stated that Britain and France had declared war on Germany in 1939 and that Britain had committed an aggressive act in 1940 by laying mines in Norwegian coastal waters. This would be very damaging to the Allies' standing, and it would no longer be possible to find a definition which put the Germans in the wrong, and not the Allies, without leaving an impression of manipulation of the law.

A shaky compromise was finally agreed. The criminal offence of aggressive war was drafted so generally that, in theory, Allied aggression was included, but the jurisdiction of the Tribunal was limited to the defeated. It goes without saying that the victors did not submit themselves to the court.

This emergency solution flagrantly violated the principle of equality, which is of fundamental importance in international law. Of course, it did nothing to alter the fact that aggressive war, according to the practice of states and according to the international law applicable, is a crime, and that political leaders of a state may not be prosecuted for their political acts by a form of judicial proceedings conducted by alien states. This was and still is the position under international law. In spite of this, a clause was adopted in the IMT Charter establishing this very accountability under criminal law.

Moreover, two days before the London Agreement was signed, the Americans had dropped the first nuclear bomb in world history on the Japanese city of Hiroshima and, in breach of the non-aggression pact between the two states of 13 April 1941, the Soviets had declared war on Japan. The second and, up to now, last nuclear bomb was dropped by the Americans on 9 August on the Japanese city of Nagasaki, one day after the conclusion of the London Agreement. Directed against a nation already prostrate and defeated, this was a morally abominable and arbitrary act which claimed almost at one blow 100,000 dead and wounded. Although Article 6b of the IMT Charter included, among war crimes, the wanton destruction of towns and villages, the United States was not called to account for its deeds.

Dr Dieter Blumenwitz, Professor of National and International Law at Würzburg, established in 1974 in a legal opinion[4] that the International Military Tribunal of Nuremberg was a 'court under international law' deriving its authority from a treaty under international law, but that this did not mean that it accorded with international law or the practice of states. In fact, the objections to the legality of this 'court' could be summarized in the following twelve points:

1. The four Allies had no right to pass judgement on German nationals on German soil. Treaties under international law create rights and obligations only *inter pares* (among equals), and cannot therefore act to the detriment of or to the advantage of third states. The London Agreement established an obligation to submit themselves to the IMT; that is, only between the signatory states.
2. Germany gave none of the Four Powers authority to conclude this agreement on behalf of Germany. Neither was such

authority implied in or consequent upon the unconditional capitulation of the German land air and sea forces of 8 May 1945, referred to by the Allies themselves as purely an 'act of military surrender'.

3. Germany did not subsequently accede to the London Agreement. Neither was this situation altered by the fact that the Allied Control Commission, which in 1945 had taken over supreme authority in Germany in the name of the four victors but had not itself participated in the conclusion of the London Agreement, incorporated this Agreement into its legislation. Under the general rules of international law, the Four Powers had no authority whatsoever to act for Germany in general.

4. The General Assembly of the United Nations approved the judgements of Nuremberg under its Resolution of 11 December 1946, and so also the exercise of jurisdiction by alien states over Germans. But it did not have authority to establish norms under international law. Neither did its Resolution create any international common law, because the United Nations could not decide to submit themselves to judgement under the Statutes.

5. Moreover, the IMT Charter created no new international law, since it was limited geographically to Europe, chronologically to the Second World War and personally to the so-called major war criminals of the European Axis.

6. Neither can the judgements of Nuremberg be justified under the general principles of international law. The principle of territoriality (punishment of acts committed in the territory of the state of the court) and the passive principle of personality (only those crimes committed by foreigners against the citizens of the state of the court are punishable) recognized under international criminal law do not accord with the Charter's offence of 'crimes against peace'.

7. The protective principle of international criminal law should also not be extended to the criminal prosecution of an illicit aggressive war. The so-called Act of State Doctrine in fact says that individuals cannot be made responsible for acts openly committed by them as agents of a foreign state. Neither did the four victors rely upon their national criminal law, which might have justified application of the protective principle. Incidentally, this national law does not recognize the offence of 'crimes against peace' in the USA, the Soviet Union, Britain or France.

8. Moreover, in relation to the punishment, no general law of war could be enlisted, although the authority of belligerents to punish the opponent's war criminals after capture according to their own criminal law is recognized. This authority does not however extend to so-called 'crimes against peace'.

9. Neither should punishment result from so-called *occupatio bellica* (armed occupation). According to this, only war crimes committed during the period of occupation are punishable.

10. The IMT certainly argued that it claimed, exceptionally, legal justification in departing from the Hague Land Warfare Convention. But it failed to acknowledge the purely military nature of the German capitulation, it confused the military conquest of Germany with its annexation-like subjugation, and it did not take into consideration the special need for protection of a militarily defenceless nation.

11. The references to collective punishment by which the Nuremberg judgements were, incidentally, justified are impermissible according to the Hague Land Warfare Convention.

12. The principle of a general declaration of outlawry, as envisaged by Churchill for Hess in 1941, is not to be found in any peace settlement of the 20th century.

What is true of the Nuremberg Tribunal and its grounds for punishment as a whole is particularly true, therefore, of the offence of 'crimes against peace' – it was and still is incompatible with international law and the practice of states. The Charter of the League of Nations to which Germany belonged until 1933 contained no general prohibition of war, but only a ban on war against members, which subjected themselves in advance to the decision of certain arbitration authorities. Although the Geneva Protocol of 1924 outlawed aggressive war as a breach of international solidarity, it was never ratified by its 19 signatory states. The League of Nations Resolution of 1927, referred to above, was of moral significance only.

Did Germany's attacks on Poland, France and the Soviet Union satisfy the requirements of a 'crime against peace', at least according to the Briand–Kellogg Pact of 1928? This question must also be answered in the negative. It is true that this Pact condemned war morally as a means of resolving international disputes, but the signatory states also undertook to exclude war as an instrument of national policy in their relations with other states. The Pact had become fully effective under international law by ratification, but it did not outlaw any form of warlike use of force. Self-defence, for example, was permissible, and the states continued to be their own judges of whether the employment of military force was to be evaluated as unlawful aggression or as permissible self-defence.

The USA, which had also signed and ratified the Briand–Kellogg Pact, even considered the defence of the Western Hemisphere against intervention by external powers (the so-called Monroe Doctrine) as self-defence. The Pact accordingly even covered the defence of a sphere of interests by use of force, as Hitler had demanded in relation to Europe. Moreover, the Briand–Kellogg Pact established no penalties for politicians. It provided no form of sanctions mechanism in the event of its contravention. Under these terms also, Nuremberg could not be justified.

There had been no state practice in the 1930s and early 1940s for the conviction of individual politicians of foreign powers for conducting a policy leading to war. At the London Conference, France in fact put forward the view that, even if it were a crime for a state to conduct an aggressive war, this did not mean that those persons who had started it were criminals. In 1944, even the USA advanced the opinion that no individual liability to punishment existed for institutional rulers, i.e. politicians active in state institutions. In spite of this, Article 6 of the IMT Charter postulated individual criminal liability for crimes against peace. Professor Blumenwitz therefore comes to the conclusion:[5] 'The victors who in 1945 claimed that the Nuremberg principles were valid international law were at no time prepared to accept them as binding on themselves. Neither under general international law nor under the law of war (occupation laws and regulations) were the Four Powers entitled to convict German politicians for crimes against peace.' The same applied to the two other offences tried at Nuremberg: crimes against humanity and war crimes in the narrower sense, i.e. as a contravention of traditional rules and customs of war. Blumenwitz says:[6] 'Punishment of crimes against peace, crimes against humanity and war crimes became in 1945 the unilateral punishment of members of the defeated states, and a unilateral reservation of amnesty for members and helpers of the victors. This represented a contravention of the principle of equality and reciprocity under international law; this represented, finally, the danger that only a lost war is and always will be a crime.'

In conclusion, Professor Blumenwitz submitted yet another criminological argument against Nuremberg which is of special and topical importance in today's world, threatened as it is by nuclear extinction. The offence of 'crimes against peace' does not have the effect of deterring war, as was asserted by the Allies in 1945, but on the contrary it encourages war. Since it is directed, under the Nuremberg model, only against the defeated, it presupposes the defeat of one of the two or more combatants. To avoid this, any warring power will strive now and in the future to decide the war – however high the price might be – to his advantage.

From whatever angle we look at it, Nuremberg law was victors' law. It did not and does not accord with international law and the practice of states. It was unique. What was the point, then, in arranging for almost everything to run along the more or less well-ordered rails of judicial proceedings? Each of the Four Powers signing the London Agreement nominated a judge and an alternate. Each of the accused was given a defence counsel. Each of the accused was given a copy of the indictment 'at a suitable time' before commencement of the proceedings. Judgements had to be substantiated. But this, and the defects in the proceedings nevertheless present, did not compensate for the great flaw, overriding all else and therefore grave also in its political effect, that no justice was done at Nuremberg. Neither was peace established. It was merely a repetition of Versailles by different means.

In three respects, however, Nuremberg went beyond even Versailles. First, the Americans bound up the legally non-existent offence of 'crimes against peace' with a conspiracy theory. According to this, since the formation of the NSDAP in 1921, the National Socialist leadership had conspired against peace. Second, they accused not only the Gestapo, the SA (Storm Troopers), the SS (Blackshirts), the SD (Secret Service) and the National Socialist leadership of being 'criminal organizations', but also the German General Staff, the Supreme

Command of the Wehrmacht and the Reich Government. Not only did German history after the First World War accordingly lose its entire dignity, but the political and military élite of the German Reich since 1933 were represented as nothing more than a criminal consortium like any group of Chicago gangsters. Third, the Americans ensured that the Nuremberg Tribunal, which was to lead to a total break of the Germans with their past, was carried through to a conclusion, and did not get bogged down in its preliminaries like the Allies' similar efforts after 1919. In this respect, Nuremberg was a super-Versailles.

Even before the London Conference, the British and the Russians had submitted preliminary lists giving names of those National Socialist leaders they considered to be major war criminals. Since Hitler was no longer alive, these lists were headed by Göring, Hess and Ribbentrop. The lists were altered on various occasions, compared one with another and extended. Publication of the names before the indictment was ready caused a bitter dispute between the Americans and the Russians, which somewhat endangered the Potsdam Conference. There was finally a list of 24 politicians, military men and industrialists accused of four alleged offences in various combinations:

I. 'Common plan or conspiracy' (to commit the crimes referred to in the other counts of the indictment).
II. 'Crimes against peace'.
III. 'War crimes' (contravention of the law of war and conventions of war).
IV. 'Crimes against humanity' (inhuman acts against the civilian population in occupied territories, and persecution of people for political, racial and religious reasons).

To give a brief but informative survey of Nuremberg and its consequences, the following table sets out in detail the defendants, the charges against them, the judgements passed on them, the punishment imposed on them and – in the case of those given time sentences – the term of imprisonment.

Nuremberg and Spandau at a glance[7]

Name	Charged under count				Guilty under count				
	I	II	III	IV	I	II	III	IV	
Göring	√	√	√	√	√	√	√	√	Death (suicide)
Hess	√	√	√	√	√	√	–	–	Life imprisonment (still in prison)
Ribbentrop	√	√	√	√	√	√	√	√	Death (executed)
Ley	Suicide before commencement of proceedings								
Keitel	√	√	√	√	√	√	√	√	Death (executed)
Kaltenbrunner	√	–	√	√	–	–	√	√	Death (executed)
Rosenberg	√	√	√	√	√	√	√	√	Death (executed)
Frank	√	–	√	√	–	–	√	√	Death (executed)
Frick	√	√	√	√	–	√	√	√	Death (executed)
Streicher	√	–	–	√	–	–	–	√	Death (executed)
Funk	√	√	√	√	–	√	√	√	Life imprisonment (released 16.5.1957)
Schacht	√	√	–	–	–	–	–	–	Acquitted (released)
Krupp	Proceedings postponed								
Dönitz	√	√	√	√	–	√	√	–	10 years (released 1.10.1956)
Raeder	√	√	√	–	√	√	√	–	Life imprisonment (released 26.9.1955)
Schirach	√	–	–	√	–	–	–	√	20 years (released 1.10.1966)
Sauckel	√	√	√	√	–	–	√	√	Death (executed)
Jodl	√	√	√	√	√	√	√	√	Death (executed)
Bormann	√	–	√	√	–	–	√	√	Death (sentenced in absentia)
Papen	√	√	–	–	–	–	–	–	Acquitted (released)
Seyss-Inquart	√	√	√	√	–	√	√	√	Death (executed)
Speer	√	√	√	√	–	–	√	√	20 years (released 1.10.1966)
Neurath	√	√	√	√	√	√	√	√	15 years (released 6.11.1954)
Fritzsche	√	–	√	√	–	–	–	–	Acquitted (released)

Those of the 24 so-called war criminals whom the Western Allies had held in their prisoner-of-war camps or seized somewhere in occupied Germany were first interned in Bad Mondorf/ Luxembourg, and later transferred to Nuremberg on 12 August 1945. Schacht and Speer joined them from Burg Kransberg in the Taunus. Hess was flown in from Britain. Raeder arrived in Nuremberg from Berlin and Fritzsche from Russian captivity at the last moment before the trial commenced. After an intense search, Martin Bormann remained missing, and his uncertain fate continued to occupy journalists for decades. One of the defendants, Robert Ley, evaded the Tribunal by suicide. The proceedings against Krupp were postponed for health reasons. In effect, therefore, only 21 defendants remained to participate from beginning to end in the proceedings before the Nuremberg Military Tribunal.

One of these was Rudolf Hess. He had been charged by the Allies under all four counts. Although he remained in the Third Reich only until May 1941, the former Deputy Führer was included among those most incriminated, alongside Göring, Ribbentrop, Keitel, Rosenberg, Frick, Funk, Dönitz, Sauckel, Jodl, Seyss-Inquart, Speer and Neurath. In contrast to the others sharing his lot, however, Hess at first refused to allow himself to be represented by counsel, and Dr Günther von Rohrscheidt was assigned to his defence by the court. Hess and Rohrscheidt, however, did not establish a relationship of trust, and finally Hess asked the Munich lawyer Dr Alfred Seidl, already representing Frank, to take over his defence also.

But by then the proceedings had already commenced.

'. . . NOT GUILTY!'

On 20 November 1945 at 10.00 hrs., Marshal of the Court Charles W. Mays shouted into Room 600 of the Nuremberg Law Courts, 'Attention, the Court!' Everyone stood up – the four chief prosecutors and their deputies, the 21 defendants and their defence counsel, and the secretaries, interpreters, stenographers and journalists attending from all over the world. The judges entered – first the Frenchmen, Henry Donnedieu de Vabres and Robert Falco, in their red robes, then the Americans, Francis A. Biddle and John J. Parker, and the Britons, Geoffrey Lawrence and Norman Birkett, in simple gowns, and finally the Russians, Iola T. Nikitchenko and Aiexander F. Voltschkov, in their military uniforms.

Behind the two-row dock stood American Military Police wearing white helmets and white belts, with white truncheons in their white-gloved hands. The judges bowed slightly to the onlookers and prosecutors, and everyone resumed their seats. Since the Tribunal was conducted according to Anglo-Saxon rules of procedure, the defendants and their counsel sat facing the judges. To the left of the elevated judges' bench, the four prosecutors with their deputies and assistants had placed themselves at long tables. Opposite to them on the other side of the Court was the wooden lectern employed as a witness stand. With almost 300 people present, the artificially-lit room appeared almost overfull. The newsreel floodlights blazed and the cameras whirred. It was hot and stifling, because at first the air-conditioning was not operating. Everyone taking part in the proceedings was connected to the simultaneous interpreters by headphones, with a little device by which the desired language could be selected.

Lord Justice Lawrence opened the proceedings by declaring, as President of the Tribunal, that everyone present in the Court was required to do his duty without fear and without prejudice 'pursuant to the hallowed principles of law and justice', since millions of people were watching the proceedings. The indictment was then read. Each of the chief prosecutors then addressed the court on a different count in the indictment – Jackson on conspiracy, Shawcross on crimes against peace, Menthon on war crimes and Rudenko on crimes against humanity. This lasted five hours. The reading went on into the afternoon session, and the air was so exhausted that finally the defendants were not alone in fighting against sleep.

The first paragraphs read by Jackson made it clear from the outset that not only was the law of the victors to be administered here but that history, as seen by the victors, was to be written. He said that since the Versailles Diktat the defendants had conspired against peace. They had not only developed their strength with conspiratorial intent but had extended their aims and objectives; they had become increasingly able to threaten force and war. Finally, these aims had become so monstrous that they could no longer be attained by 'opportunistic methods' such as fraud, deceit, threat, intimidation, propaganda and the activities of the Fifth Column, but only by force of arms and aggressive war. The National Socialist conspirators had therefore, with premeditation, decided upon and unleashed their aggression by methodical violation of international treaties, agreements and guarantees. The implementation of their conspiratorial plans had led to war crimes and the violation of the conventions of war, to murder, the ill-treatment and deportation of civilians, hostages and prisoners, and to pillage, destruction and devastation, allegedly not for reasons of military necessity. The true aim of the conspirators, however, had been crimes against humanity in Germany and in the occupied territories, murder, destruction, enslavement, deportation and persecution of people, before and during the war, on political, racial and religious grounds – all this 'in execution of the plan for preparing and conducting aggressive or unlawful wars'.[1]

Since we are concerned here with the Hess case, which his counsel Alfred Seidl has described in full in his book 'The Rudolf Hess Case, 1941–1984' (Universitas Verlag, Munich, 1984), we can ignore the details in the indictment which relate to the other defendants. After it had been read, on the second day of the hearing the 21 defendants were called upon to say whether they considered themselves guilty or not guilty under the terms of the indictment. The first to be named, Hermann Göring, then stood up. He was the dominant figure in the dock. From the judges' viewpoint, he was sitting in the front row in the left-hand corner.

Göring wished to make a statement. He had not completed his first sentence when Lawrence let his gavel fall gently upon the judges' bench and interrupted Hitler's former Deputy and head of the Luftwaffe by saying that the defendants were not allowed to make statements:[2] 'You must plead guilty or not guilty.'

In answer to this, Göring, still wearing his dove-grey Luft-waffe uniform, but without medals or braid, said: 'In the terms of the indictment, I plead not guilty.'

The next in line was Rudolf Hess. He was in Seat No. 2 in the dock between Göring and Ribbentrop, Hitler's former Foreign Minister. Like the previous speaker, he was clearly emaciated. He was wearing jacket and trousers with shirt and tie, items that had been lent him. He got up briefly and said: 'No.'

All the other defendants also replied in the negative when asked whether they pleaded guilty in the terms of the indictment.

Following this, the chief prosecutors made their opening speeches, and began to present their evidence by submitting documents and by questioning witnesses. Since the proceedings were conducted predominantly on the basis of documentary evidence, the tables were finally sagging under the weight of the material. A total of 29 witnesses were heard and 2,000 documents introduced during the trial. A series of newsreels and documentary films which the Allies had collected were shown on a screen in the court.

Although the Court tried to adhere to its rules of procedure, it could scarcely be alleged that there was any equality in the arsenals of the prosecution and the defence. The prosecution was supported by staff and technical aids of all kinds, whereas the defence counsel acted mostly as lone combatants. They saw many of the incriminating documents – and the prosecutors submitted only incriminating material – too late, or only extracts of them, or in foreign-language translations. But the defence of the accused was made additionally difficult in many other respects by the rules of procedure and the practical circumstances under which the Tribunal was conducted. What was even worse for the defence counsel was, of course, that the entire tribunal contravened international law and the practice of states. This meant that it was conducted on lines to which they had to adapt in the interests of their defendants, but which were incompatible with their legal training. This led on 19 November 1945 to a submission to the Court signed by all defence counsel. In this submission, counsel conceded that, for very many years past, world opinion had, it is true, demanded with increasing force the outlawing of war. But they pointed out that 'even today' this was still 'not accepted international law'.[3]

They also pointed out that the judges had been appointed only by states which had themselves taken part in the War. They therefore requested that the Court should obtain opinions on the legality of the proceedings from internationally recognized specialists in international law. The Court, however, refused to consider this submission in detail. The reason it gave was that objection to the authority of the Nuremberg Tribunal was precluded under the IMT Charter.

Counsel then asked one of their members, Professor Dr Hermann Jahrreiss, one of the two counsel representing Colonel-General Jodl, to test this legality within the framework of his pleadings. His conclusion was of course negative, and he further considered that the Allies could not establish retroactive criminal law at Nuremberg. Finally, he spoke against the compression of German history to cover the careers of a few criminals. Although the Court appeared to be impressed by Jahrreiss's intellectual acuteness in presenting his arguments, it did not pursue them.

It was not of course easy for Seidl to defend an accused who asserted that he had lost his memory. The Court was also concerned that, in the case of Hess, public opinion might reproach it for trying a man not of completely sound mind. Hess's

[216]

appointed counsel even in fact applied for the proceedings against his client to be discontinued because he was unfit to plead. But, after the victors' specialists had examined the defendant and declared that he was fit to plead, on 30 November 1945 Rudolf Hess addressed the Court and delivered the following statement:[4]

'Mr President, I wish to state as follows: . . . In order to prevent my being declared unfit to plead, although I wish to participate in the further hearings and receive the verdict together with my comrades, I submit to the Court the following statement, although it was originally my intention to deliver it at a later point in the proceedings:

'From now onwards, my memory is once again available, even to the outside world. The reasons for my feigning loss of memory are of a tactical nature. It is true that my ability to concentrate is somewhat reduced, but my ability to follow the proceedings, to defend myself, to ask questions of witnesses or to answer questions myself is not affected by this.

'I wish to stress that I bear full responsibility for everything I have done, signed or jointly signed.

'My basic attitude, that the Court has no jurisdiction, is not affected by the above statement.

'I have so far also persisted in my loss of memory in relations with my official defence counsel. He has therefore represented this in good faith.'

This made it clear once and for all that Hess had merely simulated his loss of memory. He probably intended to make it more difficult for the victors to organize a trial he considered unjust. But Hess did not follow through his announcement that he wished to defend himself and to question witnesses. Apart from the former Minister of the Interior, Frick, he was the only defendant who did not give evidence in his own defence at Nuremberg, and apart from a final statement he did not utter one word more throughout the trial. Although he soon gained confidence in Seidl, he did not even tell his counsel whether Hitler knew in advance of his flight to Britain.

On 7 February 1946, Lt.-Colonel J.M.G. Griffith-Jones, one of the British counsel for the prosecution, began to submit evidence against Hess to show that the former Deputy Führer was guilty of the 'conspiracy against peace' charge and of contributing to aggressive war. Griffith-Jones supported his accusations by references to the important political position in the Third Reich occupied by Hess, for example as a member of the Reich Defence Council (from 20 August 1939). What the Englishman saw as important, however, was to show that Hess had had close contacts – via a liaison officer – with the Wehrmacht and – via the Foreign Organization of the NSDAP – with foreign policy. Hess was also 'connected with the anti-Jewish policy of the Nazi Government' through the Party's Office for Racial Policy.[5]

The British prosecutor finally presented a series of laws signed by Hess as a Reich Minister, such as the law combining the office of Reich President with that of Reich Chancellor, the law against malicious attacks on State and Party, and one of the Nuremberg Laws. This was also intended to provide documentary proof of Hess's prominent position in the National Socialist hierarchy.

To prove Hess's role in the preparation of aggressive war, Griffith-Jones introduced various documents, for example a speech in which Hess had included Göring's call for 'guns, not butter'. Hess was also said to have organized the Third Reich's 'Fifth Column' – by which Griffith-Jones meant the Foreign Organization. He was alleged to have played a crucial role in Austria's incorporation into the Reich by appointing a man named Reinthaler to the post of Austrian farmers' leader and by appearing in Vienna with Himmler on 12 March 1938 as one of the senior German leaders. Griffith-Jones alleged that the same applied to the surrender of the Sudetenland to the Third Reich. Both events – 'the occupation of Austria and of Czechoslovakia' – had subsequently 'unleashed' aggressive war, according to the Englishman's somewhat strange logic.

Hess had allegedly also played a decisive part in the attack on Poland. To prove this, Griffith-Jones quoted from a speech given by the then Deputy Führer on 2 August 1939 to Germans living abroad, in which he praised Hitler's patience towards Poland. Glossing over this, however, the Englishman added that the document 'at least shows that he (Hess) took part in the official propaganda hurled against the world at that time, two days before the declaration of war'.[6] After the victory over Poland, Hess had also signed regulations for the re-integration of Danzig into the Reich and for the incorporation and administration of the conquered Polish territories. Griffith-Jones himself probably considered that the material he was submitting was not very convincing, since after he had once more referred to Hess's Fifth Column, the fairly harmless National Socialist Foreign Organization, he added defiantly: 'But I maintain that he was connected in the most forceful manner with the planning and preparation of aggressive war.' But where was there evidence of this?

Griffith-Jones also submitted material intended to prove Hess's participation in war crimes and crimes against humanity. The Court itself, however, found this evidence so little impressive that it later acquitted Hess on these charges.

Finally, the British prosecutor turned to the peace mission which had taken Hess to Great Britain in May 1941. This, of course, was a delicate point, since for Griffith-Jones what was important was to prove Hess's participation in a conspiracy against, and not in favour of, peace. Indeed, he almost forgot to refer to Hess's declaration that 'Germany would be prepared to conclude peace with Britain' when he came to the Deputy Führer's conversations with Hamilton and Kirkpatrick. This was in strong contrast to the indictment, and exonerated Hess.

Griffith-Jones did not, of course, refer to the Secret Service background to the affair, nor to the conversations Lord Chancellor Simon and Minister of Supply Beaverbrook had had with Hess, nor to Churchill's disgraceful attempt to drive Stalin into war against Germany by bogus negotiations with the former Deputy Führer. Although he believed that Hess 'probably was not out for fun when he flew to Scotland' – a rather silly description of a peace mission in which Hess had risked his life – the British prosecutor made it plain that on the whole he considered the Deputy Führer's enterprise as purely and simply an attempt to ensure that Germany's rear would be in no danger when it attacked Russia.

Dr Seidl realized immediately that the 'evidence' on which it was intended to convict his client was rather thin. As concerns Counts III and IV of the indictment, scarcely anything could be established in the way of specific acts by Hess which would be sufficient for a conviction. The real danger, diagnosed Seidl, was rather the high position occupied by Hess as Hitler's deputy within the National Socialist hierarchy, since if the prosecution intended to represent the whole of the Third Reich as a band of conspirators against peace there was a danger here that Hess would be punished. Seidl therefore decided primarily to attack the legality of the Nuremberg Tribunal in order to shake the prosecution.

Three weapons were available to him for this purpose:

1. The legal tenet of *nullum crimen, nulla poena sine lege* (no person can be punished for an act not liable to punishment at the time of its commission);
2. the flagrant injustice of Versailles;
3. the secret supplementary protocol to the Hitler–Stalin Pact of 23 August 1939.

In Counts I and II of the indictment, Hess was accused of having participated in a conspiracy whose alleged aim was to conduct an aggressive war and a war in contravention of international treaties (conspiracy and crimes against peace). In fact, however, at the outbreak of war, on 1 September 1939, there was no tenet of international law under which a ' head of state, minister, general or business leader could be called to account personally and criminally by foreign powers for such actions, and brought before an international criminal court. No such legal tenet under international law exists even today, and it is extremely doubtful whether such a tenet would act as a deterrent to war. Also, since 1945 the practice of states has been completely clear-cut on this question. In no war conducted since 1945 was it even considered that the statesmen responsible might be called to account personally or criminally. If Versailles was an injustice, Seidl's argument continued, then the National Socialists' struggle against Versailles could only be lawful and in no way unlawful, as implied by the wide-ranging accusation of conspiracy against peace. But it was very soon shown that the Court was not in any way interested in entering into a discussion on Versailles. Just after the prosecutor had argued the case for the conspiracy against peace by stating that the Nazis had taken up the struggle against Versailles, it suddenly occurred to Lawrence, the British President of the Court, that 'the entire subject was in any event far too remote' to call for detailed treatment by Seidl. The Court obviously accepted the crass contradiction in the prosecution's argument, since it rejected as 'immaterial evidence' statements by leading politicians from the period before 1933 whose assistance Seidl had intended to call upon to establish the injustice of the Treaty of Versailles.

Matters were somewhat different when it came to the secret supplementary protocol. This could not be dismissed quite as easily; it shook the very foundations of the whole Tribunal, and Seidl had succeeded in discovering a witness in the former head of the German Foreign Office's legal department, Dr Friedrich Gaus. Gaus affirmed by statutory declaration that the Secret Protocol had in fact provided for the division of Poland between Germany *and* Russia. Under cross-examination by Seidl, Ribbentrop testified that Hitler and Stalin had agreed in 1939 that this division was to be effected 'by force of arms', if all attempts at a peaceful agreement between Germany and Poland failed.[7]

It was of course very embarrassing for the Russians here in Nuremberg to be suspected of being aggressors themselves. If the victors were to take seriously their demand that they should sit in judgement on the leading National Socialists, according to principles generally recognized in law, then Seidl's indication that one of the adjudicators should actually be in the dock would have serious consequences for the further progress of the proceedings. Seidl's position was further strengthened by the fact that, one day, even the text of the Secret Protocol to the Hitler–Stalin Pact and the German–Soviet Frontier and Friendship Treaty of 28 September 1939 came into his hands. (The latter treaty made provision for the Soviet Union's annexation of most of Lithuania, which had in fact occurred during the War.) Seidl was never able to discover the identity of the person who, in the corridor of the Nuremberg Law Courts, slipped these typed copies into his hands during a break in the proceedings. His guess is that it was an agent of the American Secret Service, which in 1946 perhaps had an interest in intensifying the East–West conflict already in the offing. In any case, the Munich lawyer caused a genuine world sensation when he presented the Secret Protocol and Gaus's affirmations.

The Soviet prosecutor, Rudenko, reacted at first by reminding his American, British and French colleagues that the former Allies had in any event decided at the 1945 London Conference not to discuss the politics of the victors at Nuremberg. He was also successful in preventing Seidl from giving further corroboration of his evidence to the Court. Although, in this way, the victors prevented the worst from happening – i.e. proof that at least one of the parties to the Nuremberg trial representing itself as legislator, prosecutor and judge should in fact be in the dock – the whole affair was very embarrassing to the Soviet Union. And, moreover, Seidl had vitally wounded the authority of the International Military Tribunal.

The fact that Hess kept silent throughout the trial should not be interpreted as a failure to follow the proceedings very attentively. On the contrary, he appeared to observe the behaviour of individual co-defendants very keenly, and in some respects very critically. He occasionally performed physical exercises to relax his muscles. Although Göring sometimes defended himself so cleverly and confidently that he inflicted serious rebuffs on Jackson, the American chief prosecutor, other defendants broke down in the face of the incriminating material collected by the Allies. Others tried to weave their way between condemnation as National Socialists and a certain amount of approval from the Allies because of their indications of regret. Prominent among these was Speer, the former Armaments Minister. Hess treated him with complete contempt.

A note made by Hess on the subject of Speer's behaviour at Nuremberg gives eloquent evidence of this.[8] Speer had maintained before the Court that Hitler had in no way fully exhausted the potential of the German labour force during the War. 'With this, this fake assertion', Hess commented, 'he knocks the ground from under the argument that Germany acted in the face of a national emergency when it introduced compulsory labour for foreign workers. And it doesn't even do Speer any good.'

Speer in fact maintained that, from a certain date, there had even been a surplus supply of labour. Göring and Hitler's plenipotentiary for the deployment of labour, Fritz Sauckel, commented on this at Nuremberg with the words, 'Shameless' and 'What a scoundrel!'. This Hess also noted. Göring even hoped that 'one day there will be a German court which will hang all "these people", i.e. Speer etc.', noted Hess.

Speer's decision in late 1944/early 1945 to take a million workers in the occupied western areas out of the production industries but to continue to pay them shocked Hess even more. The reason for this, Speer told the Court, was the altered situation in the war, i.e. the imminent victory of the Allies. Hess wrote indignantly: 'He is changing his attitude and to some extent working for the benefit of the Allies! Göring tells me that Speer saw a lot of him until the very last, and acted like a man specially devoted to him. A few days before the end, Speer had even flown to see the Führer to express his loyalty. And now he behaves like this! Speer incriminates one major defendant after the other.'

In early July 1946, after the hearing of evidence was completed, defence counsel began to address the Court. The first to speak was Dr Stahmer, counsel for Göring who had played the role of *primus inter pares* among the defendants. He was followed by Dr Seidl, who opened his address by saying: 'Mr President, honourable judges! When in 1918 the German armies laid down their arms after more than four years of heroic struggle, they did this trusting in President Wilson's assurances, which he had given repeatedly in 1918. In his address to Congress on 8 January 1918, the President of the United States of America had set out 14 points, including open peace treaties agreed in public.' At this point, Seidl was interrupted for the first time by President of the Court Lawrence:[9]

'Dr Seidl, as you must know, the Court has already made it clear that the matter of the 14 points and the matter of the justness of the Treaty of Versailles are immaterial. We do not intend to listen to this. You have already been told this, and many documents dealing with these subjects have been rejected.'

Seidl replied: 'Mr President, I have no intention of expressing an opinion on the question of whether the Treaty of Versailles is or is not just. I am concerned with the following: The prosecution has submitted the Treaty of Versailles in evidence. It has placed the Treaty of Versailles at the centre of the indictment, in particular in relation to Count I of the indictment. The object of my analysis is, first, did the Treaty of Versailles come into existence legally? Second, did. . .'. Once again Seidl was interrupted by Lawrence: 'I have only spoken about the injustice of the Treaty of Versailles. But it is even more immaterial to ask whether the Treaty of Versailles is or is not a legal document. We have no intention of listening to your representation that the Treaty is not a legal document. There are many points of importance to your clients which you should argue before us, and this is not one of them.'

'Mr President', replied Seidl, 'I cannot leave the Court in doubt about the fact that the Treaty of Versailles and the effects resulting from it, in particular the causal connection beteen the seizure of power by National Socialism as a consequence of the effects of the Treaty of Versailles, form an essential part of my case, and also as far as I am concerned. . .'.

'Dr Seidl!' intervened the President. 'I have told you that the Court will not listen to you if you represent that the Treaty of Versailles was not legal or was in any way unjust. We do not wish to hear you on these points.'

The Court had here struck against a central point in Seidl's defence strategy, since the Munich lawyer indeed wished to demonstrate the connection between the injustice of Versailles and Hitler's rise to power. This was a very important point, intended to invalidate the accusation that the struggle of Hitler, Hess and most of the other defendants, from as early as the 1920s, for a revision of Versailles had been a long-planned conspiracy against peace. But since the Court refused to hear Seidl on the Diktat's legal basis, he had to skip the first five pages of his manuscript. He was forced to begin his pleadings at page 6.

Seidl had scarcely pointed out that the burden of reparations laid down at Versailles threatened to overwhelm the German economy, when he was again interrupted by President of the Court Lawrence. Counsel had apparently here again touched on the forbidden subject of legality. But by this stage it was clear that the Court wished to hear nothing at all about Versailles. The President was now looking for an argument which sounded semi-convincing to throttle Seidl's pleadings. Seidl himself was now beginning to doubt whether he would be able to continue his address under these circumstances, but this he nevertheless did, continually trying to get back to Versailles.

Finally, Lawrence decided to put an end to this – for the Tribunal – lamentable exhibition by a judicial ban on further speech.

'One moment, Dr Seidl', he interjected when counsel was about to pass from page 10 to page 12. 'Dr Seidl, since you are obviously incapable of redrafting your address in such a way that it accords with the directions of the Court, the Court will not hear you further at this stage. It will carry on with the case of the next defendant. You will then have an opportunity to reformulate your statement. And you will submit your address for translation before you present it.' Lawrence thereby muzzled Hess's defence.

The Nuremberg judges were of the opinion that the justice or injustice of Versailles had nothing to do with Germany's conduct of aggressive war, nor with the war crimes and crimes against humanity with which the defendants were charged. Superficially, they were perhaps correct in this. But, first, it was the judges themselves who had established a direct connection, going back to the foundation of the NSDAP in 1921, between Versailles and the alleged conspiracy against peace with which they charged the National Socialists. And, second, neither the ideology and policies of the National Socialists nor the outbreak of war in 1939, with all its consequences, could plausibly be explained by the defence without bringing in Versailles. This was the very crux of the matter. The Nuremberg Military Tribunal wanted simply no explanation of Hitler's deeds, which was a prerequisite for a proper understanding of the defendants and might have led to lighter sentences. The Tribunal wanted draconian condemnation of the defendants, with no argument.

Seidl was therefore instructed to draft new pleadings and to submit them to the Court for examination. This he did over the next few days. Seidl delivered his manuscript, and the Court deleted quotations, allusions to the injustice of the Versailles Diktat and other parts which it considered had no bearing on the matters in hand at Nuremberg. On 25 July 1946, Hess's counsel was allowed to collect the result of the judicial censorship from the Secretary-General of the International Military Tribunal.

When he looked at the passages he was no longer permitted to present orally, Seidl found that the Court had far exceeded the original reason for its reprimand. Crucial passages on the legal importance of the Secret Supplementary Protocol to the Hitler–Stalin Pact were now also missing from pages 59 to 63. The Court had thereby overthrown the second pillar of the Hess defence.

The London publication *The Economist* summarized the Tribunal's method of simply pushing aside Seidl's unwelcome argu-

ments in the following words:[10] 'During the trial, defence lawyer Dr Seidl produced witnesses, including Baron von Weizsäcker, permanent Secretary of State in the German Foreign
Office from 1938 to 1943, who testified about a secret treaty
attached to the Nonaggression Pact and providing for territorial
partition of six European states between Germany and the
Soviet Union. The prosecution made no attempt to disprove this
evidence; nevertheless, the judgement completely ignores it.
Such silence unfortunately shows that the Nürnberg Tribunal is
only within certain limits an independent judicature. In ordi-
nary criminal law it would certainly be a remarkable case if a
judge, summing up on a charge of murder, were to avoid men-
tioning evidence on the part played by an accomplice in the
murder because the evidence revealed that the judge himself
had been that accomplice. That nobody thinks such reticence
extraordinary in the case of Nürnberg merely demonstrates how
far we still really are from anything that can be called a 'reign of
law' in international affairs.'

At this point in his draft, Seidl had initially established that the
offence of a crime against peace did not exist under the international law applicable – an opinion with which, after the end of
the Tribunal, many politicians and jurists, even on the West's
side, were to agree. But then Hess's counsel came to the vital
conclusion that the Secret Supplementary Protocol providing for
the division of Poland by force complied precisely with the
elements of this offence. Seidl therefore concluded, incisively,
that either the indictment had lost its basis as concerns the
charges of 'conspiracy against peace' and 'crimes against peace',
or 'the position is that at least one of the signatory Powers to the
London Agreement of 8 August 1945 appears in the present
proceedings not only as author of the law constituting the court,
as originator of the penal standards, as prosecutor and judge
. . . but that this one signatory power is also a participant in a
plan and a contracting party to an agreement which, under
Article 6, Para. 2a (of the IMT Charter) renders those responsible
liable to punishment'.[11]

Seidl had thereby made the central point of his pleadings the
tenet that no one can be judge in his own cause. If it had yielded
to Seidl's arguments, the Tribunal would have had to liquidate
itself, or halt the proceedings under the two disputed charges, I

and II, of the indictment, or restrict itself to considering genuine war crimes.

But the four victors had no intention whatsoever of doing this. In spite of the East–West conflict already emerging, their joint interest in a judicial condemnation of Hitler's Germany was for the moment even greater than the Western Powers' interest in putting Stalin in the wrong. In other words, in spite of all the factors that already divided them, the four victors were not prepared to allow themselves to be split by, of all people, one of the defence counsel for the so-called major war criminals. For this reason, Seidl was not allowed to present the deleted passages in his oral pleadings.

For a moment, the angry lawyer thought of using this unacceptable restriction of his rights as grounds for causing a commotion. He wanted to resign from Rudolf Hess's defence, make a suitable statement in a public session of the Tribunal, and then leave the Court slamming the door hard behind him. But Hess did not agree with this procedure. He thought that Seidl's pleadings still contained so many good points, apart from the deleted passages, that it would be a pity if they were not submitted. Göring also did his best to persuade Seidl to change his mind. Seidl therefore decided, with a heavy heart, to appear on 25 July 1946 to make his final plea for Hess.

Seidl introduced his exposition by reviewing Germany after the First World War. It was unavoidable that this part of his submission should suffer from the fact that he was not allowed to bring out sharply enough the importance of the Versailles Diktat to Germany's internal development, but he left no doubt whatsoever that many of the important circumstances – the reparations policy, increasing unemployment, the world economic crisis and the victors' failure to disarm – which led to the destruction of the Weimar Republic had been brought about by the victors of that time and of the present, and that the rise of Hitler and the NSDAP could in no way be described as a long-planned conspiracy against peace.

It was important for Seidl to establish that the so-called seizure of power in 1933, and the subsequent change in political structures in Germany by the introduction of dictatorship, had occurred entirely by legal means. Reich President Hindenburg himself had signed the crucial decree for the protection of the people and state which abolished fundamental human and civil rights, and none of the foreign states maintaining diplomatic relations with the German Reich at the time had indicated, by breaking off such relations, that they were not in agreement with these developments.

He had explained on behalf of his client, Seidl continued, that Hess accepted full responsibility for all laws and decrees signed by him in his capacity as Deputy Führer, as a Reich Minister and as a member of the Reich Defence Council. These, however, related to the internal affairs of a sovereign state, and were in no way associated with crimes against peace and the conventions of war, as the prosecution maintained. Turning to the law reintroducing general conscription, also signed by Hess, the prosecuting authorities clearly did not regard this as an independent criminal act but only as a component of their conspiracy theory. The prosecution had not succeeded in proving that Hess had built up the NSDAP's Foreign Organization into a 'Fifth Column', Seidl continued. The contrary was true; Hess had strictly forbidden it to interfere with the internal affairs of other states. Moreover, there was no causal connection between this organization and the outbreak of war.

Seidl then turned to German foreign policy under Hitler. He contested that Hess had played a leading part in the incorporation of Austria and the Sudetenland. The same applied to the outbreak of war itself, said Seidl, and he described the development of German–Polish relations and the British attempts to interfere which finally led to the outbreak of war. In this context, he briefly referred to the Secret Supplementary Protocol, without further underlining its explosive significance to the Tribunal.

Seidl then referred to the individual charges in the indictment, pointing out that the International Military Tribunal's Charter contained only three criminal offences, whereas the indictment contained four – i.e. an additional offence of conspiracy. Counsel concluded from this that the offence did not in fact exist at all, since it was the intention of the four victors that the Charter only was to be considered as the legal basis of the Nuremberg Tribunal. Nevertheless, Seidl contested in detail this accusation of conspiracy.

He was convinced that the prosecution's description of developments in Germany since 1933 rested not only upon a complete disregard of circumstances in Germany as a consequence of Versailles but also on a failure to consider the essence of any policy. When the victors failed to disarm after the First World War, as they had promised in the Convenant of the League of Nations, said Seidl, Germany had had a right to re-arm to achieve equal status. This was in no way linked with any conspiracy to unleash the Second World War. Nor was the accusation of conspiracy corroborated by the so-called Hossbach Protocol, one of the ten so-called 'key documents' submitted by the prosecution, since Hitler's time-table, referred to in this Protocol, for the military solution of his foreign policy problems did not accord with the actual course of subsequent events. 'Under these circumstances, the existence of a specific and clearly defined plan seems very unlikely for a person like Adolf Hitler', maintained Seidl.

Moreover, there was no other document in the indictment referring to a common conspiracy between the Reich government, the NSDAP leadership and the Wehrmacht, continued Seidl. The power of the Third Reich had been exclusively in the hands of Hitler. For this reason alone, there was no place for an assumption that a common conspiracy had ever existed.

Since the prosecution had referred to a number of discussions and decisions as of evidentiary value in proving that such plans had existed, Seidl particularly emphasized that Hess had participated in none of these discussions and decisions. He was not present on 23 May, 22 August, or 23 November 1939, when Hitler explained his plan of attack to Wehrmacht commanders. Neither did Hess have any part in the *Barbarossa* directive for the attack on Russia. The same was true of discussions on 4 April and 2 May 1941.

If it was borne in mind that Hess had been Deputy Führer, it could be concluded from these facts alone that a conspiracy in the form alleged by the prosecution had in no way existed, counsel declared. Neither had any evidence come to light as yet to show that the German Supreme Command 'had an all-embracing strategic plan'. Again, there was no evidence of a common strategic plan between Japan and Germany. Even among Hitler's closest circle, there was no agreement on the next steps in the individual stages of the war.

[229]

Apart from the unleasing of war, the prosecution had claimed that the annexation of certain regions was an objective of the alleged conspiracy. But in Seidl's opinion the existence of such a plan could not be inferred, either from the incorporation of Austria or the annexation of the Sudeten–German regions into the Reich. In addition, both regional gains had come about not by war, but in one case by plebiscite and in the other under the Munich agreement between Germany, Italy, Britain and France.

Seidl complained that the prosecution had expressed itself very vaguely on the appropriation of *Lebensraum*, one of Hitler's oldest and most disputed aims. The matter of more *Lebensraum* depended simply upon the size of the given territory and the population of the state concerned, and in the case of Germany this relationship had been particularly unfavourable. Even in 1943, there was still no unanimous view among the leaders of the Third Reich on how this problem could be resolved. Moreover, Rudolf Hess was one of those who as late as 1936 wished to solve Germany's territorial problems by the acquisition of colonies.

In his legal dissection of the indictment, Seidl did not hesitate to criticize sharply the International Military Tribunal's Charter. He had already in some respects anticipated the objections later expressed by Professor Blumenwitz, for example. In some areas, Seidl added his own emphasis. He considered the self-enacted claim of the International Military Tribunal further to develop international law as incompatible with the penal code of almost all civilized states. Seidl also dismissed the attempt to convict Hess of conspiracy to commit war crimes and crimes against humanity on the basis of two – in themselves not very convincing – documents.[12]

Seidl also submitted that it was impossible to declare Hess a member of a criminal organization and to condemn him for it, although he could personally be charged with no punishable acts whatsoever. Hess had been *Obergruppenführer* (Chief Section Leader) in the SA and the SS, two organizations not declared criminal by the four victors. In the defendant's case, however, his rank had been of a purely honorary nature. Seidl also said that, as a member of the Reich Government, Rudolf Hess had conducted himself irreproachably – quite apart from the fact that the Cabinet did not meet after 1937.

Seidl finally spoke of Rudolf Hess's flight to Scotland. This flight had been a 'sacrifice', and relieved Hess from any accusation of having driven the German people into war. If there had been anything like a 'conspiracy' – Seidl assumed here that the Tribunal would come to a conclusion differing from his own – then this peace mission proved that Hess had withdrawn from such a conspiracy. If this withdrawal was in itself grounds for not punishing Hess, then he could in no way be made responsible for those acts of war which occurred after his flight to Britain. In the opinion of Seidl, who again supported his case by the statement made by Hess's former secretary, Fräulein Hildegard Fath, the former Deputy Führer had also had no knowledge of the imminent attack on Russia. The British prosecutor's argument that Hess's peace negotiations with Britain were designed merely to secure Hitler's rear for a new war therefore collapsed.

Seidl asked the judges to consider whether it would really serve the cause of peace if the Nuremberg Tribunal put itself in fundamental conflict with the accepted legal principles of all civilized peoples. In particular, contravention of the generally acknowledged principle of *nulla poene sine lege* (no act can be punishable for which there was no corresponding law at the time of the act) throws doubt on the concept of justice in general. Counsel refrained from demanding acquittal for his client in the terms of the indictment, but urged the International Military Tribunal to consider as grounds for its verdict 'only the international law actually applicable at the time of the act'.[13] This concluded Alfred Seidl's address.

The court adjourned.

The prosecution then presented its concluding speeches directed against the individual defendants. The American, Jackson, reaffirmed his conspiracy theory. The Englishman, Shawcross, emphasized the moral aspect of the proceedings. The Frenchmen demanded severe penalties. The Russian, Rudenko, considered that the hour of reckoning had struck. After this, the machinery of the trial started up again to convict the defendants of membership of 'criminal organizations' such as the Reich Government, the leadership of the Wehrmacht, the leadership of the NSDAP, the Gestapo, the SA, the SS and the SD. Although behind the scenes there had been a violent tug-of-war between judges and prosecutors about whether such proceedings against organizations were in any way legally meaningful and useful, the taking of evidence recommenced. The court thus consciously disregarded all the misgivings advanced. Finally, addresses to the court were resumed.

On 31 August, the defendants made their final statements. Göring, Ribbentrop, Kaltenbrunner, Rosenberg, Frick, Streicher and Seyss-Inquart rejected the accusations brought against them. Schirach and Speer showed some understanding of them. Hess, who had so far maintained his stubborn silence, began a long statement. Because of his weakened state of health, he was allowed to remain seated. After twenty minutes he was interrupted by Lawrence, the President, who urged him to be brief.

Hess ended his statement with the words: 'Statements made to the Court by my counsel in my name I permitted for the sake of the future verdict of my people and for the sake of history. Only this is important to me.

'I am not defending myself against the accusers, whose right to bring charges against me and my fellow Germans I deny. I do not argue against accusations concerned with events which are domestic German matters, and therefore nothing to do with foreigners. I raise no objection to statements aimed at attacking my honour or that of the entire German people. I consider such offensive remarks by adversaries as compliments. I had the privilege of acting for many years of my life under the greatest son my country has produced in its thousand-year history. Even if I could do so, I would not wish to expunge this time from my life.

'I am happy to know that I have done my duty towards my people, my duty as a German, as a National Socialist, as a loyal follower of my Führer. I regret nothing.

'If I were standing once again at the beginning, I would act again as I acted, even though I knew that at the end I would burn at the stake. No matter what people may do, one day I shall stand before the judgement seat of God Eternal. I will justify myself to Him, and I know that He will absolve me.'[14]

The court adjourned to consider its verdict.

'ANYTHING IS POSSIBLE!'

AFTER A HEARING lasting 216 days, the verdicts at Nuremberg were pronounced on 30 September and 1 October 1946. The journalists Gerhard Gründler and Arnim von Manikowski described the scene:

'American armoured cars surround the Nuremberg Court building. The guards have been trebled. Everyone entering the building must repeatedly show his identity card. Many are frisked for weapons. On this day, the judges arrive in bullet-proof vehicles.

'All seats in the courtroom are taken. The platform is crowded. High-ranking Allied officers, invited representatives of the German Länder Governments, press representatives from all over the world and the defendants themselves look tensely at the eight judges. Journalists unable to find a seat in the courtroom sit closely packed in the German and British press rooms, following the events on loudspeakers.'[1]

The verdicts were read in two stages, the four chief judges taking turns. First came the verdicts on organizations; then on the defendants. The Reich Government, the General Staff and the SA were acquitted of the criminal association charge, but this charge was upheld, although modified, in relation to the leadership of the NSDAP, the Gestapo, the SS and the Security Service (SD).

Eighteen of the 21 defendants before the Court were found guilty on all four, or fewer, of the counts in the indictment.

(Against Martin Bormann, also found guilty, the Court had proceeded *in absentia*.) In the cases of Schacht, Papen and Fritzsche, the proceedings ended in acquittal. They were immediately released.

In announcing the individual penalties, the Court had an original idea: each of the convicted defendants was to approach the bench individually on the afternoon of 1 October. This was to avoid demonstrations. Those observing the proceedings, however, saw this process as an indirect rejection by the Allies of the collective-guilt theory feared by many Germans.

During this afternoon session, those defendants found guilty were brought up to the Court from the basement one after the other in the Nuremberg Courthouse lift. There, on the first floor, a narrow sliding door behind the empty dock in Room 600 opened, and from it the 18 men, escorted by guards, stepped individually to face their judges. Eleven times was 'death by hanging' pronounced, three terms of life imprisonment were awarded, and four defendants received shorter terms of imprisonment.

Although, of course, the Tribunal was unable to put aside its inherent defects, the judges had attempted to do justice to each individual case, and brief reasons were given for each sentence. The judgement against Hess did not follow the pattern of the others; the one-time Deputy Führer was the sole member of the defendants who – apart from 'conspiracy' – was found guilty only of 'crimes against peace'. Rudolf Hess of all people! The only one among those present who had tried to rescue peace by a personal effort! In fact, in no better way could the absurdity of the Tribunal, which basically assumed the defendants' guilt from the outset, be demonstrated.

In his book *Reaching Judgment at Nuremberg* published in 1976, the American historian Bradley F. Smith examined the Nuremberg judges' motives which led to, inter alia, the conviction of Rudolf Hess:[2] 'The surviving records throw no light on how the Court came to this peculiar conclusion, but they do indicate the process that led to the decision to sentence him to life in prison. In the preliminary session that occurred on September 2, all the Tribunal members agreed that Hess should be found guilty on Counts One and Two (conspiracy and crimes against peace) but the Western judges indicated that they harbored some hesitation about convicting him on Counts Three and Four (war crimes and crimes against humanity). Nikitchenko (the Soviet judge) also paused over these counts but was inclined toward conviction. Only the Soviet alternate, Volchkov, argued strongly that Hess be convicted on Counts Three and Four, and he cited Hess's signature on the Nuremberg decrees (the harshly discriminatory legal code against Jews established in 1935) as evidence that Hess was guilty of the mass murder of Jews – a comment that caused Biddle (the American judge) to remark in his notes that the Soviets were indeed going to be 'extreme'. When the Hess case came up for final consideration on 10 September, Falco, the French alternate, opened the consideration by arguing that he was guilty on all four counts and should receive a life sentence. Donnedieu de Vabres (the other French judge) then voted Hess guilty on Counts One and Two (conspiracy and crimes against peace) and not guilty on Counts Three and Four (war crimes and crimes against humanity), and spoke in favor of a sentence of approximately twenty years. Parker and Biddle (the American judges) advocated convicting Hess on Counts One and Two, but not on Counts Three and Four, and sentencing him to life. The two Soviet members voted him guilty on all four counts and called for a death sentence. Norman Birkett (the British judge) was not present for the vote, presumably because of his work drafting the general opinion, but Lord Justice Lawrence (the other British judge and President of the Court) held Hess guilty on all four counts and wanted him to be given a punishment of life imprisonment. Hess was therefore found guilty on Counts One and Two, but, on the basis of the rule that a two-two tie meant acquittal, he was found not guilty on Counts Three and Four, because the votes of Donnedieu de Vabres and Biddle cancelled out those of Lawrence and Nikitchenko.

'Since the Tribunal was also deadlocked on the question of an appropriate sentence, Falco recommended that first they vote on whether to impose death, then on life imprisonment, and, finally, in a term of years, with the understanding that the first sentence to receive three votes by senior members would be final. This suggestion was adopted, and the death penalty quickly lost, with Nikitchenko outvoted three to one. After an initial two-two standoff on a life sentence, Biddle's notes indicate that Nikitchenko switched his vote and joined Biddle and Lawrence to overcome Donnedieu de Vabres and a life sentence was imposed on Hess by a three to one vote. The Soviet judge presumably realized that if he had not supported a life sentence, the two-two deadlock might have been resolved by an Anglo-American compromise agreement with Donnedieu de Vabres for a sentence of twenty to thirty years.

'The voting method used in the Hess case had a number of ironic and significant consequences. By advocating this procedure, the French alternate, Falco, was able to obtain the sentence on Hess that he wanted, life imprisonment, while thwarting the effort of the senior French judge to grant him a lighter sentence. Whether Falco clearly foresaw that this would be the result of his suggestion is impossible to say, but the incident should provide a note of caution to those who are eager to assert that the judges' actions simply implemented the policies of their respective Allied governments. The subsequent Soviet reaction to the life sentence that was given to Hess points even more strongly in the same direction, for this was the only individual sentence on which the Russians issued a public dissenting opinion, and we now know not only that Nikitchenko voted for life, but that his was the deciding vote. Nikitchenko apparently had found himself in a difficult and unforeseen situation without adequate instructions when he faced the two-two deadlock and he had made the best decision he could. Only later, in conjunction with the three individual acquittals and the rulings on the High Command and the Cabinet, did the Soviet government decide to issue public dissents. The Soviet statement on the Hess case would therefore appear to have been a last-minute afterthought and no weight should be attached to the argument advanced therein when trying to trace the steps that led to the verdict and sentence, except as it points to the general views held by Soviet officials. Predictably, the dissent stressed that Hess's mission to Great Britain was part of the plan to attack the Soviet Union and it also held him guilty for contributing to the development of the SS system and the harsh occupation rules in the conquered Eastern territories. The dissent was another episode in the Soviet *idée fixe* that Hess had to be eliminated because he symbolized the threat of a Western coalition against the USSR.'

It is questionable whether Smith was correct in concluding that Hess had chiefly the Soviets to thank for his life imprisonment. After all, it was the Frenchman Falco who proposed it, against the wishes of his fellow-countryman de Vabres, and the two Americans and Lord Justice Lawrence agreed. Instead of seeking responsibility for Hess's life imprisonment simply and solely among the Soviets, Smith might also have found it among the Western Powers, since, after all, a great coalition of the victors represented by Falco, Biddle, Lawrence and Nikitchenko had voted for 'life', although it was perhaps the Russian who gave the casting vote. And had not the Russian every reason to suspect a sinister manoeuvre on the part of the West?

Hess also was led through the sliding door into the courtroom on 1 October. Two guards with white helmets, white belts and white gaiters placed themselves behind him to his right and left. Hess refused the earphones handed to him by one of the soldiers, and stood to attention. He appeared tense as he looked straight ahead with studied indifference and head raised.

'Defendant Rudolf Hess, in consideration of the crimes for which you have been found guilty, the Tribunal sentences you to life imprisonment', said Presiding Judge Lawrence in English.

Hess did not move.

One of the two military guards tapped him on the shoulder from behind. Hess relaxed his rigidity and left the courtroom.

In the evening of 1 October 1946, those sentenced to imprisonment were moved to other cells. The death sentences were carried out in the early hours of 16 October 1946. A few hours before this, Göring had succeeded in taking his own life by poison. The eleven corpses were cremated under false names in a Munich crematorium. Their ashes were strewn in the River Isar.

Rudolf Hess had awaited the verdict with great calm. It was what he had expected, since as early as 2 September 1946, nearly a month before, he had written to his wife in one of the few letters from Nuremberg that have survived: 'As to the verdict, of course, anything is possible: death, prison or asylum. Karli [i.e. Karl Haushofer, W.R.H.] once told me that the physician Dr von Gudden had told Father H. (Haushofer) that care should always be taken, unless one day lunatics seize hold of the few sane people and lock them up to be safe from them. His concern was only too justified, except that his royal lunatic on Lake Starnberg not only locked him up but carried out the "death sentence" on him.'[3] (Rudolf Hess was here referring to the mysterious deaths of Ludwig II of Bavaria and his neurologist.)

At this time, in early autumn 1946, Hess took several decisions which were to prove to be of significance to his later life. First, on the day after sentencing, he told his defence counsel Seidl that under no circumstances should he submit any petition for mercy to the Allies – however long his imprisonment might last. The lawyer has kept to this throughout, and has worked for the release of his client only by legal argument.

Hess later wrote to his wife that for the moment he did not wish to see his family. Shortly before the sentences were announced, the victors had decided that family members might visit the defendants. These visits in fact took place in most cases, the prisoners and their wives and children – separated by close-mesh wire-netting and guarded by American soldiers – sitting opposite one another for a short time without being permitted to touch or to exchange a few words in private. This procedure was very distasteful to Hess. He wrote to his wife: 'I have firmly refused to "meet" you or anyone else under circumstances I consider undignified. Between ourselves, we might perhaps say, well, we once met in Landsberg under not very pleasant circumstances. But there is a great difference between sitting beside one another for half-an-hour or an hour in a room with only a worthy German policeman in the corner, who even goes to sleep now and again, or in his nice way pretends to be asleep, and just looking at one another through a grid with guards on either side, who are certainly not asleep and above all are not worthy German policemen.'[4]

Hess acknowledged with relief that his wife and mother showed understanding for his attitude. 'I have, thank God, no need whatsoever for this "family shock" ', wrote Hess to Ilse Hess on 26 September 1946.[5] 'It is wonderful how emotionally balanced I feel – in spite of all the physical complaints which plague me from time to time and which certainly go where they belong – to the devil!'

Perhaps Hess was practising renunciation in the hope that he would soon be free again, since in the letter to his wife he dreamt of 'an island surrounded by freedom on which we live as free people among free people'. He could not of course know that for the next forty years, in practice until the end of his life, he would be sitting in Spandau. He believed in his lucky star.

And he believed that his case would very soon be unravelled before all the world. Hess wrote: 'One day, no longer distant, everything will be unravelled for you at a stroke, right back to 1941, as it will for all the others who are also suffering downright incomprehension. It will "fall away like scales from your eyes", and you will draw a boundless and happy sigh of relief, since it will then all be behind you like a nightmare.'

But meanwhile Rudolf Hess still had the nightmare of Spandau before him.

'SPECIAL TREATMENT'

FOR THE SEVEN men sentenced to imprisonment at Nuremberg, difficult times began directly after the execution of their fellow-sufferers. In the night of 16/17 October 1946, they were ordered to go to the Nuremberg prison gymnasium where the gallows stood. Here they were made to clean the place of execution of the traces left by the activities of the American executioner, John C. Woods. While doing this, they learned that an American soldier had attacked the body of Hermann Göring and beaten it with a stick. For no apparent reason, another soldier on guard abused Hess next morning through the cell door by shouting 'Schweinehund!'

Nuremberg had aroused emotions, and the death of the other eleven so-called major war criminals was undoubtedly the cause of severe mental anguish to those remaining alive. This strain was reinforced by the fact that they were now being treated as convicts. The American guards removed tables, chairs, spare underclothes, books and writing materials from their cells. In spite of the autumn cold which had already set in, the heating was turned off for 70 hours, and thereafter was turned on only for such short periods that the cells did not really become warm before it was turned off again. The prisoners shivered with cold, and they could no longer sleep properly at night.

Rudolf Hess's reaction to all this took the form of violent stomach and intestinal cramps, an attack of which he suffered on 17 October 1946 at about 18.00 hrs. He called for a doctor, but the only reply he received from the sergeant who came running in to him was that he was a prisoner and was not entitled to immediate medical care; he must wait until the American doctor made his usual rounds at about 21.00 hrs. This visit did not take place, and Hess asked to see the German doctor. He had to repeat this request seven times before the doctor came to see him at about 23.00 hrs. He had only just been told of Hess's cries for help.

After a cursory examination, Hess was promised a dose of bicarbonate of soda the next evening. When the doctor did not appear with this on the evening of 18 October, Hess asked an officer of the guard to remind him, but the officer considered that Hess was not entitled to tablets. Hess then asked to see the officer's superior. He was busy, he was told. Hess must make do without his medicine until next morning. The pains were so severe during the night that he groaned loudly, and the American soldiers who crowded to his cell door revelled in his cramps and mimicked his groans.

Although Hess was already suffering from a heavy cold and bronchitis, he was taken to an unheated cell with open window on the afternoon of 17 October – wearing only underpants and overcoat. The prisoner's protests were at first in vain, and he feared that he might develop pneumonia. Only after an hour was he given a blanket. The cell had scarcely warmed up when Hess was moved to another cell, again cold. A large hole gaped in the window-pane. Hess's request that he should be left in the heated cell because of his health was met with mockery. While Hess shivered with cold, the American guards came in at short intervals and asked ironically: 'How do you feel?' The damaged window was not repaired for an hour. Hess was moved from this cell on 20 October 1946. Again, the new cell was unheated and its window was open and broken. Hess pointed this out immediately to the duty officer, but again he had to wait for 24 hours before his request was attended to. He had the not unfounded suspicion that these were deliberate annoyances associated with 'special treatment', which he believed the Americans probably justified by 'the events that took place in Germany's concentration camps'.[1] Hess's attitude towards all this is revealing: 'Since the Nuremberg trial, I am of course aware that the treatment given to concentration camp prisoners was largely not in accordance with the prison methods of German penal institutions, and was to some extent even inhuman to the very end. But, as I explained in my final statement, I am convinced that the people responsible for this were lunatics. Moreover, I consider it very improbable that it is the intention of a large part of the American, British or French people that those responsible for inhuman treatment should be punished by inhuman treatment. I am certain that it does not accord with the wishes of the overwhelming majority that inhuman treatment should be revenged by inhuman treatment against people who can in no way be held responsible for such acts. According to the verdicts of the Court, none of the prisoners concerned have been held responsible for what occurred in the concentration camps. According to their statements, and from their very nature, it is clear to anyone who knows them intimately that they knew nothing at all about these events, or if they did they opposed them, as was established in the verdict of the Court in the case of Herr von Neurath. It is therefore inhumanly cruel to make them atone for these events by special treatment, which is in some cases contrary to the treatment of prisoners in all civilized states.'

This 'special treatment' was not only inhuman, but also in some instances grotesque. For example, after the execution of the so-called major war criminals, the Americans removed the chairs and tables from the Nuremberg cells. Hess suffered particularly from the simultaneous removal of his books and writing materials; he could no longer occupy his mind. Moreover, he had from that time onwards to eat his meals on the floor, because the mattress and blankets on his bed were so filthy that he did not want to risk soiling them even more, which was inevitable if he balanced his food bowl on his knees. Hess therefore decided to put the bowl on the floor and to sit or lie to eat. The American guard watching this through the peephole in the cell door asked him mockingly why he did not use the table.

In the autumn and winter of 1946/47, however, the greatest and most dangerous problem was of course the cold. It exposed the prisoners, already weakened, to the risk of acute and dangerous illnesses, and to long-term health damage such as rheumatism. The American prison authorities clearly disregarded these consequences, since not only did they wantonly expose Hess to cold draughts in the unheated cell but they also reduced the number of blankets provided for each prisoner from five to three, and removed the cold-insulating mats from the stone floors. They had already taken away the prisoners' warm clothing, as well as their gloves and headgear, and given them thin drill suits instead. Not even hair could still provide some warmth: the seven prisoners' hair, in so far as they had any, was cropped to a length of three millimetres.

Another problem was the supply of drinking water. At Nuremberg, the prisoners received fresh water once in the morning and once in the evening. Before the death penalties were carried out, when they were – so to say – on remand, they each had two mugs for this. When imprisonment proper began, one of the mugs was removed and the absurd regulation was introduced that any prisoner who did not hand over an empty mug at midday received no lunch.

This meant that the prisoners had to drink all their water during the morning if they wanted to eat at midday. Anyone who kept some water back to drink at midday, or even for the evening, had to go without lunch. Moreover, the one small shelf in every cell was placed directly above the open WC bowl. Anyone who, like Hess, found it unhygienic to keep his mug there had to put it on the floor.

Hygiene also left much to be desired. During the initial period, after the commencement of imprisonment proper, it was impossible for Hess to wash because his towel had been removed. Then the previously compulsory use of the prison shower once a week ceased. The chalk Hess had so far used for brushing his teeth was also taken from him. The tube of toothpaste given to him as a replacement was empty. When Hess was able to wash again, having been given a towel, he found that there was not a single nail or hook in his cell on which he could hang it. Since there was nothing else available to hang it on, such as a table or a chair, Hess had to spread his towel on the floor to dry it.

On 20 October 1946, in a petition of several pages to the prison authorities – written, in the absence of a table, mostly lying on the floor – Hess demanded under 14 points that all these deficiencies and harassments, some of them serious, should cease. The first and second points of his long list of requests reflected his yearning for physical and mental work. Since, according to the 1945 certificate of an Allied medical committee, Hess suffered from a serious heart condition, he was interested in light physical work only, such as cleaning the prison floors.

What he missed chiefly, however, was his books, writing materials, and in general the chance to study. He had borrowed books from the prison library, making extracts in pencil and notes on a variety of subjects. It was important for this to have several pencils available, since if he had only one he had to stop work while the guard took it away to sharpen it. And that could take hours. It is not known whether the petition was successful, but the Americans must gradually have shown more consideration. When in summer 1947 Hess was moved with his companions-in-misfortune to the prison at Berlin–Spandau, he brought with him extensive notes he had prepared in Nuremberg. This material, which has as yet been seen only by the American Director at Spandau, Eugene K. Bird,[2] showed Hess in a completely new role – a politician pondering on his own and Germany's future.

It appears that Hess did not carry out this work entirely unsolicited, although we still know nothing precisely in the absence of documents. In fact, there is a veil of uncertainty over Rudolf Hess's political destiny between 1944 and 1952 which reminds one in many respects of the riddles linked to his flight to Scotland. Hess had then, with Hitler's consent, undertaken a mission, which was abused by Churchill. Having learnt his lesson once and for all from that experience, Hess did not allow himself to be enticed a second time into political tightrope-walking at the transition from the Third Reich of the Second World War to the divided Germany of the post-war era.

The Allies had originally agreed on the necessity of destroying the type of state that had produced the Hitler regime. But the longer the war lasted and the more brittle the unity of the anti-Hitler coalition became, the more clearly did the differences of opinion on Germany's future emerge. In early 1942, Stalin was the first to differentiate in public between 'Hitler's clique' and the German people. And although, in public, the governments of Britain and the USA persisted undiscriminatingly in their maximum objectives of Germany's military capitulation, economic elimination and moral condemnation, certain political circles even in those countries gradually changed their views.

This change was gradually emerging among the same Conservative and financial groups in Britain which had advocated at least a temporary understanding with Hitler before the outbreak of war. But as Germany's defeats increased on all fronts, the movement among these groups towards a negotiated peace declined. At the same time, however, the British middle classes' fears of Bolshevist penetration into Central Europe increased. While Churchill insisted on the relentless destruction of National Socialist rule and Prussian militarism, those opposing his undifferentiated all-or-nothing policy began to look for alternatives. Finally, during the last weeks and months before the German collapse, even Churchill appeared to have become concerned about Stalin's growing power.

In principle, there were two possible ways of saving Europe before the division of Germany: the Western Powers could either try to encourage internal resistance against the Hitler regime, or they could support any tendencies towards schism within the National Socialist leadership – both with a view to stopping the Red Army at the eastern frontier of the Reich. Although the contacts between Britain and the German Resistance were not severed throughout the War, there was bitter and even scornful disappointment on the island – depending upon one's attitude – towards the inactivity of, chiefly, the German military. The unsuccessful attempt to assassinate Hitler on 20 July 1944 was felt to confirm this scepticism.

In contrast, the split among the Italian Fascists which led to Mussolini's overthrow and Italy's defection from the Axis in 1943 had raised hopes in Britain that something similar might happen in Germany. In July 1944, the London *Times*, always the mouthpiece of sober British power interests, spoke vaguely of a 'German counter-government'.[3] It is true, however, that the newspaper withdrew immediately, saying that, following the successful landings in Normandy (June 1944), public opinion in the West was agreed that Germany, now staggering, must be finally beaten to the ground by the exertion of even more military pressure, if only to prevent a second 'stab in the back' myth. But Churchill for his part had no wish to give Stalin any pretext for negotiating a separate peace with Germany, and London's concern about the westward advance of the Red Army remained. If the whole war was to have been worthwhile for Britain, which from time immemorial had contested any one power's supremacy on the Continent of Europe, the march of communism had to be checked one way or another before it reached the Rhine.

In this context, some circles in the British capital clearly saw it as a stroke of luck that Rudolf Hess was in custody. The erstwhile Deputy Führer had been publicly branded as a 'Nazi'. He was given top ranking on all lists of German war criminals under preparation for the Allies' Tribunal. Stalin demanded that he should be sentenced immediately. This was not without reason, as we know today, since there is an indication that certain groups within the Conservative Party – perhaps even in a roundabout way the Churchill Government itself – tried to influence their prominent prisoner behind the scenes to win him over for their own purposes.

In January 1945, the head of the SS Foreign Secret Service, Walter Schellenberg, prepared a memorandum on some information just conveyed to him from Switzerland.[4] It read: 'In discussions with members of the British House of Commons in mid-December 1944, it has been established that right-wing British politicians tried to induce Hess to take over a so-called transitional government, on the assumption that he would meet with more response among the German people than any pre-war German emigrant.'

'This project is said to have been finally abandoned because circles in the British Government and on the Left opposed the plan, and Hess himself also refused to accept it.' Schellenberg's informant was incorrect in believing that it had been agreed in Britain that Hess was not to be tried as a war criminal, but the core of the message was very probably correct. Instead of Hess, the Social Democratic group of exiles around Erich Ollenhauer went over to Britain in 1945 to govern post-war (West) Germany.

The assumption that towards the end of the war Britain tried for a second time to play Hess as a trump card against Stalin unfortunately cannot as yet be confirmed. The British archives, which should contain documentary proof of this, remain embargoed until the third millennium . . . ! But there is no doubt that this unabated interest in Hess formed the background to the political reflections which occupied the Deputy

Führer in 1946/47 at Nuremberg, and probably later at Spandau.

In any event, as soon as the American guards had provided him with a typewriter Hess began to fashion his second political career while he was still in the Nuremberg prison. He was apparently still convinced that he would leave prison a free man in the not-too-distant future. Then, he hoped, the victors would make him Germany's new Führer.

The result of his endeavours was a series of proclamations, directives and memoranda, and above all a so-called 'Bulletin No. 1'. This was to present to the world the political programme of a Hess government. It is reproduced in the book written by the former US Director of Spandau, Eugene K. Bird, and is quoted here with every reservation, since Bird has as yet refused to hand over this important document to the one-time Deputy Führer's family.[5] Hess considered that Germany's position in the early years after the Second World War was even more desperate than after the First World War in 1918/19. Nevertheless, he believed in a deliverance as in 1933. At that time, millions of Germans had given up all hope. Nonetheless, Hitler had transformed Germany's decline into resurgence. 'The change in the fate of our people would have been permanent if war had not come,' wrote Hess laconically.

Without going deeper into the pre-history and course of the Second World War, Hess drew from these events a conclusion contrasting with that of the German political parties after the First World War. The German nation could not be saved either by a struggle one against the other or by blaming one another. There would have to be a clean break with the past. All people of good will must act together to 'help solve the terrible need of the people and to start rebuilding everything from the beginning'.

In order to avoid from the outset any incorrect trends in domestic policy, Hess turned to 'the mass of my National Socialist Party members'. He did not want them 'to take any sort of revenge on those who have charged us with slander or back-biting. My wish is', continued Hess, 'that everybody now sees in the former opponent a member of the same big folk community, with the same fate, with the same needs and with the same duty. That duty is to concentrate together on great aims.'

To achieve this programme of national reconciliation under the keynote of duty, Hess saw it as very important to establish relationships as trouble-free as possible with the former Allies. Clashes with the Occupying Powers, particularly with provocative intent, were to be avoided. Only in this way could 'peace and discipline be practised'. Provocateurs were to be treated with forbearance as idiots. If the provocations were caused by foreigners, the Occupying Powers would have to intervene. Relations with them must therefore be 'fully correct. Their orders must be carried out, and the German people will be quiet and dignified', read the manifesto. 'The sooner they do this the sooner they will receive help in their hour of need – and the sooner we shall gain a lasting peace for our people.'

In order to construct the 'Fourth Reich', Hess wished to secure the release of all former Nazi leaders – provided they had not already been hanged. These included, in his opinion, primarily former members of the German Reichstag, all former Secretaries of State and former military leaders. The former Vice-President of the Reichstag, Hermann Esser, should be released from a camp near Ludwigsburg and go immediately to Munich with Hess's friend Max Hofweber. Hess's wish was that the Bavarian capital should be the future capital of the new Germany. Other leaders of the Third Reich, such as former Finance Minister Lutz Graf Schwerin von Krosigk, Messerschmidt the aircraft engineer and Hitler's former adjutant Fritz Wiedemann, also imprisoned at Nuremberg, were to report to Hess immediately. All Gauleiters and senior officials of the NSDAP were to resume their posts at once.

Germany's future was to begin there and then in 1946/7 in the Nuremberg Central Law Courts. Hess asked the Americans for a room from which he could communicate with the world about him by teleprinter, telephone and letter. He considered that all kinds of electronic apparatus, radio receivers and a radio transmitter should be made available to him without delay, so that he could address the German people. He would, of course, also need suitable rooms in Nuremberg for domestic conferences.

The new German Reichstag was to have 500 members. They were to be accommodated temporarily in barracks. As an armed force, Hess planned a constabulary equipped with light weapons such as pistols, machine pistols and machine guns, to preserve internal peace only. The former Armaments Minister Speer was to eliminate the supply crisis among the German civilian population and the soldiers returning home. So-called feeding stations were to be established everywhere, at which hot food and blankets would be available. Hess was to announce his government's programme in an address to the new Reichstag.

Hess's 'Bulletin No. 1' was also concerned about public opinion. Its organization was to be different from that of Hitler and Goebbels. 'Control of press and radio should be changed so that they speak for the majority of the people and not for a minority. It will not be controlled as it was under Hitler, where nothing appeared unless it was approved by Goebbels.'

Hess wanted to call upon German journalists directly to co-operate in the new Germany. He apparently also wished to introduce a certain degree of press freedom, writing explicitly: 'Press and radio have made attacks on former domestic and foreign opponents. They must stop this immediately. It is not their mission to keep old wounds open or to open new ones.' He apparently valued unity among the people as of primary importance. As concerns the Jews, Hess evidently feared that, now as never before, the Germans would make them responsible for all the hardships suffered. In any event, he wrote in his Bulletin: 'If Jews ask or plead or request to save themselves from the rage of the German population, and wish to go into protective camps, this should be fulfilled. In this way, everything will be done to save the Jews from acts of violence. . . . It is up to them to make their life as pleasant as possible and to their own taste within the camp. The situation in such a camp must be as humane as possible. If necessary, the Occupying Powers will have to be asked for food and other necessary items for the people in these camps.'

Turning to the graves of his comrades in misfortune, meanwhile executed, Hess envisaged guards of honour on them. He clearly did not know that their ashes had already been scattered in the River Isar. Göring, Keitel and Jodl were to have their decorations with them in their coffins. Later, all former Nazi leaders executed by the Occupying Powers were to be laid to rest in a large tomb with a common guard of honour.

It was too early for Hess to draft a complete constitution for the Fourth Reich. He apparently wished to appoint himself Führer only temporarily, since he wrote in his 'Bulletin': 'Later, the people will tell me whether they are content with my leadership and will back me up as the Führer.' No provision seems to have been made for proper elections. But Hess was not clear whether he should appoint himself 'Führer' from the beginning.

Hitler had once expressed the wish, when discussing the succession with him, that the title should continue. Hess commented on this: 'I will fulfil this wish of the Führer for a certain time, but I cannot call myself 'Führer' until I am the Führer to the whole of Germany.' In his opening address to the new Reichstag, Hess wished chiefly to remember Adolf Hitler, 'the originator and leader of the National Socialist Reich', to whom millions of Germans felt bound.

This 'Bulletin' and the draft opening address annexed to it were probably, and regrettably, proof of the loss of reality which Hess had suffered during his years of isolation. His 'Fourth Reich' was no more than a new edition of the Third Reich, with a few modifications in important areas such as foreign policy. For reasons which are today manifest, Hess's thoughts in many ways missed the political realities of 1946/47, and offered no realistic future perspective for a defeated, divided and humiliated Germany. Nevertheless, the desire for continuity contained in these preparations for a 'Fourth Reich', as far as we know them, is more clearly embodied than it is in the two eventual German sub-states. One might almost speak of a political programme of contrasts compared with the make-up of present-day Germany.

The Americans were not apparently interested in Hess's plans. To them, co-operation with old Nazis was, at least initially during the enforced 're-education' phase, out of the question. But it is possible that later, when Hess was in Spandau and they had him directly in their grasp, the Russians remembered the former Deputy Führer. Indeed, had not Stalin, as early as 1943 when the German General at Stalingrad, Walter von Seydlitz-Kurzbach, founded the 'Association of German Officers' while imprisoned in Russia, steered towards an understanding with supporters of the old middle-class, nationalistic Germany?

The story allegedly dates from 1952, and it sounds incredible. At the time, the United States and the Soviet Union, preoccupied with the Cold War, each made efforts to incorporate 'their'

German sub-state into their own system of alliances. They were bent on German rearmament and the involvement of the Germans in the East-West confrontation. In March 1952, Stalin proposed a peace treaty and free elections for a neutral and unified Germany to prevent the Federal Republic of Germany from joining the West's defence organization, which he considered a threat to Soviet security.

As reported by the historian Werner Maser[6] – I repeat this merely as a curiosity and with the utmost reservation – senior officials of the German Democratic Republic met Rudolf Hess one March night in 1952 somewhere in the German Democratic Republic, possibly near Weimar or Dresden, to discuss with him a prominent role in the reunification of Germany. To this end, Hitler's former deputy had been temporarily released from his cell at a time when the Soviets happened to be in command at the Berlin–Spandau Allied Military Prison.

On the German Democratic Republic side, the Deputy Minister-President Lothar Bolz and the Minister of Trade and Supplies Karl Hamann took part in this secret discussion. But Maser also believes that he has leads which indicate that even the East Berlin Head of Government, Otto Grotewohl, was present. Perhaps there were even more participants – Maser knows nothing precise. Bolz was also Chairman of the German National Democratic Party (*Nationaldemokratische Partei Deutschlands* = NDPD), and Hamann was leader of the German Liberal Democratic Party (*Liberaldemokratische Partei Deutschlands* = LDPD), two nominally independent 'middle-class' parties which nevertheless had to bow to the claims to political leadership of the German Socialist Unity Party (*Sozialistische Einheitspartei Deutschlands* = SED). The background to this secret meeting, unknown until today, is said to have been Stalin's wish 'to temper justice with mercy in the Germany matter and to grant Hess a prominent position within the framework of reconstruction and the efforts towards the reunification of Germany'.

According to Grotewohl's statement, Stalin had reached this decision in spite of his belief that, on Hitler's instructions, Hess had flown to Britain in 1941 only to free Germany's rear for the attack on the Soviet Union, originally planned for mid-May. In his view, Hess's mission was merely part of Germany's offensive preparations, and it was not until Hitler realized that his deputy's mission had failed that he fixed 22 June 1941 as the date for the attack.

Grotewohl included strong attacks on the Western Powers in his statement, reports Maser. He accused them of 'warmongering', criticized their opposition to reunification and complained that the destruction of reactionary forces was obstructed in the western part of Germany.

During the night-time discussion, the German Democratic officials offered a golden bridge over which the Deputy Führer could step into Germany's future, the Socialist future of a reunited Germany.

The function of the NDPD, the LDPD and the German Democratic Farmers' Party (*Demokratische Bauernpartei Deutschlands* = DBB), still then in existence as a vote-catcher among the middle-class farming camp, was explained in detail to Hess. Maser's impression was that the persons meeting Hess 'had shifted' the programmes of the three parties mentioned 'suspiciously close to the 25-point programme of the NSDAP of 1920', which had had 'anti-capitalistic' features. The DDR officials wanted to kill two birds with one stone by their favourable description of DDR domestic politics. Hess was at first to be used 'as a vehicle for the introduction of the New Policy' (Maser). The East Berlin Government was at that time trying to replace the anti-Fascist democratic order of the early post-war years by dictatorship of the proletariat and by accelerating the build-up of Socialism. But enforced collectivization was meeting with massive resistance among the population of the DDR. Hess was to calm down this resistance as the representative of the right-wing middle-class, and in the long term play a part – not defined in detail – as a national figure in the integration of the whole of Germany. If Hess were to declare publicly that the DDR was implementing the kind of Socialism he had had in mind throughout his life, the Soviets would release him from imprisonment immediately.

How did Hess react to this offer? Although Bolz and Hamann used honeyed words in trying to persuade him, the former Deputy Führer remained 'suspicious, stubborn and downright hostile'; it was not the first time, of course, that offers of dubious content had been made to him. Neither did he allow himself to be moved by allusions to his hobbies, such as flying. Although Hess had welcomed 'like a statesman in office' the efforts of the

DDR and the Soviet Union to preserve German patriotism, and had listened attentively to what his interlocutors had to say on the programmes of the political parties referred to, 'he had not been prepared to accept the role intended for him', said Grotewohl to Maser.

Hess had also curtly rejected an appeal to his conscience, on the grounds that he felt no guilt by reason of his political past and would do everything over again if he had the chance. He was not even impressed by the express threat that, in those circumstances, he would have to remain in Spandau until the end of his days. He had, on the contrary, 'stubbornly and arrogantly' emphasized that he could 'under no circumstances' offend Hitler, even posthumously, by accepting the communists' offer.

Grotewohl must have been rather disappointed at the result of this night raid, since he told Maser that Hess seemed to insist on burial in Spandau. He would not even allow his family to visit him, although in summer 1947 he had drafted political appeals to the German people. 'Now that he was offered the great chance of participating prominently in the rehabilitation – and above all in the reunification – of Germany as a free man', added Grotewohl, 'he drew back . . .'. The Minister-President of the DDR could not understand this at all.

At the end of the discussion, Grotewohl enjoined Maser to preserve the strictest secrecy. When Maser protested that in such circumstances no one would get anything out of the matter, Grotewohl replied: 'Wait until I am dead, and then perhaps another twenty years.' Grotewohl died in 1964, and Maser is now released from his obligation to remain silent. His revelation directs a glaring spotlight on to a particularly critical phase in Germany's post-war history, and that is probably his intention. But Grotewohl was wrong in one detail when he set his time limit for Maser's silence: Hess did not die in the meantime. He is not dead but alive, and he has now lived in Spandau for 36 years.

Part III

SPANDAU

PRISONER NUMBER SEVEN

On 18 July 1947, the seven prisoners at Nuremberg were awakened at the early hour of 4 a.m. They were:

– 53-year-old Rudolf Hess, once Hitler's deputy and a Reich Minister, sentenced to life imprisonment;
– 56-year-old Walter Funk, former Reich Minister of Economics and President of the Reichbank, also sentenced to life imprisonment;
– 71-year-old Erich Raeder, a few years previously still Chief of Hitler's Navy. He also looked forward to life imprisonment;
– 40-year-old Baldur von Schirach, former Reich Youth Leader and Gauleiter of Vienna, sentenced to 20 years' imprisonment;
– 42-year-old Albert Speer, Hitler's former Minister of Armaments and favourite architect, also 20 years' imprisonment;
– 74-year-old Konstantin Freiherr von Neurath, Hitler's first Foreign Minister, later Reich Protector in Prague, 15 years' imprisonment; and
– 55-year-old Karl Dönitz, Hitler's successor as Head of State for a short period at the end of the War, previously Commander-in-Chief of German U-boats, 10 years' imprisonment.

The seven tired, thin and seemingly exhausted men were allowed to put on their civilian clothes once again. American officers went through the prison cells deciding what they were to take with them and what they were to leave behind. Each handcuffed to a GI, the prisoners then entered two ambulances which, escorted by several troop carriers, drove them to the nearest airport. Here, an aircraft of the 'Dakota' type was waiting to take them to Berlin.

As they approached the former Reich capital, in glorious weather, Hess and his comrades-in-misfortune were able to take a nostalgic look at Germany passing beneath them. From above, the villages and towns looked peaceful and undamaged. The fields were cultivated, meadows and forests were turning green. Somewhere a train puffed along; a barge steamed along the Elbe; factory chimneys smoked.

The American 'Dakota' flew in large circles over the ruins of Berlin. In spite of the damage, the great East-West Axis that Speer had completed for Hitler's fiftieth birthday was easily identifiable. The Reich Chancellery had suffered a direct hit but was still standing; the Tiergarten was denuded of trees. Here, only shortly before, in the former Government quarter of the German capital, the seven men had sat at the centre of power. They now returned, defeated men. The plane landed late in the afternoon of 18 July at Gatow airport. On 12 May 1941 – two days after Rudolf Hess's momentous flight – Albrecht Haushofer had flown from here to Hitler at Obersalzberg. A bus with windows painted black picked up the seven prisoners and their guards. They were once again handcuffed to one another and, escorted by jeeps and armoured cars, the clumsy vehicle drove towards Wilhelmstrasse 23 in the Spandau district of Berlin. Its passengers were severely shaken about, but the journey lasted no more than 15 minutes. Finally, there was a sharp turn; the bus braked and stopped. As the seven men alighted, the large iron gate was just closing behind them. Hess, Funk, Raeder, Schirach, Speer, Neurath and Dönitz had arrived at Spandau prison.

Handcuffs were removed, and they entered the red-brick building. In a room converted into a changing room, the seven were ordered to take off their civilian clothes and put on prison uniform: light-blue trousers, a coarse shirt, a threadbare jacket, a cap and cloth shoes with thick wooden soles. As the men changed in silence, they were told that this clothing came from former concentration camp inmates. They were then pushed one after the other into an adjacent room for examination by a Soviet doctor.

The Russian did his work thoroughly and behaved correctly. After each of the prisoners had been examined he was made to pass through an adjacent door, which closed noisily behind him. This was the door to the cell wing. Rudolf Hess was the seventh and last to pass through the door. From then on, he was 'Prisoner Number Seven'.

In 1876, the German Kaiser had erected the fortress-like building, with its walls, towers, one-man cells and communal cells for a total of 600 prisoners, as a military prison in an angle between the present Wilhelmstrasse and Schmidt-Knobelsdorff-Strasse. It was later taken over by the civil prison authorities. Under Hitler, the institution served as an interrogation centre for political prisoners. A dull light fell from the circular roof lights on to the windowless corridor. One cell after another was unlocked for the prisoners. On the left, first a cell for Schirach; then one each for von Neurath, Dönitz, Speer and Funk. On the right, Hess's cell followed Raeder's. Funk and Hess were opposite one another. Viewed from the entry to the cell wing, they were farthest towards the rear.

When Hess entered his cell for the first time on that day, 18 July 1947, he found himself in a sparsely-lit room 2.30 metres wide, 2.80 metres long and nearly four metres high. Opposite the iron door, on the other narrow side of the cell at a height of 2.40 metres, was the only window, less than a metre square, of brown-tinted plexiglass with bars on the outside. It allowed through just enough light to permit reading without artificial light on bright days. It was not possible to look out because the window was too high. An unreal view of the world could be had by standing on a chair. Fortunately, a flap in the window could be opened from below by a handle to provide ventilation.

When Hess entered through the door, with its barred window and peephole, he saw to the left in the corner a white, open WC bowl with a seat of black plastic, and to the right on the opposite wall a four-legged wooden table with a crude chair before it. Hess had to pass between lavatory and chair to reach his bed on the left. This stood in the corner below the window and beside the heater. It consisted of a black iron bedstead with horsehair mattress. The springs had been worn down by former users. But in contrast to Nuremberg there were sufficient woollen blankets, a wedge-shaped bolster and two small pillows.

Opposite the bed on the right wall hung an open cupboard with one intermediate shelf. The whole fitting was no higher and no broader than 50 centimetres. Here Hess was able to place his few belongings; toothmug, tube of toothpaste, bar of soap and change of underwear. The bottom section had hooks on which to hang his towels.

Like all the other cells, the entire space of barely six square metres was painted a dull muddy-yellow to a height of about two metres. This was intended to exert a relaxing effect upon the prisoners; they were later allowed to redecorate their cells with brush and paint. The upper part of the walls and the ceiling had been white-washed. This took from the room a little of its bleak, dull and repellent effect, increased by the plain grey stone floor. All in all, it was a dreadfully bleak environment.

When in 1946 the Four Powers requisitioned the prison in Berlin–Spandau to prepare it for the so-called major war criminals, it still held 600 prisoners. Now, a year later, there were only seven – seven men who, according to Speers's calculations, were occupying 38,000 square metres of enclosed area representing an estimated building value of over one million Reichmarks per person. Speer's ironic comment was, 'Never before in my life have I lived so expensively'.[1]

Also, never before had seven men been so well guarded, and at the same time so well served, as in Spandau. In 1944/45, in their negotiations on Germany's future, the Four Powers had agreed that each of them should take over control of the Allied Military Prison three times a year – the British in January, May and September; the French in February, June and October; the Russians in March, July and November; and the Americans in April, August and December. It is true that the Directors of the Four Powers who together formed the Directorate in Spandau remained for many years in their posts, but each time a new control period commenced on the first day of the month the guards at the watch towers, gates and yards of Spandau changed with military ceremonial.

Externally, therefore, the seven prisoners were guarded from the beginning by 32 British, French, American or Russian soldiers, a total of 128 men. All around the extensive area of the prison ran a wall and an electrically-charged barbed-wire fence. There were six watch-towers evenly distributed around the wall, manned by soldiers armed with machine pistols. At night, the entire area was bathed in the glare of floodlights. Any attempt at escape was condemned to failure from the outset.

The guard system was continued by different means within the main building and its cell wing. Each cell door was double-locked. A guard was placed before the entrance to the huge corridor on to which the cells opened. Then there was an extra room in which the so-called Chief Warder sat. Finally, the table and chair standing at the entrance to the cell corridor were intended for yet another guard. In contrast to the external guards, who performed their duties in the uniforms of their national armed forces and bore arms, the three internal guards wore a blue-grey uniform with gold buttons. They carried neither pistols nor truncheons; neither did they change around regularly like their comrades outside. Some of them retained their posts for many years. Since these internal guards, who resembled normal prison warders, frequently changed shifts, there were 18 of them.

Apart from the four Directors, the 32 soldiers in the external area and the 18 internal guards, there were still more staff in Spandau, i.e. four doctors, two interpreters, two cooks, one medical orderly and a chaplain. Together with 14 other people who performed various auxiliary services or unknown activities, the seven prisoners kept some 78 people busy.

During the negotiations preceding the IMT at Nuremberg, the Allies had already prepared detailed prison regulations to which the seven in Spandau were now subjected. These regulations included[2]:

'According to Directive No. 35 of the Control Commission, the Allied Military Command is given supreme executive power over the Allied prison in Spandau. Four officers of British, American, Russian and French nationality, forming the Directorate of the prison, are entrusted with this executive power. The duty of the Directorate is to manage and supervise the entire normal staff and to ensure the maintenance of the regulations established.

'. . . It is instructed to keep all prisoners in the institution under lock and key. . . . A doctor of officer rank is appointed from each of the Four Powers. . . . The office and domestic personnel must be of the male sex, and specially selected from members of the United Nations . . .

'The prisoners must salute officers, warders and senior staff with marks of respect. They must obey all orders and regulations without hesitation, even when these appear to them to be unjust. They must answer honestly all questions addressed to them. The prisoners may approach an officer or warder only if ordered to do so or if they wish to make a request.

'The discipline of the institution provides that prisoners should adopt a standing position. The prisoner must salute an officer, an official or a warder by standing to attention or by passing him in an upright posture. The prisoner must at the same time remove his headgear . . .

'On admission, the prisoner will undress completely and his body will be carefully searched. The search, which will be in the presence of the Directorate, will be carried out by four warders. All parts of the body, including the anus, will be searched for articles which might be smuggled into the institution . . .

'Prisoners will be locked up and guarded in accordance with the verdict of the Nuremberg IMT. They will be addressed by their convict's number; in no circumstances by name. Imprisonment will be in the form of solitary confinement. The cells will be isolated, but work, religious services and walks will be carried out together.

'When awakened, the prisoner will rise immediately and make his bed. He will then strip to the waist, wash, brush his teeth and rinse his mouth. Clothing, shoes and the cell, including furniture, will be cleaned in the time provided for this purpose and in the prescribed manner. Making a noise, shouting, whistling and even approaching the window are forbidden.

'The prisoners may not talk or associate with one another, nor with other persons except with special permission from the Directorate. The prisoner may not have in his possession any articles without permission. If he should find something, he must hand it over to the warder immediately. Equipment, clothing and all articles belonging to the institution are to be treated with care, and used only for the prescribed purposes . . .

'The Directorate will establish a plan for daily activities, but in principle work will be carried out every day except Sundays and public holidays.

'According to their capacity, all prisoners are to work as well as they are able and carry out the duties assigned to them within the time prescribed. When a prisoner is given a duty, his physical condition will be taken into consideration. . . . Prisoners may receive not more than and write not more than one letter over a period of four weeks, except when the Directorate withdraws this privilege on legitimate grounds. When dispatching a letter, the prisoner must hand it over in an unsealed envelope. The Directorate will examine all the prisoners' correspondence. Copies of all correspondence sent or received by the prisoner will be kept in his personal file. No notes may be written in the margin of the letter. All correspondence must be handed over to the Directorate unopened. Even when the conditions for correspondence are met, the Directorate may keep back letters if it considers that this privilege has been abused . . .

'In its treatment of prisoners, the staff must display firmness, calm and decision, and demand strict adherence to discipline. Doors leading to yards, buildings, cells and other rooms are to be kept locked, apart from exceptional cases provided for under supplementary regulations.'

The practical course of daily life – in so far as it could be called this in Spandau – was similarly strictly regulated. At 06.00 hrs. the prisoners were awakened by their warders. They had then to get up for their morning ablutions and go to another cell, which served as a common washroom. Cells then had to be tidied. At 06.45 breakfast arrived on a rubber-wheeled trolley. Each prisoner left his cell individually and received his ration. Eating was from primitive tin utensils on a tin tray. The prisoners were given no knife and fork for any meal, because the Directorate wished to prevent suicide attempts.

After breakfast, at about 07.30 hrs., the prisoners were required to clean their cell floors or to wash their underwear. They were then in practice 'free', interrupted by a 30-minute walk in the garden or yard of the prison.

During this 'free' period, they were allowed to read, draw or write. Lunch arrived as early as 11.30 hrs.

At about 14.00 hrs. the afternoon programme began. This once again consisted mainly of free time during which the prisoners might write or read, but was again interrupted by a 30-minute walk in the garden or yard. The evening meal was distributed at about 17.00 hrs. After this there was again ample time for reading until 22.00 hrs., when a warder moved from cell to cell collecting spectacles. The light was then turned off for the eight-and-a-half hours of sleep.

Relations between warders and prisoners were at the 'coldest distance', as Albert Speer noted[3]. The warders were full of hatred, and the prisoners had first to get over the shock suffered upon admission, bearing in mind that some of them faced life imprisonment. The atmosphere was extremely frosty and tense.

By November 1948, conditions in Spandau, especially as concerns rations, had become so bad that the prison chaplain, Pastor Casalis, wrote in a report to the Directorate:

'The justice which hung the major Nazi leaders at Nuremberg is at present allowing those it did not wish to condemn to death to die slowly of starvation.'[4]

When, in December 1948, the Americans took over from the Russians, Miller, the American Director, proposed alleviations of the prison regulations which he summarized under six headings:

1. As from today, prisoners' rations are increased to 2,700 calories a day.
2. If they so wish, sick or fatigued prisoners may lie on their beds without contravening prison regulations.
3. When working together under supervision, prisoners may speak to one another.
4. Prisoners may receive one visit lasting 15 minutes each second month.
5. In bad weather, outside work will be postponed and replaced by inside work.
6. In future, prisoners' correspondence will be reasonably censored by the simple application of the regulations decreed in 1947.

In spite of protests from the Russians, and objections from the British and French that they would first have to report to their superiors, Major Miller insisted on the immediate implementation of his decision.

The meeting on the following Thursday was stormy. It looked for a moment as if there would be a breakdown in relations. But this was avoided, since neither the Western Powers nor the

Soviets wished to give up their claim on the survivors of Nuremberg. Although the French and British gave their consent to the American decisions of the previous week, the Soviets rejected them, saying that they would respect the prison regulations introduced at the beginning.

The American Director listened calmly to all this; he had received instructions from his superiors, who were in agreement with him. He declared:[5] 'As long as no orders to the contrary are given by the senior political authorities, the instructions issued by the American Director will be carried out for the period during which we are responsible for the control of Spandau.'

Since the senior political authorities were the Control Council and the Kommandantura (the Four-Power body controlling Berlin), and these no longer existed because the Russians had walked out of them, how could a countermanding order be issued? The Russians gave in. But during the months in which they occupied the Chair of the Directorate, prison regulations were carried out to the last letter with no deviation. The prisoners had even to surrender their spring mattresses, which the Americans returned the following months. This went on for nearly a year until the American Director was changed and the Russians were again in charge.

The incident described, which is confirmed by the former American Director E.K. Bird in his book on Rudolf Hess, shows that the Western Powers can achieve a great deal by firm action. The eternal reference to the Soviet veto, which is alleged to obstruct all humanitarian measures on the part of the Western Powers in Spandau, is therefore nothing more than an excuse. This excuse is employed by the Western Powers in answer to all applications for mitigations and improvements for the prisoners.

The unusual 'attack' of courage of convictions suddenly displayed by the Americans soon burnt itself out, and normal conditions returned to Spandau; that is, the Russians steered a harsh course, and the Western Powers watched what was going on but did nothing.

This caused Pastor Casalis – the courageous and humane French chaplain – to renew his protest to the prison Directorate in April 1950:[6]

'It can safely be said that Spandau has become a place of mental torture to an extent that does not permit the Christian conscience to remain silent in the face of this instrument of international justice. This is due not so much to the systematic determination of the Soviet Director to allow the prisoners to suffer, but much more to the mediocrity and weakness of the Western Directors, who because of their fear of the Russians, their indifference, or their state of health are in practice incapable of resisting the stubbornness and 'professional scruples' of their Soviet colleagues. Behind the Western Directors stand their military authorities, who contemplate the degeneration taking place in the prison with indifference, and say that it is not necessary to increase tension with the Soviets for the sake of seven men. This is how matters stand:

(a) the prisoners are in practice cut off from the world: censorship is in the hands of the Soviet Director, who withholds a book or a letter sometimes for several weeks and then cuts it down to such an extent that it is no longer recognizable;

(b) visits are entirely at the discretion of the Directorate. (The Soviet veto has the effect, here as elsewhere, that it is the minority which controls the quadripartite administration.) Visits are in the presence of between four and eight onlookers, and in a visitors' room whose double grid almost prevents the visitor from seeing the prisoner;

(c) sleep at night is continually interrupted by the cells being brightly illuminated. This happens an average of eight to ten times a night. When the Soviet guards are on duty, this disturbance can occur up to four times an hour;

(d) visits by solicitors are always forbidden. Many prisoners who are seeking to have their cases reviewed cannot even speak to their counsel. They can expect neither hope nor help from Allied justice;

(e) relations with the chaplains are in practice reduced to very few items: no conversation may take place without the presence of a warder; these are suspicious and intrusive, and in a hurry to end the conversation quickly;

(f) all tensions among the Allies affect the seven prisoners, who live in a permanent environment of uncertainty and contra-

diction, in an atmosphere of refined sadism which the incon-
sistency of disorganized action does nothing to eradicate.'

Pastor Casalis was replaced shortly after submitting this
protest. At the request of the Russians, the voice of humanity disappeared from Spandau. Here also the Western Powers consen-
ted without resistance.

In the early 1950s, influential personalities, supported by the
press, protested against the Spandau prison regulations, in particular against the most disputed paragraphs: visits at two-
monthly intervals, one letter a month and the procedure to be
employed in the event of a prisoner's death. It had been laid
down in 1948 in a secret memorandum that in the event of a
prisoner's death his body, following post-mortem, was to be
cremated and the ashes scattered.

After the Soviets left the Allied Kommandantura in July 1948,
the four Directors decided on an 'abatement' for the time being.
The ashes were to be put in an urn and locked in the prison safe.
After long discussion, it was finally decided that the urn should
be buried within the prison area.

Under pressure, including that exercised by the Church, the
three Western High Commissioners proposed a few mitigations
of conditions in Spandau to the Soviet authorities. In September
1952, Donnelly, the American High Commissioner, published
his *démarches*.

'On 5 October 1952, High Commissioner Chemitchasnov let it
be known officially that the Russians did not object to the
prisoners' receiving a monthly visit of 30 minutes' duration,
receiving one letter a week and sending one letter a week.
Medical treatment, however, was to continue to be provided
within the prison, and the procedure in the event of death was
confirmed without comment.'

The prisoners could now enjoy a few improvements, but the
main result was to demonstrate that authorities still existed
which could intervene in Spandau. Adenauer intervened once
again, but without success, and the Russians announced that
they refused any further changes.

In these merciful efforts, the voice of the prison chaplain had
not been absent. In spite of his past history as a member of the
French Resistance, the French chaplain exclaimed, 'History will

judge severely the treatment meted out to prisoners at Spandau. Those who allow the Soviets to implement their plan of mental torture become virtually accessories, and they will be unable to advance any excuse whatsoever to justify such attitudes.'

In those years, when the Allies' chicanery and mental torture reached their peak at Spandau, my father had to bear an additional mental burden. His mother died on 1 October 1951. He learned of this in a letter from his brother, who wrote:[8]

'She passed away as peacefully as one could mercifully wish. She was thus spared a fully conscious farewell. We must be thankful for this alone. . . . For any mother it would have been most inhuman at such a moment to be separated from her dearest son, and not to see fulfilled the hope in which she steadfastly believed. Coincidence or not, one day later at the same time ten years ago Father died, 2 October 1941 at 16.00 hrs . . .'.

In a letter dated 21 October 1951, Rudolf Hess replied to this sad news in a moving letter:[9]

'My dear ones,

'I thank you from my heart for the gentle way you informed me of the – so tragic – news.

So it has happened after all; the inconceivable! I had of course to reckon with this, but I still hoped that she might be with us for a few more years, and that we would see each other again – as she also believed! I am unspeakably glad to know that at least she was not conscious of her false hopes, and that she passed peacefully away, without a struggle and without the pain of parting from you, the children, the loved little grandson, and her far-away eldest child . . .

'By now she will have been given the place in the heavenly fields which she earned by her moving love for those that were hers, her devotion to everything that was good, her brave suffering of all the adversities which have burdened her from her early youth, her unswerving integrity, her active helpfulness, her deep compassion for all suffering, and not least her loyal affection for her country.

'Here is something strange. In her old age, separated by so much distance, to me scarcely more than an idea, she had almost no influence upon my life, she was no longer actively in evidence. And yet the knowledge that she no longer lives produces in me a desolate vacuum; the world is different. I think it will be long before I can reconcile myself to this. The existence of a loved one is taken for granted; one doesn't think about it, and the result is that one doesn't give so much attention to that person, doesn't cherish her so much, doesn't show her as much love as one would have wished, and would now show if only one were able when later the impossible occurs.

'All told, it is a sad world, full of suffering lurking in the background, always ready to drop on us suddenly, culminating in the "immense solemnity of the hour of death". Oh, Schopenhauer! . . .'.

In all the unending years of his Spandau imprisonment, my father has never uttered a single word of complaint, of despair, of hopelessness, neither in his writings nor during visits. His steady heart and unyielding character did not lament, even when the mental torments inflicted on him became almost unbearable. Only between the lines – as in the final paragraph of his letter – does he sometimes suggest what he must endure, what he experiences in his innermost self.

With a certain amount of relief, the seven prisoners found when they arrived at Spandau that no so-called 'prisoners' library' of tattered penny-dreadfuls and trashy romances was awaiting them. The Allied prison was at first supplied with literature by the Spandau Urban District Library, and later by the American Memorial Library in Berlin. From time to time, the prisoners received the catalogue of new publications, and they could put a cross against the books that interested them. These books were then generally obtained by the prison authorities, provided they did not deal with the history of the last fifty years, the Nuremberg Tribunal and other contemporary political matters. Books might also be sent from home under similar restrictions.

An empty cell on the same corridor as that on to which the cells of the seven prisoners faced served as a lending centre. At certain times, this cell was unlocked by the warders for Raeder and Schirach to perform their office of librarians. Each of the prisoners was allowed to borrow four books a month. If they were not being read, they were kept in the library cell. Hess mainly studied economics and political science. He did not read novels.

Reading books, using them to occupy the mind, exercising the memory by calling to mind what had been read – all this was as important to the mental health of the prisoners as was food, sleep and fresh-air exercise to their physical health.

Fourteen days following their admission on 2 August 1947, the British Director appeared in the prison yard and told the seven men pacing along there that in future they could work in the garden instead of glueing bags. Whether this was a spontaneous idea on the part of the Englishman, his sense of the need for practical activity, or the result of Allied consultations, the prisoners needed no second bidding. From that time on they worked in the prison garden both morning and afternoon. But initially the plot of five or six thousand square metres in no way resembled an area of cultivated land. It was rather a wilderness of weeds from which protruded a few tall lilac bushes and numerous old walnut trees. The French Director, who was in command of Spandau during the following month, issued the absurd order that the weeds pulled up were to be dug in again, which made any gardening futile. Everything would sooner or later have grown up again.

The prisoners first established a vegetable garden, which improved the prison kitchen's starvation ration. Potatoes, Brussels sprouts, red cabbage, carrots, peas, various kinds of lettuce, onions, parsley, radishes and chicory were grown. There were manure beds and a little greenhouse. In the first year Neurath planted a poplar, which in the following years and decades grew to a gigantic height – today a kind of landmark for Spandau.

The vegetable garden was later divided into plots. Each of the seven prisoners was given one bed to do with as he pleased. Hess planted strawberries on his little territory. Speer was in charge; as an architect, he planned the whole operation, and to a large extent carried it through himself by heavy physical work. At 42 years of age, which he had reached by the time he was transferred to Spandau, he was the next-to-youngest prisoner after 40-year-old Baldur von Schirach, and the fittest.

Thus, over the years, the flower garden with its lawn, birches, walnut trees and lilac bushes was created, giving pleasure to all the prisoners in Spandau with its waving beds of lupins in red, white and blue. The thrill of nature, with its seasonal changes of light, scents and colours, and the pigeons, crows, sparrows, pheasants and rabbits which strayed into the garden compensated a little for the bleak imprisonment in the six square-metre cells.

This prison life was interrupted when the prisoners received visits from outside, permitted since October 1952. Six of the seven Spandau prisoners made regular use of these opportunities; there was one exception: Rudolf Hess. He corresponded with his family like the others, but for 32 years he refused with iron determination to receive his wife and son in Spandau. This rested on two grounds – one human and the other political.

My father had already written to my mother from Nuremberg refusing to see her again under the degrading circumstances the victors had at that time established. As we shall see, conditions were not very different at Spandau. My father would probably have seen it as inconsistent and as a climb-down to the victors if under such circumstances he had abandoned his resistance to family visits. It would have appeared to him, politically, as a measure of capitulation. Since in any event my father disputed the victors' right to sit in judgement over Germany the loser, he was forced to see it as an act of despotism that they held him prisoner in Spandau; moreover, under such conditions.

Besides this, however, there was also a human reason linked to the psychological strategy pursued by my father at Nuremberg, and even more at Spandau, in order to preserve his equilibrium. This strategy amounted essentially to a second confinement – voluntary quarantine in addition to the enforced imprisonment of the victors. If he were to abandon the former without simultaneously ending the latter, the system he had constructed to combat latent and ever-threatening despair in the face of life imprisonment would collapse. He therefore shunned interruption of the enforced confinement by visits, however short.

THE LONELIEST PRISONER IN THE WORLD

THE YEAR 1966 was a watershed in my father's life. He was now aged 72. As long ago as in the 1950s the four victors had released four of his fellow prisoners:

– Konstantin von Neurath (15 years): 1954
– Erich Raeder (life imprisonment): 1955
– Karl Dönitz (10 years): 1956
– Walther Funk (life imprisonment): 1957.

Dönitz had served his full term. Neurath, Raeder and Funk, on the other hand, were released early because of their age and health. At the time of his release, Neurath was aged 81; he lived a further two years in freedom. Raeder was aged 79, and lived three more years in freedom. Funk was aged only 67 when he was released; he also lived another three years in freedom. The example of these three of Hess's former fellow prisoners shows that the Spandau prison administration is certainly in a position to release old and sick prisoners by agreement between all four custodial Powers.

The release of Speer and von Schirach was now imminent. On 1 October 1966, both had completed their 20-year sentences.

It is uncertain when Rudolf Hess prepared himself for the moment from which he alone would remain behind the sinister walls of Spandau. Did he in fact take this possibility into account? Or did he secretly hope that his jailers would release him also from serving the rest of his term of life imprisonment when Speer and Schirach departed? This is also uncertain. In any event, in autumn 1964 Hess suddenly asked the Directorate to allow him larger quantities of paper than hitherto. Up to that time, the prisoners had only a few thin exercise books or writing pads for making notes about what they had read. They were never allowed to hold more than a few of these notebooks at a time, which increased the difficulty of intellectual composition from the material available. Hess, therefore, also asked to be allowed to retain these notes longer than in the past – that they should not be burned immediately, as had been the practice.

On this point, Hess risked an open conflict with the French Director. Nevertheless, he and the other two prisoners were finally allowed a 190-page notebook. As time passed, Hess also arranged for his wife to send him an increasing number of specialized text-books. He was working on the link that, in his opinion, existed between liberal democracy and the aberrations of modern civilization. He eventually collected seventy books. When Schirach made a joke about this mountain of books, Hess said dejectedly: 'It is my reserve for when I am alone.'[1]

The last day of their imprisonment arrived for Speer and Schirach on 30 September 1966. On the afternoon of that day, which passed like any other, Rudolf Hess allowed himself to be locked in his cell. He wanted to be alone when his two fellow-prisoners took leave of the warders. It was the same withdrawal into himself by which for years past he had fortified his resistance against the despair of loneliness.

Two minutes before midnight, the engines of the cars which were to carry Schirach and Speer to freedom started up in the Spandau prison yard. A guard looked at his watch once again, and the large iron gate opened. A crowd of people was waiting outside. Flashbulbs blazed. Someone shouted: 'Freedom for Rudolf Hess!' Then the gate rumbled closed again.

Next morning, 1 October 1966, Hess was wakened at 06.00 hrs. sharp, like any other morning. He was handed his spectacles, which as always had been collected the night before to prevent attempts at suicide. He made his bed and went to the washroom without glancing at the two empty cells of his last comrades in misfortune. He then returned to eat his breakfast.

When the warders asked him what he had taken in of Speer

and Schirach's departure the night before, Hess answered: 'I was awake. I was lying here with my eyes open, and I heard everything going on out there, even the noise in the street.' He then added, as a reference to his two comrades: 'But I am happy for them. They have their freedom once again.'[2]

He appeared not to be very disturbed; at least, he did not evidence this to his warders.

The events surrounding 1 October 1966 have been described by my mother, while still fresh in her memory, at the end of the third volume of my father's letters, published at that time.[3] I wish to go back to this account to describe what were surely the most dreadful days and weeks my father has experienced in Spandau:

'. . . Well, let us live in hopes for October, that then at least a few brilliant and warm weeks will be granted to us. For your sake I would be pleased – and for the sake of my two companions who will soon move southwards like the swallows . . .'.

Thus ended the letter from Spandau dated 3 September 1966.

My son and I hoped of course not only for warm days; our hope was in October days that would at long last end a separation of twenty-five years; once again that tenth day of May in 1941 at Munich appeared before my eyes. That day was also 'warm and brilliant', with my husband standing at the wide-open door into the sun-drenched garden with the flowers and scents of May saying good-bye, 'just for a few days'.

Twenty-five years and four months had passed since then; fainter and fainter hopes ending in new disappointments. But for the first time since the days of the Nuremberg sentencing it seemed to me that the final release of Albert Speer and Baldur von Schirach would inevitably be followed, logically and humanely (let alone as a just outcome – after 25 years of imprisonment), by the break up of the Spandau prison and the release of my husband.

Subconsciously, however, I linked one worry with this all too understandable hope. I knew that the attitude of the Allied custodial Powers, which arrogated to themselves the aura of a just and progressive political system, had in recent decades not always been commensurate with standards of rationality and human understanding. Thus, in my eyes, if 1 October 1966 passed without realizing the hopes of release, leaving my husband the loneliest prisoner in the world behind the sinister walls of the Spandau penitentiary, it would mean for him a new, additional and difficult load to bear.

I pondered on how we could make this – in our eyes – bitter disappointment easier for him.

It is well known that during his imprisonment my husband has consistently refused visits from his immediate family. As early as Nuremberg, he saw visiting as a moral concession to those who took it upon themselves to sit in judgement upon him.

After forty years of acquaintance with his categorically un-yielding nature, I doubted whether he would abandon his refu-sal to receive a visit from me during his imprisonment. But in my desire to show him our affection as strongly as was at all possible on the first day he was alone in Spandau, I suggested to him at the beginning of September that he should permit our son to visit him at the same time as his solicitor Dr Seidl, particularly since Dr Seidl (whose regular visits for some time past had always pleased and diverted him) told us that my husband was 'thinking over once again' whether he might occasionally permit our son to visit him.

Almost ashamed, I was forced to realize from his replies of 15 September and 1 October 1966 that my doubts about his inflex-ibility had been quite unjustified:

'I am of course pleased when Dr Seidl visits me; I also am of the view that we have much to talk about. But as concerns your wish that Wolf might accompany Dr Seidl, I want to say this: my attitude towards the question of visits from you should not be entirely unknown to you. Similarly, my inclination to overturn a decision once made which is important to me has increased very little – at least as long as there is no fundamental change.

'Dr Seidl, or the "retired colleague" who allegedly conveyed my willingness via his solicitor son, must therefore have thoroughly misunderstood some remark. I have most certainly never guaranteed that I would receive a visit, but it is very possible that I said I would think about it again! If one is so pestered about a matter, one can sometimes take refuge in such a non-binding promise, leaving everything open; not very her-oic, but a proven remedy.

'Now as ever, I want no reunion behind prison walls and in

the presence of others, neither with you nor with Wolf. Apart from emotion, this is a matter of dignity.

'From your "sensible lines", and reading between them, I have of course been able to imagine where your concern lies. But, nevertheless, I would be grateful if you would in future forbear from placing me in the painful position of having to refuse such a request from you – refuse for the sake of a higher ethical attitude; it is more difficult for me than you perhaps believe.

'You cannot know what a prison and the conditions in it mean – but I do know . . .'.

But I also remembered my own short "automatic custody" in the Sonthofer County Court prison before being taken to the Göggingen labour camp in 1947; I understood with crystal clarity the attitude of a man who – sensitive, proud and just – never, not even unto death, would bow to the injustice inflicted on him or endure dishonour.

But after 1 October 1966 had passed without his return home, only one path was left for us. We abandoned the restraint we had maintained for decades and addressed our own 'Declaration' on the matter of my husband to 'all people of good will' in the world. We issued this 'Declaration' to the press at home and abroad on 3 October 1966, and sent a copy of it with a short introductory letter – a 'request for attention' – to Pope Paul VI, the Heads of State of the four custodial Powers, the World Council of Churches, and the Human Rights Commission of the United Nations in Strasburg.

We also gave Dr Seidl a copy of the 'Declaration'. He had arranged to visit Spandau, at my husband's request, on 10 October. To his surprise and to our relief, he found the 'last Spandau prisoner' full of cheerful composure and humour, lively and interested in world events as gathered from the four newspapers made available to him each day . . .

A change in the previous censorship practice meant that reports about the release of his 'retired colleagues' – as he humorously referred to Speer and Schirach in his letters after 1 October 1966 – and remarks about himself were no longer withheld from him. He had therefore read the statements the two men had made at their press conference on the night of their release. In a letter dated 8 October, he made somewhat ironic comments on reading them:

'In what way I went through "three dreadful days", when I knew that the other two were packing their things, baffles me. In fact I already knew "somewhat" more than three days earlier that the two men were treacherously to leave me on 1 October, and that packing would be part of this (ha-ha-ha!). There can be no question of "dreadful days" – quite the contrary; I was composed as always. One of my "retired colleagues" asked me whether what was happening got on my nerves, to which I replied that of course it was not exactly a pleasure to watch the others packing their things while mine remained entirely unpacked. I told them to get on and finish it so that "peace" would prevail once again here – otherwise I would be infected by their nervousness.'

He also knew about our Declaration from scanty press reports, but he did not yet know the full text. Although Dr Seidl brought him this, he was not allowed to give it to him. Hess was therefore disturbed that this 'Declaration' might be seen as a 'plea for mercy':

'I read the announcement. You had directed an appeal to Pope Paul VI, the World Council of Churches, the UN Human Rights Commission and the Heads of State of the four custodial Powers to consider my sentence of life imprisonment discharged after 25 years of internment. The announcement was detailed, and probably contained all that was essential. I have no objection to your having approached the first three institutions, but all the more objection to the inclusion of the Heads of State. As to them, it is to be feared that, in spite of the careful drafting, and although the ominous word was avoided, the public will interpret it as if I had directed 'a plea for mercy' to those with authority to release me, as if I had involved my family only that I might not be seen to contradict my earlier statements.

'As if to order, I read recently about Baron von Stein, who was outlawed by Napoleon and banished from Prussia. From his asylum in Bohemia, his wife sent a plea for mercy to Napoleon. Historical research has shown that Stein made his wife do this; indeed, he dictated it to her. This is "incomprehensible" to historians, and they deeply regret the blemish on the image of the great man.

'You know that I had nothing to do with your action – but how are you going to prove this to those around you? How can one exclude the suspicion that, by using some secret means of communication, I had a hand in it? Probability suggests this, it will be said, and moreover that it has been reported on such-and-such a date in such-and-such a newspaper. The fact is that the press is now quoted as a source by even serious historians – however incomprehensible this may be, even to someone who doubts the veracity of the media and knows how thoughtlessly conjectures are broadcast as facts. But I do understand your action, and I can understand that you have no peace. Again and again you are urged to leaving nothing undone that might at long last bring release – release for me and for you.

'But is it your wish that I also should one day enter history with a blemish on my character?

'No, you don't want that to happen! And therefore understand that my honour is more important to me than freedom!'

My husband's calling Baron von Stein to mind was certainly not pure chance. In his case also, it was a question of voluntary submission to a foreign decree. Although my husband comprehends historically the tragic role allotted to him by fate in Cell Number Seven at Spandau, he expresses an underlying and strong hope. He believes that the history of the German people is not at an end.

Many a man of our time is justly given credit for his contribution towards rescuing the essence of the German nation from the catastrophes of the twentieth century. I am sure that my husband's unswerving attitude – from the days of the Nuremberg Tribunal until now – will one day be vindicated in the survival of the spiritual strength of our nation.

Those Powers which insist on keeping open the special prison at Spandau, are they perhaps in the end to be the involuntary instruments of a higher destiny that now allows Rudolf Hess, twenty-five years after his abortive political mission and his flight to Britain in 1941, to accomplish a moral mission?

This is what my mother had to say. My father, in the letter quoted above, emphasizes his reluctance to reverse decisions once taken – at least as long as there is no fundamental change.

I am convinced that we would not have been able to visit him until this very day if this fundamental change had not occurred. It is true that this was only temporary, but my father did not intend to rescind his consent to receive visits once he had given it. How did this fundamental change come about?

Medical care in Spandau had always been unsatisfactory. A Dutch medical orderly arrived each morning and evening to distribute pills of one kind or another. His part-time occupation was to run a restaurant. Any prisoner with a minor complaint had to report to the medical room, an anteroom to the cell wing, where he was examined by the medical orderly. The four Allied medical officers arrived once a week to look at the prisoners. But as soon as treatment was involved matters became difficult. The doctors argued for minutes on end before reaching a Four Power decision on such vital matters as prescribing an aspirin. Where difficult decisions arose, such as admission to the British Military Hospital, negotiations went on not for minutes and hours but for days before a decision was reached.

In mid-November 1969, three years after the commencement of his solitary confinement, Rudolf Hess refused food, complained of unbearable pains in the stomach area and rapidly lost weight. He could no longer get up in the morning, he no longer shaved, and he lay in bed moaning.

Even the four Allied Directors appeared to believe that this was something really serious. After three days of consultations, during which Rudolf Hess suffered a 'concealed perforation' of a duodenal ulcer, unanimity was finally reached that he should be admitted to the British Military Hospital.

The 'dangerous' prisoner on the verge of death was driven to the hospital in an ambulance accompanied by heavily-armed escort vehicles.

The British Military Hospital had been constructed in the 1960s at some distance from the Heerstrasse. A so-called 'Hess Suite' had significantly been included in the original plans, and eventually built. There was no intention, therefore, of releasing Rudolf Hess; on the contrary, provision for the lonely man in Spandau had been made in good time. The Hess Suite is a wing equipped with special security devices on the third floor of the hospital. It can be reached only by a lift serving this wing alone.

Everything had been prepared in the hospital for the reception of the prominent prisoner. As Rudolf Hess was admitted on 22 November 1969, British soldiers with machine pistols stood before the entrance. The Hess Suite and the room in which Hess lay were also under strict guard. X-ray photographs confirmed the perforated duodenal ulcer. Fortunately it had closed itself again; otherwise Hess would have died during the three days before he came under proper medical care. An operation was now no longer necessary, and Hess received conservative treatment.

As a precaution, however, the four custodial Powers had already considered how they would act if the 75-year-old man died. The USA was willing to return the body to the family for burial outside Berlin, but the Russians insisted on cremation first. Meanwhile, in the watch towers of Spandau prison, Russian – and later American, British and French – soldiers stood in the cold, guarding a completely empty prison; a ludicrous symbol of a victors' right that had lost its point.

In November, the four custodial Powers had considered it unnecessary to inform the Hess family of Rudolf Hess's dangerous illness. I was at that period often away on business, and I heard about all this on the radio. I immediately sent a telegram to Willy Brandt, then Federal Chancellor, demanding the immediate transfer of the patient to a German hospital and the assistance of the German surgeon, Professor Dr Rudolf Zenker of Munich. Both these requests were rejected by the four victors.

After Rudolf Hess had recovered to the extent that his life was no longer in acute danger, the hospital's friendly and humane surroundings – so unfamiliar – began to affect him. After all those decades, he again had a proper bed, white bed linen and a pleasant room. He was cared for by friendly nurses and not ordered about by sullen prison warders. In short, he was in contact with a breath of normal life. As a result of this fundamental change in his circumstances, and urged by the American Director, Eugene K. Bird, my father began to reconsider his decision to receive no visits from his family. The serious illness he had fortunately just survived undoubtedly had a part in this. Faced with death, he perhaps suddenly looked upon the decision not to see his family in a different light.

One day, at the beginning of December, he finally called the American Director to his bed and told him of his decision. He wanted to see his family again – the first time in 28 years.

The visit was to be at Christmas. This historical decision by Rudolf Hess to give up his voluntary quarantine thoroughly upset the four victors. Where were Frau Ilse Hess and Wolf Rüdiger Hess to meet their husband and father? What were the detailed arrangements to be? How long should it last? The Four Powers on the Directorate laboriously reached an agreement on each of these points.

On 8 December 1969, Rudolf Hess at last wrote the following application to the Spandau Directorate:[4] 'I request a visit from my wife and son, if possible on the morning of 24 December. It is the first visit for 28 years, and I therefore request that no witnesses be present in the room at the beginning of the visit. The conversation I will conduct with my family can be recorded on tape . . . I also promise that I will not shake hands with them, and my family will make a similar promise. I request that it be taken into account that in the course of twenty years von Schirach and Speer received a large number of visits, but that this is my first. I therefore also ask that, since it will last only half-an-hour, we be allowed to take Christmas lunch together. It is unimportant to me whether witnesses are present during this meal. I shall also preserve silence towards everyone about all these privileges, in so far as they concern my family.'

Hess also informed his wife of the application. It was finally approved by the four custodial Powers – without the 'privileges' he had requested. In his sick-room, the French prison chaplain had meanwhile conjured up some Advent atmosphere in the form of an Advent wreath, candles and red ribbon. While my father waited for his family, he listened to classical music on the Dual record player he had brought with him to the hospital from the prison. To celebrate the occasion, he was also given a new pair of trousers. On 24 December 1969 the day had arrived. My mother and I landed at the Berlin–Tempelhof airport, and were badgered by press photographers while still on the tarmac. Then, escorted by a Berlin police car, we drove to Spandau in one of the Directorate's limousines. All went smoothly, but my mother had long since realized that 'the cruel solitary confinement was to be given a pleasant appearance by dabs of human colour'.

Ilse Hess has captured in a detailed account what then occurred:

'In front of the entrance gate to the hospital, some forty journalists and photographers had gathered, but they could do no more than photograph the car as it entered.

[281]

'We drove as far as the enclosed area, and were there received by the American Director, Colonel E.K. Bird. Colonel Bird was extremely polite and courteous. He introduced us to Colonel O'Brian, Chief Medical Officer at the British Military Hospital, and told us that, after the visit to the Big Chap [this is what my father is called by his wife – W.R.H.], we would be able to talk to Colonel O'Brian. He also asked us, in the presence of the other Directors, not to mention that we had been informed of the Big Chap's illness by the American Consulate in Munich. This the Americans had done on their own responsibility. (The American Consulate had in fact telephoned us after we had already learned from the press of my husband's transfer to hospital.)

'We went up in the lift to the third floor to get to the so-called "Hess Suite". When the British Military Hospital was planned at the beginning of the 1960s, this Hess Suite had been conceived for the accommodation of Rudolf Hess only. It can be reached only by this one lift, and is equipped with many security devices. The date the Hess Suite was planned shows that, in the early 1960s, the custodial Powers were already firmly determined not to release Rudolf Hess; for example, when von Schirach and Speer were released on 1 October 1969, or even later.

'Standing by the lift on the third floor were Mr Banfield, the British Director, Colonel Farignon, the French Director and – suddenly appearing around a corner – Colonel Toruta, the Russian Director. Banfield and Farignon greeted us with a handshake; the Russian kept his distance and merely nodded. Finally another gentleman appeared who was introduced as Toruta's interpreter. We were asked to go into the visitors' waiting room, where there were present the four Directors, Colonel O'Brian, the Russian interpreter, my son and myself. It was explained to us that we were now required just to acquaint ourselves with the visitors' regulations and sign them, after which we could go to the Big Chap immediately. The visitors' regulations, consisting of nine points, were presented to us. They were dated 28 October 1954, and read as follows:

"The following rules of conduct for visitors are taken from the prison regulations:

1. Duration of the visit is as decided by the Directorate.

2. Conversations with prisoners must be conducted in German. Other languages must be approved in advance by the Directorate.
3. Signs, gestures and other non-interpretable actions are prohibited.
4. Visitors must submit to a search of their outer clothing.
5. Handbags and other containers must be left in the waiting room.
6. Visitors are not permitted to give anything to a prisoner or to receive anything from him without advance permission from the Directorate.
7. Personal contact, i.e. hand-shaking, embracing, etc., is prohibited. Staff on duty have been instructed to terminate the visit in the event of any contravention of these regulations.
8. It is pointed out to visitors that if, after a visit, they grant press interviews and in the process report what they may have learned, the Directors will consider whether it may be advisable to permit no further visits. All visitors are to sign this document before the visit.
9. Contravention of any of the above regulations is a contravention of the regulations of the Military Government and will be treated as such. Visitors guilty of such contraventions may be arrested by the Directorate.

THE ALLIED DIRECTORATE
(Stamp)"

'After reading these regulations, my son immediately objected to Point 4. He considered it shameful to be "frisked" like a criminal. After some argument, the Directors and my son agreed that Point 4 would be met if we took off our coats, which we were still wearing.

'My son also protested against Point 8, which he had no intention of signing since he considered it a scandalous and unreasonable request. He stressed that he could not be asked to undertake to preserve silence on an event in the future, his reaction to which he did not as yet know. It might well be that he would find his father a critically-ill man, in which case he could in no way remain silent. Colonel Toruta intervened immediately to say that there could be no discussion at all on this. If my son did not wish to sign, neither he nor I would be allowed to see my husband. Also, no further visits would be permitted. My son answered him that, in that case, he would turn on his heel, go to the Hilton Hotel and call a press conference to inform the public how the Allied custodial Powers behaved here on German soil.

'After this observation, the Directors, in particular the three Western Directors, began to become uneasy. They tried by various arguments to persuade my son to be reasonable. They argued, for example, that the prison regulations had not been drafted by them but that they had to abide by them, and that they had readily been signed by all previous visitors. My son replied that what other visitors had done was not binding on him. The present case was an exception, as Rudolf Hess was seriously ill. Neither was it correct that all other visitors had readily signed, since Dr Seidl, my husband's solicitor, had also refused not to report on his impressions of my husband. Colonel Bird then referred back to Dr Seidl's signatures and stated that he had indeed signed. I pointed out in reply that Dr Seidl had signed only with reservations. Colonel Bird and Colonel Toruta both stated that a 'gentleman's agreement' had been reached with Dr Seidl at his last visit, under which Dr Seidl would report only positively on his impressions of Rudolf Hess. Dr Seidl had broken this 'gentleman's agreement', and had reported, directly after he left the prison, that he had found Rudolf Hess in a very poor state. Dr Seidl had not kept to the agreement, and the Directorate had therefore become wary. My son countered that Dr Seidl had probably merely told the truth, truth which the Directorate did not wish to become broadcast.

'Following this, my son asked Colonel Toruta a direct question. If, after the visit, he told the press that he had found his father in such-and-such a state of health, would this be a reason for refusing him further visits? Without hesitation and without consulting his colleagues, Tortura replied "Yes". Colonel Bird now intervened with a compromise proposal, in which he tried to define how far my son might go and might not go in his statements. Tortura interrupted him and said that no compromises were possible here. Bird then became very irritated and asked my son and me to leave the room.

'After about five minutes we were called back. Bird explained that unfortunately nothing could be changed, and that we would have to sign the visitors' regulations. My son stuck to his refusal, and suggested that I should sign and go in to the Big Chap to explain the position to him so that he could decide; in the face of such a difficult situation, my son did not wish to take a decision alone. Tortura also refused to consider this proposal. His Western colleagues stood there, embarrassed, but did nothing. Meanwhile, the matron appeared and asked Colonel O'Brian to step outside. O'Brian soon returned and said that the visit was already very far behind schedule. Rudolf Hess could not stay up much longer, and would soon have to be put back to bed. The visit would have to take place as quickly as possible.

'On my insistence, my son finally signed the visitors' regulations, and I also signed. The visit could then begin, after this – to me – more than agitating prelude.

'From the visitors' room and through a long passage, we eventually reached a room guarded by four soldiers with machine pistols. Behind this was a room in which a crowd of curious nursing staff had gathered, and finally, separated from this room by a glass partition, was the visiting room itself in which the Big Chap was already sitting. The visiting room measured about 4×4 metres. In the middle was a table, and to its left and right screens had been erected so that in practice the room was divided into two. On one side sat Rudolf Hess, and behind him a warder. On the other side, in front of the table, stood two chairs, and in the corners of the visitors' half of the room there were a bench on one side and two more chairs on the other side.

'I entered the room first, and instinctively I wanted to rush up to the Big Chap to shake his hand. My son shouted to me from the rear that hand-shaking was forbidden, whereupon I jerked back and sat down in the chair on the left. My son sat beside me, and the Directors, Bird, Banfield and Toruta, sat behind us in the two corners.

'The Big Chap made a surprisingly good impression. His face was a rosy colour, which probably came from the blood transfusions. He looked thin, but not haggard. The isolation from the outside world which he had experienced during all the years of imprisonment was not of course dispersed in the course of the visit. One could detect that twice he reached the edge of his self-control. He was mentally very alert and concentrated, and sometimes even a little humour sparkled. He treated the Directors very distantly, sometimes combined with a little irony. The following subjects were discussed:

1. The Christmas presents we had brought.
2. The delay in commencing our visit was briefly explained, and he approved of my son's protest.
3. He told us about his illness. He had been in pain for a long time before 19 November, when the ulcer, which he had not recognized as such, perforated. Until his admission to the British Military Hospital, i.e. in the three days between 19 and 22 November 1969, he had suffered almost unbearable pain, which subsided relatively quickly under treatment after his admission to hospital (pain-killers had probably also been given). He had received transfusions of about two litres of blood. In the first days in hospital, nourishment was given only by infusion. Also, a tube was inserted into his stomach through his nose, which he found very bothersome. The tube was apparently for sucking out stomach secretions. He was now free of pain, and although he still felt weak he was now on the mend.
4. Greetings from relations were conveyed to and returned by the Big Chap. He asked after individual members of the family.
5. The subject of further visits was mentioned, and the Big Chap at first agreed to receive visits as long as he was still in the British Military Hospital.
6. The Big Chap asked us to remember him to Freiburg, and to tell her that he was very sorry to have treated her so badly for more than twenty years. (He was referring to Fräulein Hildegard Faht, nicknamed "Freiburg", my husband's private secretary, who had been confronted with him at Nuremberg. At that time my husband was simulating loss of memory, and he insisted that he had never before seen this lady in his life, or at least he did not recognize her. This caused Fräulein Faht great distress, and she burst into tears.)
7. When he asked my son whether he had performed military service, my son told him the whole story of his conscientious objection, without interruption from my husband.

'Time passed very quickly, and before the conversation had really got into its stride visiting time was over. The warder sitting behind my husband began the countdown. 'You have five minutes left; you have four minutes left; you have three minutes left; you have two minutes left; you have one minute left . . .'. We did not allow the visit to be stopped, and took our leave while the last minute was passing.

'As we left, we were able to glance back through the glass partition. The Big Chap was standing, supporting himself with one hand on the table. He waved to us with the other, and even in the relatively dimly-lit room – the blinds had been let down so that the Big Chap should not by chance have an unobstructed glimpse of freedom – the pain, suppressed only with difficulty, and the despair with which he, the one remaining behind, sent us into freedom could be seen on his face.

'We all went back to the visitors' waiting room. Colonel O'Brian was waiting there for us with a cup of tea and a talk about the medical diagnosis.

'The Big Chap had probably had an ulcer for more than five years. On 19 November, i.e. while still in Spandau, he had had a "concealed perforation of an ulcer located in the duodenum" and, linked with this, peritonitis. The ulcer was located immediately beside the "pylorus". It could not therefore be seen in the first X-ray photographs, and further photographs had to be taken from different angles. Colonel O'Brian decided on "conservative" treatment, which had so far produced quite good results and would probably make an operation unnecessary. With patients of Rudolf Hess's age, an operation was always a risk, and was to be avoided for as long as possible.

'Hess was at first an unusually difficult patient, but as time passed he had become easier to treat. This was probably because of the change in his environment and the people around him. Further X-ray photographs were to be taken and tests carried out in mid-January. It would then be decided what more was to be done. Until then, he would be on a diet. O'Brian could not definitely say that the ulcer was not malignant, but he thought it unlikely. He also repeated that an operation might be necessary, but this would have to be decided in the light of the X-ray photographs in January.

'My son approached O'Brian about Professor Zenker (the

family had requested the custodial Powers to permit a consultation with a German doctor. Professor Dr Rudolf Zenker had said he was prepared to take over the treatment of Rudolf Hess), and told him that we did not intend by this to express any lack of confidence in him personally, the other doctors and the nurses, both male and female, at the British Military Hospital. The application submitted by Dr Seidl had stemmed from our desire to know that a German doctor was involved with whom we could discuss the findings undisturbed. O'Brian well understood what my son was trying to express, but said that so many other doctors had already been forced upon him that he had personally refused the assistance of Professor Zenker. He indicated to us that, in the treatment of the Big Chap, he was not master in his own house; and that he had to work under very difficult conditions. In this conversation, each understood the predicaments and needs of the other. We took our leave of Colonel O'Brian feeling reassured that the Big Chap was in good hands, and that he would certainly do all he could for him in the circumstances prevailing.

'Colonel Bird accompanied us along the route already described back to the hospital's main entrance, where the American chief warder, Mr Donham, was waiting with the car. Again a large number of journalists had gathered, but they had no more than a chance to photograph us inside the car. We were escorted along part of the route to the airport by a police vehicle with flashing blue lights. The flight to Munich passed off smoothly. We drove from the airport to friends at Starnberger See, and there we spent what was certainly the most unusual Christmas Eve and Christmas Day of my entire life. Talk with our friends centred on the visit, and our thoughts returned again and again to Berlin, trying to imagine how the Big Chap would end this day, alone with his thoughts. Twenty-eight years had passed by since we last saw each other.'[5]

Here my mother's account ends. My father's serious illness and his period at the British Military Hospital caused the 'Hess case' to make news headlines for weeks on end. I went to Great Britain and then to the United States to secure my father's release. The media were demanding his immediate release, particularly in Great Britain.

The British Government found itself under considerable

pressure from the public. One British newspaper commissioned an opinion poll, which found an overwhelming majority in favour of Rudolf Hess's immediate and unconditional release. Nearly 200 members of the House of Commons signed a declaration demanding release. The matter caused a great stir, and the family cherished hopes that release was at last imminent.

These hopes were brutally dashed on 13 March 1970. Barely recovered from a dangerous illness and aged 77, Rudolf Hess was returned to the Allied prison. All the protests and all the pressure from the public were in vain. In Spandau, the cynics were triumphant. The authorities were clearly conscience-stricken. Probably for this reason, if for no other, the announcement of his transfer to the prison was accompanied by a reference to what was referred to as significant mitigation of his imprisonment.

Rudolf Hess did not go back to his old cell, but was moved to the chapel, which had been made up from two cells; he was allowed to bring his bed and chair from the hospital, and he was given permission to prepare tea and coffee on his own boiling ring in his new retreat.

But a prison is still a prison, whatever the size of the cell and whatever the standard of its furnishing. What was crucial was not 'mitigation of his imprisonment', but the old man's release.

'THE FACT OF FALSE IMPRISONMENT'

DURING RUDOLF HESS'S period in hospital at the turn of 1969/1970, a letter from the one-time British chief prosecutor at the IMT, the present Lord Shawcross, in the London *Times* of 2 January 1970 contained the following remarkable sentences:[1]

'His (Rudolf Hess's) life sentence by the International Military Tribunal was, in comparison with others, by no means a lenient one. I suspect that all of us on the Western side took it for granted that it would be subject to the sort of commutation recognized in civilized systems of criminal justice and would not literally be for life.

'That he should continue to be imprisoned seems to me to be an affront to all notions of justice . . . that the British authorities in whose hospital Hess now is should accept a Soviet veto on operative procedures which the medical specialists of the United States, France and Britain consider to be necessary in order to safeguard his health is an instance of pusillanimity of a degree to which I had hoped the United Kingdom had not yet fallen in international affairs. I shall say nothing of humanity . . .'.

That is what Shawcross had to say.

According to the penal practice of the three Western custodial Powers, a prisoner serving life sentence is released at the latest after 15 to 20 years. In the case of Rudolf Hess, this period would have been completed between 1960 and 1966, and certainly when Speer and Schirach were allowed home. The former Deputy Führer, however, is not a normal case. The penalty

[290]

imposed on him is not measured in terms of legal criteria.

Quite the contrary! In the opinion of Dr Seidl and many other legal specialists in this country and abroad, the Nuremberg Tribunal and the sentences it handed down lack any basis in law. They represent acts of political despotism on the part of the four victors. In the case of Rudolf Hess they are doubly unlawful, because he alone among the so-called 'major war criminals' was indicted under all four points but was convicted only of 'conspiracy' and 'crimes against peace' – in themselves dubious. Hess of all people! Hess, who had tried to bring peace to the world! His continued imprisonment contains the facts necessary to establish a case of false imprisonment, a crime under the law of all civilized nations.

In the view of Seidl, the Hess family and very many public figures, there is only one solution: immediate release – without equivocation.

The opinion of the family and of Dr Seidl is that there is no cause to petition for mercy, since this implies a recognition of guilt and would premise a flawless court of law and a flawless verdict. There can be no question at all of this.

My father persists in his view that the International Military Tribunal was purely a victors' court; it had no right to sit in judgement on Germans. As early as 1946, he had definitively refused, via Dr Seidl, to advance a plea for mercy. He has not changed his attitude on this up to the present day, and he will not change it in the future.

His family and his counsel took up the fight for the release of Rudolf Hess soon after the Nuremberg Tribunal. On 15 November 1948, Seidl directed a petition to the Allied Control Council in Berlin, which then still formally ruled the whole of Germany. In it, he asked for the immediate release of Rudolf Hess. The application was refused.

The legal initiatives of the untiring Dr Seidl over the following 36 years can be divided roughly into four categories, which for reasons of space I must restrict to their most important points:

1. applications to the Directorate of Spandau Prison for special privileges, and requests for visits;
2. petitions and applications to the governments of the four custodial Powers, which cited new wars of aggression and

aggressive acts by the four victors as grounds for quashing
Hess's sentence;

3. applications and appeals to the European Commission for
   Human Rights in Strasburg and the Human Rights Commission of the United Nations in New York, citing violations of
   human rights in the case of Hess;

4. complaints to and pressure on Federal courts and Federal
   authorities to allow Rudolf Hess fully to enjoy his rights of
   citizenship and to effect his release.

It must unfortunately be said, at this point, that none of these
initiatives led to the desired result.

Seidl and Hess were not allowed, at any of a total of six visits,
to speak of legal matters arising from the continuing detention.
Even the most simple questions of civil law could not be
discussed. The lawyer was repeatedly admonished that he
should make no statements in public about his visits. If he did
so, he would be permitted no further visits. Applications by
Seidl for permission to discuss important legal matters with
Rudolf Hess during his visits were rejected.

After the release of von Schirach and Speer, on 3 November
1966 Seidl directed a petition to the four custodial Powers
requesting that, in view of the solitary confinement now beginning, Hess should be granted at least a number of special privileges. In detail, Seidl asked for the following:

1. the censorship of books should end, so that Frau Hess would
   no longer have to read every book she sent to Spandau for her
   husband, to ensure that it contained nothing objectionable;

2. Hess should be given permission to have a watch;

3. his periods in the garden should be increased from 30
   minutes to 60 minutes in the afternoon;

4. Seidl asked for permission to visit his client regularly every
   two months, without having to apply for a visit in advance;

5. Hess should have a bell in his cell so that he could call a
   warder in the night if he was suddenly taken ill;

6. Hess should be allowed the necessary facilities for making tea
   and coffee for himself at any time;

7. since Hess is a non-smoker, he should, in compensation, be
   allowed a few sweets each week;

8. Hess should be allowed to decide for himself when to switch off his light in the evening;
9. Hess should be permitted to take a bath whenever he wished, over and above the usual weekly bath.

None of these requests was presumptuous or unreasonable. The Directorate of the Allied Military Prison merely acknowledged receipt of Dr Seidl's letter. Not one of the nine points was approved in 1966. Only when Hess returned from hospital to the prison in March 1970 did the Allies see the need to grant these unimportant requests.

At Nuremberg, Rudolf Hess was convicted of so-called 'crimes against peace' because he had allegedly co-operated in a war of aggression, and in the opinion of the victors wars of aggression were contrary to international law.

It follows, therefore, that from then onwards all leading politicians who give orders for a war of aggression or other aggressive acts must be brought before a court – since, if this were not to happen, Hess would have to be released. If the Nuremberg 'victors' law' was genuine law, the Allied Military Prison in Berlin Spandau would be crowded. But the victors of the Second World War obviously intended not to be disturbed by the reproach of double standards.

Since the Second World War, more than 140 wars, leaving over 40 million dead, have been carried on, with none of the politicians responsible being indicted personally and criminally before an international tribunal. Seidl singled out three aggressions which he considered especially grave, because the Spandau custodial Powers were directly involved in them in one form or another. The first was the so-called 'Suez Adventure' of 1956, when Britain, France and Israel together attacked Egypt. The second was the American intervention in Vietnam in the mid-1960s. The third was the Soviet invasion of Afghanistan in the winter of 1979/80.

Dr Seidl stated, with conviction and force, that Rudolf Hess was held at Spandau on no legal grounds, because in spite of Nuremberg the four custodial Powers obviously continued to consider that war as a means of pursuing their national policies was permissible in law. He called attention to this incontestable contradiction in letters to the governments in Washington,

London, Paris and Moscow. He was not vouchsafed a reply.

On 7 June 1973, my mother delivered a complaint to the European Commission for Human Rights at Strasburg. The complaint was directed against the British Government, and asked the Commission to declare that continuation of the imprisonment of 80-year-old Rudolf Hess contravened Article 3 of the Convention for the Protection of Human Rights and Basic Freedoms, to which all West European states except France had acceded. (The USA and the Soviet Union have not acceded to it; Britain made certain reservations upon accession.) According to Article 3, no person may be subjected to inhuman or degrading punishment.

In the course of the protracted hearing before the European Commission for Human Rights, the complaint was extended to include Article 7, which says that no person may be condemned because of an act or omission which at the time of its commission was punishable under neither domestic nor international law (the principle of *nulla crimen, nulla poene sine lege*). With the aid of these complaints, Frau Hess wished to detach Britain from the four victors' front and force it to release Rudolf Hess unilaterally when the British Director was once again in command at Spandau. However, after a lengthy hearing, the complaints were rejected by the Commission on 28 May 1975 by formal argument and on feeble grounds: it had no jurisdiction to consider the Hess matter. The Commission did not in fact consider the complaints at all.

On 23 June 1979, Seidl followed this up with a complaint against Britain and France to the European Commission for Human Rights. Both states had infringed various human and civil rights by the unlawful detention of Rudolf Hess, and they were not bound to abide by an agreement between the four victors 'which is contrary to mandatory international law (*jus cogens*) and whose implementation would contravene fundamental human rights and basic freedoms, in particular the right to freedom'.[2] But here also the Commission decided that it had no jurisdiction.

Seidl's attempt in autumn 1979 to bring the Hess matter before the United Nation's Human Rights Commission fared no better. But the General Secretariat's reply of 7 November 1979 made quite apparent the political dimension of the rejection. The UN

Secretary-General based his refusal to bring the Hess matter before the Human Rights Commission on a reference to Article 107 of the Charter of the United Nations, the so-called Enemy States Article. Under this Article, the world organization cannot invalidate retrospectively or exclude for the future measures taken by the victors of the Second World War against Germany or Japan. Germany and Japan are thus still underprivileged nations.

Although the Federal Republic of Germany had meanwhile become a member of the United Nations, and any German might now claim the protection of the United Nations, Hess had to accept that this Enemy State Clause, by which the Allies had protected themselves, in practice for all time, against critical examination of their victors' justice, applied to him, although Article 107 spoke expressly only of 'measures relative to a state', not relative to a person. By refusing to bring the Hess matter before its Human Rights Commission, the United Nations thus contravened the letter of its own Statutes, as well as its established practice.

This at the same time created a potentially discriminatory and dangerous precedent for all Germans. Moreover, it also affected other sections of the statement by which the UN General Secretariat rejected Seidl's submission. How in future are Germans to resist arbitrary acts on the part of the former victors if the United Nations tolerates such discrimination in the case of Hess?

At the same time, the incomprehensible behaviour of the European Commission for Human Rights and of the United Nations inflicted severe damage on the cause of human rights all over the world, since these rights are of value only if they are inviolable and inalienable, i.e. if they apply to all people under all circumstances and cannot be rendered ineffective by inter-governmental agreement.

To some extent, all Germans were set outside the international legal system by the United Nation's negative decision in the Hess matter. This was strongly reminiscent of the *vae victis* of former times, when whole nations were declared 'proscribed', so that they were in practice outlawed. There was therefore an intrinsic logic in Seidl's accusing the Federal Republic of Germany under the 'foreign protection' clause – in the name of

Rudolf Hess – i.e. by reference to its duty to protect the rights of German citizens against unjustified interference from foreign states.

This action was originally brought before the Administrative Court in Cologne as early as 1977. It passed through all stages, and in the end, on 24 February 1981, was finally rejected by the Federal Administrative Court as unfounded.

Seidl's action was intended to force the authorities of the Federal Republic of Germany:

1. to issue an official statement condemning the continued imprisonment of his client as an infringement of human rights;
2. to take, *vis-à-vis* the four custodial Powers, all appropriate steps for the release of Rudolf Hess, including legal and political measures;
3. to initiate resolutions at the UN General Assembly which condemned the solitary confinement of Rudolf Hess at Spandau as a violation of human rights, and which directed the four victors to release the prisoner immediately.

The Federal Administrative Court's grounds for rejecting Seidl's appeal said, on this point:[3]

'In relation to this, the plaintiff considers that the lack of an appropriate precept under Constitutional law does not prevent the Federal Republic of Germany from taking far-reaching action. This may be so, but the crucial point is that the question of whether the agencies of the Federal Republic of Germany wish to go beyond what is required of them under the Constitution is governed by their duty to exercise wide discretion, that in this case such discretion has not been wrongly exercised, and that the demand for further action advanced by the plaintiff arises from neither Constitutional nor any other Federal law.

'It is not therefore a matter of whether, as the plaintiff asserts, his conviction – not for war crimes and crimes against humanity – by the International Military Tribunal was contrary to international law, which is accepted in the literature (cf. e.g. Berber, Textbook of International Law, Vol. II, Law of War, 2nd. edition, 1969, Sec. 50 pp. 250ff., 254–263; Verdross, International Law, 5th. edition 1964, p. 219f.; Verdross-Simma, Universal International Law, 1976, p. 227, with appropriate further references), or of whether his exceptionally long detention under unusual conditions is contrary to international law, which cannot in reality be excluded.'

In fact, it is apparent from the literature quoted by the Federal Administrative Court in its judgement on 24 February 1981 that the conviction of Rudolf Hess by the International Military Tribunal was contrary to international law, and that his exceptionally long detention under unusual conditions is also contrary to international law.

Two further complaints of unconstitutionality, which Seidl submitted in Karlsruhe on behalf of Hess in 1981 and 1983, were also rejected. Had he been successful, the Federal Constitutional Court would have been obliged to declare that the Nuremberg judgement against Rudolf Hess was unlawful and therefore null and void, that the continuing confinement of the prisoner in Spandau contravened mandatory international law and the Basic Law, that Bonn's contribution to the maintenance of the Four-Power prison was incompatible with the regulations on the protection of German nationals from interference by foreign states, and that continuation of the imprisonment could not be substantiated under Article 107 of the UN Charter ('Enemy States Clause'). In addition, the Federal Government would have had to take not only humanitarian but also legal and political steps for the release of Rudolf Hess.

The Federal Government had already informed Seidl on 9 March 1979, through the Foreign Minister, Hans Dietrich Genscher,[4] that 'the advanced age and the weakened health of Rudolf Hess has long justified release from his long imprisonment. The Federal President and the Federal Government have for years been working for this – as have the Heads of Government of the three Powers [i.e. the USA, Britain and France – W.R.H.]. They will continue to do so.

'I must however point out that the three Powers do not welcome the questioning of the lawfulness of the International Military Tribunal's judgement. The three Powers are of the opinion that only humanitarian grounds can be considered in relation to Rudolf Hess's release. The Federal Government shares this opinion.'

The Federal Government has not as yet moved away from this

attitude. Since the Supreme Federal Courts of the Federal Republic of Germany have in practice supported this opinion in their judgements, everything that Bonn has officially undertaken to date in the Hess matter remains restricted to the humanitarian aspect.

The reason for this is that Nuremberg represents a cornerstone of the super-Versailles imposed by the four victors upon Germany at the end of the Second World War. Any legal attack on Nuremberg, on the judgements passed there and on the incarceration for life of Rudolf Hess would be seen as extremely provocative by the governments in Moscow, Washington, London and Paris, because this would endanger the European postwar system of law and order, which rests on a divided, humiliated and suppressed Germany. The comments of the respected Professor Theodor Eschenburg on this continue to be valid:[5] 'Anyone who challenges Germany's sole guilt for the Second World War destroys the foundations of post-war policy.'

The Western Powers have for long given the impression that they are in favour of releasing Rudolf Hess – of course, only on humanitarian grounds! – and that only the Soviets are opposed to such a move. But when the Hess matter is combined with the German question, and also therefore with the balance of power between East and West, serious doubts arise as to whether this is the true position. Notwithstanding everything which has meanwhile come between them, the four victors of the Second World War appear to be determined, now as ever, to rule Germany together. And this excludes the release of Rudolf Hess, especially on legal grounds. He has become as it were a symbol of foreign powers' dominion over Germany. This attitude on the part of the custodial Powers is made clear in a letter sent by the British Prime Minister, Margaret Thatcher, to Dr Seidl on 21 December 1979 through her Private Secretary:[6]

'The Prime Minister has asked me to reply to your letter of 23 August about Herr Rudolf Hess which I acknowledged on 3 September.

'The arguments in your letter concerning the prosecution and conviction of Herr Hess and the evidence put before the International Military Tribunal have been noted. These arguments were fully considered by the Tribunal at the time. The British Government remains in no doubt about the legality of the sentence which Herr Hess is now serving.

'As you will be aware, however, the British Government, together with the Governments of the United States and France, have for the last 12 years expressed themselves in favour of the unconditional release of Herr Hess on humanitarian grounds. The Prime Minister has asked me to assure you that the British Government for its part is continuing to press for agreement among the Four Powers for his release.

'I should say, however, that in Her Majesty's Government's view, the arguments which you put forward relating to Hess's trial and conviction are likely to reinforce the Soviet Union in their opposition to Hess's release and to make it less likely that they will reconsider their very firmly held position.'

It is true that up to the present no document has come to light in which the Four Powers represent as their official and common view the link between the Hess matter and the German question. There exists, however, a British Government statement of 12 July 1974 on the Hess family's complaint to the European Human Rights Commission that makes the link clear. It can be assumed that this was agreed behind the scenes with the three other custodial Powers.[7] And this is the nature of the link: after the Wehrmacht capitulated on 8 May 1945, the governments of the USA, Britain, France and the Soviet Union published a declaration dated 5 June 1945 under which they assumed 'supreme governmental power over Germany'. Germany was divided into four zones, which were assigned to the four Occupying Powers. The former Reich capital of Berlin would henceforth be considered as a special region. It would be occupied by the Four Powers jointly, and likewise be divided into four sectors.

On 14 November 1944 and 1 May 1945, the USA, Britain, France and the Soviet Union concluded two agreements. They created the necessary apparatus for exercise of the supreme governmental powers taken over by them jointly, the so-called Control Organization. Article 1 of the 1944 agreement reads: 'Under this agreement, supreme governmental power in Germany will be exercised by the Commanders-in-Chief of the Armed Forces . . . under the direction of the government concerned in its respective Occupation Zone, and in matters which concern Germany as a whole jointly in their capacities as members of the supreme Control Organization set up under this agreement.' This means, in plain words: each Occupying Power was sovereign in its own Occupation Zone and unrestricted in its actions. But in 'matters which concern Germany as a whole' – whatever they might be – they undertook to co-operate with one another.

The Commanders-in-Chief of the four Occupying Powers formed the so-called Control Council, the supreme body for exercising co-operation. This was the supreme authority of the Control Organization acting for the whole of Germany. For the administration of 'Greater Berlin', as it was then called, the Berlin Commandants of the Four Powers set up, in addition, a joint 'Kommandantura'. The Control Council determined what the Kommandantura was to do and what it was not to do.

This was, in brief, the organization exercising the Allies' ruling power over Germany. In addition, under the London Agreement of 8 August 1945, the four victors established the basis for the Nuremberg trials. The Charter of the International Military Tribunal (IMT) was an integral part of this Agreement. Article 27 empowered the Tribunal to sentence the accused to death or to any other punishment they might consider appropriate. This Article is the legal basis for the sentence of life imprisonment in the Rudolf Hess case. But in addition there is also Article 29, and this Article forms the link with the victors' ruling power over Germany.

This Article 29 of the IMT Charter says: 'If the accused are pronounced guilty, the sentences are to be carried out in accordance with the directives of the Control Council for Germany . . .'. On the basis of this Article, the Control Council instructed the Four-Power Kommandantura in Berlin to select and to prepare within its jurisdiction – i.e. within Greater Berlin – a suitable prison for the 'major war criminals' sentenced at Nuremberg. This prison was to be under full Four-Power administration and supervision.

This Control Council instruction formed the legal foundation on which, in 1946/47, the Berlin Kommandantura established the Four-Power prison at Spandau. The Kommandantura itself retained supreme authority over this prison, but it created a Directorate in which, until this very day, each of the Four Powers has a seat and a voice – and moreover makes use of these rights. The four Directors can act, however, only on a basis of unanimous decisions.

The upper two-thirds of the Control Council-Kommandantura-Directorate pyramid broke away as early as 1948 as the division of Germany became more apparent in the growing confrontation between the USA and the Soviet Union. On 20 March 1948, the Russian Commander-in-Chief in Germany, Marshal Sokolovsky, withdrew from the Control Council, which consequently terminated its activities. On 1 July 1948, the Soviet representatives also left the Allied Kommandantura. On 21 December 1948, the Commandants of the three Western Sectors of Berlin announced that they would continue the work of the Allied Kommandantura, and that during the Soviet representatives' absence 'the three Western Allies will exercise the powers of the Allied Kommandantura, although it is clear that, because of the Soviet obstruction, it will at first be possible to implement its decisions only in the Western Sectors of Berlin'.

As we know, the Soviet 'obstruction' has continued until the present day. The Soviets have not returned, either to the Allied Kommandantura or to the Control Council.

Nonetheless, contacts and co-operation between the four victors never quite came to a standstill. The Western Powers permitted the Soviets to – as it were – select where Four-Power responsibility would survive and where it would not. The victors' Commanders-in-Chief continued to exercise, in certain fields, the rights and responsibilities of the former Allies in and over Germany, in spite of the break-up of the Control Council.

Matters became somewhat more complicated in 1949 when the Federal Republic of Germany and the German Democratic Republic were established, since the increasingly apparent division of Germany cast increasing doubt on the victors' responsibility for Germany as a whole. But the USA, the Soviet Union, Britain and France had already ensured that the link between them on the German question should not suffer complete rupture.

On 20 June 1949, one month after the establishment of the Federal Republic of Germany, the three Western Powers signed a treaty embodying a reference to earlier agreements with the Soviet Union. This treaty transferred their sovereign rights over Germany, in so far as they had previously rested with the

Commanders-in-Chief of the American, British and French Occupying Powers, to three so-called High Commissioners. From then onwards, these three High Commissioners appointed by Washington, London and Paris exercised supreme governmental authority over West Germany. They continued to maintain contact with their opposite number representing the Soviet Union in the GDR. As a consequence, notwithstanding Germany's partition, the four victors' responsibility for Germany as a whole was preserved.

This did not change when in 1955 the High Commissioners became the Bonn Ambassadors of the USA, Britain and France upon the FRG's entry into NATO. They remained in touch with the Soviet Ambassador, who has resided in East Berlin since the GDR's entry into the Warsaw Pact. The four victors of the Second World War therefore continue to exercise their rights and obligations in relation to Germany as a whole across the boundaries of the two alliances, although the FRG and GDR have been sovereign states formally since 1955. To put it another way, Germany remained subject to Allied sovereignty and remained an occupied country, even though everyday life in the Federal Republic gives one the impression that one is living in a sovereign state.

What then was the effect of these developments on the status of the Allied Military Prison at Berlin Spandau? Here also the Western Powers bowed almost without resistance to Soviet despotism. It is true that in 1948 they once again courageously declared that they exercised the authority of the Kommandantura in the three Western Sectors, but at the same time they permitted the Soviets to take almost unrestricted command of the lowest body of the pyramid, the Spandau Directorate, although the Kommandantura has authority to issue orders to this Directorate. We have only to remember the conditions in the prison when, towards the end of the 1940s, the seven prisoners there were almost starving to death.

Nothing in this grotesque situation changed when in 1962 the Soviets dissolved their headquarters in the GDR. Responsibility for the prison at Spandau was then transferred to the staff of the 'Group of Soviet Armed Forces in Germany' – i.e. the Soviet armed forces stationed in the GDR. Since then, the Western Powers' authorities in West Berlin have maintained contact with the Soviet Embassy in East Berlin on all Four-Power matters affecting Spandau.

What then is the consequence of all this? The British Government's opinion, which certainly coincides with that of the other three victors, is that Four-Power responsibility for Spandau continues undiminished. Therefore, 'certain matters' – as they are referred to in the British statement of 1974, when alluding to the possible release of Rudolf Hess – 'for which the Four Powers remain responsible can be dealt with only on the basis of Four-Power control, and not individual control'. That is, only the Four Powers jointly, and not – let us say – Britain alone, can decide to release Rudolf Hess. But such a decision needs a unanimous decision by the Spandau Directorate. Since there is 'no agreement among the Four Powers on the immediate termination of imprisonment and the release of Rudolf Hess', such a unanimous decision has as yet failed to materialize. Using this formal unanimity argument, each of the Four Powers can hide behind the others in their joint endeavour to maintain the symbol of their sovereignty over Germany.

This unanimity was again asserted in 1954, 1955 and 1957, when von Neurath, Raeder and Funk were released ahead of time. On each occasion, the Four Powers reached agreement on their release. Every attempt to curtail Rudolf Hess's life imprisonment by referring to the fact that Neurath, Raeder and Funk were released before time has up to now been rejected by the Four Powers, whose argument is that there is no unanimity.

Nevertheless, it is questionable whether the unanimity argument really holds water. In the various Berlin crises, have not the Soviets so often and repeatedly violated Four-Power responsibility that the Western Powers now have a right to withdraw from the agreements on Spandau and to release Rudolf Hess unilaterally?

On this point, Professor Blumenwitz of Würzburg, the specialist in international law, writes in his opinion, already referred to: 'The withdrawal must take place expressly and immediately.' That is, after one of the Berlin crises, the Western Powers should have immediately declared that now they also no longer felt bound by the agreements with the Soviet Union on joint responsibility for Spandau. But, as it is, they never made such a declaration. On the contrary, the Western Powers continued to emphasize the Four-Power agreements' validity, and in the course of time the Soviets have increasingly respected this attitude. In fact, in the Four Power agreement on Berlin of 1972 – the latest agreement to be concluded between them on the question of Germany – the Four Powers again reaffirmed their intention to maintain their joint responsibility for Germany and Berlin, i.e. including Spandau.

The Western Powers have here the ready excuse that it would be contrary to international law if now – many years after the Soviet infringements of the Four Power agreements – the British Government, for example, were to withdraw from joint responsibility for Spandau, renounce the principle of unanimity underlying this responsibility and unilaterally set Rudolf Hess free. If this rejoinder on the side of the Western Powers really and unequivocally reflects the situation in Berlin under international law, there remains in logic a question for the Western Powers: why did they not terminate the Spandau agreement and release Rudolf Hess when the Soviets, by building their wall and so on, grossly violated the Four Power agreement on Berlin? The Western argument relying on the Four Power agreements, which apparently prevent them from releasing Rudolf Hess, clearly rests on sand. Or are these no more than conscious pretexts, because the Western Powers also do not wish to release Rudolf Hess?

The French journalist Michel Vercel writes on page 220 of his book, referred to above, that there exists, secret up to now, a set of rules on the administration of Spandau. These rules include a Four Power decision that, if one of them were to withdraw from the joint administration of the prison, it would have to be closed and the remaining prisoners returned to the Power that brought them before the Tribunal at Nuremberg in 1945.[8] Vercel later expressly reconfirmed in a letter the existence of such a secret set of rules. There is not the slightest reason to doubt this statement. It is easy to believe that the four custodial Powers reached such an agreement, since it had always to be borne in mind that one or more of the custodial Powers might – for one reason or another – withdraw from the joint administration of the prison. Precautions had of course to be taken against such an eventuality.

The one-time American Director of the Allied Military Prison, Eugene K. Bird, also refers in his book to the existence of such an agreement:[9] 'Or, they [i.e. the Western Powers, W.R.H.] could inform the Soviets that Spandau was "closed" and hand the prisoners over to the Allies by whom they were first captured.'

Finally, the circumstance that up to the present the custodial Powers have steadfastly refused to make copies of this agreement available, or even allow a sight of it, supports the veracity of what Vercel has to say on the matter. In 1974, Professor Blumenwitz, when preparing his legal opinion on the Hess case, asked the governments of the Four Powers to allow him to see the agreements and regulations controlling the detailed administration of, and prison methods in, Spandau. But the governments of the USA, Britain and France referred Professor Blumenwitz to the Spandau Directorate, which answered, in reply to a similar enquiry from Professor Blumenwitz: 'We acknowledge the contents of your letter of 19 March 1974, and have to inform you that the Directorate of the Allied Military Prison at Spandau is not in a position to accede to your request.'[10]

It is clear that nothing has altered here up to the present day. The four victors are concealing important sections of the legal principles under which Rudolf Hess's life imprisonment is being performed. Those fighting for his release therefore do not know whether or not there is a possibility that one of the four victors may at long last set free the last prisoner in Spandau. Indeed, it must be concluded from the secrecy surrounding the prison regulations that such a possibility exists. Its secrecy is only maintained so as not to endanger the victors' sovereignty over Germany.

The bending of the law to the political end that Germany should remain under their control far into the future has characterized the Four Powers' attitude in the Hess matter from the very outset. The Nuremberg Tribunal itself violated international law and the practice of states. Rudolf Hess is being detained in Spandau for his lifetime, although each of the Four Powers has a duty to release him. Finally, the Four Powers, by the manner of their conduct of the imprisonment, even contravene their own law.

Article 29 of the IMT Charter, which is in fact an integral part of the 1945 London Agreement, says: '. . . aggravation of the punishment is not permitted'. In spite of this regulation, such an aggravation of punishment did take place. Since Speer and Schirach were released in 1966, Rudolf Hess has no longer been under normal imprisonment. He can no longer share the sorrows of his imprisonment with other fellow-sufferers. Rather, for 19 years he has been subjected to the torture of isolation, unimaginable in its cruelty and inhumanity.

FREEDOM FOR RUDOLF HESS

1 OCTOBER 1966, when his last two fellow-prisoners, Speer and Schirach, were released, inflicted a deep wound in the struggle for the release of Rudolf Hess. For many decades the members of his family had hoped, albeit with declining conviction, that one day they would again be united in freedom with their husband, father, brother, grandfather and father-in-law. Hess himself appeared to be full of hope when he wrote to his wife on 3 September 1966:[1] 'We are then looking forward to October; that at least a few brilliant and warm weeks will still be granted us . . .'.

But 1 October, the period leading up to Christmas, and Christmas itself passed without Rudolf Hess being allowed home. The family's last hopes of a humane outcome vanished with this. It was now clear that the victors intended that Rudolf Hess should remain alone behind the sombre walls of the 600-man prison at Berlin–Spandau, the loneliest prisoner in the world.

Faced with this situation, the family decided to abandon the discretion they had hitherto exercised *vis-à-vis* the public. They now took the fight for Rudolf Hess's freedom into the open, set up a formal organization, and in their methods abandoned the strictly legal path. The outcome of this was the 'Declaration of the Hess family of 1 October 1966' and the foundation of the *Hilfsgemeinschaft 'Freiheit für Rudolf Hess' e.V.* ('Freedom for Rudolf Hess' Support Association – a registered society), a world-wide citizens' initiative in defence of human rights in the

Hess matter. In the years since its foundation, these activities have become very widespread indeed.

The October Declaration was conveyed to the press at home and abroad. Copies, with a request for attention, were sent to Pope Paul VI, the Heads of State of the four custodial Powers, the World Council of Churches and the United Nations Commission for Human Rights. It was an attempt to arouse world opinion by beating the drum.

In this Declaration, the Hess family expressed its conviction[2] that 'this cruel situation, unknown until now in modern legal history, was neither envisaged nor intended by the Nuremberg Tribunal'. Rudolf Hess's punishment was described as 'founded exclusively on the historico-political accusation that he had participated in the preparation and conduct of a war of aggression'. Even if this judgement were recognized, the circumstance had to be considered that, by his flight to Great Britain, Hess had tried to bring an end to the war. For a quarter of a century, however, he had been in prison, although all civilized states restrict the term of imprisonment in a life sentence to between 15 and 20 years. Moreover, Neurath, Raeder and Funk had also been released from Spandau before time.

The fate to which Hess had now to resign himself was, for his family, 'a belated intensification of the sentence, and perhaps an even more horrible process of homicide than the sentences of death carried out at Nuremberg – carried out on a man over seventy years of age!' They appealed to all men of good will, 'to speak out against this martyrdom before it is consummated'! (The text of the 'Declaration' is in the Appendix).

There was a great response to the Declaration. The European Commission for Human Rights, it is true, again declared that it had no jurisdiction. The British Government told the Hess family that it had seriously considered the matter, and that it was expecting to discuss it with the other three Powers. The governments of France and the United States answered similarly. The Pope, the World Council of Churches and Moscow remained silent.

In those last months of 1966, when Hess's 'life imprisonment' became a literal reality, the Freedom for Rudolf Hess Support Association gradually began to take shape within the circle of our family and friends. I drafted the Association's rules, and preliminary discussions on finance and publicity were commenced. On 14 January 1967, the Support Association was formed among a small group at Frankfurt-am-Main. Its rules included the following:[3]

'The Freedom for Rudolf Hess Support Association is an international association of individuals and corporate bodies, which has as its object the promotion of measures and the support of endeavours whose purpose is the release of the former Reich Minister Rudolf Hess, detained in the Spandau Military Prison, so as to ensure that he can spend the evening of his life in freedom with his family.

'The Association has no political objectives. It is without party-political, financial and confessional commitments of any kind. The Declaration issued by the Hess family on 1 October 1966 provided the motivation for the establishment of the Association. The Declaration is therefore annexed to these rules.'

Within a short time, the Support Association succeeded in gaining a substantial number of members from all levels of society and age groups. This gave it the financial and organizational basis for beginning the self-evident tasks before it.

The Executive Committee of the Association had no doubts about the difficulty of the objective it had set itself, and it had no illusions about the possibility of success. But under no circumstances was it prepared to sit idly by as the grass gradually grew over Spandau and its solitary prisoner.

The activities of the Support Association had of course to develop essentially in two directions:
1. keeping alive an awareness of Spandau among the public by continuous information and reminders through the media:
2. increasing pressure on the authorities by regular reminders, combined with the transmission of expressions of opinion from the public.

One of the Support Association's first steps was to publish a Declaration on 1 October 1967, the anniversary of Rudolf Hess's solitary confinement. This Declaration asked all people of good will to join in the Support Association's demands by adding their signature to it. A total of some 400,000 signatures from 40 countries have so far been collected, including well-known and highly respected individuals (see Appendix).

Another main area of PR work consisted of rallies in almost every large town in the Federal Republic. These rallies not only attracted large attendances wherever they were held; they were also widely reported in the press, on television and on the radio. Gramophone records of the rallies were prepared, which, in turn, were distributed to large numbers of people. The rallies were attended by an average of nearly 1,500 people. A far larger number of people could be reached by the PR effect of the rallies. Invitations to the rallies took the form of large poster-campaigns in the regions concerned, public protest marches were organized, and banners trailing behind aircraft emphasized Rudolf Hess's unjust confinement. Part of the Support Association's work to date has been the issue and wide distribution among the public of eleven editions of the Association's newspaper-type special publication, Spandau Report. These eleven editions reached a total circulation of over one million copies. The Support Association has recently gone over to displaying – to date – six full-page advertisements in the *Frankfurter Allgemeine Zeitung*, each of which reached a readership of approaching one million people. These advertisements, for their part, evoke editorial comment throughout the world, and lead to a – sometimes heated – discussion in the correspondence columns. Herr Simon Wiesenthal again reacted to one of the recent advertisements; he had already interceded for Rudolf Hess's release on medical grounds (unfitness to remain in custody) in a *Playboy* interview.

The Support Association also commissioned opinion polls. In 1974, a poll conducted by the Allensbach Institute for Public Opinion Surveys showed that about 70% of all those questioned were in favour of Rudolf Hess's release.

Apart from these main areas of PR work, countless petitions, applications and proposals were submitted to all the authorities concerned – directly or indirectly – in the Hess matter. Correspondence with the custodial Powers alone filled innumerable files. The same is true of correspondence with the Federal Government, Church authorities and dignitaries, humanitarian organizations such as the Red Cross, etc. The members of the German Parliament and several of those of the Länder Parliaments are briefed at least once a year on the Support Association's efforts, and urged to do all in their power to obtain the old man's final release. The Support Association's continuous flow of information has led to numerous questions being asked about the Hess matter in the Federal Parliament, as well as in the Länder Parliaments.

Apart from all these activities, the Support Association commissioned a number of legal opinions on the Hess case, the most outstanding of these being the opinion, extensively quoted here, by the Würzburg specialist in international law Professor Blumenwitz. The various proceedings before the European Commission for Human Rights were organized and financed by the Support Association. Finally, the Support Association also made funds available for Wolf Rüdiger Hess's numerous journeys, to Britain and the USA in particular, to promote the demand for Rudolf Hess's release by direct contact with ministers and members of parliament in those countries.

One thing is certain: without the work of the Support Association no one today would any longer be voicing the cause of Rudolf Hess, much of the fundamental litigation conducted by Dr Seidl would not have been possible, the countless expressions of opinion which, almost without exception, denounce the anachronistic scandal of Spandau, the judgement which declared that his incarceration violated international law, and the humiliation of all those responsible would not have existed.

It is true that all this has not led to freedom for Rudolf Hess, but it has certainly contributed to the fact that he is still alive today. Although it is officially forbidden to tell him about the efforts of the family, Dr Seidl and the Support Association, he at least comes to know that he is not forgotten; that now, as ever, there are people and organizations active on his behalf. This gives him sustenance and strength to bear with honour his cruel lot, even up to the present day. The Support Association has a nucleus of members numbering several thousand, and an equally large body of sympathizers and supporters. Since it came into being, it has received contributions and donations running into six figures. This money has been used to institute the measures described above.

In its PR work, the Support Association can certainly claim to have brought itself to the notice of all those in responsible positions, and it has been engaged in this for over 15 years. In future, therefore, no one will be able to claim that he knew nothing about the Spandau tragedy. All those in responsible positions have been regularly asked to bring an end to this inhuman game; none of them has achieved the liberating step. The work of the Support Association here described would not have been possible without the assistance of the following people: The Chairman, Major-General (retired) Max Sachsenheimer, the Secretary from the very beginning, Fräulein Eva Schleusener and the subsequent Chairman, Federal Minister (retired) Dr Ewald Bucher. Two of these, Eva Schleusener and Max Sachsenheimer, are no longer alive.

Max Sachsenheimer, holder of the Knight's Cross with Oakleaves and Swords, was promoted during the Second World War from company commander through the ranks to divisional commander. He was a man of unusual energy and high ideals. His overriding principle in life was support for humanity and justice, combined with a willingness to make personal sacrifices to that end. With these ideals before him, in February 1967 Sachsenheimer took over without hesitation, at the request of the Hess family, the chairmanship of the Support Association. He was at that time fully employed as an independent businessman. Max Sachsenheimer considered it a personal duty to work for the release of the last prisoner in Spandau.

Max Sachsenheimer saw in Hess a living reminder of the victors' inhumanity. His energy and his dedication were outstanding. Sachsenheimer led the Support Association for six years from its organizing phase to its consolidation. Thanks to him, within a very short time the Association became a respected and widely recognized organization. Only four weeks before his death, he led a major rally at Bonn. On this occasion, the General Meeting, with great enthusiasm and with no dissenting votes, once again elected him Chairman. He had just reached the age of 63 when, on 2 June 1973, he was taken from us in the middle of an enterprising and fulfilled life.

From its foundation, Fräulein Eva Schleusener, the Support Association's Secretary, gave it every day unprecedented, loyal and self-denying service. No trouble was too great for her, no commission too small to deserve immediate attention. Eva Schleusener was the Support Association's 'treasure'. She expressly refused to accept any kind of payment for her unceasing efforts, even supporting others from her meagre pension.

The Support Association owes her a debt of infinite gratitude. Three days before her death, she was still sitting in the office before her typewriter. Eva Schleusener died following a short but severe illness on 7 November 1982 at the age of 84.

Following Sachsenheimer's death, the former Federal Minister of Justice, Dr Ewald Bucher, took over the Chair of the Support Association. For this alone he deserves our greatest thanks, since in 1973/4 it was in no way to be taken for granted that the former FDP Minister would lead the fight for the release of Rudolf Hess. It was clear evidence of that personal courage which had distinguished the whole of Bucher's official career.

Dr Seidl had to relinquish Rudolf Hess as a client when, in 1974, he became a State Secretary in the Bavarian Ministry of Justice. At the family's suggestion, Dr Bucher took over as Rudolf Hess's legal representative – that is, he tried to take over. Wolf Rüdiger Hess had kept his father informed, and given him some of the details of Dr Bucher's career. Shortly after, the US Commandant informed Wolf[4] that 'your father agrees with the proposal, and Dr Bucher should make the necessary arrangements for a visit to Spandau'.

This was only to be expected, since a solicitor must speak with his client if he is effectively to protect his rights. But what followed this invitation was rejection by the Four Powers.

On 8 January 1975, Bucher submitted an application for a visit, fully correct in form, to the Spandau Four Power Directorate. But instead of the expected permission he at first received two provisional replies: he was to be patient: his visit was still under discussion. Then, a month after the application, on 11 February 1975, Bucher received a final refusal.

Bucher was seized with righteous anger. The Four Powers were certainly entitled to hold Rudolf Hess in prison as a former National Socialist he wrote to the four Berlin Commandants,[5] but they were not entitled 'to employ National Socialist methods against a German lawyer'. One of the basic rights of the citizens of any democratic state was to receive professional advice from a lawyer, and any solicitor had a right to exercise his profession free from coercion. Anything else was 'a brazen impertinence' and 'a concept both grotesque and deplorable'.

Bucher's stinging protest was considered by the governments of the Four Powers, which had the audacity to inform him that they would of course have preferred to see Rudolf Hess represented by a solicitor occupying a less exposed position, or who was at least not so dedicated to the release of Rudolf Hess.

All that was lacking was for them to tell the family to choose a lawyer for Rudolf Hess who was opposed to his release! Bucher himself brought in the Federal Chancellery in Bonn, but after contacting the Allies the Chancellery informed him that there was no prospect of the Four Powers' changing their attitude. One or other of the Four Powers had exercised its veto against the US Director Keane's invitation, and the matter rested there. Bucher therefore never received a power of attorney signed by Rudolf Hess – a fine example of Allied justice!

Apart from his courageous outspokenness and his championing of justice, Bucher was still of great assistance to the Support Association. The chairmanship of this upright Liberal made it impossible for malevolent influences to push the Support Association into the right-wing extremists' camp or to spread such an image of the Association among the public. In fact, during the many years of its existence the Support Association has not permitted itself to be misused for party-political purposes. It has always remained non-partisan.

This is also evidenced by the immense correspondence the Support Association's office has conducted, covering all parts of the world. The files, today, fill rows of shelves. Those who support the demand for the release of Rudolf Hess and speak up for this in their letters come from all political camps – from the extreme Right to the extreme Left, and most certainly include the middle-class Centre. Most of these correspondents emphasize the humanitarian aspect. But other characteristics of the Support Association's correspondence are the repeated excuses, the spurious reasons and the silence employed by political authorities in reacting – or failing to react – to any appeal. If we approached the four custodial Powers, then the three Western Powers would plead the Soviet Union's 'Njet' and declare that, if it were up to them alone, Hess would long since have been released. If we approached other political decision-makers, such as the Federal Government, EEC bodies, or the United Nations, they would refer us to the four custodial Powers. Usually, it was only the Soviet Union which did not answer at all when approached.

There, have, however, been occasions when signals have come from Moscow suggesting that the Soviets were prepared at least to consider releasing Rudolf Hess from his imprisonment. In 1973/74, the Soviet side was still repeating the stereotyped formula that there was no question of release, since Hess had shown no remorse for the millions of Second World War dead; neither had he pleaded for mercy. Moscow of course knew – and still knows – that Rudolf Hess can in no way express a view on such matters because the Soviet Union itself strictly prevents his saying anything about the period between 1933 and 1945. No one knows what Rudolf Hess's thoughts are today. But in 1974/75, at the peak of the social–liberal policy towards the East, movement in the Soviet attitude suddenly appeared.

It was at this time that Bishop Kurt Scharf of Berlin first heard that Moscow was considering the release of Hess. In earlier years, when he was still Chairman of the Council of Protestant Churches in Germany (EKD), Scharf had advocated Hess's release, and had collaborated in the initiative instituted by the World Council of Churches in Geneva to this end. It was now being said that, after the closure of Spandau, the Soviets wished to establish, as a kind of substitute, an anti-Fascist museum under Four-Power control, so that they could preserve intact their presence in West Berlin. Hess was to undertake to cease political activity and to write no memoirs when he was at liberty once again. Also, he was to be given no triumphal reception when he arrived in Munich. All this was discussed in a detailed conversation with Wolf Rüdiger Hess. The assurances desired were given by the family, but the matter came to nothing.

Scarcely two years later, in January 1976, similar information reached Scharf. This time, a further condition for Hess's release was complete discretion in public from the Support Association and the family. The bishop again took me into his confidence, and we discussed together how Dr Bucher or the GDR solicitor Dr Vogel, who was well respected for his work in the ransoming of political detainees from the GDR, could be involved in order to get from Rudolf Hess an unequivocal declaration that he would abstain from political activity. But this also ran into the sand.

Three years after this, on 16 May 1979, the London *Evening News* reported on page one that the Soviets were prepared to agree to release Rudolf Hess if he would spend the rest of his life in retirement. The writer of this article was the paper's Moscow Correspondent Victor Louis, who is known for his reliable contacts with the Kremlin. Not very long after this, the Minister of State in the Bonn Federal Chancellery, Hans-Jürgen Wischnewski, received a telephone message from 'the highest level in the Soviet Union' (Secretary-General Leonid Breschnev?) for transmission to Federal Chancellor Schmidt. This was to the effect that the Soviet Union would be prepared to sanction a private conversation between Rudolf Hess and Wolf Rüdiger Hess – that is, without the usual presence of the four Spandau Directors – if an application were made for this. Moscow was further prepared to abandon its opposition to Hess's release if, in this private conversation with his son, he undertook to abstain from all pro-Nazi statements in public. The reason given for this change of attitude was that the Soviet Union did not wish to make a martyr out of Hess.

Arising from this, Wischnewski tried to reach me by telephone to give me the news; I was at the time in Saudi Arabia on business. The German Embassy searched for me all over Jeddah, and when I was eventually found Wischnewski and I agreed by telephone that I should apply for a private visit for 3 August, and that it would be best to do this from Saudi Arabia. I flew back to Germany on 31 July so as to be on hand for the visit.

The Spandau Directorate's answer was already awaiting me at my home in Gräfeling near Munich. It had approved the visit for 3 August – but 'under the conditions usual in the past';[6] that is, no private conversation. Surprised by this contradiction, I decided to stop off at Bonn on my way to Berlin to discuss the matter with Wischnewski. The Minister of State thought there must be a misunderstanding, and he suggested that I should carry on with the visit as planned. Perhaps there would be a last-minute opportunity for me to have a private talk with my father.

This hope was not however realized. As soon as I had completed my visit to Spandau, I telephoned Bonn in the presence of the Soviet Director to explain to Wischnewski how matters stood. But the Minister of State could make no rhyme or reason out of the matter.

During the month of August, Wischnewski tried to get information from Moscow on the Soviets' true attitude. He then encouraged me to make another application for a visit – this time making a direct reference to the private conversation I desired. This application appeared to create much havoc at Spandau. The Directorate called a special meeting to discuss the letter, but they could reach no agreement on Hess's son's request that he be allowed for once to talk to his father alone about the conditions under which release might perhaps be possible. I was granted only a 'standard visit' for 4 September, i.e. in the presence of the four Directors.[7]

Wischnewski, whom I immediately informed of this development, instantly tried to discover the reason for the Directorate's failure to agree. Apparently, the Soviet Director had refused to agree to a private conversation, and had also rejected his three colleagues' proposal that the talk between father and son should begin as usual, but that they would then quietly withdraw. Nonetheless, Wischnewski suggested that I make the visit on 4 September; Bonn would meanwhile do all it could to ensure that Hess Senior and Hess Junior could talk with one another unobserved for the first time in their lives. The Minister of State remained confident until shortly before 4 September.

On 4 September, however, the well-known game was played all over again. In the hope that I would after all be able to speak to my father alone, I again went to Berlin, but the visit was conducted under the usual conditions. Nonetheless, I was able at last to inform my father that negotiations were in progress for a private conversation, and to warn him not to make any statements in advance of such a conversation. Rudolf Hess assured me that there was no question of this until he had spoken to someone in whom he could trust.

Wischnewski was again told by me of the latest position from Berlin–Tempelhof Airport. But then there was a sudden change in events which made everything even more puzzling. As I was flying back to Munich, my father was suddenly, on this very 4 September, admitted to the British Military Hospital. Neither father nor son had been informed in advance of this move.

The family at first gave as little attention to this as they did to the press announcement on 10 September that, 'after a week of thorough investigation', Hess had been returned to Spandau prison.[8] They continued to concentrate their thoughts on the efforts of Federal Chancellor Schmidt and Minister of State

Wischnewski to secure Moscow's agreement to the release of Rudolf Hess. But what had at first seemed a routine procedure suddenly appeared in a new and alarming light when, eleven days after Rudolf Hess's return, the British Director, G.P.T. Marshall, unexpectedly telephoned from Spandau.

On 21 September, he telephoned my mother to say that, unfortunately, the most recent investigation by a leading British urologist specially called in showed that an immediate operation on her husband's prostate gland was necessary. But Hess Senior refused to allow this operation to take place, and Hess Junior was therefore to go immediately to Berlin to persuade his father to change his mind. Unfortunately, I had meanwhile returned to Saudi Arabia. On 27 September, Marshall followed up his telephone call by a letter to my mother in which he referred to the 'grave danger of a new urinary infection (which could lead to septicaemia) or a complete blockage of the urinary tract'. An operation had therefore to be undertaken 'now, while his general health is still good. The specialist recommends an immediate operation'.[9]

But Hess and his family remained stubborn, and the operation did not take place. Shortly after this, Marshall was removed from his post at Spandau 'for health reasons'.

What did all this mean? For a long time, we in the Hess family could not quite make sense of these ominous events, which overlapped Bonn's efforts in Moscow to secure the release of Rudolf Hess. We are today inclined to believe that, under the pretext of a vital operation, the British had attempted to steal a march by releasing Rudolf Hess. Such an explanation is possible if one follows the sequence of steps in this puzzling affair.

In July, the Soviets had signalled their willingness to release Rudolf Hess under certain conditions. In August, the British were informed by Wischnewski of the continuing endeavours during the so-called Quadripartite discussions conducted in Bonn by the Federal Government with its three main Allies, the USA, Britain and France, in rotation. September was the first month in which the British Director was again in command at Spandau, after an interval of three months.

But my efforts to speak with my father in the prison – if possible in private – had already been going on since 22 August. The British could do nothing, without facing penetrating questioning, before 4 September, when my visit to Spandau was to take place. They were waiting to move Rudolf Hess to the British Military Hospital the moment I left. The family was not informed of this move until the evening of 5 September. Before the family could properly react, my father, having refused the operation, had been brought back to the prison.

To describe fully the extent of the oddities, it should be said that when I next visited my father in Spandau on 2 October 1979 I learned that he had been forbidden to speak of his reasons for opposing the operation. Moreover, shortly before my visit, the prison administration had confiscated one of the letters he used to write once a week. It included a reference to his reasons for refusal. My requests that the medical documents showing the necessity for a prostate operation should be handed over to me, and that the Director of the Urological University Hospital in Munich should be consulted as a doctor in whom we had confidence, were rejected. The Directorate merely offered a discussion between their doctors and myself or my mother; this in turn was rejected by us because we had reason not to trust them. The family persisted in the request already made – a matter of routine among civilized peoples – that Rudolf Hess should be given an opportunity (1) to explain to his son and his wife the reasons for his refusing the prostate operation and (2) to consult, 'in his life-threatening, isolated and therefore desperate situation', a doctor in whom he had confidence.[10] But the four custodial Powers did not accede to this request.

These events cast a curious light on the efforts then in hand to release Rudolf Hess. Had the Russians wanted to relent? Had the British wished to steal a march on them? How far had they been prepared to go in this? None of these questions can as yet be answered. As if in mockery, the British Government merely stated on 27 November 1979 that all reports that Hess was sick and had had to undergo an operation were 'pure speculation'.[11] Had Director Marshall – meanwhile recalled – gone too far?

Putting aside these unanswered questions, it is true that never before or since was my father's release so tangibly close as in the summer and autumn of 1979 under the Chancellorship of Helmut Schmidt. No previous Head of Government at Bonn had given the family such a clear feeling that everything conceivable was really being done to end Rudolf Hess's martyrdom. As late as in the final days of his Chancellorship, in September 1982, Helmut Schmidt was still trying, in a telegram to the four custodial Powers, to secure the release of Rudolf Hess.

Like everything else in the past, these efforts came to nothing. The Soviet attitude again hardened. By 23 July 1981, *Isvestia*, the mouthpiece of the Soviet Government, was polemizing against the 'disgraceful play-acting staged by reactionary circles in West Germany in the so-called "Hess matter" '.[12] This article alleged that the purpose of the 'campaign' for the release of Rudolf Hess was to create an anti-Soviet front between the Federal Republic of Germany and the United States of America following the inflammatory line of the US President, Ronald Reagan. In this context, the paper criticized chiefly Dr Seidl, Hess's solicitor, who had petitioned Reagan. In this book,[13] Dr Seidl refers to this 'petition' in the following terms: 'After taking office, President Ronald Reagan levied serious accusations against the Soviet Union. He asserted that the USSR would condone any crime and any lies to achieve communist world supremacy. Secretary for the Navy Lehmann demanded that SALT 1 should be declared invalid, because the USSR had violated the treaty. Professor Richard Pipes, a member of the National Security Council (NSC), said that "détente" was dead, and added: "Either the USSR renounces its revolutionary plans, or it provokes war." At that time also, the former United States Secretary of State Alexander Haig made serious accusations against the USSR before the Foreign Policy Committee of the House of Representatives, describing Soviet adventurism as the greatest threat to world peace at that time. On 22 March 1981, the former Chairman of the National Security Council (NSC), Richard W. Allen, said in his first public speech that, in Western Europe at present, the abhorrent philosophy of "rather red than dead" was to be heard. The United States and its Western Allies must reject this form of passivism if they wished to negotiate effectively with the USSR. These statements by the American President and his closest collaborators prompted me to write to President Reagan on 30 March 1981 in the following terms:

"These declarations and the policy pursued by you have not prevented the United States of America from administering a prison at Berlin–Spandau jointly with the USSR for 36 years since the end of the Second World War, and from providing

American Army guards for this prison, in which an 87-year-old and seriously ill man is held imprisoned without legal cause; that is, unlawfully and arbitrarily. This man is the former Reich Minister Rudolf Hess.

"It is self-evident that this contradiction removes any credibility from the United States of America's policy and deprives it of its moral foundation . . .' '.

In the opinion of *Isvestia*, the important aspect of Seidl's petition was that Hess 'is not made out to be an enemy of the present-day hawks on the other side of the ocean who are obsessed with anti-Sovietism, but almost as their ally. Kindred spirits have found each other here . . .'.

These few quotations alone show that, besides the legal and humanitarian aspects, high-level politics were always involved in the Hess matter. The Soviets' concern about the incitement of public opinion against their attitude in the Hess matter is of course understandable. In the early years of its existence, the Support Association certainly described the Soviet Union as the sole obstacle to Rudolf Hess's release. But although this line will change only when the Soviet attitude toward the Hess case changes, leading members of the Support Association, and I myself, already had doubts many years ago about whether it was – and still is – in fact the Soviets that obstruct my father's release. The Western Powers also appear to bear a good measure of responsibility – if not the main responsibility.

The governments in Washington, London and Paris never of course make the Soviets' mistake of not going along with an appeal to their humanity. Even the strongly worded petitions of Seidl and the Support Association, calling into question the legitimacy of the torture of isolation, were always rejected with dignified phrases, and those governments seldom failed to name the Soviet Union as the party opposing the release of Rudolf Hess. But it seems that in the past 37 years the Western Powers have been all too ready more than once to acquiesce to the Soviet veto.

During the 1970s and 1980s I have travelled repeatedly to London and Washington to convince the authorities there of the necessity of, at long last, releasing the old man behind the sombre walls of Spandau. I was received by journalists, Members of Parliament, and now and again by Secretaries of

State and Ministers of the individual governments. Even the one-time chief prosecutor at Nuremberg Sir H. Shawcross, the prominent historian A.J.P. Taylor and Jews supported Hess's release. But what resulted from all this in the end was nothing but words, whose sincerity I must in retrospect in every case doubt. The resolutions that have been adopted from time to time in Western Parliaments also drifted away in the wind, unheard.

Whereas in the case of the Soviet Union it is relatively easy to locate those responsible for Hess's continuing incarceration in one specific place – the Kremlin – in the case of the pluralistic organizations of the Western Democracies this becomes much more difficult. One example is sufficient to show how difficult it is here to reach any watertight conclusion; it is sometimes a game of cat-and-mouse. The example related to the hitherto fruitless struggle I have conducted in respect of my father's political testament.

On 14 February 1974, the book supplement to the newspaper *Die Welt* published a report to the effect that the former US Director at Spandau, Eugene K. Bird, was about to publish a book on Rudolf Hess through the West German Desch-Verlag publishing house. 'Prisoner No. 7' had apparently made over to him his exclusive copyright. When I enquired of Desch-Verlag about the necessary power of attorney from my father, Bird arranged for a message to be conveyed to me that this document was with his London agent. A little later, the American followed this up with the information that the original manuscript, with paragraphs about Hess on every page, was with the military authorities in Washington, as was also the original of Rudolf Hess's statement that he agreed to publication. At the same time, Bird was good enough to give me the address concerned.

Meanwhile, I had obtained a photocopy of this declaration of consent, but its quality was so poor that it was scarcely of any use as *prima facie* evidence. Moreover, Rudolf Hess had given it only on condition that his notes would not be altered before publication, which no one was in a position to check without comparison with the original. When I visited my father at Spandau on 16 April 1974, he implored me to prevent Bird's book from appearing. The US Director had promised him at the time not to publicize anything of their conversations while Rudolf Hess was still imprisoned. The prisoner described this breach of trust as 'monstrous'. Shortly after this, our conversation was terminated by the Soviet Director, who was present at the visit.

Under these circumstances, it seemed proper for me to direct an application to Spandau Prison for permission for my father's solicitor and me to discuss these matters of copyright with the prisoner. The application was rejected, no reason being given. The Spandau Directorate also refused to allow Rudolf Hess to give Dr Seidl a power of attorney for the temporary injunction Seidl wished to lodge against the appearance of Bird's book.

Meanwhile, the date for publication drew nearer. Without a temporary injunction, publication of the book could not of course be prevented. In the book, Bird himself admits that it had in fact been intended to publish it only after the release of Rudolf Hess. There is, indeed, on page 2 a reference to the discovery of a cardboard carton, which had originally come to Spandau with Hess from Nuremberg. This carton – which fell into Bird's hands – was said to contain 'thick piles of typewritten pages, all initialled at the top, "RH".' There was also 'a diary recording his daily life in Nuremberg'. In these documents, Hess was said to have written down his recollections of the historic flight to Britain and his thoughts on the Nuremberg judgement.

By this means, I came to know by chance, and as it were 'by the back door', that my father had apparently somewhere left a political testament. When, for this reason, I approached Bird about a personal meeting, the ex-Director suddenly declared that he had found this testament not in Spandau but at the Western Powers' 'Berlin Headquarters', where it probably still remained. It might also meanwhile have been moved to Washington.

My initial investigations into this via the American Embassy in Bonn were in vain. Inquiries directed to various authorities in Washington about the original manuscript and alleged declaration of consent also produced no result. On 21 January 1975, the US Embassy merely informed me[14] that 'there are no documents that we can allow you to see. Moreover, the American authorities know of no material that refers to your father which they consider suitable for putting at your disposal in the manner you propose'. Although this wording prevented me from gaining any insight into my father's testament, it did not expressly exclude the existence of such a document.

This attitude was on the same lines as the embargo on documents in London and Washington referring to Rudolf Hess until the year 2017, the refusal of a sight of the rules for the Allied Military Prison, and the systematic and strict seclusion of Rudolf Hess to deny him any opportunity of expressing an opinion.

The dispute about my father's papers also shows the unco-operative – indeed, dismissive – attitude of the American authorities. They are on the verge of flatly denying the existence of these papers. But the whole episode also showed how powerless Rudolf Hess is, even in the matter of protecting his personal copyright for example. The Allied authorities even refused him the basic right of writing out a simple power of attorney for his solicitor. The family learnt a lesson from this: in 1974, the family had me appointed *curator absentis* for my father by the Munich District Court.

HALF A LIFETIME

AFTER HALF A lifetime of imprisonment, more than ten years of which had been in solitary confinement, it seemed that the cup of suffering was full for the old man in Spandau. On 22 February 1977, Rudolf Hess tried to take his own life; he tried to sever an artery with a knife. This act against his own life was followed by a period of crisis in his health, during which 'Prisoner No. 7' was more than once on the verge of death. Everything pointed to the fact that the reserves of strength of this man, a man who had borne so much during his lifetime, were gradually waning.

In the night of 28/29 December 1978, Rudolf Hess, then aged 84, suffered a stroke which seriously damaged the visual centre in his brain. When Hess awoke next morning, he was nearly blind in the right eye. The left eye had lost 25 per cent of its strength. He was immediately taken once again to the British Military Hospital, where he was examined by the US Army neurologist and the second most senior doctor of the British Army of the Rhine.

Their diagnosis was the best argument for Rudolf Hess's immediate release. The patient had a diseased heart, a painful rupture of the abdominal wall and fluid in his legs. He suffered from a cough, bladder difficulties and general exhaustion. In fact, Rudolf Hess felt so unwell that he feared he could not live much longer.

In this situation, something happened that put the Four Powers in a position to end the martyrdom at the last minute by a generous gesture. Rudolf Hess himself decided to ask the victors of former times for his release. Could there be better evidence that he yielded, if not to their right then at least to their power?

When Wolf Rüdiger Hess visited his father at the hospital on 3 January 1979, his father told him that because of the generally poor state of his health, and in particular because of his partial blindness, he wished for the first time to make an application himself for his release so that he could see his family once again, and above all his grandchildren. Rudolf Hess also referred to his former fellow-prisoners Raeder and Funk. These prisoners, also sentenced at Nuremberg to life imprisonment, had been prematurely set free by the Four Powers in the 1950s. Rudolf Hess asked his son to draft, with Dr Seidl, a suitable application to the Directorate. Rudolf Hess's stroke and his removal to the Military Hospital had already aroused interest in the media. His solicitor, Ewald Bucher, as Chairman of the Support Association, and I now decided to exercise, with the assistance of the public, maximum pressure on the four custodial Powers to persuade the leopard to change its spots. I telephoned Federal Chancellor Schmidt, who happened to be attending a summit meeting of Western Heads of Government on the Caribbean island of Guadeloupe, appealing to him to use his influence on his colleagues to persuade them to take the necessary action. Journalists, Members of Parliament and other well-known people were mobilized. My mother even appealed by letter to Pope John Paul II – through Josef Cardinal Ratzinger and Josef Cardinal Höffner – in order to take advantage of this favourable moment.

But once again all was in vain. The Four Powers again displayed their coldness of heart, although of course the West did not neglect to point at the Soviets, alleging that they bore the main brunt of the blame.

Alfred Seidl and I had already drafted an application for release on 4 January, and we recommended my father to accept it. As a result, 'Prisoner No. 7' wrote to the Spandau Directorate as follows:

'Because of the poor state of my health, and because I would like still to see my two grandchildren, I request that I be released from imprisonment. I am convinced that I have only a short time to live, and I wish to point out that in three other cases (v.

Neurath, Raeder and Funk) there was premature release. Rudolf Hess.'[1]

The uncertainty lasted forty days. Then, on 22 February 1979, when I again visited my father, I was unofficially informed that the Four Powers had rejected the application. Rudolf Hess had been informed of this – verbally only, not in writing – some time earlier. The Four Powers had thus missed this unique chance to come out of the affair with some of their humanity intact.

Other chances were to follow. On 11 November 1980, in a long letter, Rudolf Hess once again asked the Four Powers for freedom. This was essentially for the same reasons as advanced in his first request. Once again, the negative answer – this time after three weeks – was given unofficially and only verbally, as if the Four Powers shrank from putting this outrage on record.

The third and – up to present – last opportunity came on 26 August 1982. At that time, Rudolf Hess had just spent a further period in the British Military Hospital with an attack of life-endangering 'wet pleurisy'. During the summer of 1982, his heart and circulatory troubles had also dramatically deteriorated. When his son visited him in Spandau on 26 August 1982, the old man complained that his state of health was alarming. He had recently had two heart-attacks without admission to hospital, and the prison medical orderly refused to accept further responsibility for his treatment. His difficulty in breathing and intestinal cramps were worsening, and recently a skin rash, which itched continuously, had also appeared.

Hess again spoke of the precedent of the 1950s. In 1955 and 1957, Raeder and Funk were set free before time at the ages of 79 and 67 respectively, and he was already aged 88. The only real reason that Hess could think of to account for his not being released, in spite of his serious state of health, was that the custodial Powers feared he knew things which should not be revealed to the public.

Keane, the American Prison Director, and Planet, his French colleague, who were supervising this visit, listened to what Rudolf Hess said without interfering.

Rudolf Hess then came to the point which occupied him most. He had thought about how he could allay the Four Powers' misgivings, and he had come to the following conclusion. He would give his word of honour that, after his release, he would express no views on political and historical matters, and he would indulge in no further political activity. He would in any case be prevented from such activities by age and health.

Hess reasoned that in Spandau he had had in any case to keep silent. He would now prefer to give his word of honour to preserve silence even after his release, if he were permitted to spend the remaining months of his life with his family – in particular with his grandchildren.

On the same day as my visit to my father, I drew up a 'statutory declaration' embodying the content of our conversation and my father's word of honour, and I sent this to the ambassadors of the four custodial Powers in Germany. I had to take this course because there was no other way in which I could make known my father's willingness to preserve silence even after his release. This time, amazingly, the answer was even in writing. The first to write, on 15 October 1982, was US Ambassador Burns through one of his political advisers. He assured me that the United States had for many years taken all possible action to secure the release of Rudolf Hess on humanitarian grounds, but that this had been frustrated by the Russians' inflexibility. The Americans would however continue their efforts in the future, in common with the British and the French. Reading between the lines, the diplomat thereby rejected release on a word-of-honour basis, but without committing this to writing.

Rudolf Hess's health was now 'quite good', said the letter's rather brutal ending, as his son certainly already knew from his latest visit to Spandau.[2] The British and French answers were similarly negative, although not in the same words. Once again, the Russians shrouded themselves in silence.

Since then nothing has happened to encourage any hope that the Four Powers might show understanding before Rudolf Hess's fate is brought to a close. But the initiatives instituted by his family, his solicitor and the Support Association continue:

1. On 26 April 1983, shortly after *Stern* began its series on the alleged Hitler diaries, I demanded that my father should be allowed to check the authenticity of this reputed source. An application for a visit made by him in this context was

rejected. As the forgery scandal exploded, this attempt to get Rudolf Hess out of Spandau – at least temporarily – collapsed.

2. On 18 May 1983, I made an application to the four custodial Powers for my father to be granted at least a temporary respite in his imprisonment. The reason I gave was that the world-wide discussion of the forged 'Hitler diaries' again raised the question of whether the former Deputy Führer had flown to Britain on Hitler's orders, and the nature of the peace proposals he had brought with him. Rudolf Hess was the only person still alive who could answer these questions once and for all. He needed a break in his imprisonment to refresh his memory. The application was rejected.

3. Since 29 June 1983, I have been in correspondence with Federal Chancellor Helmut Kohl. On his recent visit to Moscow he demanded of former Secretary-General Yuri Andropov that my father should be released, but this was in vain. Although the Bonn Head of Government assured me that he would continue to do all he could to secure freedom for Hess, he doubted whether any legal arguments would made this easier. Neither did he believe that the Western Powers could bring themselves to act unilaterally to liberate him. Kohl met my request for close contact with Bonn by arranging for me to talk to the Foreign Office's Minister of State, Alois Mertes. This I did on 28 January 1984.

4. On 9 August 1983, Dr Seidl, on his client's behalf, submitted in Karlsruhe a complaint of unconstitutionality in the matter of granting Rudolf Hess release on licence. This complaint was founded on a decision of the Federal Constitutional Court of 28 June according to which life prisoners must be granted release on licence, whatever the severity of their guilt, age and state of health being taken into consideration. Also, a person sentenced to life imprisonment must be allowed to hope to end his days in freedom. The Supreme Federal Court further said, in its statement of reasons, that this was a requirement under the clause of the Constitution relating to the dignity of man. Seidl's complaint of unconstitutionality was intended to compel the Federal Government to renew the struggle against the Four Powers for the release of the German citizen Hess by legal argument. At the time

this book went to print, the Federal Constitutional Court's decision was still awaited.

But is there any sense at all in hoping that the Four Powers can be brought round? It became known in January 1984 that a special lift was about to be installed in Spandau prison at a cost to the German taxpayer of DM 130,000. This was to save my father from having to use the narrow iron spiral staircase, and to convey him from his first floor cell to the garden so that he could continue to take his walk. According to a report in *Welt am Sonntag* of 12 February 1984, this event is seen in Bonn 'as a sign that, coincident with his 90th birthday, Hess might no longer count on release on humanitarian grounds'.[3]

While the press speculates on whether, after Rudolf Hess's death, the prison building will be blown up, given back to the German authorities, or dedicated as a Four Power 'anti-Fascist memorial', the loneliest prisoner in the world lives on in Cell No. 17. No less than some DM 26.5 million of taxpayers' money had been expended since 1 October 1966 to maintain this macabre relic of the Allied victory of 1945 for the solitary confinement of Rudolf Hess. Since the Allies have long since been no longer allied, one asks onself, *cui bono*?

For Rudolf Hess, life under these circumstances is unparalleled torture – and sometimes a mental stress for his family reaching the very limits of tolerance. What worry it has already caused members of the family about their husband, father, father-in-law, brother and grandfather! What agitation the family has suffered as a result of the scandalous behaviour of the Four Powers! What doubts about the compatibility of right and humanity have been awakened among the family – and not only among them! Even my application to be allowed for once to speak to my father alone to establish whether he showed the 'repentance' the Soviets found lacking was for years shelved by the Four Powers and finally refused. All applications by the family for the number of visits to be increased and their length extended were rejected. Giving no reasons, the Prison Directorate refuses to this very day to give the family more precise information on the prisoner's state of health. In the half of his life that Rudolf Hess has already spent in Spandau, the sombre walls around him have not displayed as much as a chink.

The torture of isolation for this old and sick man is maintained to this very day, with relentless consequences in not only physical but also psychological and emotional terms. Apart from the deprivation of freedom, the main instruments of torture are censorship and the regulations on correspondence and visits.

It is true that Rudolf Hess is allowed to read newspapers of his own choice: *Frankfurter Allgemeine Zeitung*, *Die Welt*, *Tagesspiegel* and *Neue Deutschland*. Since mid-1978 he has also had a television set in an adjacent cell. He may receive from his family each month four books as reading matter.Nevertheless, his perception of reality outside the prison remains limited in all political, social, cultural, scientific and sporting matters.

This is because Rudolf Hess is not allowed to see news broadcasts or programmes on contemporary history. All newspaper articles that refer to the Third Reich, Nuremberg or Spandau are cut out before he can read them. The family must pre-censor all books it sends to Rudolf Hess to ensure that they comply with the Allies' regulations. If it makes a mistake in its choice – usually for undiscoverable reasons – the book concerned is confiscated without replacement.

By these means, any recollection of the historical associations of his life have been methodically erased from the prisoner's memory. One might also add that his recollections of the time when he would see through the game of the Four Powers have been systematically destroyed. As a result, an important part of Rudolf Hess's personal conception of himself is being insidiously incapacitated.

His contacts with the outside world are restricted to a minimum by the regulations on visits and correspondence. Now as ever, Rudolf Hess may write each week just one letter of a maximum length of 1,300 words to a member of his immediate family, and receive from him or her the same. Each incoming and outgoing letter is censored by the Prison Directorate. It can break off the correspondence at any time simply by withholding the letter, giving no reason. There are of course censorship regulations – never clearly formulated – in regard to the content of letters, as there are for television programmes, newspapers and books.

Once a month – twice in the Christmas month of December – Rudolf Hess may receive a visit lasting one hour from a member of his immediate family. Each visit must be applied for at Spandau two weeks in advance. This visit is granted by the Directorate, or refused by it for no stated reason. If permission is granted, the Four Powers dictate the date and time. Delays as a result of *force majeure* or circumstances beyond one's control are deducted from the visitor's time.

Normally, the grotesque ritual of the visit runs as follows. The visitor walks from Wilhelmstrasse along a drive to the large, green, double-doored, iron entrance in the gate-house of the fortress. This gate has a little door, scarcely higher than a man. To the right of it is mounted a bell, which the visitor must operate. At the loud and piercing peal, one of the outer guards opens a slide in the iron door, looks out and asks the visitor his business. Although of course he has long been expected, he must state his wish to make a visit and produce his visiting permit. Only then is the door opened.

The visitor then enters the gate-house. This is embellished on the Wilhelmstrasse side by two small towers. To the left, a few steps lead directly forward into a bleak guardroom of the kind formerly common in Prussian barracks. The visitor must here surrender his permit to the inner guard on duty and register in the visitors' book. It is the size of a ledger, and usually already open. He must enter his own name and address, the name of the prisoner he wishes to visit, his own nationality, and the time and date at which he entered the prison. His signature must be added certifying that the information is correct. Bags and other packages are taken from him, after he has removed his little gifts.

A warder then collects the visitor and leads him across the paved inner courtyard past armed guards into the prison building itself. This involves mounting 14 steps through a broad main entrance. Somewhere along the way to the visiting room, which, like the cells, is on the first floor, he is welcomed by the Directors and interpreters. Sometimes they do not enter the visiting room until the visitor is already there. At least two, but usually all four, Directors are present to supervise the one-hour visit. One or other of them is sometimes represented by a warder or an interpreter. They sit on chairs lined against the wall behind the visitor. After entering the visitors' room, the Visitors' Regulations of 28.10.1954 must be signed. The visitors' room consists of two halves, and is of unsurpassed bleakness. Through the middle of it runs a plywood partition reaching from floor to ceiling. In the centre is an opening about two metres wide, into which a table is fitted. On either side of this table, on the 'visitor's side' of which there are pencils, paper and the Visitors' Regulations, stand the chairs on which the visitor and Rudolf Hess are to sit. The table and the chairs are the only furniture in the room. The yellowing and grimy varnish on the plywood partition and the table is old and cracked; it is breaking up all over its surface, which makes it difficult to write on the table.

Rudolf Hess is led in through a second door opening on to the cell wing. During the visit he remains on the other side of the table, i.e. of the partition. Personal contact such as a handshake or an embrace, let alone a kiss, is forbidden. It is not permitted to give my father anything or to receive anything from him not approved in advance by the Directorate. It is forbidden to communicate by signs, gestures or any other means incomprehensible to the supervisory staff present. The conversation, which must be conducted in German – as if one had any intention of speaking Chinese – must not mention the Third Reich, National Socialism, my father's peace-flight, the Nuremberg IMT, or release efforts.

If these regulations are contravened, the visit is immediately brought to an end. This threat and the penalty of the visitor's arrest are used by the custodial Powers to extort the visitor's good behaviour. Moreover, of course, there hovers over the visit the danger that this will be the last if the visitor behaves in any way not to the liking of the Four Powers. As a consequence, the visit is wide open to obstruction, shortening or termination at the discretion of the Directorate, and any meeting between Rudolf Hess and his relatives takes place under the shadow of the subliminal fear that it could be the last time we see each other.

A report written by my wife Andrea on her visit of 16 August 1983 to her father-in-law makes the oppression of these meetings especially vivid:[4]

'The flight from Munich to Berlin is smooth. The taxi puts me down at the Malanchthon Church. I want to walk the final two hundred metres alone, to take another deep breath, and to think of the hours before me.

'A cyclist turns inquisitively as I make my way towards the approach to the prison. It is forbidden to approach the prison, as the large notice-boards announce in two languages! But what does he know . . . ! On this short, wide stretch of cobblestones, there comes over me repeatedly the same feeling of helplessness and impotence. The huge prison gate, barbed wire, walls and watch towers, all radiate rejection, and the road I am on leads right through the middle of this!

'The prison bell rings stridently. I hear steps on the paving. A little hatch opens at head-height. Seldom is the little door opened immediately for admission. I am solemnly asked what I want, just as if it is entirely unexpected to find me standing at the door. Remember that the visit must be applied for three weeks in advance, and that it is confirmed in writing by the prison management, giving a precise time and date.

'Inside, the same scenario is repeated. Inquisitive glances from the lounging American sentries. . . . "Please leave your bag . . ." "Please register here . . .". In the visitors' book are the recurring names of members of the family: W.R. Hess, Ilse Hess, Margerethe Rauch, Ingeborg Pröhl, Monika Hess, Andrea Hess.

'Today, I have only brought with me for Daddy a few photos, a cinefilm, chiefly of our children, and a small jar of home-made jam.

'As usual, I am fetched and led across the little courtyard into the main building. The chestnut trees rustle here; flower boxes decorate the stairway. Today my escort does not ask me the usual questions about the flight and the weather in Munich. . . .

'Inside the building, to my surprise, the American Director comes to meet us, stepping out energetically from the cell corridor. He is a short man, and his normally red face is today brick red. He greets me extremely curtly, and disappears into the Directors' room, closely followed by his "assistant", who is three times his size in height and girth. None of the other Directors is as yet present. I am led into the visitors' room. 'Please register here . . .'. This means that the usual folder is presented to me; on the left the nine points of the Prison Regulations, on the right the visitor signs, thereby acknowledging the Regulations – also that, in the event of contravention, he can be arrested. I sign. I am still alone. I leaf back in the folder and find what I am looking for. "Andrea Hess, 18.8.1976." That was my first visit; today is my tenth. Seven years have gone by since then!

'A warder collects my photos and the film for examination. Still nothing is to be seen of the Directors. My glance wanders around the barren, high room. On the table to the right of me lies a stack of white paper and four sharpened pencils. I also have paper and pencil in front of me. On the left are more chairs; there is enough room for an audience! The warder comes back, somewhat embarrassed. The Directors also want to see the – now somewhat sticky – jam jar! But of course, with pleasure! Monsieur Planet, the French Director, arrives. He greets me with his invariable friendliness. He asks after the family, and I ask after the health of my father-in-law. Respectfully he answers, "Good, very good for a man of his age". Shortly after this I am again alone. Everything is somewhat unusual today. My glance wanders around again. In the other half of the room, separated from the visitors' side by a wall with a large piece cut out, I notice for the first time that the high window is not only barred but also masked outside by a black metal screen, leaving only the upper quarter of the window unobscured. I look out on red brick walls, with shadows of birds occasionally flitting across them.

'Meanwhile, there is some agitation in the corridor. The British and Russian Directors, today in civilian clothes, appear; the greeting is brief. I stand up to await Daddy.

'The coloured warder is the first to enter the other half of the visitors' room. He carried Daddy's things. He lays the folded blanket on the chair (Daddy uses it as a cushion when he puts his legs up) and the large notebook on the table. Some time has passed since my last visit, so I am a bit nervous when Daddy comes in. He walks without assistance and easily, but very slowly. His whole appearance has become somewhat fragile. A few words of greeting are exchanged. Contact of any kind is – as ever – forbidden, and the wide table separating the visitor from the prisoner in any event makes this impossible. Before Daddy sits down he asks a warder posted beside him – in English – to tell him when the visit has five minutes to go. He then adjusts his pocket alarm clock and asks me to be seated. When I thank him, he answers me, "Thank you for standing up to receive me. And before I forget, many happy returns of the birthday you will have in three days' time. I wish you all the best, health and as much happiness as you have had in the past. You have a clever husband and three healthy little children. That, in my opinion, is a lot to be happy about!"

'Meanwhile, the American Director has noisily joined the other gentlemen. When I ask whether I may have the photos back, I am answered brusquely that they are about to come. The photos had always previously very much eased the beginning of our sixty-minute conversation. I have not learnt over the years how to begin an entirely personal family conversation with Daddy under pressure of time and under supervision, and perhaps it is impossible to learn this.

'I begin with the children. I tell him that for more than a week they have been with my parents on the moors, and will be having a wonderful time. Wolf and I will therefore be going to Bayreuth for a week to see Wagner's *Ring des Nibelungen*, presented this year in a new production, quite naturalistic; so naturalistic that the Rhine Maidens appear in their birthday suits, dressed like Adam! Archly, Daddy corrects me. "You mean dressed like Eve". He envies us; he also would like to see the Ring one fine day.

'Another subject is our first child to go to school, Friederike. Daddy enquires about the road to school, and is a little worried about this. I explain to him that it is not very far to the school, and that Friederike already knows the way, that we often walk through the district, and that the two older children can already cross the road alone with the help of the pedestrian lights. As Daddy cannot envisage pedestrian lights, he lets me explain these to him.

'We touch briefly on present-day house-building, establishing that in our neighbourhood there are very successful examples which depart from the monotonous concrete façade. I then enquire again about the photos. The Yankee points to the Russian Director, who then pulls the photos out of his jacket pocket and begins to examine them. Meanwhile, I tell Daddy about our home-made jam from our own crop, which is still with the "censor". Daddy says smilingly that he doesn't know whether he will get it! When the Russian Director eventually gives me the photos only a few remain. He points to a second batch lying on the table in front of him and says reproachfully that strange people are in these pictures; therefore they cannot be shown. I then explain, by means of the few left, that a kindergarten party was taking place on a "circus" theme. Daddy admires Friederike's suppleness as a contortionist, her appearance as a pony and Buja's mask as a savage lion, and he wants to know more about our kindergarten. The children's progress in swimming, this beautiful warm summer, also pleases him, since this is a matter that has always been very close to his heart.

'We go on to speak of game shooting, and I say that we have seen photos showing him as a proud sportsman. Daddy says he cannot remember this. When I tell him that Wolf now also wants to get a game shooting permit he says scornfully, "You must have a lot of patience for that". He asks what kind of game we hunt, and whether we have also practised pistol-shooting. No, not that; rifles and shotguns! During this conversation a pencil is scratching busily on paper behind me: everything is being taken down! All the time, the American Director is making an annoying commotion in the background by repeatedly standing up and making muffled conversation with the Russian Director – a gross discourtesy after Daddy had already asked me to speak up as he found it so difficult to hear me!

'Even though his eyes under the still-bushy grey eyebrows give a somewhat sad impression, he amazes me by suddenly asking what kind of jewellery I am wearing; he couldn't stop looking at it!

'When, at his express wish, I tell him more about the children, I refer to Katharina's growing likeness to Grandma Hess; her whole manner, her looks, her likes and dislikes. This clearly pleases him, and he says with a smile, "That's the way things go . . . !"

'At the end of this visiting hour, when Daddy with some effort gets up from the chair and puts the photos in his pocket, the American Director brusquely demands them again for stamping. The warder, very considerately and discreetly, takes the blanket and the book from Daddy and walks away in front of him. Daddy sends his love to everybody. Then he also walks away, slowly and bent, behind the warder and back to his cell.

'Taking leave of the Directors is hasty and surly. A few sparrows are bickering in the courtyard with the chestnut trees. The American sentries in the archway are still carrying out their duties quite casually.

'Just as seven years ago, I walk out through the large gate into a radiant August day. But today I leave with a feeling of powerless fury and bitterness, increased by the thought of the humiliatingly ridiculous and ill-mannered behaviour of the Directors towards an 89-year-old prisoner of the stature of Rudolf Hess!

'At home in Munich, I tell Wolf that today's issue of the *Frankfurter Allgemeine Zeitung* has a detailed article by Dr Fromme on the complaint of unconstitutionality in the matter of release on licence.

'This appears to explain the somewhat unusual atmosphere. The article had probably slipped past the censorship, and the American Director must have been rebuked for this by his Russian colleague.'

Each of these visits calls for much fortitude on both sides. The visits are made by members of the immediate family in turn in no fixed sequence. In earlier years, Frau Ilse Hess went to Spandau as often as she could. But at 84 years of age the time has now come when the long journey from her home in Hindelang in the Oberallgaü to Berlin is too tiring. The three grandchildren, whom Rudolf Hess especially loves, at his request do not come to Spandau. He wishes to spare them – and probably also spare himself – a meeting with their grandfather in the depressing surroundings of the prison.

Apart from talking to members of his family once a month and to the inner guard, 90-year-old Rudolf Hess can converse only with the French Army Chaplain, who provides him with some company for half-an-hour once a week. Otherwise, he is utterly alone with himself and his thoughts.

His daily routine continues to be regulated minute by minute. Rudolf Hess is awakened at 07.00 hrs. He gets up, makes his morning toilet, has breakfast and reads. He then walks for an hour in the garden. After lunch, this is repeated: reading, walk, supper. At about 22.00 hrs. his spectacles are taken away and the light switched off. The naked light bulb is left on a little longer only if Hess expressly asks for this.

So it has gone on, day after day, week after week, month after month, year in, year out – for 36 years. Rudolf Hess has been in Spandau for 36 years. For the last 18 years his confinement has been solitary. There is a coffin in the cellar.

This is more than any other person has ever had to bear in recent history – and he, moreover, is an innocent person.

NOTES

Abbreviations

ADAP   German foreign policy documents
BA   Federal archives, Koblenz
FRUS   Foreign Relations of the United States
HA   Hess archives
PRO   Public Record Office, London

Part I – The Flight

'When Are You Coming Back?'
1. This and the following, Ilse Hess, *England*, p. 17ff.
2. Ibid., p. 31.
3. Ibid., p. 34.
4. Ibid., p. 35.
5. Discussion between Walter Ramsay junior and Wolf Rüdiger Hess in February 1976 at Sanaa, North Yemen, HA: see p. 22.
6. PRO INF 1/912: Additional Notes on the Hess Incident by Group-Captain the Duke of Hamilton, Secret, no date.
7. Ilse Hess, *England*, p. 39.

'A New Era Has Dawned'
1. HA: Army List, Rudolf Hess.

2. 'The peace conditions of the Allies and associated govern-ments', Berlin 1919, p. 225ff. See p. 28.
3. Ilse Hess, *Reply*, p. 17.
4. Ilse Hess, *Prisoner*, p. 24f.
5. Ilse Hess, *Reply*, p. 24.
6. HA: Letter from Rudolf Hess to Hermann Fobke.
7. Ilse Hess, *Reply*, p. 20ff.
8. HA: Letter from Rudolf Hess of 17.6.20 to his parents.
9. HA: Letter from Rudolf Hess of 24.4.25 to his parents.
10. Jochmann, *Monologues*, p. 265.
11. HA: Letter from Rudolf Hess, undated, to Ilse Hess.

'The Party's Conscience' or 'Deputy Führer of the NSDAP'
1. Ilse Hess, *Reply*, p. 31.
2. Ibid., p. 29.
3. HA: Rudolf Hess, 28.6.28, to his parents.
4. HA: Telegram from Hitler dated 11.3.34 to Rudolf Hess.
5. Haushofer, *Life*, p. 41ff.
6. Hannah Arendt, *Eichmann in Jerusalem*, p. 7.
7. Ilse Hess, *England*, p. 41ff.

War or Peace with Britain?
1. ADAP D IX, No. 413: Thomsen 11.6.40, German Foreign Office.
2. Hillgruber, *Hitler's Strategy, Policy and Warfare 1940–1941*, p. 212.
3. Jacobsen, *Haushofer*, II, p. 449: Letter from Albrecht Haus-hofer of 2.8.40 to Karl Haushofer on a discussion Albrecht Haushofer had had that day with Rudolf Hess at his request.
4. Ibid.
5. Jacobsen, *Haushofer*, II, p. 458ff.
6. Quoted from Hamilton, *Motive for a Mission*, pp. 146/7.
7. The letter directed by Mrs Roberts to the Duke of Hamilton has not as yet emerged from the files. It is not therefore known whether and to what extent she knew that she was serving certain political ends.
8. This information originates from Hamilton, *Motive for a Mission*, p. 153, who for his part refers to statements made by the German Foreign Office interpreter Paul Schmidt.
9. During his interrogations in Britain, R. Hess said that in summer 1940, after the end of the French campaign, he had

got the idea during a discussion with Hitler of, if necessary, doing something personally for peace with Britain, p. 35.

10. Ilse Hess, *England*, p. 12.

11. Kempner, *Reich*, p. 104ff.: So said Bohle's statement to the International Military Tribunal in Nuremberg. The first meeting between Hess and Bohle regarding the letter was about 9.10.40. It is strange that Bohle allegedly said nothing more about the contents of the letter he translated.

12. The following is from HA: Kaden's sworn declaration of 14.5.81.

13. There is wide confusion about the number of trial take-offs in the direction of Britain or Switzerland, partly because take-offs have been included in which, although he had arranged for the reserve tanks to be filled as a matter of routine, he apparently had no intention of actually starting his journey. In his conversation with Hamilton, Hess himself gave the number of his genuine take-offs (excluding the actual flight to Britain) as three, but it is not clear when he made the third. However, Hess told Simon that between January and May 1941 he abandoned his intention to fly to Britain because of Britain's successes in North Africa. If this is true, the attempt on 30 April could not have taken place, although it has been authenticated in detail by Kaden. Since the contradiction in Hess's statements cannot be cleared up while he remains in Spandau, two genuine take-off attempts on 10 January and 30 April 1941 are assumed here. Hess also told Simon that he took off for Britain for the first time on 10 January 1941.

14. Leasor, *Rudolf Hess: the Uninvited Envoy*, p. 69ff.

The Approach to the Mission

1. Halder, *War Diary*.

2. Churchill, *Second World War*, II, 1, p. 313.

3. Martin, *Peace Initiatives*, pp. 426 and 428. Here also the quotation refers to a 'direct order'.

4. Ibid., p. 431.

5. HA: Statement by Portner, Hess's security officer, who witnessed the scene with Hitler in the latter's ante-room. After the failure of the flight to Britain, he told Frau Ilse Hess about this event, which was confirmed by Bohle at the Nuremberg Tribunal. Cf. Kempner, Reich, p. 104ff. Hitler

also mentioned the conversation with Hess in his address to the Reich leaders and Gauleiters at Obersalzberg on 13 May 1941. The only uncertainty is whether the conversation took place on 3, 4 or 5 May 1941.

6. The matter of the agreement between Hitler and Hess might also have been a euphemism for the Führer's declaring, in the event of failure, that his deputy was mad. It is probable that Göring had not understood Hitler's changed attitude, since he tried on the evening of 10 May, via Galland, to prevent the Hess flight from continuing by employing a fighter group, which was to take off immediately. Since it was too late for this, Gallard merely ordered a 'symbolic take-off'. Galland, *Memoirs*, p. 100.

7. Hassel, *Diaries*, p. 181.

8. Jacobsen, *Haushofer*, I, p. 403: Letter K.3, *Haushofer*, 12.7.41; K.3, Lammers, Head of the Berlin Reich Chancellery; the letter was written in the context of Hess's abortive flight to Britain.

9. Jacobsen, *Haushofer*, II, p. 508: Martha Haushofer's diary, entries on 3 and 5.5.41. – Haushofer archives. In a 'Draft of a family chronicle', Martha Haushofer even emphasizes the continuity with the beginning of Hess and Hitler's peace efforts in September 1940. She writes: Albrecht Haushofer had made the journey to Burckhardt 'to carry out the commission received (on) 8–9 September 1940 from R(udolf) H(ess)'.

10. Haushofer archives: Martha Haushofer, 'Draft of a family chronicle', entry under 20.4.33.

11. Jacobsen, *Haushofer*, I, p. 369.

12. Hamilton, *Motive for a Mission*, p. 114.

13. Hoffmann, *Resistance*, p. 201.

14. Hamilton, *Motive for a Mission*, pp. 202/4. Albrecht Haushofer's memorandum of 12.5.41.

15. Ibid., p. 36.

16. This was also Hassel's position. But the question is whether Haushofer also considered the circumvention or even the fall of the Churchill Government as a pre-condition for peace talks. This question cannot be answered definitively.

17. Hamilton, *Motive for a Mission*, pp. 113/117.

18. Ibid., p. 31.

19. Jacobsen, *Haushofer*, I, p. 402: Letter from Albrecht Haus-
    hofer dated 2.8.40 to Karl Haushofer on his first discussion
    with Hess of that day. Cf. also the quotation following.
20. Ibid., II, p. 463ff.: Letter from Albrecht Haushofer dated
    19.9.40 to Karl and Martha Haushofer. Cf. here also the
    quotation following.
21. Ibid., II, p. 467: Letter from Albrecht dated 23.9.40 to Karl
    Haushofer. Cf. here also the quotations following.
22. HA: Note by W. H. Stahmer, 'Truth and misunderstanding
    about Rudolf Hess', 1959.
23. Ibid.
24. Hassel, *Diaries*, p. 205: Entry for 18.5.41.
25. This assumption is not misjudged, if it is borne in mind that
    in 1943 Langbehn also tried to bring Himmler and Popitz
    together to move the Western Powers towards peace with
    Germany without Hitler. Hoffmann, Resistance, p. 349.
26. Hassel, *Diaries*, p. 218: Entry for 30.8.41. Hasssel even refers
    to Langbehn, who called on him in August, as 'Albrecht
    Haushofer's assistant'.
27. Ibid., p. 204: Entry for 18.5.41, Cf. here also the quotations
    following.
28. HA: Letter from Karl Haushofer dated 12.7.41 to Lammers.
29. BA: Schumacher collection, letter from Rudolf Hess dated
    9.5.41 to Darré.
30. Hassel, *Diaries*, p. 205: Entry for 18.5.41.

Did Hitler Know?
 1. The statements about when Pintsch arrived at Obersalz-
    berg, and when Hitler learned of his Deputy's flight, are
    very contradictory. The diaries of Walter Hewel, Hitler's
    liaison officer at the German Foreign Office, who happened
    to be at Obersalzberg, read under 11 May 41: 'In the morn-
    ing, Pintsch, Hess's adjutant, arrives. Brings a letter. Great
    excitement.' Cf. BA: Hewel's diaries. The entire literature
    relating to the Hess incident accordingly assumes that Hitler
    did not learn about his Deputy's flight to Britain until 11
    May. But this assumption has recently been shaken by a
    statement made to me on 29 February 1984 by Rudolf Hess's
    former driver, Lippert. According to this statement, he and
    the other members of the Hess escort who had gone to

Gallspach/Austria during the night of 10/11 May were arrested by the Gestapo as early as 05.30 hrs. on the morning of 11 May. Since of course Lippert remembers this incident precisely, Hewel's statement, which may be based on hearsay, cannot be correct. The relatively small distance between Augsburg and Berchtesgaden alone would have made it possible for Pintsch to reach Obersalzberg late in the evening of 10 May and hand the important letter to Hitler.

2. Like the letter Hess had translated by Bohle in November 1940/January 1941, the original of his farewell letter of May 1941 to Hitler never reappeared. The only copy was kept by my father in his private safe at München-Harlaching. My mother, who to begin with put it into safe-keeping, unfortunately destroyed it together with other important documents in spring 1945 when the French arrived. She no longer remembers its details.

3. Institute for Contemporary History: Göring's appointments diary. it contains the following entry under 11 May: '14.00 hrs.: Lunch – Führer telephones (come at once!) – 15.15 hrs. leave by special train for Munich . . . 20.45 hrs. arrive Berghof, lecture by Führer (Hess incident)'.

4. BA: *Goebbels diary*, Genoud's edition, p. 552: According to this, Goebbels did not learn about Hess's flight until 13.5.41.

5. This conflict must have been so serious in 1941 that on 8 August 1941 Himmler and Ribbentrop – perhaps following on from the Hess incident – signed at the Führer's headquarters at Rominten, thus presumably under the eyes of Hitler, a kind of conciliation agreement which laid down precisely the SS foreign agents' field of responsibility. In a telegram to SS-Gruppenführer Wolff, Heydrich expressly referred to this agreement as 'an important peace agreement'. Cf. BA NS 19/new 1633, Secret Reich Matter.

6. Hesse, *Prelude*, p. 244. The object of this meeting is unknown. According to Himmler's appointments diary, the Reichsführer-SS was at the time in Sophia, the capital of Bulgaria. Cf. BA NS 19. Hesse, however, describes the meeting so vividly that one can scarcely doubt it.

7. Hesse, *Prelude*, p. 244f. Hesse, who was friendly with Haushofer and Hess and in fact served in the German Embassy in London as press attaché, was summoned to Fuschl by

Ribbentrop on 11 May because the Reich Foreign Minister still thought it possible that he had had a hand in the affair. Hesse then had an opportunity to observe the differing reactions of Himmler and Ribbentrop.

8. BA: Schumacher Collection, telegram from Bormann dated 12.5.41 to Darré and other Reich leaders.
9. *Ciano Diaries*, p. 321.
10. Hamilton, *Motive for a Mission*, p. 116. Here also, see the quotations following.
11. Ibid., p. 189.
12. HA: Note by Karl Haushofer, 'Life's Debit and Credit, Hartschimmelhof, Winter's End 1945'. This date must be a mistake, since by that time Albrecht Haushofer had long been dead. He was shot on 23 April 1945. But in his notes Karl Haushofer writes that his son was still in prison. From this it can be concluded that Karl Haushofer wrote the note in winter 1944/45.
13. Domarus, *Hitler*, II, p. 1714.
14. HA: Reich Minister and Head of Chancery, 31.5.41, Bormann/Ilse Hess.
15. Ilse Hess, *England*, p. 24.
16. Jordan, *Experienced and Suffered*, p. 210. Bohle does not refer to this statement of Hitler's on the imminent Russian campaign. Kempner, 108ff.
17. Kempner, *Witness*, p. 109ff.
18. Hassel, *Diaries*, p. 203: Entry for 18.5.41.
19. BA: *Goebbels Diary*, Genoud's edition, p. 553: Entry for 14.5.41. Here also, see quotations following.
20. Domarus, *Hitler*, II, p. 1715.
21. BA: *Goebbel's Diary*, Genoud's edition, p. 558: Entry for 15.5.41. Here also, see quotations following.

'Has Somebody Arrived?'
1. Hamilton, *Motive for a Mission*, p. 161.
2. Ibid., p. 163.
3. Ibid., p. 163.
4. Fromm, *Germany*, p. 21.
5. Ibid., p. 109.
6. Harriman, *Mission*, p. 24.
7. Churchill, *Second World War*, III, p. 317.

The Peace Plan
1. StA Nuremberg: 'Record of an Interview with Herr Rudolf Hess, May 13, Secret'.
2. For the remainder of the paragraph we follow Kirkpatrick's memoirs, *The Inner Circle*, because this important comment is lacking in his official report.
3. Here again we follow Kirkpatrick's memoirs, since his official report contains nothing on this important point. These contradictions between Kirkpatrick's official report and his memoirs permit one to doubt whether he briefed Churchill truthfully.
4. PRO PREM 3/219/7: Note of telephone conversation, unheaded, of 13.5.41, signed 'A.C.'
5. Churchill, *Second World War*, III, p. 43.
6. Ibid., p. 45.
7. Kirkpatrick, *The Inner Circle*.
8. PRO INF 1/912: Francis Williams, 14.5.41, to Director-General MOI.
9. Eden, *Reckoning*, p. 256.
10. *Hansard*, 1940–41, Vol. 371, col. 1085.
11. Ibid.
12. PRO PREM 3/219/7: Roosevelt, 15.5.41, to Churchill.
13. StA Nuremberg: 'Record of a Conversation with Herr Hess on May 15th, 1941', signed 'I.A. K(irkpatrick)'.
14. PRO PREM 3/219/7: 'Report on the Conduct of X', 17.5.41.
15. Kirkpatrick, *The Inner Circle*. Cf. also the quotation following.
16. Ibid.
17. PRO PREM 3/219/7: Churchill, 16.5.41, to Cadogan.
18. Churchill, *Second World War*, III, 1, p. 46.

Failure of the Mission
1. PRO FO 371/26 542C610G: FO 6.2.41, Mallet/Stockholm, Secret. This telegram was the reply to a message for the minister that Göring was willing to initiate the peace negotiations referred to via Count Bonde.
2. PRO FO 371/26 542 C 2189: FO, 24.2.41, Craigie/Tokyo, Immediate. In the absence of Eden, Churchill himself drafted this telegram.
3. PRO FO 898/5: Meeting of the Ministry of Information's Policy Committee.

4. PRO FO 898/4: 'Preliminary plan for propaganda against Germany' prepared by a committee appointed by the Ministry of Information. Paragraph 'A' stated that propaganda must adapt to the strategic objectives laid down by the politicians.

5. PRO FO 371/26 542 C 1072: FO note, 31.1.41.

6. Ibid., comment by Cadogan, 3.2.41.

7. PRO FO 371/26 542 C 1322: Comments by the senior official, Roberts, and Cadogan on a telegram from the British military attaché in Madrid dated 12.2.41 to the FO. The diplomat had reported in this telegram on Spanish proposals to terminate the war by a German–British compromise peace.

8. PRO FO 898/29: Memorandum by Steed on a discussion with representatives from Chatham House, a Churchill Government wartime political objectives think tank. On the direction of Sir Robert Vansittart, chief diplomatic adviser to the Foreign Office and one of the most influential men in the Government apparatus, Steed began his work on 9.6.41. Other bodies had previously been engaged in post-war planning, since originally – despite the intervening defeat of France – Germany's collapse had been expected in autumn 1940, chiefly for economic reasons.

9. Nicolson, *Diaries*, p. 137.

10. Statement by Duff Cooper to the House of Commons, *Hansard* 1940–41, Vol. 365, col. 647.

11. PRO FO 898/5: MOI Policy Committee, meeting on 8.5.41.

12. PRO FO 371/26 565: Cadogan, 16.5.41, to all important foreign missions.

13. PRO FO 898/30: PID (E.H. Series), Propaganda Research Section, 27.5. and 10.6.41.

14. PRO PREM 3/219/1: Campbell/New York, 19.5.41, to MOI.

15. Lash, *Roosevelt and Churchill*, p. 347.

16. Ibid., p. 348.

17. PRO FO 898/30: Note by Murray, 3.6.41. to Leeper. The content of the Hess proposals is annexed under the heading: 'Attempt at a pseudonymous Italian contact in Dublin'. This may indicate that in summer 1941 the Italians, apart from the Germans, also put out feelers in Britain towards a negotiated peace.

18. PRO PREM 3/219/7: Memorandum, Cadogan, June 1941. Top Secret.

19. PRO PREM 3/219/7: Morton, 9.6.41, to Churchill.
20. HA: Record of interview, Simon-Hess. The minute is dated 10.6.41, 'Somewhere in Britain'. The version checked by Hess and corrected in a few minor points was not however prepared until 17.11.41. The reason why this was so late is not known.
21. Ibid., annex of 10.6.41 (copy).
22. These statements are therefore not included in the official minute of the interview. They are to be found in Simon's evaluation of the interview for Churchill in PRO PREM 3/219: 'Rudolf Hess – Preliminary Report', 10.6.41, Top Secret.
23. This anxiety on the part of my father had already been noted by Cadogan in his memorandum of 6.6.41. Cf. Note 18 above.

The Trap
 1. PRO PREM 3/434/7: Records of Talks at the Kremlin at Supper on October 18th 1944.
 2. AH: Letter, Ilse Hess, 16.1.83, to Seidl – Unfortunately my mother does not remember who told her this story so many years ago.
 3. PRO INF 1/912: Note by Herbert, 26.5.41, Director-General MOI, Secret. Cf. also here postal censorship's evaluation, showing the Secret Service agencies to which the letter was forwarded. There is as yet no explanation of why the letter, written on 19 September, did not reach Britain until 2 November. Another strange aspect: conflicting with the copy of the original Haushofer letter dated 3.9.41, Herbert gives the date of dispatch as 23.9.41. This is also the date on the postal censorship's evaluation form. Even more strange: the last sentence is missing here: 'My father and mother add their wishes for your personal welfare to my own. . . . Yours ever, "A".', which points to Haushofer's authorship. There is also as yet no explanation for this.
 4. Hamilton, *Motive for a Mission*, p. 148.
 5. Ibid., pp. 149/150.
 6. See following page. Cadogan had already used the expression 'low-down on Hess', which Churchill even put in quotes, without quotes in his diary, entry for 13.5.41. Cf. Dilks, *Cadogan*, p. 378.
 7. PRO INF 1/912: Sinclair, 22.5.41, to Cooper.

8. PRO INF 1/912: Studies in Broadcast Propaganda, No. 29, Rudolf Hess, Confidential. The head of the SS Foreign News Service, Walter Schellenberg, writes in his memoirs: 'Our Secret Service is of the opinion that Hess may have been motivated to decide to fly to Britain by an official of the British Secret Service who approached him years ago.' Also, the head of the Gestapo, Heydrich, thought that 'the British Secret Service had a hand in the game'.

9. The article appeared in the May edition of the publication under the heading, 'The Inside Story of the Hess Flight'. The author was 'Anonymous', and was presented by the publishers to its readers with the words: 'The writer, a highly respected observer, is known to us and we publish this article with full faith in its sources.' *Readers' Digest* published a summary in its July number for 1943, with the comment that the London correspondent of the publication had confirmed that the *Mercury* version of the Hess flight 'corresponded to the version supported by well-informed journalists in Britain'. We used a reprint from the *Journal of Historical Review*, autumn 1982, since it was no longer possible to get a copy of the original. The *Mercury* version was also reproduced, with small variations, by Paul Merker in his book, *Germany – To Be or Not To Be*, Volume 2, Mexico City 1945, p. 245ff. During the Second World War, the German Communist Merker led the KPD's illegal activities against Germany, using France as his base.

10. The former Director-General of the SID, Sir Maurice Oldfield, who has meanwhile died, stated in an interview in *The Times* of 15.3.81 that Philby's 'single most valuable service [to Stalin – W.R.H.] was to keep them [the Russians – W.R.H.] informed from 1941 to 1945 of any British moves for a separate peace with Germany'. In this context, what I was told on 2.11.83 by the former President of the German Office for the Protection of the Constitution, Otto John, who had been a member of the German Resistance, is interesting. He told me that, following the German victory over France, the Resistance was surprised that its peace proposals were no longer making their way to the proper authorities in the Churchill Government. John is now convinced that they landed in the safe of Kim Philby, who simply did not pass them on.

11. Jacobsen, *Haushofer*, I. p. 404.
12. Hamilton, *Motive for a Mission*, p. 94.
13. Conversation with Otto John, 2.11.83.
14. Cf. p. 29, 30, Note 5.
15. PRO PREM 3/219/7: Report on Interview with Herr Hess by Wing Commander the Duke of Hamilton, Sunday, 11 May, 1941, Secret. These notes were submitted to Churchill on 19.5.41. Their purpose is unknown. Perhaps the Prime Minister wanted to know more about Hess's flight, since this information was not contained in Hamilton's first report.
16. Nothing of this is included in Hamilton's report to Churchill. It is to be found, however, in the War Diary of the 13th RAF Combat Group, 245 Squadron, which was responsible for the area in question. According to this, two Hurrican fighters were dispatched at 21.35 hrs. They landed again at 22.40 hrs. and had allegedly 'nothing to report'. I must thank Mr K. Mount of Nelson, Great Britain, who has a photocopy of the War Diary, for this information.
17. So said Hamilton in his report to Churchill (cf. Note 16 above), giving the impression that everything had been done to intercept the enemy aircraft.
18. So said Hamilton in his report to Churchill. The maps of my father's route over British territory, which I have, show nothing of this, since on some sections his course on the Air Traffic Controller's radar screen coincided with the course of a British interceptor fighter, and it was impossible therefore to enter an accurate course on the maps.
19. Leasor, Rudolf Hess, *The Uninvited Envoy*, p. 110.
20. Cf. above Note 3.
21. Dilks, *Cadogan*, p. 377: entry for 12.5.41.
22. *Frankfurter Allgemeine Zeitung*, 3.1.84.
23. Dilks, *Cadogan*, p. 376f.: entry for 11.5.41. Cadogan mistakenly assumed that Churchill was at Chequers and would receive Hamilton there. As he points out, the unsuspecting Secretary of State had of course refused to receive the Scottish nobleman or even to allow him to see Foreign Secretary Eden.
24. Ibid., p. 378: entry for 14.5.41: 'Hess is the ruin of my life', groaned the already overburdened Secretary of State 'and

all my time has been wasted'. On page 384, Dilks adds, referring to the Minister's diary, a reference to Dalton.

25. Howe, *Propaganda*, p. 60.
26. Not far from here, near Bletchley Park, was also the legendary Government and Cypher School, an outpost of the SIS, successfully listening-in to German radio traffic and decoding the Wehrmacht codes.
27. Besymenski, Notes, p. 116ff.
28. On 27 April, German troops marched into the Greek capital, three days before Hess's second genuine attempt to take off. By 11 May, one day after his flight to Britain, the Greek islands had also been occupied. Crete, the seemingly impregnable bastion of British sea power in the Eastern Mediterranean, was conquered by German airborne troops between 20 May and 1 June. Perhaps, in this operation also, Hitler's objective was to support Hess's mission by military pressure.
29. Howe, *Propaganda*, p. 33.
30. Ibid., p. 114.
31. Ibid., p. 123.
32. *The American Mercury*, p. 295 – Cf. Note 10 above.
33. Hinsley, *Intelligence*, p. 310: So says the evaluation dated 31.1.41 by the Joint Intelligence Committee (JIC) of the General Staff.
34. Dilks, *Cadogan*, p. 378.
35. Ibid., p. 377: entry for 12.5.41.
36. Ibid.
37. Woodward, *Foreign Policy*, Vol. 1, p. 614: Cripps, 13.5.41, to FO.
38. Dilks, *Cadogan*, p. 378: entry for 14.5.41.
39. Ibid., p. 380: entry for 19.5.41.
40. Ibid.
41. Woodward, *Foreign Policy*, Vol. 1, p. 615: Halifax, 23.5.41, FO – ADAPP D XII 731: Woermann, head of the German Foreign Office Political Department, 25.1.41, to Ribbentrop. It had in fact just been decided in Berlin to establish a 'Central Office for Free India' and to set up in the Indian frontier area a medium-wave transmitter for anti-British propaganda.
42. Dilks, *Cadogan*, p. 382: entry for 30.5.41.

43. Woodward, *Foreign Policy*, Vol. 1, p. 620: So say the opinions of the Joint Intelligence Committee (JIC) of 9.6.41 and 14.6.41.

44. *The Mercury* reported, however, that Hess's peace proposals also had a preamble covering in detail German plans for Eastern Europe, without referring directly to a war against the Soviet Union. This again raises the question of whether the documents released for publication contain the whole truth.

45. Dilks, *Cadogan*, p. 387: entry for 11.6.41. Cf. here also the quotations following.

46. Simon had used the word 'bluff' in his minute referred to above, in which he wrote: 'He (Hess) is probably a hypochondriac and mentally unstable, and in my opinion not unlikely in this state of mind to keep up a 'bluff' independently, even when acting under instructions.'

47. Dilks, *Cadogan*, p. 388: entry for 15.6.41.

48. Ibid., p. 388: entry for 16.6.41.

49. Eden, *Memoirs*, Vol. III, p 256: Considering the enormous part played by the Hess affair internationally in May/June 1941, in his memoirs the British Foreign Secretary expresses only a perfunctory opinion on this. His assertion that 'the incident arose as unexpectedly and inexplicably for us as for the Russians' lacks credibility. Neither does it refute Stalin's fear that 'something sinister' (Eden) was concealed behind it.

50. Woodward, *Foreign Policy*, Vol. I, p. 620.

51. PRO FO 898/37: Letter, Lockhardt, 16.6.41, to Sargent.

52. Delmer, *Germans*, p. 459ff.

53. ADAP D X, No. 228: Prinz von Hohenlohe, 25.7.40, to German Foreign Office.

54. Halder, *War Diary*, II, entry for 14.9.40 (discussion with the Führer).

55. Ibid., p. 46: entry for 31.7.40.

56. OKW (High Command of the Wehrmacht) *War Diary*, Vol. I, p. 699. So said Hitler to Jodl.

57. HA: Letter, Hess, 4.11.40, to Hitler.

58. HA: Fragmentary document, undated. It is not clear whether the talk he records between Hitler and Hess took place before or after Molotov's visit to Berlin, when the

Soviet Foreign Minister first presented territorial demands which premised a common victory for the Soviet Union and the Western Powers – i.e. a successful two-front war against Germany.

59. PRO FO 371/26 542 C 1532: Campbell, 17.2., to FO. A corresponding report from Stockholm referred to imminent peace mediation by the Swedish Baron Bonde, a friend of Göring. Cf. PRO FO 371/26541: Scovell, 13.2.41. According to Jacobsen's calendar, Haushofer, Vol. II, p. 478, Albrecht Haushofer was in Sweden from 5.2.41 to 12.2.41. The purpose of his visit is not known.

60. This relates to documents PRO FO 371/26 542 C 1687 and C 1954.

61. This relates to documents PRO FO 371/26 542 C 2662, C 2785 and C 3156.

62. PRO FO 371/26 542 C 2505: Hoare, 6.3.41, to FO.

63. Hillgruber, *Second World War*, p. 63.

64. Beer, *Barbarossa*, p. 196.

65. HA: Hess memorandum, 'Germany–Britain from the viewpoint of the war against the Soviet Union', in manuscript, handed to Beaverbrook on 9.9.41.

Part II – Nuremberg

'Do You Remember'

1. *The Sunday Telegraph*, 13.12.81: So reported Hess in a letter in which he protested against the conditions of his imprisonment in Britain. For more details, cf. next note.

2. This is seen from a list prepared by Amen, the US interrogation officer, of the personal belongings my father brought to Nuremberg from Britain. Most of these revealing documents have disappeared. Some of the letters referred to in the previous and next-but-one paragraphs emerged later in America. Cf. on this *The Sunday Telegraph*, 13.12.81, which published extracts.

3. HA: Record of Beaverbrook–Hess talks on 9.9.41.

4. Records Office, House of Lords, Beaverbrook Papers.

5. *The Sunday Times*, 13.12.81: So says Hess in a note of 9.9.41, which he had apparently prepared in preparation for the

Beaverbrook visit.

6. This is reported by Leasor, *Rudolf Hess*, *The Uninvited Envoy*, p. 185. The original, a translation of which Leasor apparently used, has not as yet been made accessible to the public. I therefore use the quotation from Leasor's book without knowing whether it is correct, and whether it represents substantially the content of the letter.

7. Ilse Hess, *England*, p. 41f.

8. PRO FO 115/3544: Although a typewritten copy of this report bearing the heading 'Hess, Rudolf' is annexed to the file, it could not be established in which newspaper it had appeared. My mother's visit to Britain was of course an invention.

9. PRO PREM 3/219/7.

10. *Neue Zürcher Zeitung*, 23.9.43.

11. PRO INF 1/912: According to notes prepared by Hamilton about his first meeting with Hess on 11.5.41, Hess merely said that 'He had made three attempts to reach this country before he finally arrived.' There was no reference that Dungavel House was his target.

12. PRO INF 1/912: (Illegible; the sender was one of Bracken's closest associates), 6.4.45, to Martin, Office of the Prime Minister. Hamilton, who wished to take part in the conference as a civilian, had been given leave by the RAF for this purpose.

13. Ibid., undated, unsigned: text of the statement.

14. Ibid., Churchill, 7.4.43, to Bracken.

15. Ilse Hess, *England*, p. 48f.

16. Ibid., p. 51.

17. HA: Evidence by Rudolf Hess recorded at Nuremberg, Germany, on 30 October 1945, 10.30 hrs. to 12.00 hrs., in the presence of various other officers. Compared with the original document, 'Question' and 'Answer' are merely changed to 'Amen' and 'Hess' to improve comprehension.

The Tribunal

1. Strictly speaking there were only eight governments-in-exile which signed, i.e. Belgium, Czechoslovakia, Greece, Luxembourg, Norway, Holland, Poland and Yugoslavia. In addition, there was the 'Free France Committee' under

Charles de Gaulle, the body opposing the official Vichy Government of France which co-operated with the Third Reich. Since, however, in the interests of the Allied plans for North Africa, the USA had recognized the Vichy Government diplomatically, the 'Committee' was not considered as a government-in-exile in the Western capitals. This was a source of life-long embitterment to the eventual President of France towards the Anglo-Americans.

2. Gründler/Manikovski, *Court*, p. 28.
3. Ibid., p. 49.
4. Professor Dr D. Blumenwitz, expert opinion under international law dated 6 March 1974 on the Rudolf Hess case, in: Wolf Rüdiger Hess (publisher), *Justice*, p. 129ff.
5. Ibid., p. 164.
6. Ibid.
7. Sources: Smith, *Reaching Judgment at Nuremberg*, p. 335 and Wolf Rüdiger Hess, *Justice*, p. 24.

'. . . Not Guilty!'

1. Nuremberg Trial, 20 November 1945. Indictment of the International Military Tribunal against the 24 Nazi war criminals (offprint).
2. Gründler/Manikovski, *Court*, p. 105.
3. Seidl, *Case*, p. 45.
4. Ibid., p. 25f.
5. Ibid., p. 32.
6. Ibid., p. 38.
7. Ibid., p. 166.
8. HA: Manuscript note, Rudolf Hess, undated.
9. Seidl, *Case*, p. 190ff.
10. Ibid., p. 279.
11. Ibid., p. 197.
12. One was a letter from the Reich Minister of Justice dated 17.4.41 to the Head of the Reich Chancellery. This said that, as concerns the Jews and Poland, Hess had raised for discussion the matter of introducing corporal punishment. Seidl doubted whether Hess, as the head of a 500-strong organization, had concerned himself with this matter at all. He referred to the evidence of a former secretary of my father who at Nuremberg had doubted whether the former

Deputy Führer had ever been able to express an opinion on the introduction of such a form of punishment. Neither was the punishment introduced by the German occupation authority. The other was an instruction from Hess dated 13.3.40 on the attitude of the civilian population towards enemy aircrew and parachutists landing on the territory of the German Reich. They were to be arrested or – if offering resistance – rendered harmless. According to Seidl, the cause of this had been a corresponding instruction from the French Government. It contained nothing contrary to the customs of war normal at the time.

13. Seidl, *Case*, p. 250.
14. Ibid., p. 253.

Anything is Possible!
1. Gründler/Manikovski, *Trial*, p. 224.
2. Smith, *Reaching Judgement at Nuremberg*, p. 181ff.
3. HA: Letter, Rudolf Hess, 2.9.46, to Ilse Hess.
4. Ibid.
5. Ibid.

'Special Treatment'
1. HA: 'Rudolf Hess/Nuremberg/Prison – Findings and petitions', 20.10.46. A typed copy of this submission of several manuscript pages is available.
2. Bird, *The Loneliest Man in the World*, p. 35, and particularly p. 55ff. Bird was US Director at Spandau from 1963 to 1972, and maintains that he won my father's confidence over this period. My father allegedly gave him permission to use his Nuremberg notes in a publication. Although Bird's description sounds quite credible in many respects, as a source I consider the book to be of only limited reliability until such time as its content is confirmed by Rudolf Hess.
3. *The Times*, 22.7.44.
4. HA: Schellenberg, January 1945, to Brandt – undated 'Note' – copy.
5. Bird, *The Loneliest Man in the World*, p. 55ff.
6. HA: Note by Werner Maser, typewritten, undated, on his meeting with Otto Grotewohl, then East German Minister-President, in mid-May 1952 in East Berlin. Maser was at the

time scientific temporary assistant at the 'Institute for Research into Imperialism' under Ernst Niekisch at the East Berlin Humboldt University. He had made contact with Grotewohl over his scientific work. The conversation took place at the East German Head of Government's office in the National Chamber in the presence of Niekisch.

Part III – Spandau

'Prisoner Number Seven'

1. Speer, *Diary*, p. 73.
2. HA: Spandau Prison Regulations.
3. Speer, *Diary*, p. 112.
4. HA: Michel C. Vercel, *Les escapés de Nuremberg*, Paris, 1966, p. 142.
5. HA: Ibid., p. 143.
6. HA: Ibid., p. 158.
7. HA: Ibid., p. 142.
8. HA: Letter, Alfred Hess, 1.10.51, to RH.
9. HA: Letter, Rudolf Hess, 21.10.51, to the Hess family.

The Loneliest Prisoner in the World

1. Speer, *Diary*, p. 652.
2. Bird, *The Loneliest Man in the World*, p. 177.
3. Ilse Hess, *Reply*, p. 270ff.
4. Bird, *The Loneliest Man in the World*, p. 194.
5. HA: Ilse Hess's account of her visit to Rudolf Hess on 24.12.69.

'The Fact of False Imprisonment'

1. *The Times*, 2.1.70.
2. Seidl, *Case*, p. 296.
3. Federal Administrative Court, 7C 60.79/OVG I A 615/78.
4. HA: German Foreign Office, 9.3.79, to Seidl.
5. Quotation, Eschenburg.
6. HA: Thatcher, 21.12.79, to WRH.
7. Reprinted in Wolf Rüdiger Hess, *Justice*, p. 101ff. All subsequent quotations.
8. Vercel, loc. cit., p. 220.

9. Bird, *The Loneliest Man in the World*, p. 91.
10. Wolf Rüdiger Hess, *Justice*, p. 189.

Freedom for Rudolf Hess
 1. Ilse Hess, *Reply*, p. 270
 2. Wolf Rüdiger Hess, *Justice*, p. 25.
 3. HA: Rules of the Support Association.
 4. HA: Letter, Klaue, 19.12.74, to WRH.
 5. HA: Bucher, 18.2.75, to the Commandants.
 6. HA: Spandau Allied Prison, 26.7.79, to WRH.
 7. HA: Spandau Allied Prison to WRH, 28.8.79.
 8. *Tagesspiegel*, Berlin, 10.9.79.
 9. HA: Letter, Marshall, 27.9.79, to Ilse Hess.
10. HA: to Spandau Allied Prison, 3.10.79.
11. *Tagesspiegel*, 27.11.79.
12. HA: *Isvestia*, 23.7.78.
13. Seidl, *The Rudolf Hess Case, 1941–1984*, Munich, 1984.
14. HA: Letter, US Embassy/Bonn, 21.1.75, to WRH.

Half a Lifetime
 1. HA: Draft of application for release and letter from R.H. to I.H. stating that the draft had been submitted without amendment on 12.1.79.
 2. HA: US Embassy/Bonn, 15.10.82, to WRH.
 3. Wams, 12.2.84.
 4. HA: Report by Andrea Hess on her visit to Spandau, 16.8.83.

APPENDIX

Chronology
The imprisonment of Rudolf Hess
10 May until the present day

1941

10 May	Rudolf Hess flies to Scotland and is taken prisoner South of Glasgow.
10/11 May	During the night, Churchill informs Roosevelt of the 'successful operation'.
11 May	The Duke of Hamilton identifies Rudolf Hess in Glasgow and has the first conversation with him.
13, 14, 15 May	Sir Ivone Kirkpatrick questions Rudolf Hess in Glasgow.
16 May	Transfer of Rudolf Hess to the Tower of London.
17 May	Churchill informs President Roosevelt by telegram of the results of the first conversations with Rudolf Hess.
20 May	Transfer of Rudolf Hess to Mytchett Place near Farnborough, Kent.
29 May	Hitler sets 22 June 1941 as the date for the attack on Russia.
9 June	Lord Chancellor Simon carries out bogus negotiations with Rudolf Hess.

9 September   Lord Beaverbrook, Minister of Aircraft Production, speaks with Rudolf Hess before his negotiations on the supply of arms in Moscow.

1942
25 June   Transfer of Rudolf Hess to Abergavenny, South Wales, Mandiff Court Hospital.

1944
26 April   Rudolf Hess's 50th birthday.

1945
8 October   Transfer of Rudolf Hess from Britain to Nuremberg.

1946
2 September   Letter from Rudolf Hess to his family, with his final words.
1 October   Pronouncement of judgement at Nuremberg.
16 October   Execution of death sentences at Nuremberg.

1947
18 July   Transfer of the seven sentenced to terms of imprisonment to the Allied Military Prison, Berlin–Spandau.

1948
November   Pastor Casalis, the French Prison Chaplain, protests against the outrageous treatment of the prisoners.
15 November   Dr Seidl's petition to the Allied Control Council in Berlin. Application for the release of Rudolf Hess.

1950
April   Pastor Casalis describes Spandau 'as a place of mental torture'.

1952
5 October   After two years of discussion between the

custodial Powers, the Soviets declare their agreement to the following 'special privileges': one visit of 30 minutes a month; one letter a week of 1,300 words; medical attention in the prison; in the event of death, interment of the ashes in the prison instead of scattering in the wind.

1954

| 26 April | Rudolf Hess' 60th birthday. |
| 6 November | Release before time of Constantin von Neurath (sentence, 15 years). |

1955

| 26 September | Release before time of Erich Raeder (sentence, life imprisonment). |

1956

| 1 October | Release of Karl Dönitz (sentence, 10 years). |
| 2 November | Dr Seidl turns to the British, American and French ambassadors, and to the Secretary General of the United Nations, demanding the release of Rudolf Hess. |

1957

21 April	Article in the *Frankfurter Allgemeine Zeitung*. It is rumoured that Spandau is to be shut; Rudolf Hess is to be moved to a mental hospital.
23 April	Dr Seidl writes to the Central Legal Protection Office of the Federal Government: the Western Powers should withdraw from the Spandau administration, close the prison and return Rudolf Hess to Great Britain.
23 April	Dr Seidl sends copies of his letters of 2 November 1956 and 23 April 1957 to Federal Minister Franz Josef Strauss, with a request that he should give attention to the matter.
16 May	Release before time of Walther Funk (sentence, life imprisonment).
29 May	Dr Seidl writes to the Legal Protection Office:

now only three prisoners still in Spandau; intention to close the prison; not clear what is to happen to Hess: Baden-Wittenau Mental Hospital – allowing an irksome prisoner to disappear into a lunatic asylum?

1959

1 December — Dr Seidl's petition to the European Commission for Human Rights: the verdict against Rudolf Hess is contrary to the Convention on the Protection of Human Rights.

1960

13 January — Dr Seidl's letter to the Federal Foreign Office: the Federal Government should take action with the European Commission for Human Rights.

1964

26 April — Rudolf Hess's 70th birthday.

30 April — The US doctor John Hitchcock's medical report on Rudolf Hess; 'To sum up, he is an alert man who reveals no disturbance of thought, memory or orientation at this time.'

19 November — Dr Seidl's first visit to Rudolf Hess in the Allied Military Prison at Spandau.

1965

11 August — Dr Seidl's second visit to Rudolf Hess in the Allied Military Prison at Spandau.

2 November — Dr Seidl's letter to the British Ambassador: Subject: The Suez war; it follows from this that Great Britain and France are of the opinion that war is permissible. Therefore, either the basis of the verdict on Rudolf Hess disappears or – in the event that the IMT Charter is valid – Great Britain and France were perpetrating a crime against peace.

1966

18 May
: Dr Seidl's petition for the release of Rudolf Hess to the President of the USA, Queen Elizabeth II, the President of the French Republic and the Chairman of the Supreme Soviet of the USSR.

  Copies of the application sent to the Federal President, the Federal Chancellor, almost all Federal Ministers, a large number of Federal Members of Parliament. Also to the United Nations, New York, the President of the Committee of the International Red Cross, Geneva, the President of the German Red Cross, numerous foreign politicians such as Senator Robert Kennedy, Senator Mansfield, Senator Fulbright, Senator Morse, Mr Heath (Leader of the Opposition in the British Parliament), etc. No answer was received.

1 October
: Release of the last of Rudolf Hess's fellow-prisoners: Albert Speer and Baldur von Schirach. Rudolf Hess becomes the loneliest prisoner in the world.

1 October
: Family Hess's Declaration of 1 October 1966 directed to 'all thinking people' in the world.

September, October, November
: Correspondence with Rudolf Hess on the 'Declaration of the Hess Family, 1 October 1966.' Rudolf Hess will not petition for mercy: 'My honour means more to me than freedom.'

10 October
: Dr Seidl's third visit to Rudolf Hess at the Allied Military Prison.

14 October
: The European Human Rights Commission rejects Dr Seidl's application of 1.12.1959 on procedural grounds.

3 November
: Dr Seidl asks the Directorate of the Allied Military Prison at Spandau for special privileges for Rudolf Hess.

26 November
: Rudolf Hess writes to his family: 'Historical research will one day leave no doubt that I have rejected unconditionally any thought of asking for mercy.'

28 December	The Federal Chancellery in Bonn informs the family that it is endeavouring to obtain the release of Rudolf Hess on humanitarian grounds, and has found that the USA, Great Britain and France are in agreement with this.

1967

14 January	*Die Hilfsgemeinschaft 'Freiheit für Rudolf Hess', e.V.* (HFRH) ('Freedom for Rudolf Hess' Support Association' – a registered society) is brought into existence on the initiative of Wolf Rüdiger Hess.
4 February	Major General (retired) Sachsenheimer agrees to take over the chairmanship of the Support Association.
31 March	Major General (retired) Sachsenheimer is elected First Chairman of the Support Association by the Members Meeting at Wiesbaden.
28 April	Dr Seidl's fourth visit to Rudolf Hess in the Allied Military Prison
15-25 June	At the invitation of the *Daily Express* in Britain, Wolf Rüdiger Hess visits the places in Scotland, London and Wales (Abergavenny) where his father landed and was imprisoned. Conversations in London with Members of the House of Commons, Sefton Delmer and press representatives.
1 October	First declaration by the Support Association. Thousands of well-known people in public life both at home and abroad sign the declaration demanding the release of Rudolf Hess.
12 October	The presiding US judge of the IMT, Francis Biddle, issues a statement that, in agreement with Lord Justice Lawrence, later Lord Treventhin and Oaksey, President of the IMT, he advocates the release of Rudolf Hess.
20 December	HFRH press conference in Munich.

1968

8 January	The former President of the IMT, Lord

Treventhin and Oaksey, writes to Wolf Rüdiger Hess; 'I fully appreciate your feelings about the prolonged imprisonment of your father and I have on several occasions expressed my opinion that he has suffered enough and should now be released. I will once more express these feelings to the appropriate authorities and hope very much that it may be of some avail.'

10 May   Professor Rubin's parachute descent in the field of Floor's Farm in which Rudolf Hess landed. The pilot of the Cessna 170 in which the flight was undertaken was Mr Willi Schubert.

1 October   Press conference in Berlin on the occasion of the second anniversary of Rudolf Hess's solitary confinement. Pastor Niemöller and Sefton Delmer speak demanding the immediate release of Rudolf Hess.

1969

27 April   Professor A.J.P. Taylor, the British historian, in the *Sunday Express:* 'Hess came to this country in 1941 as an ambassador of peace.'

5 May   Application by the first Chairman of the HFRH to the Petition Committee of the Federal Parliament.

8 June   US Foreign Secretary William Rogers to Wolf Rüdiger Hess: 'In June this year the USA, Great Britain and France requested the Soviet Union to agree to the release of Rudolf Hess. The Soviet attitude is unchanged and rigid. Without Soviet agreement, there is no possibility of achieving release of your father.'

16 October   Dr Seidl's fifth visit to Rudolf Hess in the Allied Military Prison.

19 November   Rudolf Hess suffers a perforated duodenal ulcer.

22 November   Transfer of Rudolf Hess to the British Military Hospital. The family sends a telegram to Federal Chancellor Brandt.

| 24 December | Visit by Ilse Hess and Wolf Rüdiger Hess in the British Military Hospital. First reunion with Rudolf Hess since 10 May 1941. |

1970

January	Wolf Rüdiger Hess meets Airey Neave, Member of Parliament, in the Foreign Office, London. Numerous talks at high diplomatic levels. In the House of Commons, 192 signatures from members of all three parties collected for the release of Rudolf Hess.
3 February	Wolf Rüdiger Hess visits the British Foreign Secretary, Sir Alec Douglas-Home; he supports the release of Rudolf Hess.
February	Wolf Rüdiger Hess flies to the USA. Talks with Senators and Congressmen on the release of Rudolf Hess.
20 February	Wolf Rüdiger Hess with Senator Dodd, former deputy American prosecutor to the IMT; Dodd supports immediate release of Rudolf Hess.
13 March	Rudolf Hess's return from the British Military Hospital to the Allied Military Prison.
25 March	Debate in the British House of Lords on the Hess case.
31 March	President Richard Nixon's adviser writes to US Senator Strom Thurmond: the USA will bring up the Hess case 'at every possible opportunity'.

1971

| 10 May | Placards over the whole Federal area on the occasion of the 30th anniversary of the flight and imprisonment of Rudolf Hess. |
| 15 December | Demonstration in Bonn in front of the embassies of the four custodial Powers. Petition handed over in the appropriate languages to the four governments. |

1972

| 31 October | Cardinal Julius Döpfner writes to Wolf Rüdiger |

Hess: 'I think with great emotion of your father's lot, which still cannot be overcome in spite of the numerous efforts from all parts of the world.'

1973

27 April

In the name of Ilse Hess, the Support Association brings an action against Great Britain for the release of Rudolf Hess before the European Commission for Human Rights, Strasburg.

6 May

The HFRH's first protest rally in Bonn. 4,000 people from all parts of the Federal Republic take part.

2 June

Death of the HFRH's first Chairman, Major-General (retired) Sachsenheimer.

28 June

Declaration in the British House of Commons on the Hess case.

12 July

Report in *Frankfurter Allgemeine Zeitung*: The Israeli Foreign Minister Abba Eban states that he is opposed to the release of Rudolf Hess. 'When questioned in the Knesset, Eban stated that the Israeli Government was of the opinion that war criminals of the Nazi regime should serve their complete sentence. This also applies to Rudolf Hess.'

3 September

Wolf Rüdiger Hess thanks Sir Alec Douglas-Home for having again asked the Soviets, at the Conference on Security and Co-operation in Europe at Helsinki, to release Rudolf Hess. Gromyko brusquely refused this request.

10/12 October

Wolf Rüdiger Hess discusses the release of his father with the Under-secretary at the Foreign Office, London.

22 November

The German Foreign Office writes to the Support Association: 'The subject of Hess was broached in Moscow by the German side. The Soviet Government appears not to be prepared to give up its attitude to date. The Soviet side said that the prisoner shows no repentance, and has not as yet himself submitted any plea for mercy.'

2 December	Report in the *Sunday Telegraph*: Foreign Secretary Sir Alec Douglas-Home will inform Foreign Minister Gromyko in Moscow that pressure among members of the House of Commons is growing for Britain to withdraw from the Four Power Agreement on Spandau.

1974

10 January	Warning to Wolf Rüdiger Hess by the Allied Military Prison: if press interviews are repeated, visits will be forbidden.
March	Declaration by the Hess family on the 80th birthday of Rudolf Hess.
6 March	Professor Dr Dieter Blumenwitz prepares an opinion under international law on the Hess case.
April	Dr Seidl applies for a visit to Rudolf Hess 'to discuss various important legal matters'. Application refused.
1 April	Lord Chalfont, former Labour Minister, publishes in *The Times* a proposal for the solution of the Spandau question.
6 April	Election of Federal Minister of Justice (retired) Dr Ewald Bucher as First Chairman of the HFRH by the General Meeting at Bonn.
7 April	Professor A.J.P. Taylor, the well-known British historian, demands the release of Rudolf Hess in a well-publicized article in the *Sunday Express*.
22 April	Lord Chalfont in *The Times*: 'The Russians alone have decided to show no mercy. No one should misunderstand this lesson. It clearly shows what totalitarianism means, whatever the ideological flag under which it travels.'
26 April	Rudolf Hess's 80th birthday.
30 April	In a new letter, Dr Seidl approaches the embassies of the four custodial Powers with a request for the release of Rudolf Hess.
May	Karl Moersch, Under-secretary at the German Foreign Office, estimates the total cost of the

	Allied Military Prison in 1974 at about 1.2 million DM.
10 May	Valentin Falin, the Soviet Ambassador, personally to Dr Seidl: 'Your political and legal platform has long been known. Your letter shows that you have not changed this platform, and that our attitudes remain irreconcilable.'
11 May	HFRH protest rally at Bonn.
13 May	The US Embassy in Bonn again informs Dr Seidl that the unchanged Soviet attitude prevents the release of Rudolf Hess.
20 May	The British Embassy replies to Ilse Hess's letter to the Queen requesting Rudolf Hess's release on his 80th birthday. The embassy's answer is vague.
June	Dr Seidl makes a new application to be allowed to visit Rudolf Hess in the Allied Military Prison. Application refused.
October (or mid-Nov.)	Representative opinion poll conducted by the Institute for Public Opinion Surveys at Allensbach on the Rudolf Hess matter. 69% of those questioned in favour of the release of Rudolf Hess. 89% know who he is.
11 October	Conversation between Wolf Rüdiger Hess and Dr Frank, Under-secretary at the Office of the President of the Federal Republic.
1 December	HFRH protest rally at Bad Godesberg.
4 December	Debate in the Berlin Chamber of Deputies on the FDP-group resolution demanding humane treatment for Rudolf Hess.
19 December	The Allied Military Prison announces that Rudolf Hess agrees with the family's recommendation that Minister of Justice (retired) Dr Ewald Bucher should be nominated Rudolf Hess's solicitor.

1975

11 February	The Allied Military Prison rejects an application for a visit by Dr Bucher.
18 February	Dr Bucher addresses a letter of protest to the

	three Western Town Commandants in Berlin.
24 February	The Support Association informs all Members of the Federal Parliament of the refusal to agree to a visit by Dr Bucher.
12 March	The CDU Member Peter Milz takes up with the embassies of the custodial Powers the refusal to allow Dr Bucher to visit.
24/25 March	The three Western embassies answer Peter Milz: 'Decisions on visits to Herr Rudolf Hess by a solicitor require the agreement of all four Powers'.
5 April	On the occasion of Rudolf Hess's 81st birthday and Ilse Hess's 75th birthday, Wolf Rüdiger Hess applies for Rudolf Hess to be given leave of absence under his word-of-honour for the period 20 April to 28 April 1975. Application refused.
8 April	The Head of the Federal Chancellery answers Wolf Rüdiger Hess on Spandau's refusal to allow Rudolf Hess to be legally represented by Dr Ewald Bucher.
27 April	HFRH rally at Neustadt an der Weinstrasse.
25 May	HFRH protest rally at Munich. Wolf Rüdiger Hess asks to be allowed to go to Spandau in place of his father so that his father can be allowed to return home.
31 July	HFRH telegram to the Conference on Security and Co-operation in Helsinki demanding the release of Rudolf Hess.
5 October	HFRH protest rally at Essen.
17 October	Letter from Wolf Rüdiger Hess to Oskar Vetter, Federal Board of the German Federation of Trade Unions.
20 October	Debate in the British House of Commons on the Rudolf Hess case.
29 October	Announcement by the British Foreign Office: Minister of State Roy Hattersley has asked the Soviet Ambassador, Nilolai Lunkov, to visit him today to talk about Rudolf Hess.
7 November	NDR Television Third Programme: Atonement

without mercy. Discussion with Lutz Leh-mann. Justice Senator Ulrich Klug argues against Rudolf Hess.

28 November   Letter from Prime Minister Wilson's Private Secretary to Ilse Hess: Great Britain will conti-nue its efforts to secure the release of Rudolf Hess.

30 November   HFRH protest rally at Hamburg.

1976

9 January   The Chairman of the German Federation of Trade Unions, Oskar Vetter, answers Wolf Rüdiger Hess's letter of 17 October 1975.

18 February   Talk between Wolf Rüdiger Hess and Bishop Scharf in Berlin. Soviet Union no longer inter-ested in holding Rudolf Hess to the end of his life, nor in keeping open the Spandau Prison building. The Soviet Union is afraid of making a martyr!

26 March   Second conversation with Bishop Scharf in Berlin on the Soviet Union's change of attitude.

9 May   HFRH protest rally and march in Bonn in which 3,000 people take part.

12 June   Statement by Ilse Hess about her visit to Rudolf Hess on 10 June 1976: Frau Hess was not allowed to describe to her husband how a dele-gation from the British House of Commons had been treated at the Soviet Embassy in London.

September   Dr Bucher describes to the German Lawyers' Conference the ban on visits to his client Rudolf Hess.

October   Appearance of the first 'Spandau Report' in a HFRH special publication. Subsequently, eleven further issues with a total of over one million copies.

1 October   Statement by the family on the 10th anniver-sary of Rudolf Hess's solitary confinement.

1 October   Baumann, the Berlin Justice Senator, speaks against the release of Rudolf Hess: 'One cannot

hunt the pickpocket and let the big criminals go free.'

20 November	HFRH protest rally at Wiesbaden.
20 December	Debate in the British House of Commons on the Rudolf Hess case. To a question from Cyril D. Townsend, the Minister of State at the Ministry of Defence, Robert C. Brown, answers: without Soviet agreement, no release for Hess.

1977

16 February	Wolf Rüdiger Hess approaches US President Carter with an appeal for the release of Rudolf Hess.
22 February	Rudolf Hess attempts to take his own life in the Allied Military Prison.
28 February	Press conference at the Hilton Hotel, Berlin, in connection with Rudolf Hess's suicide attempt.
1 March	The well-known Jewish journalist Bernard Levin in *The Times*: 'This enfeebled old man has paid enough – for humanity's sake, set him free!'
14 March	Letter from the Allied Military Prison, Berlin–Spandau, to Wolf Rüdiger Hess: '. . . the Directors bring to your notice the offences you have committed against the Visiting Regulations, in spite of your having been repeatedly warned about this by the Directors. You are further informed that if such offences against the existing regulations are repeated your visits may be refused'.
April	The International Executive Comittee of Amnesty International resolves that Rudolf Hess's conditions of imprisonment can be described as 'cruel, inhumane and degrading treatment or punishment', which is forbidden under Article 5 of the Declaration on Human Rights.
4/5 April	Wolf Rüdiger Hess in London: reception by the Under-secretary at the Foreign Office, Frank

Judd; talks with the All-Party Committee of the House of Commons on the release of Rudolf Hess, with the German Ambassador, with the First Secretary of the US Embassy and with the Chairman of the British section of Amnesty International.

5 April   Franz Josef Strauss to Wolf Rüdiger Hess; he has 'advocated the release of Rudolf Hess' in letters to President Carter, President Giscard d'Estaing and Prime Minister Callaghan.

10 April   The former British chief prosecutor at the IMT, Lord Shawcross, in a *Bild am Sonntag* interview: The British Government must ignore the Soviet 'Njet'; The Russians can do no more than kick up a bit of a row.

26 April   Greetings to the former Deputy Führer on his 83rd birthday in three newspapers published in Windhuk, the capital of the former German colony of South West Africa. The release of Rudolf Hess is demanded on placards on walls and doors.

29 April   The three Western Allies renew their appeal to the Soviet Union to agree to the release of 83-year-old Rudolf Hess.

30 April   The Soviet Union rejects the Western Powers' latest appeal for the immediate release of Rudolf Hess.

10 May   HFRH press conference at Bonn on the occasion of the 36th anniversary of Rudolf Hess's flight. Participants: Cyril D. Townsend and Kenneth Weetch, Members of the British House of Commons; Federal Minister of Justice (retired) Dr Ewald Bucher; and Wolf Rüdiger Hess.

3 June   Amnesty International appeals to the four governments to take steps to end Rudolf Hess's solitary confinement and to provide adequate medical care.

23 November   On the occasion of the visit of the Soviet Secretary-General Breshnev, Abelein, Member

of the Federal Parliament, urges the Federal Government to discuss the Rudolf Hess case.

19 December   The Cologne Administrative Court rejects Rudolf Hess's case against the Federal Government under the legislation protecting German citizens against the actions of foreign countries.

1978

9 February   The national section of Amnesty International states that Rudolf Hess's conditions of imprisonment represent *de facto* solitary confinement, and that its continuation for over ten years is cruel, inhuman and degrading.

5 June   HFRH press conference at Bonn.

9 June   On the occasion of the Soviet Party Leader's visit to Bonn, Federal President Scheel asks him to release Rudolf Hess. Breshnev brusquely rejects this, giving as his reason that this could not be expected of the Soviet people.

13 June   The British Government again asks for Rudolf Hess's release. The Soviet Ambassador in London rejects the request.

6 July   Debate in the British House of Commons initiated by Members of Parliament Cyril Townsend, Clement Freud and Neville Sandelson, who are working for the release of Rudolf Hess. Frank Judd, Minister of State at the Foreign Office, supports the debate on behalf of the Government.

29 December   Rudolf Hess suffers a heart attack, with opacity of eyesight. Admission to the British Military Hospital once again.

1979

3 January   Wolf Rüdiger Hess (specially returned from Saudi Arabia) visits his father in the Allied Military Prison. Rudolf Hess is about two-thirds blind as a result of the heart attack.

5 January   The Chief Medical Officer at the British Mili-

	tary Hospital, Col. Thoresby, describes Rudolf Hess's state of health to Wolf Rüdiger Hess as 'very serious', and admits that further heart attacks are possible.
6 January	Telex from Wolf Rüdiger Hess to Federal Chancellor Schmidt in Guadeloupe informing him of Rudolf Hess's state of health. Appeal to the Federal Chancellor and the Heads of State of the three Western custodial Powers 'to break through, at the last minute, the vicious circle of Soviet stubbornness and Western submission'.
8 January	Telex from Wolf Rüdiger Hess to the Bonn Embassies of the three Western custodial Powers stating that the application submitted on 30 June 1978 for permission 'to speak to his father privately and without time limit' should now be treated as a matter of urgency.
	The Federal President and Federal Chancellor received copies of the telex.
11 January	Federal Chancellor's Office's reply to the telex of 6 January: 'The Federal Chancellor advocated the release of your father in Guadeloupe in talks with President Carter, President Giscard d'Estaing and Prime Minister Callaghan'.
12 January	In a letter to his wife, Rudolf Hess says that on 12 January 1979 he sent an application for release from prison to the Directorate, with a request that it should be passed on.
13 January	Wolf Rüdiger Hess sends his 'Report on Rudolf Hess's state of health' to the Dean of the Medical Faculty of the Technical University, Munich, requesting an opinion on Rudolf Hess's state of health.
22 January	The Archibishop of Cologne and Chairman of the German Conference of Bishops, Josef Cardinal Höffner, approaches Pope John Paul II requesting him to use his influence, at the Pope's coming talk with the USSR Foreign Minister, for the release of Rudolf Hess.

[375]

22 January/ 15 February/ 3 March	Dr Seidl repeatedly demands, referring to the legal action of 19 October 1977, that the Federal Government should meet its obligation to protect Rudolf Hess.
25 January	Dr Seidl's sixth visit to Rudolf Hess at the Allied Military Prison.
2 February	Frau Ilse Hess sends a letter to Josef Cardinal Ratzinger asking him to support efforts to release her husband, including via the Pope.
12 February	Josef Cardinal Ratzinger answers Frau Ilse Hess: 'I therefore hope with you that mercy will at last be granted your husband, and that he can return to your side and into the bosom of his family. In this sense, I shall be happy to help you and your husband wherever I can.'
15 February	Golo Mann in a letter to Ilse Hess: 'I have never forgotten how helpful Rudolf Hess was to my mother's (Jewish) father as long as he in any way could.'
22 February	Wolf Rüdiger Hess sends the opinion on Rudolf Hess's state of health provided by the Medical Faculty of the Technical University, Munich, to the Directorate of the Allied Military Prison.
22 February	Wolf Rüdiger Hess visits his father in the Allied Military Prison. When asked, the Directors state that Rudolf Hess's application for release dated 12 January 1979 has been rejected on the Soviet side. Rudolf Hess had been informed of this. Rudolf Hess was not given this information in writing.
22 February	When asked by Wolf Rüdiger Hess, the medical officers of the four custodial Powers admit that from a medical aspect Rudolf Hess can 'no longer be considered as fit to remain in custody'.
26 February	Rudolf Hess admitted to British Military Hospital for treatment for acute bronchitis.
9 March	The Federal Minister of the German Foreign Office writes to Dr Seidl: '. . . the Three

Powers have misgivings about questioning the legality of the International Military Tribunal's verdict at Nuremberg. The Three Powers are of the opinion that Rudolf Hess's release can be considered only on humanitarian grounds. The Federal Government shares this opinion'.

12 March
Rudolf Hess returned to the Allied Military Prison.

14 March
Question in the German Parliament by 30 members led by Dr Wittmann and Benno Erhard on the Rudolf Hess case.

26 April
HFRH press conference at Hotel Intercontinental, Berlin, with Wolf Rüdiger Hess, Dr Seidl and Eugene K. Bird, former US Director of the Allied Military Prison, Spandau.

14 May
Hearing of the appeal in the matter of Rudolf Hess's protection from the actions of foreign countries before the Higher Administrative Court at Münster. Appeal rejected, but appeal to the Federal Administrative Court permitted.

16 May
The London *Evening News* reports, via its Moscow correspondent Victor Louis, that the Soviet Union is about to abandon its resistance to the release of Rudolf Hess.

5 June
Dr Seidl again reminds the Federal Chancellor of the Federal Government's obligation to protect Rudolf Hess against the actions of foreign countries.

2 July
For reasons of principle, the Federal President is asked to support Rudolf Hess in the matter of the actions of foreign countries.

16 July
Dr Seidl writes to the Secretary General of the United Nations requesting him to bring the Rudolf Hess case before the Commission on Human Rights.

20 July
In Jeddah, Saudi Arabia, Wolf Rüdiger Hess is informed by telephone by Minister of State Wischnewski that the Soviets are prepared to release Rudolf Hess under certain conditions.

23 July
Complaint by Dr Seidl to the European Com-

mission on Human Rights directed against Great Britain and France.

2 August Wolf Rüdiger Hess visits Minister of State Wischnewski to discuss the 'signal' from Moscow.

4 August Wolf Rüdiger Hess visits his father in the Allied Military Prison, Berlin–Spandau. Contrary to indications from Moscow, the visit is subject to the usual conditions.

4 September Rudolf Hess undergoes 'routine medical examination' in the British Military Hospital. A leading urologist from Great Britain examines Rudolf Hess on 8 September. He recommends an immediate operation for Rudolf Hess because of his prostate condition. Rudolf Hess refuses to undergo the operation.

10 September Rudolf Hess is returned to prison.

7 November The UN rejects Dr Seidl's application that the Rudolf Hess case should be referred to the UN Commission on Human Rights, referring to the so-called 'Enemy States Article'.

21 December In a letter to Dr Seidl, the British Prime Minister, Mrs Thatcher, asserts that there is 'no doubt about the legality of the sentence which Herr Hess is now serving'.

1980

7 January Wolf Rüdiger Hess writes to the International Red Cross in Geneva requesting support for the release of his father.

8 January On the occasion of the Red Army's invasion of Afghanistan, Dr Seidl approaches the US President: '. . . in this case, any more than in all the other wars since Nuremberg, nobody thinks of calling to account, personally or criminally, the state institutions responsible for this war'.

14 January Dr Seidl approaches the Federal Audit Office and the Berlin Audit Office requesting investigation of the legality of expenditure on the Allied Military Prison at Berlin–Spandau.

22 January	The President of the Berlin Audit Office replies to Dr Seidl: 'In Berlin (West), supreme authority is, now as ever, exercised by the three Occupying Powers.'
2 January	Dr Seidl again writes to President Reagan about the Rudolf Hess case.
25 January	The President of the International Red Cross at Geneva, Alexandre Hay, answers Rudolf Hess and tells him that he should approach the national Red Cross Associations of the countries directly involved.
28 January	Dr Seidl submits a complaint of unconstitutionality against the judgement of the Supreme Administrative Court, Münster.
7 February	The President of the Federal Audit Office replies to Dr Seidl: 'The Federal Audit Office is not authorized to comment on the necessity and justification of the expenditure. The Occupying Powers in Berlin strictly supervise the Federal Audit Office's adherence to these provisions.'
20 February	Dr Seidl draws the attention of the Executive Committee of the Scientific Forum of the Conference on Security and Co-operation in Europe to the Rudolf Hess case.
9 June	Request by Dr Seidl to CSCE member states to add the Rudolf Hess case to the agenda in Madrid.
August	Simon Wiesenthal advocates in *Playboy* the release of Rudolf Hess for health reasons.
19 August	Wolf Rüdiger Hess in London visits the Deputy Foreign Secretary, Sir Ian Gilmour.
25 September	Dr Seidl approaches all United Nations Member States, pointing out the untenability of the UN Secretary General's decision.
11 November	Rudolf Hess writes a long letter to the Governments of the four custodial Powers in which he asks for his release. The request is founded on health, age and the desire to see his family and grandchildren once again, with

a reference to the fact that he probably has not long to live.

13 November	The European Parliament passes a resolution demanding the release of Rudolf Hess.
16 December	The Federal Constitutional Court rejects the complaint of unconstitutionality of 28 January 1980.

1981

10 February	The *Süddeutsche Zeitung* publishes the following statement by Abrassimov, the Soviet Ambassador: 'People speak of "repentance" by the war criminal Rudolf Hess, who himself however has refuted this, in that a wreath is said to have been laid on the grave of Hitler's successor, Admiral Dönitz, in his name.'
20 February	Hearing of the appeal against the judgement of the Supreme Administrative Court before the Federal Administrative Court in Berlin.
24 February	The Federal Administrative Court declares that the Nuremberg judgement against Rudolf Hess and his long imprisonment is contrary to international law.
30 March	President Reagan's serious accusations against the USSR cause Dr Seidl to approach the American President once again. No reply is received.
7 April	Rudolf Hess is admitted to the British Military Hospital with severe 'influenza'. Pneumonia is diagnosed there. On 11 April, Rudolf Hess's condition had so deteriorated that it was feared he would not survive the day.
16 April	Further complaint of unconstitutionality by Dr Seidl to the Federal Administrative Court for protection for Rudolf Hess against the actions of foreign countries.
3 May	HFRH rally at Augsburg on the occasion of the 40th anniversary of Rudolf Hess's flight to Britain. Federal Minister of Justice (retired) Dr Bucher is appointed Honorary Chairman.
7 May	Full-page HFRH advertisement in the *Frank-*

	furter Allgemeine Zeitung on the occasion of Rudolf Hess's forty years of imprisonment. Readers' response is substantial.
23 May	Complaint of unconstitutionality of 16 April 1981 rejected by the Federal Administrative Court.
May/June	Comprehensive discussion in the *Frankfurter Allgemeine Zeitung* correspondence columns on the Rudolf Hess case, occasioned by the rejection of the complaint of unconstitutionality.
10 July	The Commission for Human Rights states that the complaint of 23 July 1979 is inadmissible.
16 July	Dr Seidl requests, in the Bavarian Parliament, that efforts be made to delete the so-called Enemy States Articles 53 and 107 from the Statutes of the United Nations.
23 July	Detailed article in *Isvestia* defending the continued imprisonment of Rudolf Hess. West German circles are accused of revanchism, and Dr Seidl is strongly attacked for his manifold activities on behalf of Rudolf Hess. 'The son of the former Deputy Führer came forward. The upshot of his address was that the Nuremberg Tribunal was contrary to justice and was an act of revenge by the victors.'
6 September	In the context of the death of 76-year-old Albert Speer in a British hotel, the *Sunday Express* says that: 'Compared with Albert Speer, Rudolf Hess was as innocent as a new-born babe.'
3 October	HFRH full-page advertisement in the *Frankfurter Allgemeine Zeitung* on the 15th anniversary of Rudolf Hess's solitary confinement in Spandau.
26 October	Dr Seidl asks the Federal Minister of Justice to bring the case of Rudolf Hess before the UN Commission on Human Rights.
19 November	HFRH full-page advertisement in the *Frankfurter Allgemeine Zeitung* on the occasion of the visit of Breshnev, the Soviet Head of Government, to Bonn.

25 November	In a talk with the Soviet Head of Party and State, Leonid Breshnev, Dr Helmut Kohl advocates the release of Rudolf Hess.

1982

4 March	Resolution of the Bavarian Parliament to the Bavarian State Government: 'to exercise its influence on the Federal Government to the end that the so-called Enemy States Articles 53 and 107 of the Statutes of the United Nations are deleted'.
6 May	HFRH full-page advertisement in the *Frankfurter Allgemeine Zeitung* on the occasion of Rudolf Hess's 88th birthday and 41 years of imprisonment.
10 May	In a joint letter to the Allied Military Prison, Ilse Hess and Wolf Rüdiger Hess request that Rudolf Hess's body be handed over in the event of his death.
6 July	On the initiative of Benno Erhard and Dr Alois Mertes, members of the CDU and the CSU Alliance Party, 131 members of the Federal Parliament demand immediate release of the last of the war convicts, in particular Rudolf Hess.
26 August	Rudolf Hess tells Wolf Rüdiger Hess that he would give his word of honour not to comment on historical matters if he were released.
15 September	Rudolf Hess is admitted to the British Military Hospital with 'wet pleurisy', having suffered violent pains in the left side of the chest since 14 September.
20 September	Rudolf Hess is returned to the Allied Military Prison. The British Military Government announces that he has been discharged from hospital following satisfactory treatment for pleurisy.
24 September	A few days before his resignation, Federal Chancellor Schmidt sends identical telegrams to the Heads of State of the four custodial Powers requesting the release of Rudolf Hess.

October	The Ambassadors of the three Western custodial Powers write to Wolf Rüdiger Hess that the state of Rudolf Hess's health is again satisfactory, and that the Western Powers would continue to work for his release.
7 October	HFRH full-page advertisement in the *Frankfurter Allgemeine Zeitung* headed: 'The case of Rudolf Hess and the humanity of the victorious Powers'.
7 November	The secretary of the Support Association for many years, 84-year-old Eva Schleusener, dies in a Frankfurt hospital.

1983

26 April	On Rudolf Hess's 89th birthday, the first printing of 'Hitler's Diaries' begins. Doubts are raised about their authenticity. Wolf Rüdiger Hess requests that his father should be allowed to test their authenticity.
5–9 May	Wolf Rüdiger Hess goes to the USA to exploit, in the form of a campaign for Rudolf Hess's release, the world-wide interest in his case provoked by 'Hitler's Diaries'.
18 May	Because of Wolf Rüdiger Hess's efforts referred to above, the Directorate of the Allied Prison rejects an application for a visit by Wolf Rüdiger Hess in May 1983.
18 May	Wolf Rüdiger Hess applies to the embassies of the custodial Powers for Rudolf Hess's release on licence for one month.
1 June	The Ambassadors state that they have no authority to deal with the application, and refer him to the Directorate of the Allied Military Prison.
29 June	Dr Seidl applies to the Directorate of the Allied Military Prison, Berlin–Spandau, for Rudolf Hess's release on licence. Shortly afterwards the application is rejected, no reason being given.
12 July	Federal Chancellor Kohl writes to Wolf

	Rüdiger Hess about his fruitless efforts in Moscow to secure the release of Rudolf Hess.
9 August	Dr Seidl submits a complaint of unconstitutionality to the Federal Administrative Court on the grounds of the rejection of the application for release on licence.
15 August	Wolf Rüdiger Hess answers Federal Chancellor Kohl in a letter setting out the principles involved.
6 September	The Allied Military Prison orders for study 16 copies of the paper: *The case of Rudolf Hess and international law*.
30 September	Federal Chancellor Kohl answers Wolf Rüdiger Hess and informs him that the Federal Government could work for the release of Rudolf Hess on humanitarian grounds only.
2 November	Answering a question by Klein (CSU), Munich, a member of the Federal Parliament, the Federal Government states that over the past 12 years the Federal Government has paid out DM 17,705,169.00 for the Allied Military Prison.

1984

18 January	During a visit, Rudolf Hess tells Wolf Rüdiger Hess that a lift is to be installed in the prison to make it easier for him to reach the garden. Price: DM 130,000.
End of January	Comprehensive discussion in the correspondence columns of the *Münchener Merkur* on the Rudolf Hess case.
9 Feburary	Dr Seidl's book, *The case of Rudolf Hess, 1941–1984*, introduced to the public at a press conference in Munich.
5–9 March	Wolf Rüdiger Hess in Britain to talk once again with politicians about the release of Rudolf Hess. Meeting with Ray Whitney, Secretary of State at the Foreign Office.
9 March	Long article in *Le Monde* requesting the release of Rudolf Hess.

9 March   Question in the British House of Commons by the Conservative member Cyril Townsend about the release of Rudolf Hess.

Declaration by the Hess Family, 1 October 1966

Frau Ilse Hess and Wolf Rüdiger Hess, the only close relatives still living of the former German Reich Minister Rudolf Hess, have presented the following declaration to the public and have forwarded it to Pope Paul VI in Rome, the World Council of Churches in Geneva, the United Nations Commission on Human Rights in Strasburg and the Heads of State of the four Spandau custodial Powers:

After many weeks of hope that for the first time the release of Rudolf Hess, husband and father, was moving into the realm of the possible, it has become certain today, 1 October 1966, to our deepest dismay that he is now to continue in solitary confinement in Allied custody. We are convinced that this cruel situation, unknown until now in modern legal history, was neither envisaged nor intended by the Nuremberg Tribunal.

In its judgement of 1 October 1946, the Tribunal *acquitted* Rudolf Hess on the charges of war crimes and crimes against humanity. The verdict of guilty was founded exclusively on the historico-political accusation that he had participated in the preparation and conduct of a war of aggression. During the court proceedings, Rudolf Hess expressed no opinion on this, and we, his closest relatives, refrain from argument.

Even those who acknowledge the judgement must nevertheless recognize that Rudolf Hess, by his personal action in flying to Britain in the night of 10 to 11 May 1941, hoped to put an end to the War. Since then – that is, for more than a quarter of a century – he has been imprisoned. The Nuremberg Tribunal did not wish to inflict the maximum punishment on him, and therefore did not condemn him to death. In all civilized states, however, a sentence of 'life imprisonment' is considered as having been discharged after fifteen to twenty-five years; also, the practice followed hitherto at Spandau in releasing prisoners has taken account of humanitarian considerations. Admiral of the Fleet Raeder and Reich Economics Minister Funk – both, like Hess, sentenced to life imprisonment by the Nuremberg Court – had already returned to their families in 1955 and 1957 respectively, and were able to spend the last years of their lives peacefully; the former Reich Foreign Minister von Neurath, sentenced at Nuremberg to fifteen years imprisonment, was also released early in 1954.

But what is now to begin in Spandau in absolute isolation is in our opinion a belated intensification of the sentence, and perhaps an even more horrible process of homicide than the death sentences carried out at Nuremberg – carried out on a man over seventy years of age! We appeal to all people of good-will to speak out against this martyrdom before it is consummated.

Comments and Opinions on the 'Hess case'
A selection from the period dating
from his solitary confinement on 1 October 1966

The former British chief prosecutor at the Nuremberg trials, *Lord Shawcross*, stated in 1967: 'Most civilized people with a concern for humanity nowadays inflict punishment for retaliation or revenge. And from the humane aspect therefore it now appears to me to be necessary to release Hess. Continuation of his imprisonment is a pure act of revenge and retaliation, a disgrace to great and powerful nations . . .

'A judgement that banishes a human being behind bars for his whole life threatens to destroy his soul. Only a few who suffer such punishment are anything more than a wreck at the end.

'Imprisonment for life is more cruel than a verdict of death, since it robs the prisoner of all hope. Nevertheless, the judges came to the conclusion that Hess had brought upon himself a less dreadful measure of guilt than those condemned to death. Many states pronounce sentences of life imprisonment, but I know of no country claiming to be civilized which does not remit the rest of the sentence after a certain period of time.

'In Britain, "life imprisonment" with good conduct means 12

[386]

to 15 years. Never has a life prisoner served more than 20 years. I assume that at least the British and American judges at Nuremberg anticipated, when pronouncing a life sentence, that the procedure would be similar in the case of Hess.'

The 'Freedom for Rudolf Hess' Support Association published the following DECLARATION on 1 October 1967, the anniversary of Rudolf Hess's solitary confinement:

'In the Four Power prison at Berlin–Spandau, a year of absolute solitude is completed on 1 October 1967 for the former Reich Minister Rudolf Hess, who is still held prisoner there. He is in his 75th year and in the 28th year of his imprisonment.

'In 1946, the Nuremberg Tribunal expressly acquitted Hess of the charges of war crimes and crimes against humanity. The sentence was based exclusively on the historico-political accusation that he had taken part in the preparation and execution of aggressive wars. The undersigned refrain from expressing an opinion on this accusation; they judge the case of Hess under the humanitarian aspect of 1967, and advocate the view that this prisoner has abundantly discharged the measure of suffering imposed upon him.

'They also consider that the maintenance of a political prison by four Great Powers merely to supervise the slow death of an old man is unworthy of our time and age, which is struggling for a break-through in the field of human relations. In comparison with the great affairs of world politics to which they must daily devote their attention, the "Hess case" may seem trivial to the governments concerned – but nevertheless this challenge to human sentiment can become of tragic importance if it is not brought to a peaceful end in time, for which the signatories appeal.' Over the years, the DECLARATION has been signed by nearly 400,000 people. Some of the prominent signatories are included below.'

Lord Bourne, British Town Commandant in Berlin, 1949–1952, 8 September 1967:
Declaration on the Hess case: 'I believe this man should be released from Spandau Prison for two reasons:

1. He has spent more than 20 years of his life in the prison and is now at the age of 76 (sic) no longer any danger to anyone. According to general humanitarian attitudes, he has . . . atoned and should be released.
2. It was cruel to keep 7 men imprisoned in a prison capable of housing more than 200 (sic) people, and therefore, as the British Commandant in Berlin, I proposed in 1950 that they should be transferred to another prison. This proposal was rejected by the Russian, French and American Governments. Now, 27 [17 – German translator's note] years later, it is more than cruel to hold just one man, Hess, in Spandau.

'I appeal to all four governments to agree to the release of this old man.'

Professor Dr Otto Hahn, Göttingen (Nobel Prize-winner), 28 April 1967:

'I entirely agree with you that Rudolf Hess should be released from Spandau prison as soon as possible. And I can only say that I most certainly sympathize with the efforts of the "Freedom for Rudolf Hess" Support Association and hope that these efforts will soon be successful. As is generally known, I was a strong opponent of National Socialism; nevertheless, I consider it unjust to continue to keep Rudolf Hess of all people imprisoned.'

Pastor Schantz, Strasburg, 2 August 1967:

'Since I knew your father very well and had an opportunity to talk to him on various occasions during my period as Chaplain at Spandau Prison, I cannot be indifferent to his fate. I of course authorize you to add my name to the list of those who, for humanitarian reasons, consider it desirable that at long last this old man, now aged 75, who has been imprisoned since 1941, should now be allowed to rejoin his family. Our generation cannot be healed of its traumas if it does not decide finally to live in a spirit of genuine and sincere reconciliation . . .'

Jean Anouilh, Paris, 29 August 1967:

'I have never accepted the post of judge – even, for example, in a competition for actors – and I am not entitled to judge your father – but I consider that the deliberations preceding the judgements of the Nuremberg Tribunal (and this certainly cannot be accused of having been lenient), which did not uphold the charge of war crimes against Hess, should, if a concept of the humanity for which we were allegedly fighting still remains in this world, lead to a decision to release Rudolf Hess on the same legal grounds as were granted to others condemned to life imprisonment – on the basis of the mercy normal after 20 years' imprisonment . . .'.

Sefton Delmer, Britain, on the German 'TV Channel Two', 2 October 1967:
'If it were up to me, we would simply release the man as soon as it is our turn to take over duty at Spandau Prison, and tell the others to take a running jump at themselves!'

Bernard Levin in the *Daily Mail*, December 1967:
'The time has come to declare that 20 years of carefully regulated torture, which is what solitary confinement is, is sufficient and should be ended. And that the three nations which are prepared to do so – namely Britain, France and the United States – should act without delay. If the fourth government concerned, the Soviet Union, refuses to give its consent, it should be invited to start a Third World War on these grounds. Since the Four Powers take turns monthly in providing the guard, there is no problem in making the necessary announcement during a month in which the Western Powers are responsible for Spandau. Also, if Kosygin should really be alarmed, the thought of a Third World War is scarcely tenable. Our Foreign Office would doubtless find an acceptable and sonorous explanation.'

Sunday Express, London, December 1967:
'If he (Hess) had been a child murderer or mail-train robber held for a quarter of a century in a British prison, Trafalgar Square would resound with shouts for his release. But our protestors

are very selective in their quest for mercy and justice. Nevertheless, we are all to a certain extent responsible for Rudolf Hess.'

Lord Trevethin and Oaksey, former Lord Chief Justice Lawrence, Chairman of the IMT, Nuremberg, 8 January 1968:
'I fully appreciate your feelings about the prolonged imprisonment of your father and I have on several occasions expressed my opinion that he has suffered enough and should now be released.

'I will once more express these feelings to the appropriate authorities and hope very much that it may be of some avail.'

Professor Dr F. J. Berber (International Law), Munich, 31 January 1968:
'I acknowledge receipt of your letter 24 January 1968, and inform you that I support you in your efforts as set out in the printed declaration. At the same time, I send you my signature to this declaration.

'I wish to point out in this context that in 1962, in the international law textbook, The Law of War, p. 257ff., published by C. H. Beck'schen Verlagsbuchhandlung, Munich and Berlin, I put forward with detailed legal argument the proposition that the proceedings against the so-called criminals against peace must be said to comply in no way with valid international law.'

Dr jur. Helmut Lemke, Prime Minister of Land Schleswig-Holstein, 10 May 1968:
'I have signed with pleasure the declaration you sent me, because on humanitarian grounds I consider the further detention of Rudolf Hess as indefensible. It is my hope that the custodial Power which still refuses to grant release will also follow this precept of humanity.'

Pastor Martin Niemöller wrote:
'When, three years ago, three (Hess, v. Schirach, Speer) of the seven prisoners originally imprisoned in Spandau were still left,

I approached the four custodial Powers to help the prisoners to end their imprisonment. At the time, I received replies from the three Western Heads of Government; not from Russia. When, two years ago, Rudolf Hess was left alone I felt prompted to ask for mercy to be shown to him. On 1.3.1968, I went to Paris in the hope of speaking to President de Gaulle. I had quite a long talk with Couve de Murville, who promised to speak to de Gaulle about the Hess case. At the time, de Gaulle was the only Head of Government to answer personally. Since my trip to Paris I have heard nothing more from there.

'Russia has stuck to its negative attitude. How can one help to bring this inhuman situation to an end? I have no personal opinion on this case; I do not know Rudolf Hess personally; I got to know his son only eighteen months ago. It is well-known that I was never a friend of the Nazis; I myself was imprisoned for eight years under National Socialism.

'I support Rudolf Hess because the judgement at Nuremberg led to no consequences in international law; it was thus only the victors' act of revenge against the defeated. My concern is my sympathy for the human lot, for the inhuman, long, sneaking torture.

'A year ago I was awarded the Lenin Peace Prize. I hoped on this occasion to be able to speak to the leading men of the Soviet Union. But the prize consists only of money; and this I have used for humanitarian purposes.

'I have the idea that one of the three custodial Powers might be able to release Rudolf Hess – even if the fourth Power is opposed to this. (France would be the most suitable state to do this.) A dangerous question: will the matter be pushed on to the political level?

'I would be very happy if the Hess family, with the Support Association, were to publish this appeal, if this human request were to penetrate to the widest circles and find a response everywhere.'

Sefton Delmer, the well-known British journalist and head of propaganda transmissions against Germany during the Second World War:
'When I visited Frau Hess a few years ago to talk to her about her

husband's lot, she told me that I had always been very critical of the German position. Are you now being honest? Is this your opinion? To this I replied that I supported Rudolf Hess not because I am pro-German or anti-National Socialist but because I am pro-British. I do not want my country to share the guilt in this matter. My opinion is that we bear a large part of the guilt. When Hess parachuted into Scotland, rumours spread that he was mentally deranged . . . At the time, Churchill published nothing about the Hess case; he was passed over in silence. There was a large peace party in Britain, and Churchill probably feared that this party would throw him from his Ministerial seat because he had not agreed to Hess's peace proposals.'

The British historian, *Professor A. J. P. Taylor*, wrote, in an appeal to Prime Minister Wilson in the *Sunday Express*, 27 April 1969: 'Hess came to this country in 1941 as an ambassador of peace.

'There is a call which of itself thrusts towards the great desires of mankind. . . . It concerns just one man. But he is worthy of the attention of even a Prime Minister of Great Britain. This man is Rudolf Hess. He should be seen as a reproach to the conscience of every British citizen, since we are very largely responsible for the fate he has suffered. Hess came to this country in 1941 as an ambassador of peace. He came with the . . . intention of restoring peace between Great Britain and Germany.

'He acted in good faith. He fell into our hands and was quite unjustly treated as a prisoner-of-war. After the war, we could have released him. Instead, the British Government of the time delivered him for sentencing to the International Tribunal at Nuremberg, a British judge pronouncing the judgement of 'life imprisonment' on Hess.

'No crime has ever been proved against Hess . . .

'As far as the records show, he was never at even one of the secret discussions at which Hitler explained his war plans. Hess was Hitler's Deputy only to the extent that he represented him at events such as youth rallies or visits to factories.

'He was of course a leading member of the Nazi Party. But he was no more guilty than any other Nazi or, if you wish, any other German. All the Nazis, all the Germans, were carrying on the war. But they were not all condemned because of this.

'A courageous and resolute British Government could go even further. Hess could without doubt be released from Spandau and set free in West Germany. It is said that if that were done the Russians would take revenge on Berlin. This is an empty threat. They did nothing when they had a much better reason when the West German Government met in Berlin.

'If the Jews could abduct Eichmann from Argentina, we could abduct Hess from Berlin in the interest of a noble cause.

'The conscience of every simple man turns towards Mr Wilson. He should forget all political calculations and tactics. He should speak for mankind . . .'.

Julius Cardinal Döpfner wrote on 31 October 1972 to Wolf Rüdiger Hess:

'. . . With great emotion I think of your father's hard lot, which in spite of all the endeavours from all over the world has still not been surmounted.

'I have commissioned the head of our Bonn office, Prelate Wöste, in collaboration with Bishop D. Kunst, to take all action possible to ease your father's lot . . .'.

In the *Frankfurter Allgemeine Zeitung* of 12 July 1973, the following note appeared:
'On Wednesday, Abba Eban, the Israeli Foreign Secretary, made a statement opposing the release of Rudolf Hess. Answering questions in the Knesset, the Israeli Parliament, Eban declared that the Government of Israel was of the opinion that war criminals of the Nazi regime should serve their "complete sentence". This also applied to Rudolf Hess.'

A signatory to the 'Declaration' of 1 October 1967, himself a Jew, said that this attitude was scandalous.

On 23 October 1973, *Sir Alec Douglas-Home* replied, in a personal letter, to a letter from Wolf Rüdiger Hess:
'I sincerely regret that we were unable to meet. I really would have liked to talk to you. As you know, I have long been convinced that the continuation of your father's imprisonment is wrong, and I would sincerely welcome it if he were released as

soon as possible. I have therefore carefully considered what you say in your letter. With all sympathy, however, I know of no easy solution. I am sure that you are aware that my Government can take no independent action which would mean breaching a binding agreement – an agreement which indeed to some extent forms the basis of the Allied presence in Berlin. But I can assure you that we shall continue our efforts, together with the United States and France, for the release of your father. Meanwhile, we shall do what is in our power – which, I fear, is not very much – to ease your father's life a little.'

Lord Chalfont, former Minister in the Wilson Cabinet, in the London *Times* 1 April 1974:
'. . . Successive British Governments have for years been of the opinion that he (Hess) should be released to spend the remaining years of his life with his family and the few others who still call themselves his friends. Of the other three Powers governing Berlin, the attitude of the French and Americans is by and large the same as the British. The Russians, on the other hand, have the . . . unsentimental standpoint to be expected from disciples of dialectic materialism. Life imprisonment means imprisonment for life, they say, with a certain cold logic. . . . The Russians will permit nothing which would make it easier for him to bear his pitiable life . . . Spandau remains a Western island in the Gulag Archipelago, ignored by détente.

'I have a proposal to make to bring this senseless situation to an early end. On 26 April, Hess will 'celebrate' his 80th birthday – if celebrate is not too cruel a word here. On this day he should be released from Spandau prison into the clear spring air of Berlin, and he should be allowed to spend the few remaining days of his life if not in absolute freedom then at least in the company of other people. It is of course clear to me that this is not a proposal which would be acceptable in the eyes of the Russian Government . . .

'It is time that the three Western Powers ceased accepting a Russian veto on their wish to release Hess. . . . The three Western Powers should inform the Russian Government of their intention to release Hess from Spandau on 26 April under his strict word of honour to refrain from political activity or public appearances of any kind. It is hard to see what the Russians could do to stop this. They would presumably not be prepared to endanger the entire delicate balance of East–West relations on such an issue.

'If however the West is of the opinion that the risk involved in such action is too great, there is another way open to them. The military guard at Spandau is provided by each of the four custodial Powers monthly in rotation. . . . There is no reason why the Western Powers should not give notice that, after the end of the American duty month, the French, British and Americans do not intend to continue to provide guards for Spandau. The Russians could of course then grasp the opportunity to provide their own permanent guard. . . . But that would at least have the effect that the world would unmistakably see that it is not the West which wishes to keep Hess imprisoned for ever.

'If nothing is achieved and the pitiable man in the prison cell . . . dies, history will record that Russian soldiers were his jailers when he died. Whatever happens, no men of a British regiment should stand at the gate on that day.'

The British historian *A. J. P. Taylor* in an article in the *Sunday Express* of 7 April 1974:
'The Russians insisted that it was a pernicious act to try to conclude peace between Britain and Hitler's Germany. Hess's defence counsel replied that the Russians did the same thing when in August 1939 they concluded the 'Nazi–Soviet' non-aggression pact. This enraged the Russians. They demanded the death penalty for Hess in order to conceal their own shameful deeds. The other judges were agreed on life imprisonment. The injustice suffered by Hess weighs heavily on all of us. Those who declare that Hess was guilty of war crimes are themselves guilty.

'The British Governments which assist in keeping Hess imprisoned in Spandau are guilty. We share their guilt if we do not raise our voices to support him. Appeals have often been directed towards the Soviet Government. They were in vain and will never produce an affirmative reply. The Russians are determined to erase any connection with the 'Nazi–Soviet Pact'.

'The Russians behave quite differently where people are concerned who work for Russia instead of for their own country.

'They welcomed and protected the spies Guy Burgess, Donald Maclean and Kim Philby. They achieved the flight of the condemned spy George Blake. Surely the time has come for the British Government for once to follow the Russian example. We should by all means try once more to tread the heavy road of negotiation.

'But if all negotiations are unsuccessful, which will be so, other means must be found. To start with, the British authorities should declare that they will no longer participate in continuing Hess's shameful imprisonment. A British garrison should no longer be provided. British money should no longer be paid for the maintenance of the prison. We should go even further. If George Blake can be abducted from a British prison, Rudolf Hess can also be made to disappear from Spandau. Although he is there on the basis of an international agreement, there is no moral obligation to adhere to an agreement which is now clearly unjust.'

Allgemeinen Jüdischen Wochenzeitung (Universal Jewish Weekly) of 12 April 1974:

'. . . Frau Hess has submitted a complaint to the European Commission on Human Rights in Strasburg. She pleads that the continuing imprisonment of her husband damages her family life and contravenes the ban on inhuman or humiliating treatment. According to the Commission's statements, the complaint has already been partially successful. Because of the long period of imprisonment, the European Commission on Human Rights has asked the British Government to express an opinion. The Soviet Union, the United States and France, who are also responsible for Spandau prison, cannot, however, be accused at Strasburg as they have not ratified the European Commission on Human Rights.

'As was also said in Strasburg, the Commission on Human Rights has finally rejected Frau Hess's complaint against the procedure at the Nuremberg war-criminal trials.'

Lord Chalfont in the London *Times* of 22 March 1974:

'When three weeks ago I suggested here that Rudolf Hess should be released from Spandau prison on his 80th birthday, the ensuing events were easy to foresee. . . . To my pleasure, the great majority of those commenting on my remarks about Hess reacted positively to the proposal for magnanimous measures. . . . The most encouraging point of this discussion was the large number of readers' letters from this country and from Western Europe (including some from West Germany from people who had themselves unforgettably suffered under Hitler) which reflected the kind of compassion for Rudolf Hess that I would have expected from civilized men and women. . . . Let me first try to dispel any remaining doubts about my attitude towards the terrible tyranny in which Hess played a leading part. National Socialism was evil and cruel, and with others of my generation I happily gave some years of my life in defending the free world against all he stood for . . .

'But there are other things that must be said. First, that the concept of war crimes gives rise to serious reservations. In a certain sense, any government conducting a war of aggression is guilty of a crime. But it is not at all clear to me why the victor is best qualified to act as prosecutor, judge and court in relation to the vanquished.

'Even if we . . . accept . . . that the Nazi leaders were treated justly and correctly at Nuremberg, there is yet another consideration which should not be forgotten – that of common humanity. . . . The Western Powers have long believed that Hess has atoned for whatever crimes he committed. Only the Russians are determined to show no mercy . . .

'Cruelty, persecution and inhumanity cannot be more or less tolerated if they come from one end of the political spectrum rather than from the other. Neither should it be believed that oppression is a thousand times worse if it is imposed on a thousand people rather than on one person. John Donne has said almost all that needs to be said on this subject: If through lack of charity and human feeling we diminish Rudolf Hess we diminish all mankind.'

On 4 May 1974, the *Pope's Secretariat* answered a letter from Frau Ilse Hess and her son Wolf Rüdiger Hess:

'. . . and are pleased to inform you that the urgent matter represented will continue to receive due attention from the Holy See within the possibilities present. As you know, all efforts in this direction have as yet unfortunately been unsuccessful.'

The Soviet Ambassador in Bonn, *Valentin Falin*, to Dr Alfred Seidl, 10 May 1974:
'Hess was sentenced for taking part in preparation for the murder of dozens of millions of people. As well as this, he has up to the present shown no signs of remorse for his deeds.

'You seek to show that the preparations of Hitler, Hess and Co. for a war of aggression were thoroughly legitimate. Your political and legal platform in this respect has long been known. The letter of 30 April 1974 shows that this platform has not changed and that our attitudes remain irreconcilable.'

Dr jur. Helmut Lemke, former Prime Minister and now President of the Schleswig-Holstein Landtag, 25 November 1974:
'. . . I continue to welcome any initiative which assists in drawing attention to your father's bitter and inhuman fate. I hope your meeting will again make it clear that the 'Rudolf Hess case' should not be evaluated politically or legally, and that the treatment of your father conflicts with any sense of justice and humanity.

'The document sent me has a heading which seems to me appropriate, having regard to the incomprehensible behaviour towards your father, i.e. that "Neither justice nor humanity" has any effect.'

The Prime Minister of the Saarland, Röder, 26 November 1974:
'I wrote to you in July 1968 to say that I was happy to support your efforts for the speedy release of your still-imprisoned father. For humanitarian reasons, I consider it unjustified to continue to deprive your father, now aged 80, of his freedom after more than 33 years of imprisonment. I hope your efforts will soon be successful.'

The Chief of the Federal Chancellery to Wolf Rüdiger Hess, 8 April 1975:
'The Federal Chancellor has asked me to reply to your letter of 20 March 1975 about the legal representation of your father by Dr Ewald Bucher. As you know, Herr Bucher approached the Allied Town Commandants in Berlin directly on this matter and protested against the decision of the Allied Prison's Directorate. The reaction to this letter has been discussed with the representatives of the Three Powers in Bonn. This leads to the clear conclusion that a change in the attitude of the Four Powers, who have sole responsibility in this matter, is not to be expected. The appeal which you direct to the Federal Chancellor allows me to assure you once again that, now as ever, the Federal Government is endeavouring to obtain your father's release on humanitarian grounds.'

Mrs Wilson's Private Secretary, London, to Ilse Hess, 26 November 1975:
'Mrs Wilson has asked me to reply to your letter of 11 November about the imprisonment of your husband, Rudolf Hess. The present Government fully sympathizes with you, and, as you know, has repeatedly expressed its conviction that Rudolf Hess should be released from the Spandau Military Prison without delay. This was also the attitude of previous Governments, including that of Mr Wilson between 1964 and 1970. Furthermore, the British Government has repeatedly approached the Soviet authorities and has insistently requested its consent to the release of your husband immediately on humanitarian grounds. You may perhaps have heard that the last of these attempts was made as recently as a month ago on 29 October, when Mr Roy Hattersley, Minister of State at the Foreign and Commonwealth Office, approached the Soviet authorities about this. I can assure you that the British Government will continue in the future its efforts to free your husband.'

Declaration by *Ilse Hess*, 12 June 1976:
'On the occasion of my visit on 10 June 1976 to my husband Rudolf Hess in the Allied Military Prison, Berlin–Spandau, the

Directors of the prison did not allow me to make known to my husband the contents of the letter from Mrs Mollie Caborn of 21 May 1976, in which Mrs Caborn reports on the visit of the British Parliamentary Delegation, which included Mrs Caborn, to the Soviet Embassy in London with the object of obtaining the release of my husband. Neither was I allowed to tell my husband verbally about the delegation's visit.

'I had made an application to be allowed either to read extracts from the above-mentioned letter from Mrs Caborn to my husband or to inform him verbally of the rebukes of the Soviet Counsellor of Embassy Mr V. Kotliar on the occasion of the delegation's visit. In particular, I wished to tell my husband of the following statement made by the Counsellor and quoted in Mrs Caborn's letter:

"Not once has Rudolf Hess expressed any kind of regret for the millions killed in the war or shown the slightest sign of compassion, and this is why he deserves to remain in prison."

'The behaviour of the Directors of the Allied Military Prison, Berlin–Spandau, clearly shows that my husband will be given no opportunity of any kind to face up to the Soviet rebukes. Neither is he allowed to make any statement, either to his family or to a solicitor. Until this very day, my husband's solicitor, Federal Minister of Justice (retired) Dr Ewald Bucher, has not been given permission to talk to my husband.

'Since my husband can say nothing, the Soviet statements must be seen as mere conjecture.

'I am prepared to swear to the events referred to above on the occasion of my visit to the Allied Military Prison at Berlin–Spandau.'

Bernard Levin in *The Times*, 1 March 1977:
'This weak old man has paid enough – for the sake of humanity, release him!

'Rudolf Hess's attempt at suicide in Spandau has compelled the eyes and conscience of the Western world to recognize something that these eyes would rather not see and with which this conscience would rather not be burdened. Hess will die quite soon . . . and we shall immediately call the whole guard together and thank God that we are rid of a scoundrel.

'But his death should not fully pacify our conscience, for Hess has now been imprisoned for more than 30 years. After a whole generation has been born and grown up since his conviction, it is perhaps necessary to say here that he was justly found guilty of abominable crimes, which he had without doubt committed, but it should also be added that the manner of this, as well as the justice and the clemency, was somewhat unnatural. A man who was found guilty by a court, to which one of Stalin's judges belonged, for taking part in the aggression against Poland has some right to feel discriminated against.

'. . . who is satisfied, who is revenged, who is raised from the dead by keeping Rudolf Hess imprisoned? Or: who is deterred by it, who learns a lesson, who is impressed? How will the world be made better or worse by keeping this man imprisoned until he dies? . . .

'Clearly, no argument will make the Soviet authorities change their minds. But the Western Powers, which participate in the duty of 'guarding' one man who would probably not be able to walk out of his prison without help if the doors were opened and the walls pulled down, having declared long ago that they were not against the release of Hess, are apparently content to let the matter rest, apart from the few formal and meaningless 'representations' to the Russians which are made every few years. And this seems to me to be insufficient, notwithstanding all demands for maintaining good relations with the Soviet Union. (As if true pressure for the release of Hess would have even the slightest detrimental effect on these relations!) It is time for some kind of positive action to be taken by those countries which, faced with the senseless inhumanity of Hess's continued imprisonment, have been too long and over concerned with creating an impression that they can do nothing in this matter. But they can do a great deal in this matter.

'First, the Governments of Britain, the United States and France can . . . deliver a joint *official* declaration to the world denouncing the Soviet Union for its senseless cruelty in not agreeing to an act of pure humanity. Such a declaration could quite easily be presented to the Assembly of the United Nations – or at least the subject could be raised there . . .

'But there is a simpler way . . . I made this proposal more than five years ago in this column. I did not expect that the nations would accept it immediately, but I was interested at the time to establish that no one was inclined to make its acceptance impossible.

'Why cannot the three Western Powers, when it is their turn to guard Hess, simply release him conditionally from prison? If this is thought too dangerous, do not free him in such a way that he can go home, but at least so that he can go to a hospital in West Berlin. . . . No doubt within four months, if protocol has to be observed, he would have to be returned to Spandau for a period of one month. But this measure . . . might also represent a . . . form of pressure which would bring it to the notice of the Soviet leaders that their stubbornness no longer is an advantage. . . . The performance of bringing this old, harmless, weak man back to prison three times a year would scarcely enhance the image of the Soviet Union as an honourable nation.

'. . . Why cannot this be done? Why cannot the three Western Powers declare that any useful effect which might have been achieved by the imprisonment of Hess has been achieved long ago, and that he should no longer rot in prison during the period in which he is entrusted to them?

'Of course, I shall receive no answer also on this occasion. But this will strengthen my case and not weaken it, since it is not "my" case; it is not even Hess's case; it is the case of all humanity.'

Lord Shawcross, former British Chief Prosecutor at the International Military Tribunal, Nuremberg, in an interview with Bild am Sonntag, 10 April 1977:

Lord Shawcross: . . . The continued imprisonment of Rudolf Hess is a scandal!

Question: But you yourself prosecuted Rudolf Hess. As a result he was given life imprisonment . . .

Lord Shawcross: In no civilized country in the world is a 'life' sentence taken literally. It is still a principle of humanity that a 'life prisoner' is released after a suitable period of imprisonment. And particularly if he is sick. I had misgivings from the outset about whether Hess was fit to stand trial at all. A medical committee examined him at the time and found him of sound mind, although they admitted that his memory was disturbed.

Later, I repeatedly expressed doubts about whether the man convicted was fit to undergo detention. In any event, the severity of the sentence surprised me.

Question: What punishment would have been appropriate for Rudold Hess? When should he have been released?

Lord Shawcross: After about 15 years . . . or perhaps 20.

Question: You have suggested that one of the three Western Powers should at least move Hess to a hospital during its term of guard duty – even if the Soviets continue to refuse to give their consent. What could the Russians do in that event?

Lord Shawcross: They would kick up a fuss and protest loudly. But otherwise they can't do much about it. After all, Rudolf Hess merely serves as a pretence for them to go on holding their parades at the monthly changing of the guard at Spandau, and thus to demonstrate their presence in the West.

Question: Are you in favour of conditions being set if Hess is released – for example, that he is not allowed to give interviews or write his memoirs?

Lord Shawcross: No. Others have written their memoirs.

The Federal President, *Dr Walter Scheel*, to *Wolf Rüdiger Hess*, 12 January 1979:

'As you know, the Federal Government and I have long endeavoured to give effect to humanitarian considerations in the case of your father. Most recently, during his talks in *Guadeloupe*, the Federal Chancellor presented the case to his Western colleagues. *At the suggestion of the Federal Chancellor, they agreed to act positively in a manner there agreed.* I hope that the efforts of the Federal Government, which now will be shared by the three Western Heads of Government, will be fully successful.'

The British historian *A. J. P. Taylor* in the *Sunday Express*, 23 December 1979:

'Will Mrs Thatcher dare to release Hess for Christmas?

'We are now in the time of goodwill. "Peace on earth and goodwill to all men" we all say as we enjoy being with our families or going to church on Christmas morning.

'Quite an admirable sentiment. But there is one person to

whom we extend no goodwill. A man who is now sick and aged, who will enjoy no Christmas with his family. A man who is still condemned to the loneliness he has had to suffer for 37 years.

'This man is Rudolf Hess, the only prisoner in Spandau. Hess is at present in the military hospital. His doctors would like him to undergo a prostate operation. Hess however is reluctant . . . unless he can first be reunited with his wife and son.

'What inhuman tyrant has refused him the fulfilment of this wish, particularly at Christmas, the time of goodwill?'

'The refusal is an act of brutality . . . but this inhuman act is the work of civilized people who boast of charity and . . . of overflowing with Christmas sentiment . . .

'It is the governments of the Great Powers – Great Britain, France, Soviet Russia and the United States – who keep Hess prisoner. This crime is being committed in our name. . . . We are told that we must respect legality. In 1946, the International Tribunal at Nuremberg sentenced Hess to life imprisonment. He cannot therefore be released until all four Powers . . . give their consent. . . . What kind of hypocrisy is this! It is of course desirable to respect the law. But there are higher considerations than the law. Do we have to applaud the massacre of innocent children because the decree to do so was issued by Herod? And who would accept the Crucifixion because Pontius Pilate permitted it?

'Even if Hess had had a past of the utmost villainy, 37 years of imprisonment is too severe a punishment to be inflicted on anyone.

'. . . Hess's real crime was a crime of peace. The reason for which Hess came to Britain was what Churchill referred to as an altruistic act arising from an insane wish to do good. Hess came to establish peace between Britain and Germany.

'. . . Many applications for the release of Rudolf Hess have been addressed to the Russians. They have always been rejected. It is certain that no future application will be successful.

'The time has therefore come to act in the name of humanity . . . France and America agree. The conscience of mankind agrees . . .

'Rudolf Hess is in the military hospital in the British zone of Berlin. However much we may blame the Russians, he is now our prisoner – not theirs. Is it not time for an act of courage, which would also be an act of wisdom and humanity? . . .

'We now have a new government with a new spirit of determination. The Prime Minister has taken many bold initiatives. Let her react to the call for humanity for Hess! . . .

'If Hess is not allowed to go to his family for Christmas, our creed of charity and Christian principles becomes a farce. . . . A sick old man will not have a happy Christmas. He will be ignored by most people. But the British people cannot evade the reproach that this offence against humanity and the spirit of Christmas is being committed in its name. We are guilty, every one of us, if we do not . . . insist that Hess must have as happy a Christmas as ourselves.'

40 members of the European Parliament introduced the following Resolution at the Sitting on 13 November 1980:

'Proposed Resolution requesting consultation under the emergency procedure pursuant to Art. 14 of the Statutes for the release of Rudolf Hess from Spandau prison.

'The European Parliament . . .

calls upon the Foreign Ministers, within the framework of political co-operation,

1. to give full support to the Governments of France, the United Kingdom and the United States in their efforts to achieve the release of Rudolf Hess;

2. to ensure that the release of Rudolf Hess is always raised at meetings between the Governments of Member States and the USSR;

3. to ensure that all negotiations on relations between Germany and the Eastern Bloc are conducted also with a view to the release of Rudolf Hess;

4. requests its President to convey this Resolution to the officiating President of the Council, the Governments of Members States and the Ambassadors of the USA in the EEC.

'*Grounds*

The release must be effected without delay because Rudolf Hess has spent forty of his eighty years in prison, his health is greatly impaired, and his continued confinement in prison is expensive and is contrary to the principles of humanity.'

Sunday Express, 6 September 1981:
'The London hotel room in which Hitler's wartime Minister of Armaments, 76-year-old Albert Speer, suffered a fatal stroke was very probably paid for by the BBC . . .

'The war has been over for 36 years. Speer atoned for his crimes by 20 years in Spandau Prison. It would be absurd if hatred and hostility were to last forever. But one thing is strange. Throughout the war, Speer was at Hitler's side. He was responsible for the exploitation of slave workers. Compared with him, Rudolf Hess was as innocent as a new-born babe. He flew from Germany to Scotland before the atrocities resulting from the war took place. And now Speer was offered tea, toast and a television fee while Hess still sits in prison – after 41 years.

'It is said that it is the Russians who refuse to let him go. But is it not very strange that not one leading politician of this government – including Mrs Thatcher – or any other government has ever raised a voice in protest?'

Wolf Rüdiger Hess to the *British Ambassador* on 31 August 1982:
'I send you enclosed herewith my record of a talk I had with my father on 26.8.1982 in the Allied Military Prison, Berlin–Spandau.

'My father told me that in the event of his release he would give his word of honour that he would not express an opinion on political, contemporary or other historical matters, and also that he will not be politically active.

'The family appeals to your Government to release my father to his family for the few remaining months of his life, so bringing to an end the degrading anachronism of Spandau before it is too late.

'On 1 October 1982, 36 years will have passed since the judgement was pronounced at Nuremberg. Including his imprisonment in Britain, my father has been imprisoned without a break for nearly 42 years, 16 of which have been in absolute solitary confinement.

'I have at the same time sent this letter to the Embassies of all four Spandau custodial Powers.

Gräfelfing, 26 August 1982

'*Statutory declaration*

'Having been informed of the consequences of making a false statutory declaration, I, *Wolf Rüdiger Hess*, depose as follows:

'My father, former Reich Minister Rudolf Walter Richard Hess, born 26 April 1894 in Alexandria, Egypt, informed me of the following during my visit to him at the Allied Military Prison, Berlin–Spandau, on 26.8.1982. During my father's statement, the following were present:

– the American Prison Director Mr Darold W. Keane,
– the French Prison Director, Mr Planet,
– the interpreter regularly assigned to the Russian Director; name unknown,
– a French warder named Morel.

1. His state of health gives cause for alarm, in particular because of the following acute and chronic diseases:
   – he recently suffered two heart attacks within 4 weeks, always after meals. Both attacks were treated by the prison's medical orderly; the first with "nitroglycerin", the second, considerably more serious, with "nitroglycerin" and oxygen. During the second heart attack, his pulse rate increased to 150 a minute and remained at that level for about one hour.

   The medical officers of the four custodial Powers paid him visits after both heart attacks without taking any further action or even considering transferring him to hospital.

   The medical orderly informed him that under these circumstances he could no longer accept responsibility.

   My father stated that in his opinion the four custodial Powers' doctors could no longer bear the responsibility.
   – my father suffers from permanent night-time enterospasm;
   – my father suffers from breathing difficulty which, in his opinion, has been caused by a failure of the autonomic rhythm. The breathing difficulty is accompanied by temporary total blindness;
   – my father very quickly becomes tired when walking in the prison garden (after about 15 minutes); the right leg shows muscular weakness, so that he can walk only with a stick;
   – because of the stroke my father suffered about two and a half years ago, he is nearly 75% blind;

- my father suffered years ago a rupture of the abdominal wall, which is becoming steadily worse. He must always wear a permanent "support belt" (truss);
- his legs are badly swollen, and he must always therefore wear rubber stockings up to the knee. When sitting or lying down, his legs have to be raised;
- recently a skin rash, which itches continually, has appeared.

2. After this itemization, my father said that two fellow-prisoners condemned to life imprisonment by the IMT were already released in the mid-1950s for reasons of age and health.

[Author's note: Erich Raeder on 26.9.1955, Walther Funk on 16.5.1957].

'Since, in spite of his advanced age of 88 years and his serious illnesses, he had not yet been released, the only reason he could think of for this was that the custodial Powers assumed that he knew about matters which should not reach the public.

'He therefore gave his

WORD OF HONOUR

that in the event of his release he would express no opinions on political, contemporary or historical matters, nor indulge in political activity.

In addition, it was in any case mistaken to assume that he still could or would wish to indulge in political activity in view of his state of health and his age.

In Spandau, his mouth had been closed. Under his word of honour, it would remain closed in freedom. However, he preferred the latter situation, in which he would be able to spend the few months still perhaps remaining to him in his family circle – in particular with his grandchildren.'

The British Embassy, Bonn, 18 October 1982, to *Wolf Rüdiger Hess:*
'The Ambassador has asked me to reply to your letter of 31 August 1982. Enclosed with your letter was a note of the talk you had with your father during your visit on 26 August.

'The British authorities share your concern that your father is still kept imprisoned. As you know, every British Government has advocated, vis-à-vis the Soviet Union, that your father should be released on humanitarian grounds. We shall not relax our efforts for the release of your father.

'As concerns the enclosure to your letter, I must correct the statement that your father has recently suffered two heart attacks. The doctors who examined your father established that the high pulse rate to which you refer had been caused by "paroxysmal atrio-tachycardia", and that there had been no indications of heart failure. In both incidents, hospitalization was seriously considered, but this proved unnecessary after your father had been examined and treated in Spandau Prison. Since then, your father's complaints have not recurred.

'As you know, your father suffered an attack of pleurisy on 15 September. He was admitted the same day to the British Military Hospital, where he quickly recovered, so that he could be discharged from hospital as early as 20 September.'

Amnesty International to a member of the *Support Association*, 3 January 1983:

'I wish today to answer your letter to Helmut Frenz, since he is at present in Central America for a few weeks. I hope you will have no objection if, in reply to your questions about the initiatives Amnesty International has taken in support of Rudolf Hess, I send you a London paper in which all the activities in this direction are summarized. There is, unfortunately, no more recent information.

'Amnesty International's efforts on behalf of Rudolf Hess were directed towards securing humane conditions of imprisonment for him and the lifting of the solitary confinement which has been his for many years. In view of his advanced age and his impaired health, it would certainly be an act of humanitarianism to release him, but it appears that the Soviet Union, as one of the custodial Powers, is not prepared to put this into effect.

'But it is not possible for Amnesty International to demand his release. We make this demand – as you know – only for non-violent political prisoners. Rudolf Hess was, however, condemned as a war criminal. The old lady should not close her eyes to this fact.'

Federal Chancellor Helmut Kohl to *Wolf Rüdiger Hess*, 12 July 1983:
'Dear Herr Hess,

'Following my return from the Soviet Union, I feel driven to write to you.

'During my talks there, in particular during a personal talk with Secretary General Andropov, I once again emphatically requested the release of your father. I want to assure you that during this talk I put forward all conceivable arguments to the advantage of your father.

'I must to my great regret inform you that, following these very direct and very intensive talks, I see no chance of your father's speedy release – at least not with the present Soviet leadership.

'I am writing you this letter with great concern, since I can imagine your feelings, and I am very sorry indeed that I cannot send you any more favourable information.'